THE PENGUIN CLASSICS

FOUNDER EDITOR (1944–64): E. V. RIEU

Editor: Betty Radice

Josephus was born in about 37 A.D. He was one of the Jewish leaders at the time of the revolt of the Jews in the reign of Nero. He commanded in Galilee and was captured by the Romans, but his life was spared. Spending the rest of his life in Rome, he was given Roman citizenship and became a friend of Titus and Vespasian. His two most important works are said to be the *Jewish War* and the *Jewish Antiquities*.

G. A. Williamson was born in 1895 and was a Classical Exhibitioner at Worcester College, Oxford, graduating with a First Class Honours degree. He was Senior Classics Master at Norwich School from 1922 to 1960. He has also translated *Eusebius: The History of the Church* (1965) and *Procopius: The Secret History* (1966) for the Penguin Classics.

JOSEPHUS

The Jewish War

TRANSLATED WITH AN INTRODUCTION BY
G. A. WILLIAMSON

PENGUIN BOOKS

Penguin Books Ltd, Harmondsworth, Middlesex, England
Penguin Books, 625 Madison Avenue, New York, New York 10022, U.S.A.
Penguin Books Australia Ltd, Ringwood, Victoria, Australia
Penguin Books Canada Ltd, 2801 John Street, Markham, Ontario, Canada L3R 1B4
Penguin Books (N.Z.) Ltd, 182–190 Wairau Road, Auckland 10, New Zealand

—

This translation first published 1959
Reprinted 1960, 1967
Revised edition 1970
Reprinted 1972, 1974, 1976, 1977, 1978

—

Copyright © G. A. Williamson, 1959, 1969
All rights reserved

—

Made and printed in Great Britain
by C. Nicholls & Company Ltd
Set in Monotype Bembo

Contents

INTRODUCTION 7

Preface 21

1 Herod's Predecessors 27
2 Herod's Rise to Power 47
3 Herod Master of Palestine 60
4 Herod's Murder of Mariamme and her Children 80
5 Herod's Murder of his Heir, and Death 96
6 The Rise and Fall of Archelaus 113
7 Antipas and the two Agrippas 125
8 Florus and Agrippa II 141
9 The Outbreak of War 155
10 Josephus Governor of Galilee 170
11 The Coming of Vespasian and Titus 180
12 Josephus the Prisoner of Vespasian 196
13 Vespasian's Conquering Advance 213
14 Factions in Jerusalem 230
15 Atrocities in the City. Vespasian's Intervention 240
16 Vespasian Emperor 259
17 The Siege of Jerusalem – First Stages 276
18 Two Walls Captured 296
19 The Horrors of the Siege 312
20 Antonia Captured and Destroyed 325
21 The Temple Burnt and the City Taken 343
22 Jerusalem Destroyed: Roman Celebrations 361
23 Cleaning-up Operations 374

CONTENTS

APPENDIX

The Slavonic Additions   396
Correlation with Whiston's version   401
List of Dates   402
The Calendar   403
Money   404
Chief members of the Herodian family   405

BIBLIOGRAPHY   406

INDEX OF PROPER NAMES   407

MAPS

Palestine in the First Century A.D.   423
Jerusalem in 70 A.D.   424
Herod's Temple   425

Introduction

HISTORY, we are told, is the record of the crimes and follies of mankind. Anyone reading *The Jewish War* will certainly feel this to be true. It is a tale of unrelieved horror – of brutalities committed by Herod and the other Palestinian kings, by provincial governors, by the most enlightened and reasonable of the Roman emperors, by the leaders of the Jewish insurgents, and by Josephus himself. It is a tale of hopeless revolts, of suicidal strife between rival gangsters and warring factions, of incredible heroism achieving nothing but universal ruin and destruction. It is a tale, too, of a country filled with such a wealth of architectural and artistic splendour as has perhaps never been seen elsewhere since the world began, and reduced by crimes and follies to a desert, a mass of shapeless ruins.

Yet it is a tale of surpassing interest, a tale of achievements none the less magnificent because they ended in dust. Has any country had such a history as Palestine has had? a history so colourful, so rich in incidents that grip the imagination, stir the emotions, and haunt the memory? Does any country possess a geographical character so astounding in its diversity, so fascinating in its uniqueness? In this book we have a graphic record of the most exciting period of that history; we have too some remarkable descriptions of many of the geographical features; and a great deal of space is given up to bringing before our eyes the cities, palaces, and temples which filled this little land with beauty and made it one of the greatest creations of Hellenism, as different as could be imagined from the Palestine of our Sunday School memories. Here too we find the information that will serve as the necessary background for our understanding of recent research in Palestine – of the excavations at Jericho and Masada, and of the world-shaking discovery at Qumran both of an Old Testament manuscript a thousand years older than any previously discovered, and of the rules and doctrines of a mysterious sect, which seems to have been no other than the Essenes, that remarkable community which though never mentioned in the New Testament is so fully described in this book.

But for those who hold Palestine dear because it was the land trodden by a Saviour's feet the book has a unique interest. Here we have a work written in the same language as the gospels and at almost the same time, describing events many of which happened in the period covered by the New Testament record, while many others are most vividly foretold in the synoptic gospels. Men who figure so largely in the story of Christ and His infant church, men about whom every enquiring reader must have longed to know more – Herod the Great, Archelaus, Antipas, Pontius Pilate, the two Agrippas, Felix and Festus, Bernice – are here portrayed from a different angle and in enormously greater detail, so that new light is shed on their characters, a light that illumines but does not impair the scriptural portraits. Was Herod indeed great? Was he monster enough to order the butchery of innocent babes? And what sort of city was the Jerusalem that Christ entered in triumph and over which he wept? What sort of building was the Temple that at twelve years old He called His Father's House, and from whose courts He later drove the sheep and the oxen? To these and many such questions Josephus provides the answer.

I have referred to events foretold in the synoptic gospels. I am thinking, of course, of the destruction of Jerusalem and the signs that preceded it. Had we no other sources of information than the gospels we should be tempted to suspect that the warnings of Jesus were couched in hyperbolical language, not intended to be taken literally. Was it possible that of that mighty Temple not one stone should be left upon another, that should not be cast down? It was indeed possible; it is historical fact. The destruction was utter and complete,[1] and of the successive stages by which it was carried out Josephus gives us a full and terrible account. The whole tragic story had been foretold with startling accuracy; and of the event itself we have an eyewitness's description that omits no detail of the horror.

It was the startling accuracy of our Lord's warning that led critics of a generation ago, committed to the principle that every prophecy is written after the event – a principle of which there is not a shred of justification in science, philosophy, or experience – to allege that the great prophecies recorded by Matthew, Mark, and Luke were borrowed from later works of apocalyptic or eschatology and 'put into Christ's mouth'. These critics overlooked several facts. Leaving out of count the transparent honesty of the gospel writers, we notice that while these later works were concerned with the end of the world, Christ was obviously thinking much more about events which His own generation was to witness. The disciples, Matthew tells us, had asked Him a double question – about the destruction of the Temple and about His own final coming – and He gave them a double answer, the first part of which most vividly foretold the occurrences destined to be so fully described by Josephus. He made it clear to his audience how the imminence of those occurrences was to be recognized, and instructed them what they were to

1. The 'Wailing Wall' was never part of the Temple itself. For an excellent account of Jerusalem, ancient and modern, the reader might well consult Sir John Garstang's article in *Wonders of the Past*.

do when the warning signs were observed. This the Christians remembered and carried out: before the City was encompassed by its enemies they fled to Pella and so escaped the general destruction. It is hard to account for this escape if the prophecy was written after the event.

And here we should note that the threatened destruction of the City as distinct from the Temple was not completely carried out until the collapse of Bar-Kochba's rebellion and the capture of Jerusalem by Hadrian in A.D. 135 – a date long after the writing and circulation of all four gospels, as recent discoveries of New Testament papyri have established beyond question; so that at least some part of the prophecy must have been published before the event. We should observe also that in addition to the remarkable prophecies recorded by Matthew and Mark, and somewhat differently by Luke, we have another in John's account of our Lord's conversation with the woman of Samaria,[1] and, what is more important, the almost innumerable hints conveyed by His laments over Jerusalem, its women and unborn children, and by such unquestionably authentic passages as the parables of the Wedding Feast and the Wicked Husbandmen, and the solemn warning to those on whom the Stone should fall. The gospels are in fact interwoven with so many prophecies that no one who took the books seriously could think of tearing them out; for besides foretelling the fate of the City and the Temple, Jesus over and over again foretold His own betrayal, desertion, arrest, and trial, His crucifixion, resurrection, and ascension, the coming of the Holy Ghost, the divisions His message would cause, and the persecution and deaths of His disciples, collectively and individually. These things are of the very tissue of the gospel text.

*

What of our author himself? Unlike those of the gospel writers his identity and history are not open to question, and his character is known perhaps too well. Unlike them he figures largely in his own pages, not only because he took a prominent and highly individual part in the war, but because he enjoyed talking about himself and had a high opinion of his own excellences – no unusual trait in Roman literary circles. He was, moreover, the writer of an autobiography or *apologia pro vita sua.*

Joseph ben Matthias, who was later to call himself Flavius Josephus, taking like a freed slave the name of his master, was born in A.D. 37, the year of Caligula's accession, and lived to be 63. By birthright a priest, and on his mother's side the descendant of kings, conspicuous at 14 for his precocity and continuing his education till he was 19, he was destined to become politician, soldier, orator, and historian. His earlier years were spent in his own country, but in 64, the year in which Nero watched the

1. See John iv 21.

burning of Rome, he visited that city on a mission to the imperial government. His efforts evidently won him a reputation; for when in 66 the great rebellion was brought about by the surprising defeat of Cestius he was, in spite of his youth, made governor of Galilee. How he organized his province, how he came to be the prisoner of Vespasian, and how he thenceforth served the Romans with unswerving devotion, is fully and graphically related in the pages of this book. Readers will reach their own conclusions about his conduct, to which we must refer later. No one who reads his account will be surprised to learn that at the end of the war he became a Roman citizen and an imperial pensioner, that he accepted from Vespasian the revenues of land confiscated from his unfortunate fellow-countrymen, settled down comfortably in an apartment set aside for him in the emperor's house, followed Roman precedent by divorcing as unsatisfactory the mother of his sons and wedding an heiress, and spent the rest of his life writing successful works, of which a primary motive was to prove that the Romans had been right in what they had done, while he himself had not only been justified in going over to their side but was a loyal Jew after all.

Four works have come down to us, published, it is almost certain, in the following order, and varying greatly in style and literary quality according to the amanuenses employed to assist his halting Greek.

1. *The Jewish War* – by far the most interesting of Josephus' writings, and the most complete record we possess of an important period of Roman history; first written in Aramaic, then translated into Greek, and probably published in more than one edition, considerable additions and alterations being made. It will not escape notice that the title, identical in form with 'The Punic War' or 'The Gallic War', shows how completely the author had placed himself on the Roman side.

2. *Antiquities of the Jews* – a much longer work, overlapping the early chapters of *The Jewish War*; very dull in parts, but containing much valuable historical information.

3. *Life* – mainly an answer to the suggestion that Josephus had been the cause of the Jewish war; to disprove this he gives an account of his own doings in Galilee, at many points irreconcileable with the account in *The Jewish War*. In the opinion of some scholars this part of the book was written before the *War*, and with the addition of very brief summaries of earlier and later events published many years later as the *Life*.

4. *Against Apion* – a counterblast to an anti-Semitic outburst from Alexandria; by far the best written of the four works; published, like the *Life*, at the turn of the century.

Of Josephus himself we know nothing beyond what he tells us in his own writings. The picture that emerges is by no means a pleasant one. 'The traitor of Jerusalem', as Dr Cecil Roth calls him, has damned himself for all time by his own accounts of what he did at Jotapata – surely the most appalling story of cowardice, duplicity, and treason ever penned. What makes it the more horrifying is the absence of any sense of shame: Josephus vaunts his abominable behaviour; after claiming credit for all the heroic efforts of the Jews to hurl the Romans back, he treats his unspeakable act of desertion as his crowning achievement, the final proof of his greatness. But steadfast support of a cause was beyond him. Had he not earlier toyed in turn with all three rival philosophies of religion – those of Pharisees, Sadducees, and Essenes? And had he not virtually abandoned the faith of his fathers? For though he puts the most improbable pseudo-Jewish, monotheistic religious language into the mouth of Titus, the emissary of God Who 'now dwelt in Italy', he shows only too clearly that his own outlook has become pagan: his writings are full of allusions to Greek religious concepts, to impiety, omens, fortune, fate, nemesis, metempsychosis, and Avenging Furies.

Before his final traitorous act it is plain from his own account that he had long been seeking an opportunity to desert. The great army he had raised and trained on the Roman model had been allowed to melt away; those who were keen to fight for their country were treated as enemies and scoundrels; the towns he had fortified so strongly were left undefended; and as soon as he himself was trapped in Jotapata he did his utmost to slip away and leave his countrymen to their fate, as he tells us with such blatant effrontery.

Nor was treason his only crime. In his governorship of Galilee he practised the foulest deception on his fellow-Jews, following it up with acts of horrifying brutality, all recorded with the same self-satisfaction. Yet the atrocities committed by his pet aversion, John of Gischala, and the other fighting leaders he denounces with the utmost vehemence, though it is obvious that he thoroughly enjoyed the retailing of horrors. For instance, in spite of his pretence that he can hardly bring himself to relate the story of the woman who devoured her child, he evidently gets immense pleasure out of the long-drawn relation of this gruesome tale, adorned with a wealth of manifestly invented detail. Our author has other traits also that modern readers will find little to their taste. He moralizes over the whole agonizing tragedy of his nation, proclaiming that it was just what those abominable Jews deserved. He gloats over the terrible fate of his personal enemies, and exults over the loathsome triumphal display staged in Rome by the two conquerors whose boots he is never tired of licking. He does not express even the mildest disapproval as he records the atrocities of which they were guilty – the throwing by

Vespasian of living, fettered men into the Dead Sea by way of scientific experiment; the duplicity by means of which he lured 38,000 helpless Jews into Tiberias, there to be butchered if infirm, sold into slavery if physically sound; the killing by Titus of thousands of Jewish prisoners in theatre after theatre, in celebration of family birthdays – the horrible spectacle of innocent men thrown to the beasts, compelled to fight each other to the death, or burnt alive.

Neither errors of taste nor moral insensibility need necessarily detract from the value of a book as history or as literature; but in the case of *The Jewish War* some of the writer's faults undoubtedly do, as we shall see later, when we have tried to do justice to his merits. But first let us consider how the work came to be written. Its purpose is plainly stated in the author's own preface, and again in his final sentence. All accounts hitherto published of the 'greatest war of all time' were either ill-informed or deliberately misleading. The emperor's subjects were entitled to know the true facts, and to be in a position to appreciate the difficulties which the Romans had faced, and the genius and heroism by which they had overcome them. A new account was therefore necessary, the work of an eyewitness who could set personal feelings aside and, without flattering one side or belittling the other, do justice to both with absolute truthfulness. We are told also that the book had originally been written in Aramaic and had enjoyed a wide circulation throughout the Middle East; now it was to be available in a Greek translation for Greek and Roman readers.

Whether our existing text is simply a translation with a new preface, or is largely a new work, is a matter for speculation. Some authorities, notably Dr Eisler, hold that Josephus first wrote a short work entitled 'The Capture of Jerusalem', then prefixed an account of Herod, his predecessors and successors, and finally added the last few sections, to which, as every reader will no doubt observe, there is no allusion in the summary of the book which the author includes in his preface. There seem also to have been some omissions in the later editions. Like every wise historian Josephus consulted written authorities, including, as he himself tells us, the official Roman records of the siege and other military operations. For the first quarter of the book he had to go elsewhere, and it is believed that while he pieced together items of information gleaned from a variety of sources, he made particular use of the immensely long history of Nicolas of Damascus. Nicolas had written a full account of Herod the Great and had brought the story down to the accession of Archelaus. About the years that followed Josephus could find very little information, with the result that his narrative is sadly out of proportion. Herod's life is told at very great length, and page after page is devoted to the struggle of Archelaus to obtain recognition at Rome: the remainder of his ten-year reign is dismissed in half a dozen lines.

Unlike the gospel writers, who were content with the living language of the market-place, Josephus (or his amanuenses) wrote in a literary type of Greek very little removed from that of the great Attic writers and characterized by elaborate 'periods' and an enormous vocabulary. Though sometimes there are obscurities, on the whole the narratives and descriptions are clear. Many of the scenes are presented with great dramatic power, and the speeches, though psychologically unsound and obviously not authentic, are by no means devoid of eloquence. One characteristic of the book, which some would ascribe to the amanuenses, is the frequent lifting or adapting of phrases from classical authors. It is difficult to think that a man whose Greek was so shaky that he needed the constant help of expert assistants had read all the authors here laid under contribution. These include Sophocles, Euripides, and Meleager; Herodotus, Thucydides, and Demosthenes; Virgil and Sallust. Such reminiscences occur not only in narrative and comment but even in the speeches of Roman generals and Jewish leaders. The most remarkable instance of this borrowing is in the character sketches of John of Gischala, for which, as St John Thackeray pointed out, Josephus is indebted to the description of Catiline composed by Sallust.

Irrelevance is a fault that in an ancient author we must to some extent be prepared to overlook. Herodotus had set the example of how to record one recent war, and in so doing to relate or describe everything that in his long peregrinations he had read, heard, or seen. And how entertainingly he did it! Josephus was not quite a Herodotus, and he had the advantage of knowing how differently Thucydides had written, and how much was to be said for sticking to a theme. But because he had ample information he prefixed to the history of a four-years' war a detailed account of the two previous centuries, with full particulars of Herod's building operations, his domestic tangles, his crimes and follies, and the sordid story of his death. It may be that some will feel this to be justified on the ground that it really does account for the subsequent course of events; but what shall we say of all the anecdotes, the accounts of curious topographical and biological phenomena, the detailed descriptions of works of art, of Jewish sects, of priestly dress and Temple ceremonies, of events in far off Rome with no repercussions in Palestine? By no stretch of imagination can these be judged essential parts of an organic whole. Yet it is no rare thing for an author's irrelevances to be both interesting reading and sources of valuable information; and the digressions of Josephus are amongst the most precious things in his book, for which readers of every generation must be profoundly grateful.

Irrelevance can be forgiven if a historian fulfils his one essential duty of telling his readers the truth. Can we say that of Josephus? It must be confessed that our book contains much that has not the stamp of truth, though fortunately the discerning reader is in little danger of being imposed on. From one who boasted so proudly of his own achievements in the art of deception we should hardly expect a high standard of objectivity. Many statements in the *War* are contradicted in our author's other works, and we cannot always say 'He had new sources of information and corrected his mistakes', for he gives irreconcileable accounts of events in which he himself was the chief actor, and we cannot escape the conclusion that in one account or both he is perverting the truth, and perverting it for a purpose. Where we do not find contradictions the account may still fail to convince us. He obviously draws freely on a vivid imagination for events that he did not witness, such as the mass-suicide at Masada, and many details of the horrors that earlier took place inside Jerusalem, in which he constantly generalizes from the particular. Figures of every sort he habitually exaggerates. In my footnotes I have ventured to draw attention to several instances, and it should be observed that so far from correcting these figures in his later works, he often increases them – like a story-teller who in each retelling of the tale feels compelled to make it more impressive still.

Of course Josephus was not a critical historian: he swallowed open-mouthed the statements of his informants. A man who could accept and repeat the account of the mysterious root in the ravine at Machaerus[1] must have been credulous indeed. But did Josephus really believe that a shot knocked off a man's head and carried it 600 yards? His battle-casualties are reminiscent of newspaper accounts of the Spanish civil war, or of more recent battles in Algeria. But it is not only figures that he exaggerates. His passion for hyperbole enables him to write of rivers of blood that extinguished the fires of Jerusalem, and so on. But perhaps the chief reason why he departed from the truth was personal prejudice: everything that Josephus did was right; anything that John or Simon did was wrong. All the people he disliked were scoundrels, bandits, terrorists, tyrants, agitators, and the like – we of this generation have become only too familiar with the application of such words to men whom in other circumstances we should call resistance leaders, patriots, heroes of the maquis, and so forth. As for Titus, the flattery poured upon him by Josephus is distasteful in the extreme, and we tire of reading of battle after battle won single-handed by that immaculate and infallible hero.[2]

But when all this has been admitted the fact remains that while, as all scholars agree, we must use the greatest caution in accepting at its face value any statement that Josephus makes about himself or his personal enemies, when he has no axe to grind and is not indulging in patent

1. See the description in Chapter 23.

2. The adulation of Titus is extended to his dreadful brother Domitian and to his kinsman Cerealis, both of whom are portrayed disingenuously.

exaggeration he is an informative and reliable historian. As regards the principal facts recorded we can certainly accept his account as essentially trustworthy. How could he, writing in Rome for Roman readers and under the eye of the late commander-in-chief, now a model emperor, do other than record truthfully the war in which so many potential readers had taken part? He has, indeed, not only set down both clearly and accurately the main course of events, but has recorded the long-drawn agony of the war and of the happenings that preceded it with such a wealth of detail that his work is indeed a major contribution to the history of a critical century. Not only does it fill a conspicuous gap left in that history by his Roman contemporaries, who hardly troubled to mention the tremendous happenings in Palestine, but it adds incidentally in no small measure to our knowledge of the Roman Empire in general, its rulers and their struggle for power, and its military organization and methods of training, battle, and siege.[1] In fact, it would be hard to name one historian of those stirring times to whom we owe a greater debt, one writer the loss of whose works would have been a greater disaster.

*

At the time when this translation was begun, anyone who wished to study the writings of Josephus was faced with a serious difficulty. The scholarly and most readable bilingual edition by St John Thackeray in the Loeb Classics, which happily is once more on sale, was out of print, and second-hand copies were almost unobtainable, the fortunate possessors stead-fastly refusing to part with them. If the student had the desire, the ability, and the patience to study the author's works in the original language, he might lay his hand on a copy printed at Geneva in 1611, or at Basle in 1544 – in lovely type, but full of mysterious abbreviations and fancy combinations of letters. If he wished to read an English translation, he was unlikely to find anything in the bookshops except Whiston's famous version, already over two centuries old, though he might be lucky enough to light on a copy of Traill's Victorian version, with its many beautiful but not very helpful illustrations. To Whiston we owe a debt of gratitude, for it is through his labours that generations have been able to study not only *The Jewish War* but all Josephus' writings. But it would be untrue to suggest that his translation is either scholarly or readable. It is frequently inaccurate, sometimes grossly so; in passage after passage the meaning is obscure or non-existent; and in spite of quaint expressions and occasional felicitous phrases it is very clumsy and a poor specimen indeed of eighteenth-century prose. Nor did Whiston exercise any restraint over

1. In addition to the description of the Roman Army in Chapter 11 students of the art of war will find the descriptions of siege tactics at Jotapata, Gamala, Jerusalem, and Masada of enthralling interest.

his own loquacity: his principle seems to have been never to use one word if two or three would do.

Translations of ancient books are intended to serve a variety of purposes. The Victorian 'crib' gave a word-for-word rendering, often in deplorable English, the object of which was to assist struggling schoolboys to 'construe' the allotted portion: as long as they found out which word was which they were not required to produce a version in recognizable English. Other translations, intended for the use of more mature scholars, succeeded in avoiding 'translationese' while remaining fairly literal. A third type is intended for the ordinary reader, who knows no Greek or Latin but wants to know what the authors had to say. Such versions need not be literal; they may be free paraphrases and yet give a far truer impression of the original; but they are written in the living language, they have the true flow, and they may even be works of literature. Nowadays very few can read Greek, even if Greek texts are available, and the present translation is naturally intended for the ordinary reader. For that reason my first aim has been to make it lucid and readable, but I trust I have not departed too far from the original to be of service to any who may wish to use it in conjunction with the Greek.

In my anxiety to make the translation readable I have devoted special care to the speeches. These, except where the style is peculiarly stilted, I have endeavoured to turn into the English that is really spoken, allowing the speakers to seem like human beings. I cannot understand how a first-rate translator in this twentieth century could put into their mouths such moth-eaten expressions as 'verily', 'to boot', 'scurvy villain', or 'perdition take thee, most impious wretch'!

In order that what Josephus wrote may be intelligible to the ordinary reader I have departed in several respects from the practice of my predecessors. In the first place I have changed many expressions that are no longer part of our language, and in some cases not likely to be understood. Cubits have been converted into yards, feet, or inches, stades or furlongs into miles, *amphorae* into gallons. In the second place the hours of the day and watches of the night, varying according to the time of year and so mystifying to readers of Caesar or St Mark, have been replaced by the a.m. and p.m. system, which, the reader may be interested to note, must have been actually in use during our author's lifetime if we are to make sense of the allusions to time in the Fourth Gospel. The third liberty I have taken is with the names of places. I see no point in employing unusual spellings just because Josephus has done so, and all names known to readers of the New Testament appear in this version in their familiar form. Non-Biblical names that have changed little appear in their modern form, e.g. Berytus as Beirut, while those that have changed beyond recognition retain their Greek form, for instance Sebaste and

Scythopolis. I hope that this is a sensible compromise. I have retained the name Syria, which, e.g. in Chapter 9, covers all Jewish areas of what we loosely call Palestine. As regards Jewish names of men I have used the Old Testament spellings, such as Elijah and Jeshua, not Elias and Jesus.

Lastly, I have divided the book into chapters which correspond, I hope, to the natural divisions of the subject matter, and have provided them with carefully chosen titles. Any reader who may wish to compare this version with Whiston's will find in the Appendix the necessary correlation of my chapters with his.

In the first edition of this book a further liberty was taken, more presumptuous than any of these. Numerous passages of varying length which interrupt the narrative and obscure the connexion of thought were removed from their positions in the manuscripts. The nine longest of these passages were transferred to the end of the book and printed as excursuses; the many short ones appeared as footnotes, in Roman type to distinguish them from my own comments and explanations, which were printed in italics. My object may be stated in Josephus' own words – 'to secure coherence and continuity in the narrative.' In the present edition, however, in deference to the wishes of Dr Rieu's successor, Mrs Betty Radice, these passages have all been restored to their original positions. In order, therefore, to enable the reader who may wish to do so to study some of Josephus' very interesting descriptions, without having to dig them out of the long narrative in which they are hidden away, I append here a list of the ten longest, with the chapters in which they occur.

Jewish Sects	Chapter 7
Ptolemais and its crystalline sand	7
Galilee, Peraea, Samaria and Judaea	11
The Roman Army	11
Gennesareth	13
Jordan Valley and the Dead Sea	16
Jerusalem and the Temple	17
Machaerus	23
The Defences of Masada	23
The Temple of Onias	23

*

May I, in conclusion, express the confident hope that students of history, and most of all those to whom any new light shed on the New Testament is precious, will find the reading of Josephus' *Jewish War* amply worth while?

G. A. W.

1970

THE JEWISH WAR

Preface

THE war of the Jews against the Romans was the greatest of our time; greater too, perhaps, than any recorded struggle whether between cities or nations. Yet persons with no first-hand knowledge, accepting baseless and inconsistent stories on hearsay, have written garbled accounts of it; while those of eyewitnesses have been falsified either to flatter the Romans or to vilify the Jews, eulogy or abuse being substituted for factual record. So for the benefit of the Emperor's subjects I have decided to translate into Greek the books which I wrote some time ago in my native language, for circulation in the Middle East. I myself (Josephus, son of Matthias) am a Hebrew by race, and a priest from Jerusalem; in the early stages I fought against the Romans, and of the later events I was an unwilling witness.

This upheaval, as I said, was the greatest of all time; and when it occurred Rome herself was in a most unsettled state. Jewish revolutionaries took advantage of the general disturbance; they had vast resources of men and money; and so widespread was the ferment that some were filled with hope of gain, others with fear of loss, by the state of affairs in the East; for the Jews expected all their Mesopotamian brethren to join their insurrection. From another side Roman supremacy was being challenged by the Gauls on their borders, and the Celts were restive – in fact after Nero's death disorder reigned everywhere. Presented with this opportunity many aspired to the imperial throne, while the soldiery were eager for a transference of power as a means of enriching themselves.

I therefore thought it inexcusable, when such issues were involved, to see the truth misrepresented and to take no notice. Parthians, Babylonians, Southern Arabians, Mesopotamian Jews, and Assyrians, thanks to my labours, were accurately informed of the causes of the war, the sufferings it involved, and its disastrous ending. Were the Greeks and those Romans who took no part in it to remain ignorant of the facts, deluded with flattery or fiction? Yet the writers I have in mind claim to be writing history, though beside getting all their facts wrong they seem to me to miss their target altogether. For they wish to establish the greatness of the Romans while all the time disparaging and deriding the actions of the Jews. But I do not see how men can prove themselves great by overcoming feeble opponents! Again they are not impressed by the length of the war, the vastness of the Roman forces which endured such hardships, and the genius of their commanders, whose strenuous endeavours before Jerusalem will bring them little glory if the difficulties they overcame are belittled.

However it is not my intention to counter the champions of the Romans by exaggerating the heroism of my own countrymen: I will state the facts accurately and impartially. At the same time the language in which I record the events will reflect my own feelings and emotions; for I must permit myself to bewail my country's tragedy. She was destroyed by internal dissensions, and the Romans who so unwillingly set fire to the Temple were brought in by the Jews' self-appointed rulers, as Titus Caesar, the Temple's destroyer, has testified. For throughout the war he pitied the common people, who were helpless against the partisans; and over and over again he delayed the capture of the city and prolonged the siege in the hope that the ringleaders would submit. If anyone criticizes me for the accusations I bring against the party-chiefs and their gangs of bandits, or for my laments over the misfortunes of my country, he must pardon my weakness, regardless of the rules of historical writing. For it so happened that of all the cities under Roman rule our own reached the highest summit of prosperity, and in turn fell into the lowest depths of misery; the misfortunes of all other races since the beginning of history, compared to those of the Jews, seem small; and for our misfortunes we have only ourselves to blame. How then could I master my feelings? If anyone is disposed to pass harsh judgement on my emotion, he must remember that the facts belong to the story, and only the grief is the writer's.

On the other hand criticism may fairly be levelled at those Greek scholars who, knowing that the wars of the past fade into insignificance beside the astonishing events of their own times, sit in judgement upon the latter and severely censure those who make an effort to record them. For though their own flow of words is greater, their historical sense is inferior. They write histories themselves about the Assyrians and Medes, implying that the earlier writers did not do the work properly. Yet they are no more a match for them as writers than as thinkers. For the old historians were all eager to set down the events of their own lifetimes, and their participation in these events gave vitality to their account, while it was impossible to depart from the truth without being detected. Surely to leave a permanent record of contemporary events for the benefit of posterity is worthy of the highest praise; and the real worker is not the man who merely changes the order and arrangement of another man's work, but the one who has something new to say and constructs a historical edifice of his own. I myself have gone to great trouble and expense, though an alien, so that I may offer to the Greeks and Romans a permanent record of their triumphs: native writers on the other hand, though the chance of profit from litigation finds them possessed of ready tongue and an unlimited flow of words, when they turn to history (which requires them to speak the truth after laboriously collecting the facts) appear to be gagged, and pass over to inferior writers unaware of the facts the task of recording the achievements of the great. I am determined therefore to respect the truth of history, though it has been neglected by the Greeks.

An account of the early history of the Jews, their origin, their exodus from Egypt, the extent of their wanderings and subsequent conquests, and their removal from their country, would, I think, be out of place here, and in any case unnecessary; for many Jews before me have accurately recorded the doings of our ancestors, and their accounts have been translated into Greek with very few mistakes. But where the Greek historians and our own prophets left off I shall begin my story; and the events of the war I witnessed I will relate in greater detail and with all the completeness of which I am capable, whereas events before my time will be run over in brief outline.

Starting with Antiochus Epiphanes, who stormed Jerusalem and after holding it for three and a half years was driven out of the country by the Hasmonaeans, I shall explain how their descendants by their struggles for the throne forced Pompey and the Romans to intervene; how Antipater's son Herod brought in Sossius and put an end to the Hasmonaean dynasty; how the people revolted after Herod's death, when Augustus was Roman Emperor and Quintilius Varus the local governor; and how in the twelfth year of Nero's reign the war broke out, with disastrous results to Cestius and remarkable successes for Jewish arms in the early encounters.

The fortification of the neighbouring towns will occupy us next; and the decision of Nero, in whom Cestius' defeats had aroused fears for the whole Empire, to give Vespasian supreme command; the invasion of Jewish territory by Vespasian assisted by his elder son; the size of the Roman army and allied contingents with which he overran Galilee; the capture of the Galilaean towns, some by all-out assault, some by negotiation. At this point I must explain the Roman system of military discipline and legionary training, and describe the dimensions and features of the two Galilees and the limits of Judea, with the peculiarities of the country, especially the lakes and springs. Of the fate of each of the captured towns I shall give an exact account based on my own observations and the part I played. It would be pointless to draw a veil over my own misfortunes, with which my readers are so familiar.

Next will come the death of Nero at the moment when Jewish hopes were waning; the interruption of Vespasian's advance on Jerusalem by his summons to the throne; the encouragement he received from portents, and the upheavals in Rome; the insistence of his soldiers on making him emperor despite his protests; the outbreak of party strife among the Jews following his departure for Egypt to settle the affairs of the Empire, the tyranny and dissensions of the party chiefs.

An account must next be given of the second invasion, mounted in Egypt by Titus; the method, place, and size of his troop-concentrations; the state of the party-riven City when he arrived; the series of assaults and the erection of the platforms; the siting and measurements of the three protecting walls; the defences of the City and the plan of the Temple and Sanctuary; all the exact measurements of these and of the altar; certain customs of the feasts, the seven grades of purity, the priestly ministrations, the priestly and high-priestly vestments; the description of the Holy of Holies. I shall conceal nothing, and add nothing to the published facts.

Then I shall contrast the brutality of the party-chiefs towards their countrymen with the clemency of the Romans towards aliens, and the persistence with which Titus showed his anxiety to save the City and the Sanctuary by inviting the insurgents to come to terms. In discussing the sufferings of the people and the calamities that led to their final defeat, I shall consider how far they were due to enemy action, how far to party strife, how far to starvation. My account will include the misfortunes of the deserters and the punishments inflicted on the prisoners; the burning of the Sanctuary despite Caesar's disapproval and the number of sacred treasures snatched from the flames; the capture of the entire City and the signs and wonders that preceded it; the arrest of the party chiefs, the number of people enslaved and the fates that befell them; the way in which the Romans disposed of the last remnants of the war, demolishing the ramparts of every fort; the progress of Titus through the whole country to establish order, and his return to Italy and triumphal celebrations.

All this I have embraced in seven books.[1] To those who took part in the war or have ascertained the facts I have left no ground for complaint or criticism; it is for those who love the truth, not those who seek entertainment, that I have written. I will now begin my story where I began my summary.

1. *We cannot say for certain where the author's seven books began and ended, nor should the usual division into 110 chapters be attributed to him.*

CHAPTER I

Herod's Predecessors

AT the time when Antiochus Epiphanes was disputing the control of Palestine with Ptolemy VI, dissension broke out among the leading Jews, who competed for supremacy because no prominent person could bear to be subject to his equals. Onias, one of the chief priests, forced his way to the top and expelled from the City the sons of Tobias. They fled to Antiochus and implored him to use them as guides and invade Judaea. This was just what the king wanted; so setting out in person with a very large force he stormed the City, killed a large number of Ptolemy's adherents, gave his men permission to loot as they liked, took the lead in plundering the Sanctuary, and stopped the continuous succession of daily sacrifices for three and a half years. The high priest Onias fled to Ptolemy, from whom he obtained a site in the district of Heliopolis. There he built a little town on the lines of Jerusalem and a Sanctuary like the one he had left. All this will be referred to again in due course.

Antiochus was far from satisfied with his unexpected capture of the City, the loot, and the long death-roll. Unable to control his passions and remembering what the siege had cost him, he tried to force the Jews to break their ancient Law by leaving their babies uncircumcised and sacrificing swine on the altar. Meeting with a blank refusal he executed the leading recusants; and Bacchides, who was sent by him to command the garrison, finding in these monstrous instructions scope for his savage instincts, plunged recklessly into every form of iniquity, torturing the most worthy citizens one by one, and publicly displaying day after day the appearance of a captured city, till by the enormity of his crimes he drove his victims to attempt reprisals.

Matthias (son of Asamonaeus) a priest from the village of Modein, raised a tiny force consisting of his five sons and himself, and killed Bacchides with cleavers. Fearing the strength of the garrison he fled to the hills for the time being, but when many of the common people joined him he regained confidence, came down again, gave battle, defeated Antiochus' generals and chased them out of Judaea. By that success he achieved supremacy, and in gratitude for his expulsion of the foreigners his countrymen gladly accepted his rule, which on his decease he left to Judas, the eldest of his sons.

As Judas did not expect Antiochus to take this lying down, he not only marshalled the available Jewish forces but took the bold step of allying himself with Rome. When Epiphanes again invaded the country he counter-attacked vigorously and drove him back; then striking while the iron was hot he hurled himself against the garrison of the City, which had not yet been dislodged, threw the troops out of the Upper City, and shut them into the Lower – the part of the town called the Citadel. Then taking possession of the Temple he cleansed the whole area and walled it round, ordered a new set of ceremonial vessels to be fashioned and brought into the Sanctuary as the old ones were defiled, built another altar, and resumed the sacrifices. No sooner was Jerusalem once more the Holy City than Antiochus died, leaving as heir – both to his throne and to his hatred of the Jews – his son Antiochus.

The new king got together 50,000 foot, about 500 horse, and 80 elephants, and marched through Judaea into the hill country. Bethsaron, a small town, fell into his hands, but at a place called Bethzachariah, where the road narrows, he was met by Judas and his army. Before the main bodies engaged, Eleazar, Judas' brother, noticed the tallest of the elephants fitted with a large howdah and gilded battlements, and assuming that Antiochus was on its back ran out a long way ahead of his own lines, and hacking a way through the enemy's close array got near to the elephant. To reach the supposed king was impossible because of his height from the ground, so he struck the beast's under-belly, bringing it down on himself so that he was crushed to death. He had done no more than make a heroic attempt, putting glory before life itself. The rider of the elephant was in fact a commoner; even if he had happened to be Antiochus, Eleazar would have achieved nothing by his daring but the reputation of having in the mere hope of a brilliant success gone to certain death. To his brother the tragedy was a presage of the final issue. Determined and prolonged as was the Jews' resistance, superior numbers and fortune's favour gave the king's soldiers the victory; most of his own men dead, Judas fled with the remnant to the toparchy of Gophna. Antiochus went on to Jerusalem, where he remained only a few days, till lack of supplies compelled him to withdraw, leaving a garrison that he thought adequate, and taking the rest of his forces to winter quarters in Syria.

After the king's retreat Judas did not let the grass grow under his feet. Large numbers of Jews flocked to his standard, and he had already rallied the survivors of the battle; so near the village of Acedasa he challenged Antiochus' generals. In the battle that followed he fought magnificently and inflicted heavy casualties on the enemy, but lost his own life. Only a few days later his brother John fell victim to a plot of the pro-Syrian party.

John was succeeded by another brother, Jonathan, who did everything possible to strengthen his authority in his own country, securing his position by his friendship with Rome and by making a truce with Antiochus' son. Unfortunately none of these precautions could guarantee him security. Trypho, guardian of the young Antiochus and virtually regent, had long been plotting against the boy and endeavouring to eliminate his friends; and when Jonathan came with a very small escort to Ptolemais to see Antiochus, he treacherously seized and imprisoned him, and launched a campaign against the Jews. Then repulsed by Simon, Jonathan's brother, he avenged his defeat by murdering Jonathan.

Simon's conduct of affairs was most efficient. He reduced Gazara, Joppa, and Jamnia in the neighbourhood of Jerusalem, and demolished the Citadel after overwhelming the garrison. Later he allied himself with Antiochus against Trypho, whom Antiochus was besieging in Dora before marching against the Parthians. But he did not cause the king to modify his ambitions by helping him to destroy Trypho: it was not long before Antiochus sent an army under his general Cendebaeus to ravage Judaea and reduce Simon to subjection. Simon in spite of his years showed a young man's vigour in his conduct of the campaign; he sent his sons ahead with his stoutest men, while he himself at the head of a section of his army took the offensive in another direction. He also placed large numbers of men in ambush all over the hill country and was successful in every onset; so brilliant was his victory that he was appointed high priest, and after 170 years of Macedonian control gave the Jews their freedom.[1]

He too was the victim of a plot: he was assassinated at a banquet by Ptolemy, his son-in-law, who after locking up Simon's wife and two of his sons sent a party to murder the third son, John Hyrcanus. Warned of their approach the youngster made a dash for the City, having great

1. *A number of errors in the foregoing paragraphs Josephus later corrected in his Antiquities: several statements cannot be reconciled with* 1 *Maccabees.*

confidence in the people, who remembered what his father had achieved and were disgusted with Ptolemy's iniquitous conduct. Ptolemy hurled himself against another gate but was thrown back by the citizens, who had already welcomed Hyrcanus with open arms. Ptolemy at once retired to one of the forts above Jericho, called Dagon; Hyrcanus, invested with the high priesthood like his father before him, offered sacrifice to God and then hurried after Ptolemy to rescue his mother and brothers.

His attack on the fort started promisingly enough, but was held up by his natural feelings. Every time Ptolemy was in a difficulty, he brought out John's mother and brothers on to the ramparts where they could be seen by all, and began to torture them, threatening to throw them headlong unless John broke off the siege forthwith. This atrocity filled Hyrcanus with anger, and still more with pity and fear; but neither torture nor the threat of death could make his mother flinch – she stretched out her arms and implored her son on no account to let her cruel sufferings induce him to spare the vile creature; better death at Ptolemy's hands than life without end, so long as he paid for his wrongs to their house. Whenever John, thrilled by his mother's fortitude, listened to her entreaties, he launched a fresh attack; but when he saw her flesh torn with the lash, his resolution weakened and his feelings overcame him. This dragged out the siege till the Year of Rest came round, for like the seventh day, the seventh year is observed by the Jews as a time of rest. This freed Ptolemy from the siege, and after putting John's mother and brothers to death he fled to Zeno Cotulas, the autocrat of Philadelphia.

Antiochus, eager to avenge his defeat at Simon's hands, marched into Judaea and pitching his camp before Jerusalem besieged Hyrcanus. Hyrcanus opened the tomb of David, the wealthiest of kings, and removed more than 3,000 talents. With a tenth of this sum he bribed Antiochus to raise the siege. With the balance he did what no Jew had ever done before; he maintained a body of mercenaries.

When later Antiochus marched against the Parthians, giving him a chance to retaliate, he at once launched a campaign against the towns of Northern Palestine, correctly assuming that he would find no first-class troops in them. Medabe and Gamaea with the towns nearby submitted, as did Sichem and Gerizim. He was successful also against the Cuthaeans, the people living round the copy of the Temple at

Jerusalem. In Idumaea a number of towns submitted, including Doreon and Marisa.

Advancing to Samaria, where now stands Sebaste, the city built by King Herod, he constructed a wall right round and entrusted the siege to his sons Aristobulus and Antigonus. They pressed it relentlessly, bringing the inhabitants so near to starvation that they resorted to the most unwonted food. They appealed for aid to Antiochus the Aspendian. He readily agreed, but was defeated by Aristobulus and his men. Chased by the brothers all the way to Scythopolis he managed to escape; they, returning to Samaria, again shut the people inside the walls, then took the city, demolished it, and enslaved the inhabitants. As success followed success they lost none of their ardour, but marching their forces as far as Scythopolis overran that region and ravaged all the country inland from Mount Carmel.

Jealousy of the continued success of John and his sons aroused the bitter hostility of their fellow countrymen, who gathered in large numbers and engaged in active opposition, which at last flared up in open war and ended in defeat. For the rest of his natural life John enjoyed prosperity, and after no less than thirty-three years of admirable administration he died leaving five sons, blessed if ever a man was and with no cause to blame fortune as far as he was concerned. He alone enjoyed the three greatest privileges at once – political power, the high priesthood, and the prophetic gift. So constant was his divine inspiration that no future event was hidden from him; for instance, he foresaw and foretold that his two eldest sons would not retain control of the state. Their overthrow is a story worth telling, so far they fell below their predecessor's prosperity.

When their father died, the eldest of them, Aristobulus, turned the constitution into a monarchy, and was the first to wear a crown, 471 years three months[1] after the return of the nation to their own land, set free from slavery in Babylon. To the next brother, Antigonus, of whom he seemed very fond, he assigned equal honours; the rest he imprisoned in fetters. In fetters too he placed his mother, who contested his claim to supremacy, as John had left her in supreme charge, going so far in brutality as to let her die of starvation in the dungeon.

Vengeance overtook him in the loss of his brother Antigonus, of whom he was so fond that he had made him sharer of his royal auth-

---

1. *As usual, Josephus' figure is too large – this time by 40 years.*

ority. He killed even him as the result of slanders invented by un-scrupulous courtiers. At first their tales were disbelieved by Aristobulus, who, as we have said, was very fond of his brother and put down most of their lies to jealousy. But when Antigonus returned with full cere-mony from a campaign to attend the feast at which it is an old custom to put up tabernacles to God, it happened that Aristobulus was ill at the time. At the end of the feast Antigonus went up to the Temple with his bodyguard and in full regalia to offer prayers, mainly for his brother's recovery. Meanwhile the unscrupulous courtiers went to the king and told him all about the escort of soldiers and the proud bearing of Antigonus, improper in a subject; he was coming, they said, with a huge force to murder him, unable to rest content with the shadow of royalty when he could grasp the substance.

These tales by degrees overcame the reluctance of Aristobulus, who took care to hide his suspicions but at the same time to guard against any unseen danger. While he himself was confined to bed in the fort at first called Baris and later Antonia, he stationed his bodyguard in one of the underground passages, with orders to leave Antigonus alone if un-armed, but to kill him if he came in arms; then he sent men to warn his brother to come unarmed. To counter this the queen contrived a very cunning plot with the conspirators. They bribed the messengers to suppress the king's warning and tell Antigonus that his brother had heard he had secured some wonderful armour and military equipment in Galilee. Owing to his unfortunate illness he could not come and see them himself; 'However,' he went on, 'now that you are just leaving, I should very much like to see you in your outfit.' Hearing this, and aware of nothing in his brother's disposition to make him suspect any harm, Antigonus set off in his armour to have it inspected. When he came to the dark passage called Strato's Tower, the bodyguard killed him – convincing evidence that no natural affection is proof against slander, and that none of our better feelings are strong enough to hold out against envy indefinitely.

The incident had another surprising feature. Judas was an Essene born and bred, who had never been wrong or mistaken in any of his predic-tions. On this occasion, when he saw Antigonus passing through the Temple, he called out to his acquaintances – a number of his pupils were sitting there with him – 'O God! the best thing now is that I should die, since truth is dead already, and one of my predictions has proved false. There, alive, is Antigonus, who was to have been killed today. The place where he was fated to die was Strato's Tower, and that is 70 miles away; and it is already 10 o'clock! The time has made nonsense of my prophecy.' Having said this the old man remained lost in gloomy thoughts – and a few minutes later came the news that Antigonus had been murdered in the underground strong-point, which was actually called Strato's Tower, like the coastal town of Caesarea. So the prophet's mistake was natural.

Aristobulus, bitterly regretting this foul crime, at once fell into a swift decline; at the thought of the murder his mind became unhinged and he wasted away, until his entrails were ruptured by his uncontrollable grief and he brought up quantities of blood. While carrying this away one of the servants waiting on him, impelled by divine providence, slipped at the very spot where Antigonus had been struck down, and on the blood-stains – still visible – of the murdered man he spilt the blood of the killer. At once a shriek went up from the spectators, as if the servant had poured the blood there on purpose. Hearing the cry the king asked the reason, and when no one dared tell him he insisted on being informed. At last by threats he compelled them to tell him the truth. His eyes filled with tears, and groaning with the little strength that was left he murmured: 'So it is. I could not hide my unlawful deeds from God's all-seeing eye. Swift retribution pursues me for the blood of my kinsman. How long, most shameless body, will you contain the soul that has been adjudged my mother's and my brother's? How long shall I pour out my blood to them, drop by drop? Let them take it all at once: let heaven mock them no more with these libations from my entrails.' The next moment he was dead, having reigned no more than a year.

His widow released his brothers and enthroned Alexander, the eldest, and seemingly the most balanced character. But on ascending the throne he executed one brother as a rival claimant: the survivor, who preferred to keep out of the public eye, he held in honour. He also came into conflict with Ptolemy Lathyrus, who had seized the town of Asochis; he inflicted many casualties but Ptolemy had the advantage. But when Ptolemy was chased away by his mother Cleopatra and withdrew to Egypt, Alexander besieged and took Gadara and Amathus, the biggest stronghold east of the Jordan, where were stored the most valuable possessions of Zeno's son Theodorus. But by a sudden counter-attack Theodorus not only recovered his property but captured the king's baggage-train, killing some 10,000 Jews. However, the blow was not fatal, and Alexander turning towards the coast captured Gaza, Raphia, and Anthedon, which King Herod later renamed Agrippias.

After his enslavement of these towns there was a Jewish rising at one of the feasts – the usual occasion for sedition to flare up. It looked as if he would be unable to crush this conspiracy, but his foreign troops came to the rescue. These were Pisidians and Cilicians: Palestinians he did not recruit as mercenaries because of their innate detestation of all Jews. After putting to the sword over 6,000 of the insurgents he attacked Arabia, overrunning Gilead and Moab and imposing tribute on the inhabitants. Then returning to Amathus he found that Theodorus had taken fright at his victories and abandoned the fortress; so he demolished it. He next took the field against Obodas of Arabia. But the king had laid an ambush near Gaulane and Alexander fell into the trap, losing his entire army, which was crowded together at the bottom of a ravine and crushed by a mass of camels. He made good his own escape to Jerusalem, but the completeness of the disaster fanned the smouldering fires of hatred and the nation rose in revolt – only to be worsted again in a succession of battles which lasted six years and cost the lives of as many as 50,000 Jews. He had little cause to rejoice over these victories, so ruinous to his kingdom; so suspending warlike operations he attempted to reach an understanding with his subjects by persuasion. But they were still more embittered by his change of front and unstable behaviour; and when he asked in what way he could satisfy them, they replied: 'By dying; even a dead man would be hard to forgive for such monstrous crimes.' Without more ado they called on Demetrius the Ready for help. He at once agreed – in the hope of enlarging his kingdom – and arrived with an army, joining his Jewish allies near Sichem.

The combined army was opposed by Alexander with 1,000 cavalry and an infantry force of 8,000 mercenaries, reinforced by loyal Jews to the number of 10,000. The other side consisted of 3,000 cavalry and 14,000 infantry. Before battle was joined the two kings issued proclamations intended to detach supporters from the other side, Demetrius hoping to win over Alexander's mercenaries, Alexander Demetrius' Jewish contingent. As the Jews would not abandon their bitterness or the Greeks their loyalty, there was nothing for it but an appeal to force. Victor in the battle was Demetrius, in spite of a magnificent display of determination and prowess by Alexander's mercenaries. The outcome of the engagement, however, was not at all what either side had expected. Demetrius, the victor, was deserted by those who had called him in, whereas through sympathy for the man who was down Alexander, after fleeing to the hills, was joined by 6,000 Jews! This swing of the pendulum was too much for Demetrius: convinced that Alexander was now fit to take the field again and that the whole nation was flocking to his standard, he withdrew. The departure of their allies did not cause the rest of the people to lay aside their quarrel: they waged war unremittingly with Alexander till after very heavy losses the remnant were driven into Bemeselis; when this town fell, the survivors were taken as prisoners to Jerusalem. So unbridled was Alexander's rage that from brutality he proceeded to impiety. Eight hundred of the prisoners he impaled[1] in the middle of the City, then butchered their wives and children before their eyes; meanwhile cup in hand as he reclined amidst his concubines he enjoyed the spectacle. Such terror gripped the people that the next night 8,000 of the king's opponents fled right out of Judaea, and remained in exile till his death. By such deeds he at last gave his kingdom an uneasy peace, and hung up his weapons.

But fresh troubles were in store for him – the work of Antiochus Dionysius, brother of Demetrius and last heir of Seleucus.[2] This man launched a campaign against the Arabs, alarming Alexander, who dug a deep trench stretching from the hillside above Antipatris to the beach at Joppa, raising a high wall in front of the trench with wooden towers built into it to ward off attacks at the weak points. But Antiochus was not to be stopped: he burnt the towers, filled in the trench, and marched his army across. Deciding to deal later with the man who had tried to stop him he went straight on to attack the Arabs. Their king retired to better defensive positions, then suddenly faced about with his cavalry force of 10,000 men and fell upon the army of Antiochus while in disarray. A bitter struggle followed. While Antiochus survived his men fought on, though they suffered appallingly at Arab hands; when at last he fell as a result of risking his life all the time in the forefront to help his struggling soldiers, the entire line broke. Most of his army was destroyed in the engagement or in the subsequent flight; the survivors took refuge in the village of Cana, where lack of food killed off all but a handful.

At this point the people of Damascus, through hatred of Ptolemy son of Mennaeus, brought in Aretas and made him king of Coele-Syria. He promptly marched into Judaea, defeated Alexander in battle,

1. Or crucified.   2. *Actually last but one.*

agreed on terms, and withdrew. Alexander took Pella and advanced
against Gerasa, once more coveting Theodorus' possessions. After
shutting up the garrison within a triple wall he occupied the place
without a battle. He went on to overwhelm Gaulane and Seleucia and
the 'Valley of Antiochus', and captured the strong fortress of Gamala,
dismissing its commander Demetrius who was accused of many
crimes. Then he returned to Judaea, after three whole years in the field,
and was warmly welcomed by the nation in view of his successes. But
the end of the war proved to be the beginning of physical decay.
Afflicted with a quartan ague he thought he could get rid of his sickness
by resuming a strenuous life. He threw himself into ill-judged campaigns, and by making impossible demands on his bodily strength
wore himself out completely. He died in the midst of storm and stress,
after reigning 27 years.

He had left his throne to his wife Alexandra, confident that the Jews
would most readily submit to her, since by her freedom from any trace
of his brutality and her constant opposition to his excesses she had
gained the good-will of the people. And he was right in his expectations; woman though she was she established her authority by her reputation for piety. She was most particular in her observance of the
national customs, and offenders against the Holy Law she turned out of
office. Of the two sons she had borne Alexander she appointed the
elder, Hyrcanus, high priest, in view of his age and his natural dis-
inclination to interfere with state affairs; the younger, Aristobulus, who
was an impulsive character, she kept out of the public eye.

Alongside her was the growing power of the Pharisees, a Jewish sect
that appeared more pious than the rest and stricter in the interpretation
of the Law. Alexandra, being devoted to religion, paid too great heed
to them and they, availing themselves more and more of the simplicity
of the woman, ended by becoming the effective rulers of the state, free
to banish or recall, to release or imprison, at will. In short, the privileges
of royal authority were theirs, the expenses and vexations Alexandra's.
She was very shrewd in making major decisions, and by regular
recruiting doubled the size of her army, collecting also a large mer-
cenary force, so that beside making her own country strong she inspired a healthy respect in foreign potentates. But while she ruled
others, the Pharisees ruled her. Thus Diogenes, an eminent man who
had been a friend of Alexander, was put to death by them on the charge
of having abetted the king in his impaling of 800 citizens. Then they

pressed Alexandra to execute the rest of those who had incited Alexander against them: her superstitious nature made her give way, and they killed whom they would. The most prominent of the threatened citizens sought the aid of Aristobulus, and he persuaded his mother to spare them in view of their station, expelling them from the City if not sure of their innocence. Thus granted impunity they scattered over the country.

Alexandra dispatched an army to Damascus on the ground that Ptolemy was regularly meddling there; but the army returned with no particular success to its credit. However, while Tigranes the Armenian king was encamped before Ptolemais besieging Cleopatra, she won him over by bargaining and bribery. But he had to withdraw in hot haste to deal with troubles at home, Lucullus having invaded Armenia. Meanwhile Alexandra sickened; the younger son Aristobulus seized his chance, and with his numerous servants – all devoted to him because of his impulsive character – got all the strongholds into his power, and with the money found there raised a force of mercenaries and proclaimed himself king. This so upset Hyrcanus that his mother felt very sorry for him, and locked up the wife and children of Aristobulus in Antonia. This was a fortress adjoining the Temple on the north side; as stated already, it was first called Baris and later renamed when Antony was supreme, just as the cities of Sebaste and Agrippias were named after Sebastos (Augustus) and Agrippa. But before Alexandra could proceed against Aristobulus for the unseating of his brother, she died, after ruling the country nine years.

The heir to the throne was Hyrcanus. While still alive Alexandra had put the kingdom in his hands, but in ability and enterprise he was no match for Aristobulus. Near Jericho the two met in battle for the crown, but the bulk of Hyrcanus' army deserted him and went over to Aristobulus. Hyrcanus with those who stuck to him immediately sought shelter in Antonia, and seized as hostages for his security the wife and children of Aristobulus. However, final disaster was averted by a compromise: Aristobulus was to be king and Hyrcanus, having abdicated, was to retain his other dignities as the king's brother. On these terms they were reconciled in the Temple, and surrounded by the people they warmly embraced each other and exchanged residences, Aristobulus taking over the palace, Hyrcanus Aristobulus' house.

Fear seized the enemies of Aristobulus when he so unexpectedly triumphed, most of all Antipater, whom he had long detested. He was by race an Idumaean, and ancestry, wealth, and other sources of strength made him the natural leader of his nation. He advised Hyrcanus to seek the protection of Aretas, king of Arabia, and so win back his kingdom, at the same time urging Aretas to receive Hyrcanus and restore him to his throne. He heaped abuse on the character of Aristobulus and lavished praise on Hyrcanus, and argued that it was the right thing for the ruler of so splendid a kingdom to extend his aid to the wronged; wronged indeed was Hyrcanus, deprived as he was of the crown that was his by right of birth. Having prevailed on both men, he slipped out of the City in the dark with Hyrcanus, and making all speed arrived safely at Petra, the capital of Arabia. There he handed over Hyrcanus to Aretas, whom by dint of much persuasion and carefully chosen presents he induced to provide an army to restore the exile – 50,000 horse and foot.[1] For such a force Aristobulus was no match; worsted in the first clash he was chased into Jerusalem, where he would quickly have been captured after a successful assault had not Scaurus the Roman commander intervened in the nick of time and ended the siege.

Scaurus had been sent into Syria from Armenia by Pompeius Magnus, who was at war with Tigranes. Arriving at Damascus immediately after its capture by Metellus and Lollius, he packed off these officers, and learning how things were in Judaea lost no time in seizing this heaven-sent opportunity. As soon as he set foot on Jewish soil delegates arrived from both brothers to request his aid. The rights of the case were outweighed by Aristobulus' gift of 300 talents. Accepting this sum Scaurus sent a herald to Hyrcanus and the Arabs, threatening them with Pompey and the Romans unless they raised the siege. Back from Judaea to Philadelphia fled Aretas in a panic, and back to Damascus went Scaurus. Aristobulus was not satisfied with his escape, but collected his entire army and pursued the enemy; near Papyron he engaged them and killed over 6,000, among whom was Antipater's brother Phallion.

Hyrcanus and Antipater, deprived of Arab help, transferred their hopes to the other side, and when Pompey entered Syria and arrived at Damascus they sought his protection. They brought no presents but relied on the same arguments as they had used with Aretas, begging him to repudiate the violent methods of Aristobulus and to restore to his throne the man to whom, as the elder and better of the two, it

1. As usual, this incredible figure undergoes further expansion in Antiquities.

belonged. Nor was Aristobulus behindhand, knowing that Scaurus could be bribed. He too presented himself, decked out in all his royal splendour. But he turned sick of servility and could not bear to abase himself in order to secure his ends at the cost of his dignity; so at Diospolis he turned back.

This conduct stung Pompey, who yielding to the importunity of Hyrcanus and his friends set off in pursuit of Aristobulus at the head of the Roman army and numerous auxiliaries from Syria. Bypassing Pella and Scythopolis he came to Coreae, where travellers from the interior cross into Judaea. Informed that Aristobulus had sought safety in Alexandreum, a most elaborately equipped fortress perched on a lofty eminence, he sent orders to him to come down. Summoned thus peremptorily the king was more inclined to try a fall than to submit, but he saw that the people were frightened to death, and his friends begged him to realize that Roman power was irresistible. Taking their advice he came down to Pompey, attempted at great length to justify his claim to the throne, and went back to his stronghold. At his brother's invitation he came down again, argued the rights and wrongs of the case, and went away without hindrance from Pompey. Hovering between hope and fear he came down repeatedly in the expectation of talking Pompey into putting everything into his hands, and as often returned to his citadel to avoid the appearance of yielding too soon. Finally however Pompey insisted on his evacuating the forts, and as the commanders had instructions to take no notice of any order not written by Aristobulus himself, he forced him to send each one of them a written order to march out. Aristobulus complied, but withdrew to Jerusalem in a rage and prepared for war with Pompey.

Pompey allowed him no time for these preparations but followed at once, stimulated by news of Mithridates' death, received when he was near Jericho. This is the most fertile spot in Judaea, rich in palms and in balsam: the stems of the balsam trees are slashed with sharp stones and the resin collected where it is exuded from the cuts. After spending one night in camp there, at dawn he set off rapidly for Jerusalem. Panicking at his approach Aristobulus met him as a suppliant, and by promising money and putting the City and himself in his hands appeased his anger. But no part of this agreement was carried out: the officer sent to receive the money, Gabinius, was prevented by Aristobulus' partisans from even entering the City.

Stung once more by his treatment Pompey kept Aristobulus in

custody, and advancing to the City reconnoitred the possible lines of attack, observing the almost impregnable strength of the walls, the formidable ravine in front of them, and within the ravine the Temple, with its fortifications so strong that if the town was captured it would provide a further refuge for the enemy. While Pompey took time to make up his mind party strife broke out in the City, supporters of Aristobulus calling for war and the rescue of the king, those of Hyrcanus urging the opening of the gates to Pompey. The numbers of the latter were swelled by fear, when they saw the perfect discipline of the Romans. Worsted in the struggle, the opposite faction retired into the Temple, destroyed the bridge linking Temple and City, and prepared to fight to the death. The others invited the Romans into the City and surrendered the Palace, to which Pompey sent Piso, one of his senior officers, and a large body of men. Piso posted sentry-groups about the City, and as none of the men sheltering in the Temple could be persuaded to come to terms, he removed all obstacles in the vicinity in readiness for an assault, finding the supporters of Hyrcanus most free with advice and assistance.

Pompey himself on the north side was busy filling in the trench and the entire ravine with material collected by the troops. This was a formidable task, as the depth was immense and the Jews interfered from above in every possible way. The Romans would never have reached the end of their labours if Pompey had not availed himself of the Seventh Day, on which for religious reasons the Jews will not set their hands to any work, raising the level of his earthworks while keeping his men out of all armed clashes; for only in self-defence will Jews fight on the Sabbath. When at last the ravine was filled in he erected high towers on his artificial platform, brought up the engines he had fetched from Tyre, and began to batter the walls while the stone-throwers prevented any interference from above. But for a long time little impression was made on the towers, which in this sector were massive and splendid to a degree.

While the Romans were suffering severely Pompey was amazed at the unshakable endurance of the Jews, especially their maintenance of all the religious ceremonies in the midst of a storm of missiles. Just as if deep peace enfolded the City the daily sacrifices, offerings for the dead, and every other act of worship were meticulously carried out to the glory of God. Not even when the Temple was being captured and they were being butchered round the altar did they abandon the ceremonies ordained for the day. In the third month of the siege the Romans at last overthrew one of the towers and swarmed into the Temple. The first who ventured to surmount the wall was Sulla's son, Cornelius Faustus. Next came two centurions, Furius and Fabius, followed by their respective units, which completely surrounded the Temple court and killed some as they fled to the Sanctuary, others as they put up a short-lived resistance. Many of the priests, though they saw the enemy approaching sword in hand, quietly went on with the sacred rites and were cut down as they poured libations and offered incense, putting the service of God before their own preservation. Most who fell were killed by their own countrymen of the rival faction; others beyond number threw themselves over the precipices; some, maddened by their hopeless position, fired the buildings round the wall and perished in the flames. The Jews lost 12,000 dead; of the Romans very few were killed, but a good many wounded.

Among the disasters of that time nothing sent such a shudder through the nation as the exposure by aliens of the Holy Place, hitherto screened from all eyes. Pompey and his staff went into the Sanctuary, which no one was permitted to enter but the high priest, and saw what it contained – the lampstand and the lamps, the table, the libation cups and censers, all of solid gold, and a great heap of spices and sacred money totalling 2,000 talents. Neither on this nor on any other of the sacred treasures did he lay a finger, and only one day after the capture he instructed the custodians to purify the Temple and perform the normal sacrifices. He appointed Hyrcanus high priest again, because he had shown himself most helpful during the siege, especially by holding off the crowds of countryfolk anxious to fight for Aristobulus. In such ways he proved his worth as a general, and by relying on considerateness rather than severity won the goodwill of the citizens. The prisoners included Aristobulus' father-in-law, who was also his uncle. The chief authors of the war were beheaded. Faustus and the men who had given him such splendid support received magnificent rewards. The country and its capital were laid under tribute.

Pompey next deprived the Jews of the towns they had occupied in Coele-Syria, putting them under a Roman governor specially appointed; this meant that the nation was confined within its own boundaries. He rebuilt Gadara, which the Jews had razed to the ground, as a favour to a Gadarene among his own freedmen. He also freed from their rule all such inland towns as they had not already destroyed – Hippus, Scythopolis, Pella, Samaria, Jamnia, Marisa, Azotus, and Arethusa; likewise the coastal towns, Gaza, Joppa, Dora, and the city which at first was called Strato's Tower and later was re-built by King Herod on the most magnificent scale and renamed Caesarea. All these towns he gave back to their legitimate citizens and added to the province of Syria, which with Judaea and the whole area as far as Egypt and the Euphrates he entrusted to Scaurus, with two of his legions. He himself marched rapidly through Cilicia on his way to Rome, taking with him Aristobulus and his family as prisoners. Of the two sons and two daughters, one son, Alexander, escaped en route; the younger, Antigonus, and his sisters were conveyed to Rome.

Meanwhile Scaurus invaded Arabia, but was held up at Pella by the difficult terrain, and though he ravaged the country around he suffered severely in doing so as he ran completely out of food. From this plight he was saved by Hyrcanus, who sent supplies by Antipater. He as an old friend of Aretas was dispatched by Scaurus to persuade him to buy peace. The Arab agreed to pay 300 talents, and on those terms Scaurus removed his army from Arabia.

The son of Aristobulus who had slipped out of Pompey's hands, Alexander, in time collected a large force which undermined Hyrcanus' position by overrunning Judaea, and it looked as if he would quickly dethrone him; for he advanced to Jerusalem and brazenly began rebuilding the section of the wall thrown down by Pompey. But Gabinius had been sent to Syria as successor to Scaurus, and after show-ing his worth on many other occasions he marched against Alexander. He, in alarm at his approach, recruited vigorously till he had 10,000 heavy infantry and 1,500 cavalry, and fortified carefully chosen posi-tions, Alexandreum, Hyrcanium, and Machaerus near the Arabian hills. Gabinius sent Mark Antony ahead with a detachment of his army, and followed in person with the main body. Antipater and his picked men, with the other Jewish forces under Malichus and Peitholaus, put themselves under the command of Mark Antony's officers and made contact with Alexander. Soon afterwards the heavy infantry arrived with Gabinius at their head. The united forces of his enemies were too much for Alexander, who retreated until near Jerusalem he was forced to give battle, losing in the engagement 6,000 men, half of them killed, half of them prisoners. With the survivors he fled to Alexandreum, where Gabinius on his arrival found many of them encamped. By promising to pardon their past offences he tried before using force to win them over; as they refused any compromise he killed a large number and shut the rest into the stronghold. In this battle Mark Antony displayed superlative courage; on every field he had invariably proved his worth, but never so convincingly as now.

Gabinius left enough men to reduce the fort and went off himself to settle the towns that had not been sacked and to rebuild those that had been destroyed. On his instructions Scythopolis, Samaria, Anthedon, Apollonia, Jamnia, Raphia, Marisa, Adoreus, Gamala, Azotus, and many other towns were re-established, each of them attracting an influx of eager colonists. These arrangements complete, he returned to Alexandreum and intensified the siege till Alexander, abandoning hope entirely, sent a herald to implore pardon for his offences and to surrender his remaining fortresses of Hyrcanium and Machaerus. Finally he handed over Alexandreum as well. All these Gabinius at the instigation of Alexander's mother demolished, that they might never be used as bases for a second war. The lady had come to ingratiate herself with him in her anxiety for the prisoners at Rome, her husband and remaining children. Gabinius next reinstated Hyrcanus in Jerusalem, entrusting him with the custody of the Temple, and set up a political system based on aristocracy. He divided the whole nation into five unions, one centred round Jerusalem, one round Gadara, one under the protection of Amathus, the fourth assigned to Jericho, the fifth based on Sepphoris, a town in Galilee. Only too pleased to be freed from the domination of one man, the Jews were thenceforth ruled by an aristocracy.

It was not long before trouble broke out for them. Aristobulus escaped from Rome, and again rallied a number of Jews, some eager for political change, others long devoted to him. His first act was to seize Alexandreum and to attempt its refortification; but when he learnt that Gabinius had sent an army under Sisenna, Antony, and Servilius to attack him, he retired towards Machaerus. Shaking off a mass of useless followers he kept only those properly equipped, about 8,000. Among these was Peitholaus, chief of staff in Jerusalem, who had deserted to him with 1,000 men. The Romans followed close behind, and battle was joined. For a long time Aristobulus and his men offered a fierce and successful resistance, but in the end they were overwhelmed by the Romans and lost 5,000 killed. Some 2,000 escaped on to a hill and the remaining thousand led by Aristobulus hacked their way through the Roman ranks and drove on to Machaerus. There, as he bivouacked the first night among the ruins, the king dreamt of raising another army, if only he was granted a breathing-space, and he began to fortify the position after a fashion; but the Romans soon attacked, and after holding out for two days beyond his strength he was captured, and with Antigonus, the son who had escaped with him from Rome, he was brought in fetters to Gabinius and by Gabinius sent back to Rome. He himself was imprisoned by the Senate, but his children were allowed to return to Judaea, as Gabinius sent a written statement that he had promised this to Aristobulus' wife in return for the surrender of the strongholds.

Gabinius had already sent off an expedition against the Parthians when he was stopped by Ptolemy. He turned back from the Euphrates and restored that monarch to the Egyptian throne, supported throughout the campaign by all the resources of Hyrcanus and Antipater. Money, weapons, corn, and auxiliaries were furnished by Antipater, who also persuaded the Jewish frontier guards at the Pelusian Approaches to let Gabinius pass. In the absence of Gabinius there were risings all over Syria, and the Jews were again stirred to revolt by Alexander, Aristobulus' son, who collected a huge army and started a massacre of all the Romans in the country. This alarmed Gabinius, who had already hurried back from Egypt on hearing of the upheaval in Palestine. He had sent Antipater ahead to win over the rebels, and met with some success; but 30,000 remained loyal to Alexander, and he was determined to fight. So when Gabinius took the field the Jews met him, and in a battle near Mount Tabor lost 10,000 killed, the rest fleeing in all directions. Gabinius visited Jerusalem, where he reconstituted the government according to Antipater's wish; setting out from there he defeated the Nabataeans in battle. Mithridates and Orsanes, refugees from Parthia, got away with his connivance, 'giving him the slip', as he informed the soldiers.

At this point Crassus arrived to take over the governorship of Syria. For the campaign against the Parthians he removed all the gold from the Sanctuary in Jerusalem, including the 2,000 talents Pompey had not touched. He crossed the Euphrates and perished with his army, but that is irrelevant to our story. After their victory the Parthians swept forward to cross the river into Syria, but were driven back by Cassius, who had escaped to the Roman province. Having secured the province he hurried towards Judaea, capturing Tarichaeae, where he enslaved some 30,000 Jews and at Antipater's suggestion executed Peitholaus, who was trying to rally Aristobulus' partisans. Antipater had married a distinguished lady from Arabia called Cypris, who bore him four sons, Phasael, the future King Herod, Joseph, and Pheroras, and a daughter Salome. He had won influential support on every side by kindness and hospitality; above all he had by his marriage made the Arab king his friend, and when he undertook the war against Aristobulus it was to him that he sent his children for safe keeping. Cassius, after forcing Alexander to give a written undertaking to keep the peace, went back to the Euphrates to prevent a Parthian crossing. A fuller account will be given in a later work.[1]

When Pompey and the Senate fled across the Adriatic, Caesar became master of Rome and the Empire. He at once released Aristobulus from prison, put two legions at his disposal, and sent him posthaste to Syria, in the hope that he would easily bring over that province and the whole Judaean area to his side. But malice frustrated both Aristobulus' enthusiasm and Caesar's hopes; poisoned by Pompey's adherents, for a long time the king was even denied burial in his native land, his body lying preserved in honey till Antony delivered it to the Jews to be buried in the royal sepulchres. Death came also to his son Alexander by the axe of Scipio in Antioch, by order of Pompey, after he had been tried for the damage he had done the Romans. His brother and sisters were taken under the wing of Ptolemy, son of Mennaeus and ruler of Chalcis under Lebanon, who sent his son Philippion to fetch them from Ascalon. Philippion tore Antigonus and his sisters away from Aristobulus' widow, and after taking them to his father fell in love with the younger and married her – only to be killed on her account by his father, who after murdering his son married Alexandra himself! This marriage made him take still greater care of her brother and sister.

On Pompey's death Antipater changed sides and courted Caesar, and when Mithridates of Pergamus while leading an army to Egypt was warned off the Pelusian Approaches and held up at Ascalon, as a friend of the Arabians he persuaded them to assist, and arrived himself with 3,000 Jewish infantry. He further won the support of two influential Syrians, the Ptolemy resident in Lebanon, and Jamblichus, who easily induced the towns in their neighbourhood to join the war. All doubt dispelled by the additional strength which Antipater had provided, Mithridates pushed on to Pelusium, and finding the way

---

1. *No such account has come down to us.*

barred laid siege to the town. In the assault too chief honours went to
Antipater; he broached the wall in front of him and was the first to dash
into the town followed by his men. Pelusium fell; but as Mithridates
advanced he was again held up by the Egyptian Jews who occupied the
district called after Onias. But Antipater induced them not only not to
oppose the army but even to furnish supplies; consequently at Memphis
too the people refrained from opposition and volunteered to serve
under Mithridates. He now rounded the Delta and met the rest of the
Egyptians in battle at a place called 'Jews Camp'. As the fight raged he
with the entire right wing was in grave danger, when he was rescued
by Antipater who, after routing his opponents on the left where he was
in command, made his way round by the river bank. He fell on
Mithridates' pursuers, killed a great many and pursued the survivors so
far that he even took their camp. He lost only 80 of his own men,
whereas Mithridates in the rout had lost about 800. Saved thus from
imminent destruction, he bore whole-hearted testimony before Caesar
to Antipater's achievements.

Thereupon Caesar by praise and promise incited the veteran to face
further hazards on his behalf. In all these he proved himself the most
intrepid of fighters, and wounded again and again he bore on almost
every part of his body the marks of his valour. Later, when order had
been restored in Egypt and Caesar returned to Syria, he bestowed Roman citizenship on him and exempted him from taxation, and by other
honours and marks of friendship made him an object-lesson to all. For
his sake also Caesar confirmed the high-priesthood of Hyrcanus.

CHAPTER 2

Herod's Rise to Power

SOON after this Antigonus, son of Aristobulus, had an interview with Caesar which had the unexpected result of winning Antipater further advancement. His wisest course would have been to express grief for his father, who was thought to have been poisoned because of his differences with Pompey, and indignation at Scipio's brutal treatment of his brother, and not to mix his appeals for sympathy with an outburst of bitterness. But he went on to accuse Hyrcanus and Antipater, openly alleging that in a most iniquitous fashion they had driven him and his sisters right out of their native land; that in their insolence they had treated the whole nation outrageously; that they had sent assistance to Caesar in Egypt, not out of loyalty to him, but through fear springing from old differences and in the hope that their friendship with Pompey would be forgotten. Antipater retorted by throwing off his garments and exposing his countless scars. Of his loyalty to Caesar, he said, he need say nothing; his body shouted it aloud without his saying a word. The impudence of Antigonus passed belief; the son of an enemy of Rome – and a fugitive from Rome – inheriting from his father a craving for revolution and sedition, he had the sauce to accuse other people before the Roman commander, and to try and feather his own nest when he was lucky to be alive! His present lust for power did not arise from his being in want; his ambition was to stir up sedition among the Jews and so to bite the hand that fed him. Having listened to both, Caesar declared Hyrcanus the better candidate for the high priesthood, and allowed Antipater to choose his own office. Antipater left it to the bestower of the honour to decide its magnitude, and was appointed Commissioner for all Judaea, with authority to rebuild the demolished walls of the mother-city. These honours Caesar ordered to be engraved in the Capitol, to commemorate his own justice and Antipater's splendid services.

As soon as Antipater had escorted Caesar out of Palestine he returned to Judaea. There he began by re-erecting the wall of the mother-city which Pompey had demolished, and proceeded to suppress disturbances in various parts of the country, using in every case both threats

and advice – if they supported Hyrcanus they would live in prosperity
and quiet, enjoying their own property and general peace; but if they
were deluded by the frigid hopes of those who for private profit were
eager for revolution, they would find him not a protector but a master,
Hyrcanus not a king but an autocrat, Caesar and the Romans not leaders and friends but enemies; they would never stand by while the Jews
turned out of office the men they had appointed. While he talked in
this way he was organizing the country along his own lines, knowing
that Hyrcanus was too lethargic and spineless to be a real king. Phasael,
his eldest son, he appointed governor of Jerusalem and district; the
next one, Herod, he sent with equal authority into Galilee, though he
was quite young.[1]

Herod, overflowing with energy, soon found scope for his active
spirit. Finding that Hezekiah, a bandit chief, was overrunning the
district adjoining Syria with a very large gang, he caught and executed
him along with many of his bandits. This stroke won Herod the gratitude of the Syrians; in all the villages and in the towns his praises were
sung – had he not won back for them their peace and property? A
further result was that he became known to Sextus Caesar, a kinsman of
the great Caesar and governor of Syria. His reputation also served to
arouse a spirit of friendly rivalry in his brother Phasael, who became
steadily more popular in Jerusalem and by force of personality kept the
City quiet without any blundering misuse of his powers. Consequently Antipater was revered by the nation as if he were king, and
honoured by all as undisputed head of the state; yet his own loyalty and
faithfulness to Hyrcanus remained unchanged.

But in prosperity there is no way of avoiding jealousy. Hyrcanus,
though he did not show it, was cut to the heart by the fame of the young
men; he was grieved most of all by Herod's achievements, and by the
stream of messengers announcing one success after another. His bitterness was aggravated by the malignity of numerous courtiers, offended
by the moderation either of the sons or of Antipater; to the three of
them had gone by default the management of affairs while Hyrcanus
sat helpless, retaining only the name of king without the authority.
How long would he be so foolish as to rear kings to his own hurt?
They no longer pretended to be viceroys but were the unquestioned
heads of the state while he had ceased to count; for without his giving
any order, verbal or written, Herod had put all these people to death in

1. *Twenty-six.*

defiance of the Jewish Law. If he was not king but a private citizen still, he ought to be put in the dock and in the king's presence justify his breach of the ancestral laws which forbade execution without trial. By these suggestions Hyrcanus was gradually inflamed, and at last in an outburst of fury he sent for Herod to stand his trial. He, advised by his father and emboldened by the success of his own policy, posted garrisons about Galilee and presented himself in Jerusalem, accompanied by a strong escort – not so swollen a force as to suggest the intention of dethroning Hyrcanus, nor small enough to leave him helpless in face of jealousy. But Sextus Caesar, fearing that the young man would run into a hornets' nest, sent Hyrcanus a categorical order to acquit Herod of the charge of homicide. The king, who as an admirer of Herod was in any case anxious to do this, found him not guilty.

Herod, believing that the king was mortified by his escape, withdrew to Sextus' headquarters in Damascus, with the intention of disobeying if summoned again. The malignant courtiers renewed their incitement of Hyrcanus, alleging that Herod had gone away in a rage and was ready to attack him. Swallowing the bait the king was at a loss what to do, as he saw the superiority of his opponent. But when Sextus Caesar actually appointed Herod commander-in-chief of Coele-Syria and Samaria and not only the loyalty of the people but the forces at his disposal made him formidable, Hyrcanus was paralysed with fear, every minute expecting Herod to march against him with an army at his back. And he guessed right. Herod, furious at the threat implied in his trial, collected an army and set out for Jerusalem to dethrone Hyrcanus. And he would soon have done it, if his father and brother had not hurried out and calmed him down, urging him to confine his revenge to threats and ferocity and to spare the king under whom he had grown so powerful. If he felt sore at being put in the dock, he ought at the same time to be grateful for his acquittal, and not, when the sword had been hanging over his head, to be ungrateful for his escape. And if it was true that in war God held the balance, Herod's military strength would be outweighed by the wrong he was doing. So he had better not be too certain of victory, when he was going to join battle with his king and comrade, often his benefactor, who had never been harsh, except when he had been driven by malignant advisers to try to scare him with a shadow of injustice. Thus advised Herod gave way, satisfied that he had made his future secure by giving the people a demonstration of his power.

Meanwhile for the Romans near Apamea peace was shattered and civil war broke out. Caecilius Bassus in loyalty to Pompey treacherously killed Sextus Caesar and took over his army. Caesar's other generals in revenge for the murder assailed Bassus with all their forces. Antipater, for the sake of the dead Caesar and the living, friends of his both, sent them assistance by his sons. While the war dragged on, Murcus arrived from Italy as successor to Sextus. It was at this time that Rome's Great War broke out through the action of Cassius and Brutus, who treacherously murdered Caesar when he had ruled the Empire for only three years seven months. A tremendous upheaval resulted from the murder and the most powerful citizens were divided into two camps, every man joining the party that promised him most. Cassius in particular went to Syria to take over the forces near Apamea. He patched up the quarrel between Bassus and Murcus and between the opposing legions, and brought the siege of Apamea to an end. Then taking command of the troops himself he went from town to town levying tribute and demanding more money than they were in a position to pay. When the Jews were ordered to contribute 700 talents, Antipater, frightened by Cassius' threats, divided the responsibility for its speedy collection among his sons and some of his acquaintances, including Malichus, one of his enemies, in view of the pressing necessity. First to satisfy Cassius was Herod, who brought his quota of one hundred talents from Galilee and earned Cassius' hearty approval. The others Cassius abused for their slowness, and then poured forth his fury on the unfortunate towns. Gophra, Emmaus, and two less important places he enslaved, and he was on the point of executing Malichus for his failure to levy the tribute at once, when his death and the destruction of the other towns were prevented by Antipater's prompt appeasement of Cassius with a present of one hundred talents.

When, however, Cassius was out of the way, Malichus, so far from showing gratitude to Antipater, devised a plot against the man who had so often saved him, anxious as he was to remove this obstacle to his career of crime. Antipater, alarmed at the strength and cunning of the man, crossed the Jordan with the intention of raising a force to crush the plot. Caught in the act, Malichus by sheer impudence got the better of Antipater's sons: Phasael, warden of Jerusalem, and Herod, responsible for arms and equipment, were deceived by a stream of excuses and oaths into undertaking to intercede on his behalf with their father. Thus Malichus was saved a second time by Antipater, who persuaded Murcus, then governor of Syria, to abandon his intention of executing him as a revolutionary.

When war was declared on Cassius and Brutus by young Caesar and Antony, Cassius and Murcus raised an army in Syria, and as they hoped for valuable assistance from Herod they put him for the time being in charge of all Syria with a body of horse and foot under his command, Cassius promising that when the war was won he would make him king of Judaea. Antipater's destruction was the direct outcome of the actual and prospective dominance of his son. Fearing Herod's rise, Malichus bribed one of the royal cup-bearers to give Antipater poison. It was a triumph for the scheming Malichus; for after the banquet Antipater died. He had at all times shown energy and initiative in the management of affairs, above all in putting Hyrcanus back on his throne and keeping him there. Malichus, suspected of the poisoning, quieted the angry citizens by denying it and made himself more secure by raising a body of infantry; he did not suppose that Herod would take it lying down, and indeed Herod arrived almost instantaneously with an army to avenge his father. But as his brother Phasael advised him not to settle accounts with the man openly, for fear of provoking a riot, for the time being he accepted Malichus' explanation and agreed that no suspicion attached to him. Then he performed the funeral rites for his father with magnificent ceremonial.

He next turned his attention to Samaria which was torn by party strife, and after putting matters there to rights turned back to Jerusalem to attend the feast, accompanied by his armed forces. Hyrcanus, at the instance of Malichus who had panicked at Herod's approach, sent orders that he was not to bring foreigners among the nationals when they were purified. Herod showed his contempt for the pretext and the man who issued the order by entering during the night. Malichus again approached him and bewailed Antipater. Herod met cunning with cunning, though he could hardly contain his anger; but he sent letters deploring his father's murder to Cassius, who hated Malichus already. The Roman wrote back that he should settle accounts with his father's killer, and gave secret instructions to his tribunes to help Herod 'pay a debt of honour'.

After the capture of Laodicea the leading men of every district gathered at Cassius' headquarters, bringing him crowns and other gifts. This was the moment chosen by Herod for his revenge. Malichus was suspicious, and when he was in Tyre where his son was held as a hostage he determined to get him out by stealth, and made arrangements for his own escape to Judaea. His slender chances of survival acted as a spur; his ambitions soared, and he saw himself leading his nation in revolt against the Romans while Cassius had his hands full with the war against Antony, and setting the crown on his own brow after quickly disposing of Hyrcanus.

But fate had the last laugh. Herod, perceiving his game, invited him and Hyrcanus to dinner, and then calling one of his attendant slaves sent him home as if to prepare the meal, but really to warn the tribunes to come out and put the ambush into effect. They had not forgotten Cassius' instructions and came out to the sea-shore in front of the city sword in hand, and there surrounded Malichus and hacked him to death. Hyrcanus promptly fainted from shock and collapsed; when at last he recovered consciousness and asked Herod who killed Malichus, one of the tribunes answered 'Cassius's orders'. 'Then Cassius,' returned Hyrcanus, 'has saved me and my country too, by destroying the mortal enemy of both.' Whether he really thought this or was too frightened to dispute an accomplished fact, will never be known. Anyway, Herod's account with Malichus was now settled.

When Cassius withdrew from Syria strife again broke out in Jerusalem. Helix, backed by a body of soldiers, rose against Phasael with the intention of avenging Malichus by punishing Herod through his brother. As it happened, Herod was with Fabius at his Damascus headquarters, and though anxious to help he was immobilized by sickness. Meanwhile Phasael overpowered Helix without assistance, and denounced the ingratitude of Hyrcanus in collaborating with Helix and permitting Malichus' brother to seize the forts. He had indeed seized many of these, among them the strongest of all, Masada. But he was helpless against the might of Herod, who as soon as he was well again recaptured all the forts and kicked him out of Masada grovelling. Next he expelled from Galilee Marion the autocrat of Tyre, who had already possessed himself of three of the strongholds, sparing every Tyrian he captured and even sending some away laden with gifts, so ensuring that the citizens were devoted to him and bitterly hostile to their own ruler. Marion had received his authority from Cassius, who had appointed an autocratic ruler of every district; through hatred of Herod he had brought back from exile Aristobulus' son Antigonus – in any case he could not resist Fabius, who had been bribed by Antigonus to work for his recall. All expenses were met by Ptolemy, the brother-in-law of Antigonus. These confederates Herod met and defeated in the approaches to Judaea; then banishing Antigonus again he went back to Jerusalem to receive universal congratulations on his success. Even those who had hitherto regarded him coldly now warmed towards him in view of his marriage into the family of Hyrcanus. He had previously married a Jewess of good birth named Doris, who bore him a son Antipater; now he wedded the daughter of Alexander, the son of Aristobulus, and grand-daughter of Hyrcanus, Mariamme, so becoming a connexion of the king.

When at Philippi Cassius had met his end, Caesar went back to Italy, Antony to Asia. Numerous cities sent deputations to Antony in Bithynia, and with them came influential Jews to accuse Phasael and Herod of obtaining control of affairs by force and leaving Hyrcanus a mere figurehead. To counter this propaganda Herod appeared on the scene, and coaxing Antony with huge bribes so worked upon him that he would not let Herod's enemies say a word. Thus for the time being they were silenced. But later on a hundred Jewish officials arrived at Daphne near Antioch to appeal to Antony, now a slave to his passion for Cleopatra. They put forward the most highly esteemed and eloquent men among them to accuse the two brothers. Messala replied for the defence, backed by Hyrcanus because of the marriage-connexion. Antony listened to both sides, and then asked Hyrcanus which party was the more fit to govern. When Hyrcanus recommended Herod and his associates, Antony was delighted, – years before he had been the guest of Herod's father, who had given him a right royal welcome when Gabinius and he were invading Judaea. So he appointed the two brothers tetrarchs, with the task of administering all Judaea.

The delegates exploded with fury, and Antony arrested fifteen and locked them up, with the fixed intention of putting them to death; the rest he sent packing with a flea in their ear. The result was greater turmoil in Jerusalem. A second delegation – a thousand strong – was sent to Tyre, where Antony was resting on his way to Jerusalem. His reply to their clamour was to send out the governor of Tyre with instructions to execute all he could catch and to back up the authority of the men he had appointed tetrarchs. This procedure was forestalled by Herod, who went on to the beach with Hyrcanus and strongly advised them not to bring about their own destruction and land their country in war by senseless strife. This made them more furious still, so Antony dispatched a body of infantry, who killed or wounded many of them: Hyrcanus saw to it that the dead were buried and the wounded cared for. Even so the survivors would not keep quiet, but created such disorder in the City that Antony was actually goaded into executing the prisoners.

Two years later Barzapharnes, the Parthian satrap, serving under Pacorus the king's son, seized Syria. Lysanias, who had succeeded his late father, Ptolemy son of Mennaeus, by promising 1,000 talents and 500 women, persuaded the satrap to bring back Antigonus and make him king, dethroning Hyrcanus. Pacorus accepted the bribe, and choosing the coastal route for himself, instructed Barzapharnes to drive through the interior. Of the seaside towns Tyre would not admit Pacorus, though Ptolemais and Sidon did so. Then to one of the royal cup-bearers who had the same name as himself he entrusted a detachment of cavalry, ordering him to gallop on into Judaea, to reconnoitre the enemy position and give all necessary aid to Antigonus.

While the troopers plundered Carmel, Jews flocked to Antigonus' standard, eager to take part in the invasion. He sent them ahead to seize a position called The Oaks. Here they clashed with the enemy, drove them back and chased them helter-skelter to Jerusalem, and having attracted strong support advanced to the Palace. Hyrcanus and Phasael met them with a powerful force and battle raged in the marketplace. Routing the enemy, Herod's forces herded them into the Temple, and to keep watch on them posted sixty men in the houses nearby. These guards the party opposed to the brothers assailed and burnt to death; Herod, furious at their destruction, attacked and killed many of the citizens; and day after day they sallied out against each other in small groups and bloodshed continued without pause.

Now came the Feast of Pentecost, and all the vicinity of the Temple – in fact the whole City – was filled with people from the countryside, most of them armed. Phasael was guarding the wall; Herod, with a handful of men, the Palace. The latter sallied out against the disordered enemy in the northern suburb, inflicted very heavy casualties, routed them all, and herded some into the City, some into the Temple, and others into the entrenched camp outside. At this stage Antigonus requested the admission of Pacorus as mediator, and Phasael agreed to open the gates to the Parthian with an escort of 500 horse, and made him welcome. Pacorus had come avowedly to end the strife, but in reality to assist Antigonus; he cunningly persuaded Phasael to go and discuss with Barzapharnes means of re-establishing peace, though Herod did his best to dissuade him and urged him to kill the schemer, not walk into his trap: one should never trust a foreigner's word. Phasael went, taking Hyrcanus with him. Pacorus, to silence suspicion, left with Herod some of the so-called Yeomen Cavalry, and with the rest escorted Phasael.

On reaching Galilee they found the inhabitants in a state of armed revolt. They had an interview with the satrap, a very subtle rogue who wrapped up his scheming in friendly protestations. He bestowed gifts on them, and then as they departed set a trap for them. The nature of the plot dawned on them when they arrived at one of the seaside towns, called Ecdippon. There they heard of the promised 1,000 talents, and how most of the 500 women dedicated by Antigonus to Parthian use were of their own race; how they themselves were spied on by the foreigns troops every night, and would have been kidnapped long ago if they had not been waiting to seize Herod in Jerusalem first, before news of what had happened to them put him on the look-out. This was no longer just a rumour: they could now see sentries not far away. But though Ophellius, who had learnt every detail of the plot from Saramalla, the richest Syrian of his generation, did his best to persuade Phasael to make his escape, nothing could induce him to desert Hyrcanus. He went straight to the satrap and told him plainly what he thought of the plot, and especially of his sinking so low for the sake of money; moreover, he himself was prepared to pay more for his life than Antigonus for his crown. The Parthian made a cunning and plausibly reply, denying the suspicion on oath, and then went to Pacorus. In accordance with his orders some of the Parthians left behind at once kidnapped Phasael and Hyrcanus, who cursed them bitterly for their perjury and broken faith.

Meanwhile the cup-bearer who had been sent to kidnap Herod was trying to carry out the plot by enticing him outside the walls, as instructed. He, however, had from the beginning suspected the invaders, and, learning now that a letter notifying him of the plot had fallen into enemy hands, he refused to go outside, though Pacorus argued most convincingly that he ought to meet the bearers of the dispatch, which had not come into the enemy's possession and made no reference to a plot, but merely recorded Phasael's doings. But as it happened, Herod had previously learnt from another informant that his brother had been kidnapped; and he was visited by Hyrcanus' daughter Mariamme,[1] the shrewdest of women, who implored him not to go outside or trust himself to the foreigners, now openly trying to bring him down. Pacorus and his staff were still seeking some crooked means of carrying out their scheme, it being impossible to get the better openly of a man so alert, when Herod forestalled them by setting out at night with those to whom he was most attached, in the hope of reaching Idumaea undetected. The Parthians, learning what had happened, went in pursuit. Herod made his mother and sisters,[2] the girl he had promised to marry, with her mother, and the youngest of his brothers, go straight on, while he and his servants protected them by vigorous rearguard actions. Every time he attacked the enemy he inflicted heavy casualties, finally making a dash for Masada.

In his flight he had less trouble with the Parthians than with the Jews, who harried him all the way, and seven miles from the City began a pitched battle, which lasted quite a long time and ended in their utter defeat. Here later on Herod commemorated his victory by building a city graced with a palace on which no expense was spared, and defended by a citadel of enormous strength. This city he called after himself Herodium. For the rest of his flight he was daily joined by large numbers, and at Thresa in Idumaea his brother Joseph met him and advised him to disburden himself of most of his followers, as Masada could never hold so big a number – over 9,000. Herod agreed, and sent those who were of no use to him to various parts of Idumaea, providing them with food for their journey; then keeping the toughest fighters as well as his family and close friends, he arrived safely at the fortress. Leaving 800 men there to protect the women, with provisions sufficient for a siege, he hurried on to Petra in Arabia.

The Parthians in Jerusalem turned to looting, breaking into the houses of those who had fled and into the Palace, and sparing only Hyrcanus' money, which did not exceed 300 talents. The total sum found fell short of their expectations; for Herod, long suspicious of Parthian trustworthiness, had already transferred the most valuable of his treasures to Idumaea, an example followed by all his friends. The looting finished, the Parthian conduct became so outrageous that they filled the whole country with war to the death, blotted out the city of Marisa, and after making Antigonus king, actually handed over to

1. *Has Josephus confused daughter and grand-daughter?*
2. *The MSS all read 'brothers'.*

him Phasael and Hyrcanus in fetters to be tortured. When Hyrcanus fell down at his feet, Antigonus with his own teeth mutilated his ears, that never again in any circumstances might he resume the high priesthood; for a high priest must be physically perfect.

But Phasael was too quick for him; he bravely dashed his head against a rock, as he was not free to use sword or hand. Thus he showed himself a true brother of Herod and Hyrcanus a cowardly poltroon; he died like a hero, crowning his life's work with a fitting end. A rival version of the incident states that he revived after the first shock, but a doctor sent by Antigonus 'to look after him' filled the wound with noxious drugs and finished him off. Whichever version is correct, all honour to him for his attempt. It is said that before he breathed his last he was told by some woman that Herod had escaped. 'Now,' he whispered, 'I shall die happy, as I'm leaving behind me a living man to avenge me.' So he died. The Parthians had missed their main target – the women – but put Antigonus at the head of affairs in Jerusalem and carried off Hyrcanus in fetters to Parthia.

Herod was driving on farther towards Arabia, thinking his brother was still alive and anxious to get money from the king, as without it he could not hope to save Phasael by appealing to Parthian cupidity. He reckoned that if the Arab was too forgetful of his friendship with Herod's father and too close-fisted to make him a gift, he could borrow the ransom from him by leaving in pledge the son of the man to be ransomed, as he had his nephew with him, a boy of seven. He was further prepared to give him 300 talents, putting forward Tyrian intermediaries. But fate had forestalled his earnest efforts; Phasael was dead, and Herod's brotherly affection was of no avail. Nor did he find any friendship now among the Arabs. Their king Malichus sent him orders to leave the country forthwith, on the pretext that the Parthians had formally demanded the expulsion of Herod from Arabia; in actual fact he had made up his mind to keep what he owed Antipater, and not to be shamed into repaying Antipater's generosity by any kindness to his children in their distress. He was abetted in his shameless behaviour by men equally anxious to embezzle the money Antipater had deposited with them – the most powerful of his courtiers.

Meeting with the hostility of the Arabs for the very reason that had led him to expect their warmest friendship, Herod gave the messengers the answer suggested by his disappointment and turned back towards Egypt. The first night he bivouacked at one of the country's temples, after picking up the men he had left behind. The next day he went on to Rhinocorura, where the story of his brother's death reached him. Anxiety for what might happen displaced by grief for what had happened already, he marched straight on. Belatedly regretting his behaviour, the Arab king hastily sent messengers to recall the man he had wronged. But Herod had already reached Pelusium, where he was refused a passage by the sailors in the harbour, so appealed to their superiors; they, impressed by his rank and reputation, conducted him to Alexandria. When he entered the city he received a splendid welcome from Cleopatra, who hoped to employ him as commander in a projected campaign; but he evaded the queen's pressing request, and fearing neither a voyage in midwinter nor the turmoil in Italy sailed for Rome.

In serious danger off Pamphylia he jettisoned the bulk of the cargo and with difficulty made Rhodes, which had suffered grievously in the war against Cassius. There he was received by his friends Ptolemy and Sapphinius. Shortage of money did not prevent his having a very large trireme built; in this he sailed with his friends to Brundisium. From there he hurried on to Rome, where he first applied to Antony as the friend of his father, telling him of his own and his family's misfortunes, and how he had had to leave his nearest and dearest besieged in a fortress while he endured a winter crossing to appeal for his assistance.

Antony was very grieved at the change in his fortunes: recalling Antipater's hospitality and filled with admiration for the heroic character before him, he decided on the spot that the man he had once made tetrarch should now be king of the Jews. If regard for Herod moved him, dislike of Antigonus moved him just as much; he considered him an agitator and an enemy of Rome. Caesar Herod found even more ready to help than Antony: the Egyptian campaigns which Antipater had shared with his father[1] were fresh in his mind, as were his hospitality and unshakable loyalty; and he could see Herod's appetite for action. He convened the Senate, to which Messala, supported by Atratinus, introduced Herod, and gave a full account of his father's services and his own loyalty to Rome, at the same time making it clear that Antigonus was their enemy, not only because he had quarrelled with them before, but because he had now accepted the crown from the Parthians in defiance of the Romans. These revelations angered the

1. *Octavian was the adopted son of Julius.*

Senate, and when Antony rose to suggest that the Parthian war was an added reason for making Herod king, they all voted in favour. The House adjourned, and Antony and Caesar went out with Herod between them, the consuls and other magistrates leading the way in order to offer sacrifice and to deposit the decree in the Capitol. This first day of Herod's reign Antony celebrated with a banquet.

CHAPTER 3

Herod Master of Palestine

ALL this time Antigonus was besieging Masada, whose defenders had plenty of supplies of every other kind but were short of water. In view of this, Joseph, Herod's brother, with 200 of his men planned to make a dash for Arabia, being informed of Malichus' desire to make amends to Herod. He would actually have left the fortress had it not happened that on the night of his departure rain fell in torrents; the reservoirs were filled to the brim, and he had no further wish to escape. They began to make sorties against Antigonus' forces, and now engaging them in the open, now luring them into ambushes, destroyed large numbers. Of course they did not succeed every time; sometimes they were worsted and had to retreat.

Meanwhile Ventidius, the Roman commander sent from Syria to check the Parthians, after dealing with them had crossed into Judaea, professedly to assist Joseph, but really to get money out of Antigonus. He encamped very close to Jerusalem, and after lining his pockets to his satisfaction withdrew with most of his troops; but he left Silo in command of a detachment, for fear that the removal of the whole army might make it only too evident what he had been after. Antigonus meanwhile, in the hope of further help from the Parthians, courted Silo to avoid any interference with the fulfilment of this hope.

But by this time Herod had sailed from Italy to Ptolemais, and having raised a substantial force of Jews and foreigners was marching through Galilee against Antigonus, with the cooperation of Ventidius and Silo, whom Dellius on Antony's behalf had induced to assist Herod's return. But Ventidius was busy settling sporadic disturbances resulting from the Parthian occupation, and Silo remained in Judaea, bribed with Antigonus' money. Not that Herod lacked support: as he moved on his strength steadily grew, and apart from a few localities all Galilee took up his cause. The most urgent task facing him was Masada; he must first of all rescue his family and friends from the siege. Joppa stood in the way; it was in enemy hands and must be reduced first; otherwise while he went on to Jerusalem his opponents would remain in possession of a stronghold behind his back. He was joined by Silo only too pleased to have found a pretext for leaving Jerusalem. The Jews followed in pursuit but Herod swooped on them with a handful of men, routing them easily and rescuing Silo, whose efforts at defence were feeble. He then took Joppa and hurried on to Masada to rescue his friends. Some of the country-folk were drawn to him by their friendship with his father, some by his own fame, some by the desire to repay the kindnesses of both, the largest number by the prospect of a stable monarchy; consequently he had now got together an almost invincible army. Antigonus tried to check his progress by laying ambushes at suitable points on his route, very ineffectively, as it turned out. Herod had no difficulty in freeing his friends in Masada and recovering the fortress of Thresa. He then set out for Jerusalem, and was joined by Silo's men and many Jews from the City, alarmed at his strength.

Having pitched their camp west of the town, Herod's men became the target for the arrows and javelins of the guards on that side, while others made organized sorties to test the strength of his outposts. Herod at once had proclamation made all round the walls that he came for the good of the people and the preservation of the City; that he would take no action even against his undisguised enemies and would grant even his bitterest foes an amnesty. Antigonus' staff countered this appeal by forbidding anyone to listen to the proclamations or to cross over; so Herod gave his men leave from then on to return the shots from the battlements, and they hurled their missiles to such effect that the towers were quickly cleared of defenders.

At this point Silo's venality became evident. He put up a number of his men to raise a clamour about short rations and demand money for food, and to insist on being marched to winter quarters in a suitable locality; there was nothing to be had anywhere near the City as Antigonus' men had taken the lot! Silo thereupon began to strike camp in an attempt to withdraw. But Herod approached the Roman officers, and then appealed to the rank and file not to leave him in the lurch when he had come with the authority of Caesar, Antony, and the Senate. That very day he would supply their wants. He had no sooner ended this appeal than he set out in person for the country-side, returning with supplies in such abundance as gave the lie to all Silo's pretexts; and to guard against any possible shortage in the coming days he requested the people living round Samaria, this city having espoused his cause, to bring corn, wine, oil, and cattle to Jericho. Hearing of this,

Antigonus sent orders round the country to block or ambush the food-convoys. The people obeyed, and a large number of armed men gathered above Jericho, and stationed themselves on the hills to watch for the supply column. However Herod was not idle; he set off with ten cohorts, five Roman, five Jewish, with a sprinkling of mercenaries and a few of the cavalry, and arrived at Jericho, which he found deserted; but the high ground had been occupied by 500 men with their wives and families. These he captured but set free, while the Romans poured into the rest of the town and looted it, as they found the houses full of luxuries of every kind. Leaving a garrison in Jericho the king returned, and sent away the Roman contingent to winter in districts that had come over to him – Idumaea, Galilee, and Samaria. Antigonus for his part by taking advantage of Silo's venality persuaded him to billet a portion of his army in Lydda – a sop to Antony.

While the Romans enjoyed every comfort and a complete rest from fighting, Herod was not idle. He occupied Idumaea with 400 horse and 2,000 foot led by his brother Joseph, to forestall any movement in support of Antigonus. His own task was to transfer his mother, and all the kinsmen and friends he had brought out of Masada, to Samaria; when he had settled them safely there, he marched on to secure the remainder of Galilee and expel Antigonus' garrisons. Forcing his way through a blizzard to Sepphoris he occupied the city without opposition, the defenders fleeing at his approach. There he refreshed his followers, battered by the storm, with the plentiful supplies available, setting out next against the bandits who lived in caves and over-ran a great part of the country, causing the inhabitants as much misery as a war could have done. Sending on three infantry brigades and one troop of cavalry to the village of Arbela, he joined them six weeks later with the rest of his army. His coming failed to frighten the enemy, who went out armed to meet him with all the skill of warriors as well as the fearlessness of bandits, and joining battle routed Herod's left wing with their right. Promptly swinging round his own right wing, Herod came to the rescue, made his fleeing troops face about, and falling on the pursuers brought their advance to a halt, finally by frontal attacks breaking their resistance and putting them to flight. He pursued them to the Jordan, attacking all the way and destroying a large proportion of them, the survivors scattering beyond the river. Galilee could now breathe again; the only bandits left were lurking in caves, and it would take time to deal with them. So Herod's next act was to bestow on his soldiers the fruits of their toil, awarding each man 150 silver drachmas and sending much larger sums to the officers in the various camps in which they were wintering. Pheroras, his younger brother, he appointed to lay in stores of provisions for them and to fortify Alexandreum. Both tasks Pheroras faithfully performed.

At this period Antony was living near Athens, and Ventidius sent for Silo and Herod to take part in the Parthian war, instructing them first to settle the problem of Judaea. Herod was delighted to second Silo to Ventidius, while he himself took the field against the bandits in the caves. These caves opened on to almost vertical slopes and could not be reached from any direction except by winding, steep, and very narrow paths; the cliff in front stretched right down into ravines of immense depth dropping straight into the torrent-bed. So for a long time the king was defeated by the appalling difficulty of the ground, finally resorting to a plan fraught with the utmost danger. He lowered the toughest of his soldiers in cradles till they reached the mouths of the caves; they then slaughtered the bandits with their families and threw firebrands at those who proved awkward. Wishing to save some of them Herod invited them to come up to him. Not a man voluntarily surrendered, and of those who were brought out forcibly many preferred death to captivity. One old man, father of seven children, was begged by the children and their mother to let them come out as their lives were guaranteed. His response was terrible. One by one he ordered them to come out, while he stood at the cave-mouth and killed each son as he emerged. Herod, in a good position to watch, was cut to the heart, and stretched out his hand to the old man, begging him to spare his children; but he, treating the suggestion with contempt, went so far as to sneer at Herod for his lack of guts, and after disposing of the last of his sons and killing his wife too, flung their bodies down the precipice and finally leapt over the edge himself.

Master now of caves and cave-dwellers, Herod left what he deemed a sufficient force to deal with any rising, with Ptolemy in command, and turned back towards Samaria with 600 cavalry and 3,000 heavy infantry to settle accounts with Antigonus. His departure removed all restraint from the habitual trouble-makers in Galilee; they killed his general Ptolemy in a surprise attack and systematically ravaged the country, establishing their lairs in the marshes and other inaccessible places. Informed of the rising Herod speedily came to the rescue, destroyed a large number of the insurgents, reduced by siege all their fortresses, and as a penalty for their fickleness made the towns pay a fine of 100 talents.

By now the Parthians had been driven out and Pacorus killed; so Ventidius was able at Antony's suggestion to send support to Herod in his struggle with Antigonus – two legions and 1,000 horse. Their commander Machaeras received a letter from Antigonus begging him to come to his aid instead, complaining bitterly of Herod's unscrupulous use of force against his kingdom, and promising to make it worth his while. Machaeras however was not prepared to disobey higher authority – especially as Herod was offering more; so he refused to turn traitor, and simulating friendship went to spy out Antigonus' position, disregarding Herod's warnings. Antigonus was not deceived, but shut the City gates in his face and shot at him from the ramparts as an enemy, till the crestfallen general returned to Herod at Emmaus, so furious at his failure that he killed every Jew he met on the way, not sparing even Herod's men but treating everyone as a supporter of Antigonus. This made Herod so angry that he was on the point of attacking Machaeras as an enemy, but mastering his rage set out for Antony's headquarters to expose the outrageous conduct of his subordinate. Machaeras, realizing his mistake, followed on the king's heels and by eating humble pie mollified him. But Herod continued his journey all the same; and when he heard that Antony was conducting a large scale attack on Samosata, a well-fortified city near the Euphrates, he increased his speed, seeing an excellent chance of showing his mettle and placing Antony under an obligation. And so it proved. As soon as he arrived he finished the siege for them, killing masses of the enemy and capturing quantities of booty, so that Antony's old admiration for his prowess was greatly strengthened, and he heaped new honours upon him, confirming his hopes of mounting the throne; while King Antiochus was forced to surrender Samosata.

Meanwhile a heavy blow befell Herod's fortunes in Judaea. He had left his brother Joseph in complete charge, instructing him to make no move against Antigonus till his return, since the unreliability of Machaeras as an ally was evident from what he had done. But as soon as Joseph heard that his brother was a long way off, he disregarded his instructions and marched towards Jericho with five cohorts contributed by Machaeras; he went with the intention of seizing the corn-crop at the height of summer. In hilly and difficult country he was set upon by his adversaries; he himself was killed after playing a hero's part in the battle, and the Romans perished to a man. The cohorts were new levies from Syria, with no stiffening of veterans to strengthen the morale of raw recruits. Not satisfied with his victory, Antigonus went to such an extreme of fury that he even mutilated Joseph's corpse. Having got possession of the bodies of the dead he cut off his head, although his brother Pheroras offered to redeem it for 50 talents. Antigonus' victory was followed by such an upheaval in Galilee that his partisans dragged the more important of Herod's adherents to the lake and drowned them. Many parts of Idumaea too changed sides, though Machaeras was there, rebuilding a stronghold called Gittha.

Not a word of all this had yet come to Herod's ears. After the fall of Samosata Antony had made Sossius governor of Syria, instructing him to assist Herod against Antigonus, while he himself returned to Egypt. Sossius accordingly sent two legions ahead to reinforce Herod in Syria, following on his heels with the rest of his army. But while Herod was at Daphne near Antioch, vivid dreams informed him of his brother's death, and as he sprang in alarm from his bed messengers came in with news of the disaster. For a brief while he gave vent to his distress, then postponing further mourning hurried off at a killing pace in the direction of his enemies. Arriving at Lebanon he was reinforced by 800 of the hillmen and joined by one Roman legion. Without waiting for daylight he led this mixed force into Galilee, where he was met by the enemy but drove them back to their base and began a continuous assault on its fortifications. Before he could take it a phenomenal storm compelled him to seek shelter in the village nearby. When a few days later the second legion sent by Antony joined forces with him, his increased strength alarmed the enemy, and in the night they abandoned the stronghold. Herod next passed through Jericho, determined to take the speediest vengeance on his brother's killers. There thanks to providence he had an astonishing and miraculous escape, which gained him the reputation of the darling of heaven. Many of the local magistrates had dined with him that evening, and when the banquet was over and everyone had left, the building promptly caved in. Deeming this a joint portent of dangers and deliverance in the coming campaign, at dawn he set forward with his army. About 6,000 of the enemy charged down from the hills and engaged his advance guard: they did not feel too inclined to meet the Romans hand to hand, but pelted them at long range with stones and javelins, wounding a large number, including Herod himself, who as he rode along was struck by a javelin in the side.

It was the wish of Antigonus to give the impression that his men were superior not only in daring but also in numbers; so he sent Pappus, one of his associates, with an army to Samaria. Their task was to oppose Machaeras. Herod for his part overran the enemy country, reduced five little towns, destroyed 2,000 of the inhabitants, fired the houses, and returned to his camp near the village of Cana.[1] He was joined by a steady stream of Jews from Jericho and other places, some through hatred of Antigonus, some impressed by Herod's successes, most in the grip of an unaccountable longing for change. Herod was impatient for a fight, and Pappus, completely confident in the face of superior numbers and Herod's extraordinary energy, advanced against him eager for the fray. When the clash came, most of the enemy line stood firm for a time; but Herod, remembering his murdered brother and risking everything to get his revenge on the murderers, quickly mastered the troops facing him and then attacked in turn all the groups that still held out, till in the end the whole army was in flight. The carnage was frightful, the enemy driven back into the village from which they had set out, Herod mercilessly assailing their rear and killing more than could be counted. Along with the enemy he rushed into the village, where every house was packed with armed men and the roofs crowded with defenders who threw missiles down at him. First defeating those outside, he tore the houses to pieces and dragged out those within. On a great many he pulled down the roofs, destroying them en masse; those who crawled out of the ruins were met by the soldiers sword in hand: so vast were the piles of corpses that the streets were blocked to the victors. Such a blow the enemy could not survive; those who reassembled after the battle, seeing the destruction in the village, fled in all directions. Emboldened by his victory, Herod would at once have driven on to Jerusalem, if he had not been held up by a most violent storm. This circumstance robbed him of his crowning success and final defeat of Antigonus, who was already planning to abandon the City.

In the evening Herod dismissed his weary comrades to refresh themselves while he himself, still hot from the fight, went to take a bath like any other soldier, attended by a single slave. He was on the point of entering the bath-house when one of the enemy dashed out in

1. *Surely impossible. According to* Antiquities, *Isana.*

front of him sword in hand, then a second and a third, with others in their train. These men had fled from the battlefield into the bath-house fully armed. There they had cowered unnoticed for a time, but when they saw the king, they lost their nerve entirely and ran past him, un-armed as he was, shaking with fear, and dashed for the exits. As it happened, no one else was there to seize the men and Herod was con-tent to have come to no harm, so they all got away. Next day he cut off the head of Pappus, Antigonus' general, who had perished in the fight-ing, and sent it to his brother Pheroras as reparation for their murdered brother; for it was Pappus who had killed Joseph.

When the storm died down Herod drove on towards Jerusalem and brought his army up to the walls. It was now the third year since he had been proclaimed king in Rome. He pitched his camp opposite the Temple, as from that direction an attack could be launched, and it was from there that Pompey had captured the City. Dividing the task among the troops, he stripped the suburbs of trees and ordered three artificial platforms to be raised and towers erected on them. Then, leaving his most competent subordinates to supervise the work, he went off to Samaria to fetch Alexander's daughter, whom he had promised to marry, as mentioned before. He made his wedding inci-dental to the siege – he no longer took the enemy seriously. The wedding over, back he went to Jerusalem with still stronger forces. Sossius too joined him at the head of a very large army of horse and foot which he had sent on by the inland route while he himself marched through Phoenicia. The combined forces totalled eleven infantry brigades and 6,000 cavalry, not counting the Syrian auxiliaries, who added considerably to the strength. They encamped together near the north wall, Herod relying on the senatorial decrees appointing him king, Sossius on Antony's decision to send the army under his com-mand to support Herod.

The Jewish masses throughout the City were variously affected by their agitation. Crowding round the Sanctuary the feebler creatures behaved as if possessed, and feigning inspiration poured out a mass of 'prophecies' to fit the situation; the bolder spirits went out in gangs to carry out raids of every kind, and especially to seize all supplies within reach of the City, leaving no food for man or beast. Of the fighting-men the more disciplined were organized to resist the besiegers; from the ramparts they hindered the raising of the platforms and coun-tered the engines with a succession of new devices: in nothing did they score so much over the enemy as in their mining-operations. The king parried the raids by devising ambushes which put a stop to their excursions; he overcame the food shortage by fetching supplies from a distance; and he got the better of the fighting-men by using Roman tactical skill, though they showed amazing audacity. In broad daylight they would hurl themselves against the Roman lines to certain death, and through their mine-shafts they would suddenly appear in the middle of Herod's men; and before any section of the wall was battered down they would build another in its stead – in short, with neither hand nor brain did they show the slightest weariness, determined as they were to hold out to the last. Indeed despite the overwhelming strength of the besieging army, they maintained their resistance for more than four months.

Finally some of Herod's storm-troopers ventured to scale the wall and leap into the City, followed by Sossius' centurions. First to be captured was the area round the Temple; then the army poured in and there was frightful carnage everywhere, as the Romans were furious at the length of the siege, and Herod's Jewish soldiers determined that not one opponent should survive. They were massacred by the thousand, crowded together in streets and houses or fleeing to the Sanctuary. No mercy was shown to infants or the aged, or to defenceless women. Although the king sent round imploring them to discriminate, no one stayed his hand, but as if raging mad they vented their fury on every age alike. At this point Antigonus, paying no regard to his past or to his present position, came down from his palace and fell at Sossius' feet. The Roman, not in the least moved by his changed situation, laughed uproariously and called him Antigone. But he did not treat him like a woman and let him go free: he put him in fetters and kept him in custody.

Herod's first problem after mastering his enemies was to master also his foreign allies; for the alien masses were determined to see the Temple and the sacred things inside the Sanctuary. The king appealed to some, threatened others, and drove yet others back by force of arms, thinking victory more terrible than defeat if such people got a glimpse within the Veil. At the same time he stopped all looting in the City, telling Sossius with the utmost emphasis that if the Romans stripped the City of money and men they would leave him king of a desert, and that for the slaughter of so many citizens he would regard a worldwide empire as inadequate compensation. When Sossius insisted that after the strain of the siege it was only right to let the men pillage, he undertook to distribute rewards to the whole army out of his own pocket. Ransoming thus what was left of his mother-city he kept his promises; he rewarded every soldier handsomely, and the officers in proportion, Sossius himself right royally, so that no one went short of money. Sossius dedicated to God a golden crown and then bade farewell to Jerusalem, taking Antigonus in fetters to Antony. The fallen ruler, clinging to life to the very end though hope was dead,[1] died as such a coward deserved – by the axe.

King Herod did not make the mistake of treating all the citizens alike: by bestowing honours on those who had taken his side he increased their devotion; the supporters of Antigonus he liquidated. As money was now tight, he turned all his personal treasures into cash and sent it to Antony and his staff. Even so he could not buy freedom from all trouble: Antony, ruined by his passion for Cleopatra, had become the complete slave of his desire, while Cleopatra had gone right through her own family till not a single relation was left alive, and thirsting now for the blood of strangers was slandering the authorities in Syria and urging Antony to have them executed, thinking that in this way she would easily become mistress of all their possessions. She even extended her acquisitiveness to Jews and Arabs and worked in secret to get their kings, Herod and Malichus, put to death.

Antony was sober enough to realize that one part of her demands – the killing of honest men and famous kings – was utterly immoral; but he cut them to the heart by withdrawing his friendship. He sliced off large parts of their territory, including the palm-grove at Jericho in which the balsam is produced, and gave them to Cleopatra along with all the cities except Tyre and Sidon on this side of the river Eleutherus. Mistress now of this domain she escorted Antony as far as the Euphrates on his way to fight the Parthians, and then came via Apamea and Damascus into Judaea. Herod placated her hostility with costly gifts, and leased back from her the lands broken off from his kingdom, at 200 talents a year! Finally he escorted her all the way to Pelusium, showing her every attention. It was not long before Antony reappeared from Parthia, bringing a prisoner – Artabazes the son of Tigranes – as a present for Cleopatra, to whom, along with the money and all the booty, the unfortunate Parthian was immediately handed over.

1. *Literally 'cold', which conceals a feeble pun.*

When the war that ended at Actium broke out, Herod prepared to take the field with Antony, having settled all disturbances in Judaea and captured Hyrcania, a fortress till then in the hands of Antigonus' sister. But he was prevented by Cleopatra's cunning from sharing Antony's dangers; as mentioned already she was scheming against the kings, and now she persuaded Antony to entrust Herod with the war against the Arabs – if he won she would become mistress of Arabia, if he lost, of Judaea, and she would be using one ruler to get rid of the other.

It was Herod, however, who benefited by her scheme. He began by plundering enemy country, then got together a large force of cavalry and sent them into battle near Diospolis, emerging victorious despite determined resistance. This defeat led to feverish activity among the Arabs, who gathered at Canatha in Coele-Syria in enormous strength and awaited the Jews. There Herod arrived with his army, and endeavouring to conduct his campaign with great circumspection ordered a camp to be fortified. His soldiers, however, disregarded his commands, and elated by their earlier success attacked the Arabs, routed them at the first charge and followed in pursuit. But in the pursuit Herod was the victim of treachery, the inhabitants of Canatha being sent against him by Athenio, one of Cleopatra's generals who was permanently hostile. Their onslaught restored the morale of the Arabs, who turned about, and joining forces on rocky, difficult ground routed Herod's men, slaughtering them wholesale. Those who escaped from the battle sought shelter in Ormiza, but their camp was surrounded and captured with all its defenders by the Arabs.

Soon after this disaster Herod brought up reinforcements, but he was too late. Responsibility for the tragedy rested with his undisciplined subordinates; if battle had not been joined prematurely, Athenio would have found no opportunity for treachery. Still, Herod got even with the Arabs later by repeatedly overrunning their country, so that they often had reason to remember their one victory. But while he was settling accounts with his enemies another disaster befell him, an act of God occurring in the seventh year of his reign at the height of the Actian War. At the beginning of spring there was an earthquake which destroyed 30,000 people and numberless cattle. The army escaped unhurt, as it was camping in the open. At once Arab confidence was stimulated by rumour, which always makes disasters seem worse than they are. Convinced that Judaea was one vast ruin, the land deserted and at their mercy, they descended on it, first offering as sacrificial victims the envoys who had just arrived from Judaea. This invasion completely demoralized the people – their spirit was broken by the succession of overwhelming disasters; so Herod brought them together and tried by the following appeal to awaken the spirit of resistance.

'It is surely quite unnecessary to take fright like this. To be upset by an act of God was natural enough; to be equally upset when men attack you shows a very poor spirit. I for one am so far from being alarmed because the enemy have come after the earthquake that I believe God sent it to trap the Arabs, and make them pay us the penalty for what they have done. It was not so much their own strength and skill as our accidental misfortunes that gave them confidence to come here – and it is a poor hope that depends not on one's own ability but on other people's troubles! No one can count on either bad luck or good going on for ever – everybody knows how fickle fortune is. You can see an example of that very near home. You won the first battle, they won the second; now they expect to win and are pretty certain to lose. Cock-sure people are caught napping, those who scent danger keep their eyes open; so your nervousness makes me feel all the safer. When you were overbold and went for the enemy against my wishes, Athenio seized his chance to catch us out; now that you hang back and seem down in the mouth, I am dead certain we shall win. That is how you *should* feel while waiting for something to happen: when it does happen, you must see red, and show these dirty louts that nothing God or man can do to us will ever damp the fighting spirit of Jews as long as they have breath in their bodies, and that no Jew will stand by while his property goes to an Arab who time and time again has only just missed becoming his prisoner.

'Again, you needn't turn a hair at the upheavals of the physical world, or imagine that the earthquake is a warning of another disaster to come. These elemental disturbances are quite natural and do us no harm beyond the immediate damage. Plague, famine, and earth tremors may perhaps be foreshadowed by some slighter indication, but the actual calamities are too big to go beyond their own limits. Do you think we could suffer more than we did in the earthquake, even if we lost the war? No; it is our enemies that have received the clearest warning of the coming crash, not from some natural occurrence or the action of someone else, but from their own guilty consciences. In defiance of international law they have brutally murdered our envoys; such are the victims they have sacrificed to get God on their side! But they will not escape His all-seeing eye and invisible right arm; they will soon pay us the penalty, if we show something of the spirit of our fathers and rouse ourselves to give these treaty-breakers what they deserve. Let every man take up arms to champion, not his wife, his children, or his threatened country, but our murdered envoys; they will be more inspiring leaders in the war than we who are alive can ever be. For my part, if you will obey my orders, I will be in the forefront of the battle; you know well enough that unless by some rash act you injure your own cause, your gallantry is irresistible.'[1]

By this speech Herod put new spirit into his soldiers, and satisfied with their enthusiasm he sacrificed to God, immediately afterwards crossing the Jordan with his army. Pitching his camp near Philadelphia[2] quite close to the enemy, he began skirmishing with them for the possession of a fort in No Man's Land, being anxious for an early trial of strength. It happened that the enemy had sent a party forward to seize this strongpoint; the king's men quickly drove them back and occupied the hill. Herod himself daily led out his forces, deployed them for battle, and challenged the Arabs. Not a man came forward to oppose him – they were in a state of utter panic, and even more than the rank and file their general Elthemus was incapacitated by terror – so he advanced to their palisade and began to tear it down. At that they had to do something, and they came out to battle in disorder, infantry mixed with cavalry. In numbers they had the advantage of the Jews, but in enthusiasm they could not be compared, though desperation made even them show reckless courage. So as long as they stood their ground their losses were few, but when they turned tail many were killed by the Jews and many trampled to death by their friends. 5,000 fell in the rout; the remainder lost no time in crowding within their palisade. Surrounded and besieged by Herod, they would have fallen to an assault if the failure of their water-supply had not forced them to send envoys at once. These the king treated with contempt, and the offer of 500 talents only made him intensify his attacks. Parched with thirst, the defenders came out en masse and voluntarily gave themselves up, till after five days 4,000 were in Jewish cages. Next day in desperation the remainder came out to give battle. Herod engaged

1. Josephus, dissatisfied with this effort of composition, in Antiquities provides Herod with a different speech.
2. Amman.

them and killed about 7,000 more. By this overwhelming blow he settled his account with Arabia and humbled the pride of her people so triumphantly that the nation chose him as their Protector.

No sooner was that difficulty overcome than Herod's whole future was in the melting-pot because of his friendship with Antony, whom Caesar had defeated at Actium. Actually he occasioned more alarm than he felt; for Caesar was not sure that Antony was finished while his ally Herod remained. But the king determined to come to grips with his danger, and sailing to Rhodes where Caesar was at the time, sought an audience without his crown, in the dress and with the appearance of a commoner, but with the haughtiness of a king. He kept back nothing and spoke as man to man.

'It was Antony, Caesar, who set me on the throne, and I freely admit that to Antony I have rendered every possible service. Nor do I hesitate to say that you would certainly have found me fighting loyally by his side if the Arabs had not prevented it. As it was I sent him all the reinforcements I could and many thousand sacks of corn; and not even after his defeat at Actium did I desert my benefactor – I gave him the best possible advice, as it was no use sending any more soldiers; I told him there was only one way of retrieving his disasters – Cleopatra's death. If he would kill her I promised money, protecting walls, an army, and my active participation in the war against you. But there it is! His ears were stopped by his insane passion for Cleopatra – and by God who has given the victory to you. I am defeated with Antony and with his fall I lay aside my crown. I have come to you placing my hope of safety in my unblemished character, and believing that you will wish to know not whose friend, but what sort of friend, I have been.'

Caesar replied: 'You are perfectly safe, and your throne is now more securely yours. You deserve to rule over many subjects after showing such loyalty to your friend. Try to be as faithful to those who enjoy better success; for my part, I see a dazzling prospect for such a bold spirit as yourself. It is a very good thing that Antony listened to Cleopatra and not to you: we have gained you through his folly. It seems I am already in your debt, as Quintus Didius writes to tell me you have sent a contingent to help him deal with the gladiators.[1] I now therefore issue a decree that the throne is securely yours. Before long I shall endeavour to show you some further favour, so that you may not have lost anything with Antony.'

1. *Summoned to her aid by Cleopatra.*

After addressing these gracious words to the king and setting the crown on his head, he published a decree announcing the award and expressing with the utmost generosity his high opinion of the beneficiary. After placating him with presents Herod interceded on behalf of Alexas, a friend of Antony, who had asked for mercy. But Caesar's anger brooked no opposition; he vigorously and bitterly condemned the petitioner, firmly rejecting Herod's appeal. Later, when Caesar travelled to Egypt via Syria, Herod welcomed him for the first time with all his kingly wealth, rode by his side when he inspected his army near Ptolemais,[1] and gave a banquet for him and all his Gentlemen, finally providing a feast of good things for the rest of the army. As the troops were to march through the desert to Pelusium and back, he took care to supply water in abundance, and the army lacked nothing in the way of supplies. The thought naturally occurred to Caesar and his men that in view of his generosity Herod's kingdom was far too small. So when Caesar arrived in Egypt, and Cleopatra and Antony were now dead, he showered honours upon him, restored to his kingdom the area sliced off by Cleopatra, and added Gadara, Hippus, and Samaria, with the coastal towns Gaza, Anthedon, Joppa, and Strato's Tower. He further made him a present of 400 Gauls, to be his bodyguard as they had formerly been Cleopatra's. Of all his liberality there was no more potent cause than the open-handedness of the recipient.

After the first Actiad[2] Caesar added to Herod's kingdom Trachonitis, Batanaea that adjoined it, and Auranitis. This is how it came about. Zenodorus had leased the estate of Lysanias, and he never stopped sending bandits from Trachonitis to waylay the Damascenes. These sought the protection of Varro, governor of Syria, and begged him to bring their plight to the notice of Caesar; Caesar's response was to authorize the destruction of the nest of bandits. Varro therefore mobilized his forces, cleared the district of these rogues, and dispossessed Zenodorus; to prevent it from again becoming a base for raids on Damascus, Caesar later transferred it to Herod. When after an interval of ten years he paid a second visit to the province, he made him procurator of all Syria, with power to veto any decision of the other procurators; and when Zenodorus died he assigned to him also the whole area between Trachonitis and Galilee. What counted still more

1. Acre.
2. An Actiad was a four-year period culminating in athletic sports, on this occasion held in 24 B.C.

with Herod was that in Caesar's affections he was second only to Agrippa, in Agrippa's second only to Caesar. From then on he climbed to the very heights of prosperity, while his moral stature increased and his superb generosity was largely devoted to works of piety.

In the 15th year of his reign[1] he restored the existing Sanctuary and round it enclosed an area double the former size, keeping no account of the cost and achieving a magnificence beyond compare. This could be seen particularly in the great colonnades that ran round the entire Temple and the fortress that towered over it to the north. The former were completely new structures, the latter an extremely costly reconstruction, as luxurious as a palace, and named Antonia in honour of Antony. His own palace, built in the Upper City, consisted of two very large and very lovely buildings which made even the Sanctuary seem insignificant: these he named after his friends, one Caesareum, one Agrippeum.

But it was not in buildings only that he enshrined their memory and names; through his lavish generosity whole cities came into being. In the district of Samaria he built a city with magnificent walls over two miles long, settled in it 6,000 colonists, allotted to them some land in excellent heart, and in the centre of the new town erected a vast shrine with precincts dedicated to Caesar 300 yards in length. The town he called Sebaste, and to the citizens he granted a very special charter. At a later date, when Caesar had enriched him by the addition of further lands, there also he erected a shrine of white marble dedicated to his patron, near the sources of the Jordan at a place called Paneum. There is a mountain here whose top is lost in the clouds; in the lower slopes is a cavern with its mouth concealed by vegetation, inside which a sheer precipice descends, nobody knows how far, to a cavity filled with still water: no plummet has ever reached the bottom, however long the cord. From the roots of the cavern outside well up the springs which some consider to be the head-waters of Jordan. A true account will be given later.[2] At Jericho, between the fortress of Cypros and the old palace buildings, he built others, better and more comfortable for visitors, named after the same friends. In fact I cannot think of any suit-

1. *In two different books of* Antiquities *we are told that it was the 18th year. This seems to be correct. Reckoning from Herod's capture of Jerusalem in 37 B.C. we get 20 as the date of the founding of Herod's temple. From St John ii 20 we should then deduce that the first cleansing took place in A.D. 27, a date confirmed by St Luke iii 1.*

2. *See page 220.*

able spot in his kingdom that he left without some tribute of esteem for Caesar. When he had filled his own country with temples these tributes overflowed into his province, and in city after city he erected a Caesareum.

He noticed on the coast a town called Strato's Tower, in a state of decay, but thanks to its admirable situation capable of benefiting by his generosity. He rebuilt it entirely with limestone and adorned it with a most splendid palace. Nowhere did he show more clearly the liveliness of his imagination. The city lies midway[1] between Dora and Joppa, and hitherto the whole of that shore had been harbourless, so that any-one sailing along the Phoenician coast towards Egypt had to ride the open sea when threatened by the south-west wind; even when this is far from strong, such huge waves are dashed against the rocks that the back-wash makes the sea boil up a long way out. But the king by lavish expenditure and unshakable determination won the battle against nature and constructed a harbour bigger than the Piraeus, with further deep roadsteads in its recesses. The site was as awkward as could be, but he wrestled with the difficulties so triumphantly that on his solid fabric the sea could make no impression, while its beauty gave no hint of the obstacles encountered. He first marked out the area for a harbour of the size mentioned, and then lowered into 20 fathoms of water blocks of stone mostly 50 feet long, 9 deep and 10 broad, sometimes even bigger. When the foundations had risen to water-level he built above the surface a mole 200 feet wide; half this width was built out to break the force of the waves and so was called the Breakwater; the rest supported the encircling stone wall. Along this were spaced massive towers, of which the most conspicuous and most beautiful was called Drusium after Caesar's step-son.

There was a row of arched recesses where newly-arrived crews could land, and in front of these in an unbroken circle was a stone ledge forming a broad walk for those disembarking. The harbour-mouth faced north, as in that locality the north wind is the gentlest, and on either side rose three colossal statues standing on pillars; those on the left of ships entering were supported by a solid tower, those on the right by two upright stones clamped together, even higher than the tower on the other side. Adjoining the harbour were houses, also of limestone, and to the harbour led the streets of the town, laid out the same distance apart. On rising ground opposite the harbour-mouth

1. *Much nearer Dora.*

stood Caesar's temple, of exceptional size and beauty; in it was a colossal statue of Caesar, no whit inferior to the Olympian Zeus[1] which it
was intended to resemble, and one of Rome comparable with the Hera
of Argos. Herod dedicated the city to the province, the harbour to
those who sailed these seas, the honour of his new creation to Caesar;
and Caesarea was the name he gave it. The rest of the buildings –
theatre, amphitheatre, and market-place – were on a scale worthy of
that name. The king also instituted four-yearly games and called them
too after Caesar, gracing the first contest – held in the 192nd Olympiad
– with the personal gift of very valuable prizes, the royal bounty
extending not only to the winners but to those who came second and
third.

Herod also rebuilt Anthedon, a coastal town destroyed in war,
and renamed it Agrippeum. So devoted was he to his friend Agrippa
that he even engraved his name over the gate which he had erected in
the Temple.

If ever a man was full of family affection, that man was Herod. In
memory of his father he founded a city, choosing a site in the loveliest
plain in his kingdom with an abundance of rivers and trees, and naming
it Antipatris; and the fortress overlooking Jericho he refortified, making it outstandingly strong and beautiful, and dedicated it to his
mother under the name Cypros. To his brother Phasael he erected the
tower in Jerusalem that took his name; its design and tremendous
size we shall describe later. He also founded another city in the valley
running north from Jericho and called it Phasaelis.

Having immortalized his family and friends he did not neglect to
make his own memory secure. He built a fortress in the hills facing
Arabia and called it Herodium after himself, and seven miles from
Jerusalem he gave the same name to an artificial hill, the shape of a
woman's breast, adorning it more elaborately than the other. He encircled the top with round towers, filling the enclosed space with a
palace so magnificent that in addition to the splendid appearance of
the interior of the apartments the outer walls, copings, and roofs had
wealth lavished on them without stint. At very heavy cost he brought
in an unlimited supply of water from a distance, and furnished the
ascent with 200 steps of the whitest marble; the mound was of considerable height, though entirely artificial. Round the base he built
other royal apartments to accommodate his furniture and his friends,

1. *One of the seven wonders of the world.*

so that in its completeness the stronghold was a town, in its compactness a palace.

After this spate of building he extended his generosity to a great many cities outside his boundaries. For Tripolis, Damascus, and Ptolemais he provided gymnasia, for Byblus a wall, for Beirut and Tyre halls, colonnades, temples, and market-places, for Sidon and Damascus theatres, for the coastal Laodicea an aqueduct, for Ascalon baths, magnificent fountains, and cloistered quadrangles remarkable for both scale and craftsmanship; in other places he dedicated woods and parks. Many towns, as if they belonged to his kingdom, received gifts of land; other he endowed with revenues to finance for all time the annual appointment of a gymnasiarch – Cos, for instance – that the office might never lapse. Corn he bestowed on all who needed it. To Rhodes he over and over again gave money for naval construction, and when the temple of Apollo was burnt down he rebuilt it with new splendour out of his own purse. What need be said of his gifts to Lycia or Samos, or of his liberality to the whole of Ionia, sufficient for the needs of every locality? Even Athens and Sparta, Nicopolis and Mysian Pergamum are full of Herod's offerings, are they not? And the wide street in Syrian Antioch, once avoided because of the mud, did he not pave – two and a quarter miles of it – with polished marble, and to keep the rain off furnish it with a colonnade from end to end?

It may be suggested that all these benefits were enjoyed only by the particular community favoured; but his endowment of Elis was a gift not only to Greece in general but to every corner of the civilized world reached by the fame of the Olympic Games. Seeing that the games were declining for lack of funds and that the sole relic of ancient Greece was slipping away, he not only acted as president of the four-yearly meeting held when he happened to be on his way to Rome, but endowed them for all time with an income big enough to ensure that his presidency should never be forgotten. We should go on for ever if we tried to list the debts and dues he paid for others, as when he relieved Phaselis, Balanea, and the smaller Cilician towns of part of the burden of their annual taxation. However, his superb generosity was severely limited by the fear or arousing jealousy, or of being suspected of an ulterior motive for doing more for the cities than did their own masters.

Herod's bodily strength was as great as his power of mind. He had always excelled in hunting, owing his success mainly to his horsemanship. On a single day he once brought down forty beasts: the country breeds boars, and stags and wild asses are still commoner. He was also an incomparable fighter; on the training-round many were amazed to see his accuracy in throwing the javelin, and the regularity with which his arrows found the target. Beside his bodily and mental advantages he enjoyed the best of luck; he met with very few military defeats, and for these he was not to blame – they were due either to his soldiers' rashness or to someone's treachery.

CHAPTER 4

Herod's Murder of Mariamme and her Children

FOR his public successes fortune made Herod pay a terrible price in
his own house. His woes began with a woman whom he loved
passionately. At the start of his reign he had divorced the wife he had
married when a commoner, a native of Jerusalem called Doris, and
wedded Mariamme, the daughter of Aristobulus' son Alexander. She
was the cause of the divisions in his house, which began early and grew
worse after his return from Rome. First of all he banished from the City
his son by Doris, Antipater, for the sake of his children by Mariamme,
permitting him to return for the festivals alone. Next he executed his
wife's grandfather Hyrcanus on his return from Parthia, accusing him
of conspiracy. Hyrcanus had been taken prisoner by Barzapharnes
when he overran Palestine, but freed at the request of his sympathetic
countrymen beyond Euphrates. If only he had taken their advice not
to go across the river to Herod, he would not have perished when
innocent; but he was lured to his death by his grand-daughter's marriage, relying on that and unable to resist the pull of his homeland. He
provoked Herod not by claiming the throne, but because the throne
was really his.

Of Herod's five children by Mariamme two were girls and three
boys. The youngest of the boys died while at school in Rome; the two
eldest he brought up in royal style on account of their mother's noble
birth and because he was king when they were born. A more compelling reason was his passionate love of Mariamme, which every day
consumed him more fiercely, blinding him to the calamities his beloved
was bringing upon him; for Mariamme hated him as passionately as he
loved her. She had good reason to be revolted by his actions and could
speak freely because of her hold upon him, so she openly took him to
task for what he had done to her grandfather Hyrcanus and her
brother Jonathan. For he had not spared even him, child as he was; he
had given him the high-priesthood in his seventeenth year and after
bestowing the honour had immediately executed him, because when
he put on the sacred vestments and approached the altar during a
feast, the whole crowd had burst into tears. The boy was therefore sent

at night to Jericho and there, by Herod's commands, the Gauls took
him to a swimming-pool and drowned him.

These were the things for which Mariamme took Herod to task;
she then turned her attention to his mother and sister and heaped abuse
upon them. Herod was muzzled by his infatuation, but the women
were furious, and knowing that it was the most likely way of rousing
Herod brought against her the baseless charge of adultery. Among
much false evidence concocted to convince him, they accused her of
having sent a portrait of herself to Antony in Egypt, and in her over-
mastering licentiousness exposed herself, in spite of the distance, to a
man who was woman-mad and able to get his way by force. Herod
was thunderstruck; in his passionate love he was tormented by
jealousy; and he thought of the terrible skill with which Cleopatra
had disposed of King Lysanias and the Arab Malichus – he knew he
was in danger of losing not only his queen but his own life. So, as he
was bound for foreign parts, he put Mariamme in the care of Joseph,
husband of his sister Salome, a trustworthy man, loyal because of their
kinship, giving him secret instructions to kill her if Antony killed
Herod himself. Joseph, with no evil intention but simply to prove to
her how passionately the king loved her, as he could not bear that
even death should part them, disclosed the secret. On his return Herod,
during intercourse, protested with many oaths his devotion to her,
the only woman he had ever loved. 'And a nice way,' she exclaimed, 'to
show your love for me – giving Joseph instructions to kill me!' When
he learnt that the secret was out, Herod was frantic, and declared that
Joseph would never have revealed his instructions unless he had
seduced her. Blind with rage he leapt from the bed and rushed wildly
about the palace. This opportunity for slander his sister Salome seized
with both hands, assuring him that his suspicion of Joseph was true.
Driven mad by uncontrollable jealousy he ordered the instant execution of them both. But rage quickly gave way to remorse, and as anger
died down love was rekindled. So hot was the flame of his desire that he
could not believe her dead, but in his sickness of mind talked to her as if
still alive, until time revealed to him the terrible truth, and filled his
heart with grief as passionate as his love had been while she lived.[1]

The mother bequeathed her bitterness to her sons, who, aware of the
blood on their father's hands viewed him as an enemy, first at the time

1. *This unconvincing story is told again in* Antiquities *with wide differences and at
immense length.*

of their schooling in Rome, and still more when they returned to Judaea. As they approached manhood this feeling grew steadily stronger; and when they reached an age to marry and one wedded the daughter of his aunt Salome, the accuser of their mother, and the other the daughter of King Archelaus of Cappadocia, they made no further attempt to conceal their hatred. This boldness gave slanderers their chance, and more open suggestions were made to the king that both sons were plotting against him, and that the son-in-law of Archelaus, relying on his father-in-law, was getting ready to flee in order to accuse his father before Caesar. Stuffed with these slanders Herod, as a bulwark against his other sons, recalled his son by Doris, Antipater, and began in every way to show him preference.

This new attitude was more than the two sons could stomach: when they saw the commoner's son promoted, pride in their own birth made their anger uncontrollable, and every new annoyance called forth an outburst of wrath; so that they provoked increasing hostility while Antipater was now winning favour by his own efforts. He was very clever at flattering his father, and concocted a variety of slanders against his brothers, putting some of them into circulation himself and getting his close friends to broadcast others, till he destroyed any chance of his brothers' coming to the throne. Both in his will and by his public actions Herod declared him to be the heir: he was sent in royal state to Caesar, with the robes and all the other trappings except the crown. In time he was in a position to bring back his mother to Mariamme's bed; and by employing two weapons against his brothers, flattery and slander, he cleverly coaxed Herod into contemplating the execution of his sons.

Alexander was dragged by his father to Rome to be charged before Caesar with an attempt to poison him. Having at last a chance to bring his grievances into the open before a judge more experienced than Antipater and better balanced than Herod, the accused kept a respectful silence about his father's faults, but vigorously combated the imputations against himself. Having next made it clear that his brother and companion in danger was as innocent as he was, he went on to denounce the villainy of Antipater and the wrong done to his brother and himself. He was aided not only by a clear conscience but by the vigour of his oratory – he was a very effective speaker. Declaring as his peroration that his father was free to put them both to death if he was satisfied that the accusation was true, he reduced the whole court to tears, and so moved Caesar that he dismissed the charges and effected an immediate reconciliation, on the understanding that the sons should obey their father in everything and that he should be free to choose his successor. The king then took his leave of Rome, to all appearance abandoning the charges against his sons, but still retaining his suspicions; for he was accompanied by Antipater, who had inspired his hate, but dared not openly reveal his enmity through respect for the reconciler. As he skirted Cilicia Herod landed at Eleusa and was hospitably entertained by Archelaus, who expressed delight at his son-in-law's acquittal and the greatest satisfaction at the reconciliation: he had previously written to his friends in Rome to stand by Alexander at his trial. He escorted Herod to Zephyrium and gave him presents to the value of 30 talents.

Back in Jerusalem Herod assembled the citizens, presented his three sons, explained his absence, and expressed his deep gratitude to God and to Caesar for setting his troubled household to rights and bestowing on his sons something more precious than the throne – concord. 'That concord,' he went on, 'I shall myself knit together. Caesar made me lord of the realm and judge of the succession, and I while acting in my own interest will requite his kindness. I proclaim these three sons of mine kings, and call first on God, then on you, to confirm my decision. The succession belongs to one by priority of birth, to the others by their noble parentage: my kingdom is big enough for more than three. Whom Caesar has joined together and their father nominates you must defend, honouring them justly and equally, but each according to his birthright: to pay one more respect than his age entitles him to would give less pleasure to him than annoyance to the one neglected. The Counsellors and Gentlemen of the Household who are to attend each king I shall myself choose, appointing them securities for the preservation of concord, since I am well aware that divisions and rivalries are engendered by the malignity of the companions of princes, but if companions are good men they encourage feelings of affection.

'I must insist, however, that not only these officials but also the officers in my army place their hopes for the present in me alone: it is not kingship, but the honour due to kingship that I am bestowing on my sons. The sweets of power they will enjoy, but the burden of responsibility is mine, however unwelcome. Let each of you consider my age, my way of life, my piety. I am not so old that an early end is in sight, or given up to self-indulgence, which cuts men off even in their prime, and I have served the Almighty with such devotion that I may hope for a very long life. So any man who puts himself at the service of my sons in order to bring me down I shall punish for their sakes too: it is not meanness towards my own children that makes me limit the reverence to be paid them; it is the knowledge that to the young, adulation is a temptation to presumption. If everyone who comes into contact with these young men reflects that if he upholds what is right I shall reward him, but if he promotes division not even the man he is serving will give him any recompense for his malice, then everyone, I think, will be loyal to me – and that means to my sons; for it is in their interest that I should be on the throne, and in mine that their concord should be unbroken.

'You, my good sons, turn your thoughts first to the sacred laws of nature, which keep even beasts in the bonds of affection; then to Caesar, who brought about our reconciliation; and lastly to me, who entreat when I might command – and continue as brothers. I give you henceforth the robes and attendants of kings; and I pray that God will maintain my settlement, if your concord remains.'

So saying he gave each of his sons an affectionate embrace and dismissed the people, some of whom said Amen to his prayer, and others, who wanted a change, pretended they had not even heard it!

However, the brothers did not leave their divisions behind but parted still more suspicious of each other, Alexander and Aristobulus resenting the confirmation of Antipater's rights as the eldest, Antipater grudging even second place to his brothers. Antipater however was extremely shrewd and kept his mouth shut, concealing with the utmost cunning his detestation of the other two; whereas they, proud of their birth, made no secret of their feelings, goaded all the time by their 'friends', many of whom nosed their way in to spy on them. Every word uttered in Alexander's circle was immediately repeated in Antipater's, and passed on, with additions by Antipater to Herod. The young man could not make the most innocent remark without getting into trouble; everything he said was given an incriminating twist, and if he spoke unguardedly mountains were manufactured out of molehills. Antipater employed a succession of agents to draw him on, so that his own lies should have some foundation of truth, and if any one of the statements attributed to Alexander was proved authentic the rest were taken for granted. All his own friends were either naturally secretive or induced by gifts to divulge absolutely nothing: Antipater's life might fairly be described as a mystery of wickedness. Alexander's companions, on the contrary, had succumbed to bribery or subtle flattery, Antipater's invariable weapon, and become informers who betrayed all his actions and words. By the most adroit stage-management Antipater showed himself a pastmaster in the art of making slander sink into Herod's ears, himself acting the part of an affectionate brother and leaving the tale-bearing to others. Whenever a story was told to the discredit of Alexander, he would make his entrance and act his part, first tearing the story to pieces, then subtly confirming it and stirring the king to anger. Everything was turned into proof of conspiracy, and nothing did so much to win acceptance for the slanders as Antipater's appeals on his brother's behalf.

Thus deceived Herod grew savage, and every day cared less for the youths and proportionately more for Antipater. The courtiers followed his example, some willingly, some under compulsion, for instance Ptolemy his most valued friend, the king's brothers, and all his family. Antipater was everything and – the bitterest pill for Alexander to swallow – so was Antipater's mother, his fellow-conspirator and the cruellest of stepmothers, who hated her stepsons the more because their mother had been a princess. It followed that everyone fawned on Antipater now in the hope of advantage, and was encouraged to turn against Alexander and his brother by the king's command forbidding his most distinguished subjects to go near them or have anything to do with them. His word was law not only in his own kingdom but among his friends abroad: to no other king had Caesar given the right to demand the extradition from another sovereign state of a fugitive national.

Blissfully ignorant of these slanders the youths exposed themselves to them all the more, as their father never openly took them to task; but gradually the truth dawned on them, as they perceived his coldness and growing exasperation over petty annoyances. Antipater also poisoned against them the mind of their uncle Pheroras and aunt Salome, whom he coaxed and prodded as if she had been his wife! Her enmity was further stimulated by Alexander's wife Glaphyra, who vaunted her noble lineage and claimed precedence over all the ladies at court, as the descendant through her father of Temenus, through her mother of Darius Hystaspes; while she was never tired of sneering at the low birth of Herod's sister and wives, all of them chosen for their looks, not their parentage. He had many wives, as Jewish custom had always allowed polygamy, and the king was strongly in favour ! Every one of these, provoked by Glaphyra's contemptuous boasting, detested Alexander.

Salome, enraged already by Glaphyra's abuse, was alienated by her own son-in-law Aristobulus, who was constantly sneering at his wife for her humble origin, and lamenting that he had married a commoner and his brother Alexander a princess. Between her sobs she repeated this to her mother Salome, adding that Alexander and Aristobulus were threatening, when they succeeded to the throne, to force the mothers of the other brothers to work at the loom with the slaves, and to make the brothers village clerks – a mocking allusion to their careful schooling. Unable to contain herself Salome repeated the whole story to Herod: she was naturally believed as it was her son-in-law she was accusing. A further slander was brought at the same time to the king's ears, adding fuel to the flames. He was informed that the two brothers were constantly invoking their mother, bewailing her loss while they called down curses on him, and that often, when he distributed some of Mariamme's garments among his newer wives, they would threaten that instead of royal robes they would soon be wearing haircloth.

These tales made Herod fear the temper of the young men, but he still had hopes of correcting their faults; and on the eve of a voyage to Rome he summoned them before him, and after briefly threatening them as their king admonished them at great length as their father, urging them to love their brothers, and overlooking their offences in the past on condition that they behaved better in the future. They replied with a complete denial of the charges, declaring them to be baseless, and assuring him that they would prove their statements true by their actions; at the same time it was his duty to put a stop to tittle-tattle by being less ready to swallow it; there would never be an end to the lies told about them, as long as there was someone to believe them.

As he was their father they soon convinced him by these declarations and rid themselves of their immediate fears; but their anxiety for the future was increased now that they knew of the hostility of Salome and their uncle Pheroras. These two were dangerous enemies, especially Pheroras, who shared all the appurtenances of royalty except the crown. He had a private income of 100 talents, and enjoyed the revenue of all trans-Jordan, a gift from his brother, who beside obtaining Caesar's permission to appoint him tetrarch, honoured him with a royal marriage by giving him the hand of his own wife's sister. On her death he promised him his eldest daughter with a dowry of 300 talents; but Pheroras ran away from the royal marriage for love of a slave-girl. This enraged Herod, who married his daughter to his nephew, later killed by the Parthians. But before long he got over his annoyance with Pheroras and pardoned his love-sickness.

Pheroras had at an earlier date, when the queen was still alive, been falsely accused of conspiring to poison Herod; and now great numbers of informers came forward, so that Herod, though a most devoted brother, began to believe their stories and to take fright. After torturing many suspected persons he came finally to Pheroras' friends. None of these made a direct admission that there was a conspiracy, but they said that Pheroras was preparing to snatch up his loved one and make a dash for Parthia, partnered in his projected flight by Costobar, Salome's husband, to whom the king had given her hand after the execution of her former husband for adultery. Nor did Salome escape slander: her brother Pheroras accused her of pledging herself to marry Syllaeus, regent for Obadas, king of Arabia and a bitter enemy of Herod. Found guilty of this and every other offence with which Pheroras charged her, she was nevertheless pardoned. Pheroras himself was acquitted by the king on all counts.

The storm that threatened Herod's house struck Alexander, bursting about his head with all its violence. There were three eunuchs whom the king valued most highly, as is plain from the offices entrusted to them. One was detailed to pour out his wine and one to serve his dinner, while the third put him to bed and slept in his room. These Alexander by large presents had induced to minister to his unnatural lust. When this came to the king's ears he put them to the torture, and they at once confessed their criminal association, disclosing also the promises which had tempted them to it; they had been deceived by Alexander, who told them not to rest their hopes on Herod, a shameless old man who dyed his hair, unless that made them really think he was young; but to turn to Alexander, who would succeed to the throne whether Herod liked it or not, and at no distant date would settle accounts with his enemies and bring prosperity and happiness to his friends, above all to themselves. They added that leading citizens had secretly offered their services to Alexander, and that the generals and other officers of the army were conferring with him behind closed doors.

These revelations so alarmed Herod that he dared not immediately publish them, but sent out secret spies, night and day, to investigate all that was done or said; all suspects were at once executed. Complete anarchy reigned in the palace; to suit his personal animosity or hatred everyone invented slanders, and many availed themselves of the royal lust for blood to get rid of their rivals. Any lie found immediate acceptance, and the punishment came more swiftly than the slander. The man who had just accused another was himself accused; and he and his victim were led off to execution together; for the king's enquiries were cut short by the danger to his life. He became so embittered that he never smiled even at those not accused and was ready to bite the heads off his friends; many of these he debarred from the court, and those who were safe from his hand felt the lash of his tongue. On top of Alexander's misfortunes came Antipater, who with the collaboration of his Counsellors slandered him in every imaginable way. To such a pitch of terror was the king reduced by his ingenious lies and fabrications that he was convinced that Alexander stood over him sword in hand. So he suddenly arrested and imprisoned him and proceeded to put his Gentlemen to the torture. Many died without a word, or after saying only what they knew to be true; others were driven by their agonies to tell lies, and said that Alexander and his brother Aristobulus were plotting against him and awaiting a chance to kill him during the chase and make a dash for Rome. This improbable story, extemporized under pressure, the king was glad to accept, feeling more comfortable about the imprisonment of his son now that it seemed justified.

When Alexander saw there was no way of shaking his father's belief, he determined to come to grips with his perils, and composed a four-volume indictment of his enemies, admitting the plot but naming most of them as accomplices, of whom the chief were Pheroras and Salome; the latter, he alleged, had one night actually forced her way into his room and had intercourse with him against his will. These volumes, full of clamorous and dreadful allegations against the highest in the land, came into Herod's hands, and shortly after Archelaus made a hurried journey to Judaea, in alarm for his daughter and son-in-law. In assisting them he showed remarkable tact, and by using guile he brought the king's threats to nothing. The moment he met him he let fly. 'Where is that perishing son-in-law of mine? Where shall I find that damned parricide? I will flay him alive with my own hands; and I will do the same to my daughter along with her charming husband! Even if she had no finger in the pie, she is his wife, and tarred with the same brush. I can't understand how you, the intended victim, can take it so calmly – if it is true that Alexander is still alive! *I* came full speed from Cappadocia expecting to find he had paid the penalty long ago, and to ask your advice about my daughter, whom I gave away to that scoundrel because of your great name; but now we must put our heads together about the pair of them, and if you are too much of a father or haven't the nerve to give your son what he deserves, we had better change places and carry out each other's sentences.'

Seeing the force of this argument Herod for a time transferred his anger from Alexander to Pheroras, the chief villain of the four volumes. He, observing this sudden change in the king's attitude and his complete acceptance of the suggestions of his friend Archelaus, saw no hope of saving himself by honest means, so decided to do it by sheer impudence. He dropped Alexander and applied to Archelaus. That monarch answered that he didn't see how he could plead for a man mixed up in such a shady business – which made it as plain as could be that he had plotted against the king and brought all the lad's present troubles on him – unless he was prepared to abandon his tricks and denials and plead guilty to the crimes he was charged with, and then ask pardon of his brother, who was still fond of him: if he would do that, he would help him in every possible way.

Pheroras took his advice, and after making careful preparations to look as woebegone as possible, clothed in black and with streaming eyes, grovelled at Herod's feet and begged for mercy – as he had done successfully on several previous occasions! He admitted he was a dirty scoundrel, guilty on every count, but blamed his unbalanced and frenzied state of mind, brought on, he said, by his passionate love for his wife. Having thus brought Pheroras to accuse and give evidence against himself, Archelaus now began to plead for him, and mitigate Herod's anger by quoting parallels in his own house: why, he himself had suffered much worse treatment at his brother's hands, but had never let revenge weaken the ties of blood; kingdoms were like fat men – one member or another was always getting inflamed because of the weight it carried; but this called, not for the surgeon's knife, but for a dose of medicine.

These arguments and others to the same effect softened Herod's

anger with Pheroras, but Archelaus continued to fume against
Alexander and insisted that he would divorce his daughter and take her
home, until he brought Herod round to the point of pleading with him
on the lad's behalf, and once more requesting the hand of his daughter
for his son. With a most convincing appearance of sincerity Archelaus
gave him leave to marry her to anyone he pleased – except Alexander;
he was most anxious to preserve the marriage links between himself
and Herod. The king replied that he would be receiving back his son as
a gift from him if he refrained from breaking the marriage; they already had children and the lad was most devoted to his wife; if she
stayed with him she would help him to be ashamed of his misdeeds,
but if she was torn from him his despair would be complete: a reckless
spirit was tamed when diverted by domestic affection. After long hesitation Archelaus gave in, was reconciled to the young man, and reconciled his father to him. However, he said it was necessary to send
him to Rome for an audience with Caesar, to whom he had himself
dispatched a detailed report.

Thus the stratagem by which Archelaus rescued his son-in-law was a
complete success. After the reconciliation they spent their time in
feasting and mutual entertainment. When he said goodbye Herod
made him a present of 70 talents, a golden throne set with precious
stones, eunuchs, and a concubine called Pannychis,[1] and rewarded all
his Gentlemen according to their rank. By the king's command all his
Counsellors similarly gave Archelaus magnificent gifts. Finally he was
escorted by Herod and the nobility all the way to Antioch.

Alas! it was not long before Judaea was visited by a man who could
do far more than the stratagems of Archelaus, and who not only
brought to an end the reconciliation Archelaus had contrived for
Alexander but actually compassed that young man's destruction. He
was a Laconian by birth named Eurycles, whose intrusion into the
kingdom was due to his passion for money: Greece no longer satisfied
his extravagance. He brought splendid gifts for Herod as a bait to
secure his ends, instantly receiving much bigger in return; but he had
no use for a straightforward gift unless he could make a profit out of the
kingdom by bloodshed. So he got round the king by compliments,
subtle suggestion, and hollow flattery. He quickly summed up Herod's
character, and playing up to him in all he said and did he soon became one of his closest friends: the king and all his court were only

1. 'All-night Entertainment'!

too glad to show special regard for this Spartan for his country's sake.

He soon became thoroughly acquainted with the rotten state of the royal house, the brothers' quarrels and their father's attitude to each, and though Antipater in view of his hospitality had the first claim on his gratitude, he professed friendship for Alexander, falsely claiming that he had long been an intimate friend of Archelaus. This won him instant acceptance as a proved ally, and an early introduction to Alexander's brother Aristobulus. Playing first one part and then another, in various ways he won the confidence of everybody; but his favourite rôles were those of hireling to Antipater and traitor to Alexander. He cried shame on Antipater if he, the eldest son, stood by while other people were after his expectations; and on Alexander if he, whose mother and wife were kings' daughter, allowed the crown to pass to a commoner's son, and that when he had the influential backing of Archelaus! The lad trusted him as a counsellor since he claimed the friendship of Archelaus; so, keeping nothing back, he told him of all the wrongs Antipater had done him, and of the likelihood that after killing their mother Herod would deprive him and his brother of her kingdom. With these grievances the tender-hearted Eurycles pretended to sympathize. Then he tricked Aristobulus into saying the same things, and having involved both in criticism of their father he went off to repeat their private conversation to Antipater, adding the lie that his brothers were after his blood and on the point of swooping on him sword in hand. These efforts having earned him a handsome dividend, he sang the praise of Antipater to his father. Finally terms were agreed for him to compass the death of Aristobulus and Alexander, and he undertook to accuse them before their father.

Presenting himself before Herod he declared that he was offering him life in return for his kindness, the light of day to repay his hospitality; a sword had long since been sharpened against him and Alexander had braced his arm – he himself had delayed the blow by feigned collaboration. He had heard Alexander say that Herod was not content to sit on a throne belonging to others, and after murdering their mother to squander her empire, but was actually dragging in a bastard as his successor and offering the kingdom of their grandfather[1] to that worm Antipater. But he would take the law into his own hands and avenge the spirits of Hyrcanus and Mariamme: he would never stoop to succeed such a father on the throne without bloodshed. Day after

1. *Josephus means their great-grandfather Hyrcanus.*

day he was subjected to constant annoyance, so that he could not make the most casual remark without its being turned against him. If other people's ancestry was mentioned, his father went out of his way to make insulting remarks such as 'Only Alexander has any ancestors: he thinks his father came out of the gutter!' At the hunt his very silence gave offence; if he paid a compliment he was accused of sarcasm. Everywhere he found his father impossible to please, and with no feeling for anyone but Antipater; so he would gladly die if he failed in his attempt. If he succeeded, his safety was guaranteed, first by Archelaus his father-in-law, to whom he could easily escape, then by Caesar, who was not yet aware of Herod's true character; he would not, as on a former occasion, stand before him intimidated by his father's presence, or confine himself to the discussion of his personal grievances; he would first of all openly proclaim the miseries of his people, bled white by taxation, and then reveal the luxuries and excesses on which all this blood-money was spent, the sort of men enriched at the expense of himself and his brother, and the means by which certain towns had won privileges. And while he was there he would demand an enquiry into the fate of his grandfather and his mother, and mercilessly expose the filth and corruption pervading the whole kingdom. There would be no question then of his being adjudged a parricide!

When he had concluded this scandalous diatribe against Alexander, Eurycles delivered a lengthy eulogy of Antipater as the only son with any affection for his father, and for that reason an obstacle to the plot hitherto. The king, who had not yet got completely over the earlier shocks, boiled over with uncontrollable anger. Antipater again seized his chance, and sent a fresh set of hush-hush informers to accuse his brothers of having held secret conferences with Jucundus and Tyrannus, once officers of the king's cavalry, but now because of some offences deprived of their commissions. At this Herod lost his temper completely and at once put the two men on the rack. They admitted none of the charges; but a letter was produced as sent by Alexander to the commandant at Alexandrium, requesting him to admit Aristobulus and himself to the fortress when he had killed their father, and to let them use the weapons and other resources of the place. Alexander protested that this letter had been forged by Diophantus the king's secretary, a man without scruples and very clever at imitating any hand, who after a lifetime of forgery was ultimately executed for that very offence. Herod put the commandant to the torture, but failed to extract

any information from him about the allegations. He found the evidence
unconvincing, but nevertheless kept his sons under surveillance though
still at liberty. The curse of his house and stage-manager of the whole
filthy business, Eurycles, he called Saviour and Benefactor and rewarded with 50 talents. Thus enriched he did not wait for the truth to
come out, but hurried off to Cappadocia, where he got money out of
Archelaus too by brazenly asserting that he had reconciled Herod to
Alexander. Then crossing to Greece he employed his ill-gotten gains in
promoting further mischief. Twice accused before Caesar of fostering
sedition all over Achaia and fleecing the townships, he was deported.
So he paid the penalty for what he had done to Alexander and Aristobulus.

How different from the Spartan was Evarestus of Cos! One of
Alexander's closest friends, he was in the country at the same time as
Eurycles, and when the king put to him the allegations made by the
latter he declared on oath that he had not heard the youngsters say any
such thing. But he could do nothing to help the unfortunate pair:
Herod was only too eager to listen to evil tongues and no others, and
welcomed only men as gullible and irascible as himself.

His savage treatment of his children received a further impetus
from Salome, the aunt and mother-in-law of Aristobulus, who wishing
to involve her in his own dangers sent her a hint to look after herself;
the king, he said, was ready to kill her on the charge previously brought
– that in her determination to wed the Arab Syllaeus she had treacherously disclosed to him the secrets of the king his enemy. This proved to
be the final gust that sent the storm-tossed youths to the bottom.
Salome ran to the king and reported the hint she had received. Herod,
finally giving way, put both his sons in fetters and in solitary confinement; then losing no time he sent Volumnius the military tribune and
one of his Gentlemen, Olympus, to Caesar with Salome's report in
writing. They sailed for Rome and delivered the king's dispatches.
Caesar was very grieved for the youths, but did not think that he ought
to undermine the father's authority over his sons; so he wrote back
leaving the matter to Herod's discretion, but recommending him to
convene a joint committee of his own Counsellors and the provincial
governors to enquire into the alleged conspiracy: if the charges were
proved, he should put his sons to death; if they had merely intended to
abscond, a lesser penalty would suffice.

Accepting this suggestion Herod went to Beirut, the place indicated by Caesar, and convened the court. In obedience to the Emperor's written instructions the bench was occupied by Roman officers, Saturninus and his legates (Pedanius and another), together with Volumnius the procurator. Also present were the king's Counsellors and Gentlemen, Salome, and Pheroras, and finally the nobility of all Syria, with the sole exception of King Archelaus, who as Alexander's father-in-law was distrusted by Herod. The sons were not brought into court – Herod was too shrewd for that, knowing they had only to be seen to melt all hearts, and if in addition they were allowed to speak Alexander would easily refute the charges. So they were kept in custody at Platana, a village near Sidon.

The king rose and, as if they were present, launched out into a bitter attack. His attempts to prove the charge of conspiracy were weak, owing to the lack of evidence; but he emphasized the insults, mocking speeches, outrages, and offences without number directed against him, harder to bear than death itself, as he told the court. Then he invited his silent audience to pity him, in that he himself was the sufferer even if he did win a bitter victory over his sons. Finally he asked them for their several opinions. First to reply was Saturninus, who was for condemning the youths, but not to death: it would not be right for a man with three children in court to vote for the execution of another man's children. His two legates voted the same way, and several others followed their lead. Volumnius was the first to advocate the death sentence, and all who spoke after him were for condemning the lads to death, some from flattery, some from hatred of Herod, no one from conviction that the accused were guilty. And now all Syria and Judaea were in suspense, waiting for the last scene of the drama; but no one guessed that Herod would be so barbarous as to murder his children. He however dragged his sons to Tyre, and after sailing from there to Caesarea weighed the possible methods of putting the lads to death.

There was an old soldier of the king called Tiro, whose son was a bosom friend of Alexander, and who was very fond of both lads himself. He was so overcome with indignation that his reason gave way and he went round shouting that justice had been trampled underfoot, truth was no more, nature in confusion, life in a state of anarchy – and anything else that occurred to a man deeply moved and without a thought for his own life. At length he went boldly to the king: 'You miserable wretch!' he thundered, 'that is what I think of you! To turn against your own flesh and blood at the bidding of utter scoundrels!

Over and over again you have condemned Pheroras and Salome to death – and now you take their word against your children! Don't you see they are cutting off your legitimate heirs and leaving you with only Antipater, choosing a king they can twist round their little finger? Take care, take care the army doesn't one day hate him as it hates you, because of his brothers' death: there is not one private who doesn't pity the lads, and many of the officers are cursing you openly.' He proceeded to give their names; and the king at once arrested them, along with Tiro and his son.

Directly after this one of the court barbers, called Trypho, sprang forward in the grip of some frenzy and informed against himself. 'I am in it too,' he shouted, 'Tiro here told me to cut your throat with my razor when I was shaving you, and promised that Alexander would pay me well.' Hearing this Herod examined Tiro, with his son and the barber, on the rack, and when the first two denied everything and the other had nothing to add, ordered Tiro to be racked still more severely. At last the son, greatly distressed, promised to tell the king everything if he would spare his father, and when Herod agreed he stated that his father had been persuaded by Alexander to plan his death. Some people thought that he had made this up in order to end his father's agony, others that it was true.

Herod called a mass meeting, at which he accused the officers and Tiro and enlisted the help of the people to dispose of them; along with the barber they were killed then and there with clubs and stones. Then he sent his sons to Sebaste, which was not far from Caesarea, giving orders that they should be strangled. The order being instantly carried out, he gave instructions for the bodies to be brought to the fortress of Alexandrium, to be buried by the side of Alexander, their mother's father. So ends the story of Alexander and Aristobulus.

CHAPTER 5

Herod's Murder of his Heir, and Death

ANTIPATER, now undisputed heir, had called down on his own head the utter loathing of the nation; for everyone knew that all the slanders directed against his brothers had originated with him. And he was filled with secret but terrible fear when he saw the dead men's children growing up. Glaphyra had borne Alexander two sons, Tigranes and Alexander; Bernice, Salome's daughter, had borne Aristobulus three sons, Herod, Agrippa, and Aristobulus, and two daughters, Herodias and Mariamme. Glaphyra Herod sent back to Cappadocia with her dowry after the execution of Alexander; Aristobulus' widow Bernice he married to the brother of Antipater's mother: it was to placate the hostility of Salome that Antipater arranged this marriage. He tried also to get round Pheroras with gifts and other attentions, and round Caesar's friends by sending large moneys to Rome. Saturninus and his staff in Syria all received more than enough of his presents. But his gifts made him the more hated, as it was obvious they were not spontaneous expressions of generosity but insurances against foreseen dangers. The result was that while the recipients liked him no better than before, those to whom he gave nothing became more bitter enemies. Yet he made his largesse daily more lavish, as he saw the king negativing his efforts by taking care of the orphans and showing his remorse for the murder of his sons by his tenderness towards their little ones.

One day Herod assembled his Counsellors and Gentlemen, set the children before them, and with brimming eyes began: 'The fathers of these children were snatched from me by some malignant spirit: they themselves are commended to my care both by natural ties and by pity for their orphanhood. I will try, though I have been most unfortunate as a father, at any rate to show myself a more devoted grandfather, and when I die to leave in charge of them those most dear to me. I betrothe your daughter, Pheroras, to the elder of Alexander's two boys, and so make you automatically his guardian; and to your son, Antipater, I give Aristobulus' daughter, so that you will become father to the orphan girl. Her sister my own Herod shall have, since on his mother's side he had a high priest for grandfather. Let my wishes be carried out in this way, and let no one who cares for me go against them. I pray God to seal these unions to the good of my kingdom and of my descendants, and to look with gentler eyes on these little children here than He ever looked on their fathers.' And now the tears flowed faster and he joined the children's hands; then after warmly embracing each in turn he dismissed the gathering.

His decision struck a sudden chill into Antipater, who made no attempt to hide his mortification. He felt that the honour shown by his father to the orphans meant the end of his hopes, and that his prospects of succession would again be in danger if not only Archelaus but Pheroras, a tetrarch, supported Alexander's heirs. He thought of the nation's hatred for himself and compassion for the orphans, of the devotion the Jews had felt for his brothers while they lived, and their tender memories of them now that thanks to him they were dead. So he made up his mind by fair means or foul to break these betrothals. He was afraid to try any tricks on a father so difficult and so prone to suspicion, so he took the bull by the horns and asked him direct not to rob him of the honour already conferred, or to give the name of king to him, the power to others; he would never be in control if with Archelaus as his grandfather Alexander's son should also have Pheroras as his father-in-law; as the Royal Family was so large, would he please reconsider the proposed marriages?

The king, indeed, had nine wives and children by seven of them. Antipater himself was the son of Doris, Herod of Mariamme, the high priest's daughter, Antipas and Archelaus of Malthace the Samaritan, their sister Olympias being married to Herod's nephew Joseph. By Cleopatra of Jerusalem he had Herod and Philip and by Pallas Phasael. He had other daughters, Roxane and Salome, the first by Phaedra, the second by Elpis. Two wives were childless, a cousin and a niece. Apart from these there were the two sisters of Alexander and Aristobulus, children of Mariamme.[1] The family being of such exceptional size, Antipater asked for the marriage arrangements to be reconsidered.

On realizing how Antipater regarded the orphans the king was extremely angry, and it flashed across his mind that the murdered men might also be victims of Antipater's slanders. So for the moment he made a long and bitter reply and sent the fellow packing. Later however he succumbed to his flatteries and altered the arrangements,

1. Not included in the nine wives.

marrying Aristobulus' daughter to Antipater himself and Pheroras'
daughter to his son. How effective was his flattery in this instance can
be seen from Salome's failure in a like case. She was Herod's sister, and
was backed by Caesar's wife Julia[1] in her repeated requests to marry the
Arab Syllaeus; but Herod swore he would count her his worst enemy
if she did not abandon this ambition, and ended by marrying her
against her will to Alexas, one of his Gentlemen, and one of her
daughters to Alexas' son, the other to Antipater's mother's brother. Of
his own daughters by Mariamme one wedded his sister's son Antipater,
one his brother's son Phasael.

Having cut off the orphans' hopes and arranged the marriages for
his personal benefit, Antipater felt that his own hopes were safely in
port, and, as confident now as he was wicked, became insufferable. To
overcome the detestation in which he was universally held was beyond
him, so he relied on terror to maintain his security. He was aided by
Pheroras, who had no doubt now that he would be king. There was
too a group of women who stirred up fresh troubles at court. Pheroras'
wife, with the cooperation of her mother and sister and of Antipater's
mother, began to throw her weight about in the palace, even daring to
affront two of the king's daughters, making him thoroughly disgusted
– though his aversion did not prevent their tyrannizing the rest. The
only one who stood up to this conspiracy was Salome, who denounced the gang to the king as a danger to himself. Informed of this
denunciation and of Herod's displeasure, they left off meeting openly
and exchanging friendly greetings, and instead pretended to quarrel
with each other in the king's hearing: Antipater joined in the pretence
by publicly disagreeing with Pheroras. But they held secret meetings
and caroused in the night, the watch kept over them only serving to
strengthen the conspiracy. But every detail of their doings was known
to Salome and duly passed on to Herod.

The king blazed with anger, especially against Pheroras' wife, whom
Salome accused most vehemently. He convened a committee of his
Counsellors and Gentlemen and laid a great many things to the
woman's charge, especially the affront to his daughters, accusing her
also of paying money to the Pharisees to spite him, and turning his
brothers against him by the use of powerful drugs. Finally he turned to
Pheroras and told him he must choose one or the other, his brother or

1. *Called Livia in her husband's lifetime. According to* Antiquities *she opposed the
marriage.*

his wife. When Pheroras replied that he would die rather than give up his wife, Herod, at a loss, went off to Antipater and forbade him to hold any converse with Pheroras, his wife, or anyone connected with her. Antipater conformed with this command in public, but in secret he spent the night with them. Afraid however of Salome's watchful eye he arranged through friends in Italy to visit Rome. They wrote that Antipater ought in the near future to be sent to Caesar, and without hesitation Herod sent him off with a splendid retinue, a vast sum of money, and his will, which named Antipater as the next king, and as Antipater's successor Herod, son of Mariamme the high priest's daughter.

To Rome sailed also Syllaeus the Arab, in disregard of Caesar's commands and with the intention of arguing against Antipater the case about which he had previously been arraigned by Nicolaus. There was also a serious dispute between him and Aretas, his own king, as he had executed a number of his friends, among them Soaemus, the most powerful man in Petra. By a heavy bribe he won over Fabatus, Caesar's treasurer, using his help against Herod too. But Herod by a still heavier bribe detached him from Syllaeus and attempted with his aid to extract from that rogue the money Caesar had ordered him to pay. Syllaeus would not pay a penny, and even accused Fabatus to Caesar, saying his treasurer treasured not his interests but Herod's! Furious at this, and still high in Herod's favour, Fabatus betrayed Syllaeus' secrets, telling the king that Syllaeus had bought the services of his bodyguard Corinthus, on whom he must keep an eye. As Corinthus, though brought up in his kingdom, was by birth an Arab, the king took the hint and immediately arrested both him and two other Arabs found with him, one a friend of Syllaeus and the other a tribal chief. Under torture they admitted that Corinthus had given them heavy bribes to murder Herod. After further examination by Saturninus, governor of Syria, they were sent under escort to Rome.

Herod maintained his relentless pressure on Pheroras to divorce his wife, but could find no means of punishing the woman, many as were his motives for hating her, till he lost his temper and banished her, along with her brother. Pheroras swallowed the insult and went off to his tetrarchy swearing that the only end to his exile would be the death of Herod – never while he lived would he go back to him! He did not return even when his brother was sick, despite the most pressing invitation; for Herod wanted to leave him certain instructions, believing himself on the point of death. But he unexpectedly recovered, and soon afterwards Pheroras fell sick. Herod showed himself less adamant; he went to him and looked after him sympathetically. But he could not master the sickness and after a few days Pheroras died. Herod had loved him till his dying day, but for all that it was rumoured that he had poisoned him. However, he conveyed the body to Jerusalem, ordered prolonged mourning by the whole nation, and honoured him with the most magnificent funeral. Such was the end that came to one of the murderers of Alexander and Aristobulus!

But arising out of Pheroras' death retribution was at last finding the true author of that crime. Some of the dead man's freedmen came in a dejected state to the king and declared that his brother had been deliberately poisoned; his wife had brought him a most unusual dish, and as soon as he had eaten it he had been taken ill. Two days earlier her mother and sister had called in an Arab woman with a knowledge of drugs to prepare a love-potion for Pheroras; instead she had given him deadly poison at the instance of Syllaeus, to whom she was known.

Plagued with suspicions of every kind, the king put the maid-servants and several free women to the torture. One of them in her agony cried out: 'May God, the ruler of heaven and earth, visit our sufferings on their author, Antipater's mother!' Seizing on this hint the king went still further in his search for the truth. The woman disclosed the friendship of Antipater's mother with Pheroras and his women-folk, and their surreptitious meetings. She told how Pheroras and Antipater, after returning from the king, drank with them all night, rigidly excluding every servant whether man or woman. It was one of the free women who gave this information.

The slave-girls Herod tortured one at a time. Their evidence in every case tallied with that already given, with the addition that it was by agreement that Antipater had gone off to Rome, Pheroras to Peraea; for they had said again and again that having disposed of Alexander and Aristobulus Herod would be after them and their wives. After killing Mariamme and her sons he would spare no one, so it was better to put as many miles as possible between them and the beast. Again, Antipater had often grumbled to his mother that he was grey-haired already while his father got daily younger; as likely as not he would die without ever actually being king. When his father died – if he ever did – his enjoyment of the succession would be terribly short. And those hydra-heads were shooting up, the sons of Aristobulus and

Alexander. He had been robbed by his father of his hopes for his children, as the person nominated to succeed him when he died was not to be one of his own sons but Mariamme's Herod. In that respect anyway the king must be a complete dotard, if he imagined that in this matter his will would be carried out; he himself would see that none of the family survived. Hating his children more than any father had ever done, Herod hated his brother far more. Only a day or two ago he had given him, Antipater, 100 talents to hold no converse with Pheroras. When Pheroras asked: 'What harm were we doing him?' he himself had replied: 'I only wish he would strip us of everything, and leave us to live naked. But there is no way to escape such a murderous beast, who will not even let us show affection openly. Now we shall have to meet in secret: we can do it openly if ever we have the arms and spirits of men.'

To these disclosures, wrung from them by the rack, they added that Pheroras had planned to fly with them to Petra. Herod believed every word because of the 100 talents, which he had mentioned to nobody but Antipater. His anger descended first on Doris, Antipater's mother; he stripped her of all the adornments he had lavished on her at fantastic expense and sent her packing a second time. Pheroras' women-folk he made as comfortable as he could after their ordeal, having no further quarrel with them. But he was in constant terror and blazed up on the tiniest suspicion, dragging many guiltless persons off to torture for fear of missing any of the guilty.

He now turned to the Samaritan Antipater, Antipater's chief executive. Putting him on the rack he found out that Antipater had sent one of his companions to Egypt for a noxious drug meant for him; Antiphilus had handed it to Theudion, Antipater's uncle, who had passed it on to Pheroras, Pheroras being required by Antipater to assassinate Herod while he himself was at Rome out of reach of suspicion; and Pheroras had put the drug in his wife's hands. The king sent for her and commanded her to fetch that very moment what she had received. She went out as if to fetch it, but threw herself from the roof, to forestall inquisition by the king's torturer. However, by the providence of God who, it would seem, was resolved to punish Antipater, she did not fall on her head but on other parts of her body, and survived. She was taken to the king, who had her revived, as she was unconscious after her fall, and pressed her for the explanation, swearing that if she told the truth she would be immune from any punishment, but if she held anything back he would rack her to pieces and leave nothing for burial.

After a brief hesitation the woman answered: 'Well, why should I go on keeping these secrets, now Pheroras is dead? To save Antipater, who has ruined us all? Listen, Your Majesty, and may God listen too and witness the truth of my words, for there is no deceiving him! When Pheroras was dying and you sat beside him in tears, he called me to him and whispered: "I have been badly mistaken, my dear, about my brother's attitude to me. He loves me like this and yet I hated him, and planned to kill a man who is so terribly distressed about me even before my death. I am only receiving what I deserve for my disloyalty; you go and fetch the drug you are keeping to poison him with, that Antipater left with us, and destroy it at once before my eyes, for fear I go to Hades with a devil on my back." Thus bidden, I fetched it and emptied most of it into the fire before his eyes, but kept a little for myself in case of emergency and because I was afraid of you.'

So saying she produced the box, containing very little indeed of the poison. The king then turned his tortures against Antiphilus' mother and brother, who both admitted that he had fetched the box from Egypt, and stated that he had obtained the drug from a brother who practised medicine in Alexandria. The ghosts of Alexander and Aristobulus were prowling around the whole palace, ferreting out hidden things and bringing them to light, and dragging those most remote from suspicion before the inquisitor. Even the high priest's daughter Mariamme was found to be privy to the conspiracy; torture extracted this information from her brothers. The king punished the mother's criminal intention through her son: the name of her Herod, who was to succeed Antipater, was blotted out of his father's will.

On top of this Bathyllus came under inquisition and clinched the evidence of Antipater's conspiracy. A freedman of Antipater, he brought another concoction, a noxious compound of the poison of asps and the secretions of other reptiles, so that if the first drug proved ineffectual Pheroras and his wife should be armed with this weapon against the king. As a sideline to the intended attack on the father he brought letters forged by Antipater to incriminate his brothers Archelaus and Philip, sons of the king at school in Rome, now adolescent and proud-spirited. Determined to nip in the bud this growing danger to his hopes, Antipater forged incriminating letters in the names of their friends in Rome, and bribed others to write that they regularly criticized their father, openly denouncing the fate of Alexander and Aristobulus and protesting against their own recall; for their father had already sent for them, and this was the chief cause of Antipater's alarm.

Even before his absence from the country, while still in Judaea, he had paid for similar incriminating letters to be written in Rome, and to avoid suspicion had gone to his father on purpose to excuse his brothers' conduct, maintaining that some of the things were untrue, and others merely boyish indiscretions. Having disbursed vast sums to the writers of these incriminating letters his task now was to cover up his tracks; so he bought up costly wardrobes, elaborate tapestries, cups of silver and gold and many other valuables, in order that his huge expenditure under these heads might conceal the more dubious items. His accounts showed outgoings totalling 200 talents, attributed mostly to his legal battle with Syllaeus. All his rascalities, however small, had come to light with the major crime now that all the tortures cried aloud 'Parricide!' and the letters 'Fractricide a second time!' – yet no one arriving in Rome told him what had happened in Judaea, though between the discovery of his guilt and his homecoming seven months went by; so great was the detestation with which all regarded him. Perhaps, too, the mouths of those prepared to tell him were stopped by the ghosts of his murdered brothers. Anyway he wrote from Rome announcing the good news of his imminent arrival, and of the honour paid him by Caesar at his final interview.

Itching to lay hands on this murderous scoundrel and afraid of his being forewarned and on the look-out, the king replied in a letter which suppressed his real feelings, and with much show of affection urged him to hurry home; if he came quickly Herod would say no more about his mother's misdoings. For Antipater was now aware of her banishment from the court. He had earlier received at Tarentum a letter describing Pheroras' death and had made a great show of grief, which much impressed those who thought it was for his uncle. It is more likely that he was upset by the failure of the conspiracy and was weeping not for Pheroras but for his tool; and he was already assailed by terror of what he had done: perhaps the poison had been discovered! Now when he received in Cilicia the letter from his father mentioned above, he pushed on without delay; but as he sailed into

Celenderis he was overcome by the thought of his mother's fate, his unaided soul giving him a premonition of disaster. The more far-seeing of his Gentlemen advised him not to put himself in his father's power till he knew for certain the grounds of his mother's banish-ment: they were afraid there might be something attached to the charges against her. The less prudent, more anxious to see their own country again than interested in Antipater's welfare, urged him to push on and not by lingering to give his father an excuse for base suspicion and his enemies a handle for slander. Even if there had been a movement against him, it was due to his absence: no one would have dared if he had been there. It was ridiculous to let doubtful suspicions deprive him of unmistakable benefits, and not to put himself as soon as possible in his father's hands to take over the kingdom which depended on him alone. It was to these advisers that Antipater, guided by his evil genius, listened: he made the crossing and landed at the Augustus Harbour of Caesarea.

He was amazed to find himself utterly alone: everyone avoided him and no one ventured near him; for while he had been hated just as much in the past, now at last this hatred was not afraid to show itself. Many too were kept away by fear of the king, since every city was now full of rumours about Antipater, and the only person unaware of his situation was Antipater himself. No one ever had a more wonderful send-off than he when he sailed for Rome, or a more miserable wel-come back. He now began to suspect the disasters at home, but he was cunning enough to hide it, and though inwardly dead with fear maintained by a tremendous effort a haughty demeanour. There was no possibility now of running away or of getting his head above water; but he had no definite news of events at home because of the king's threats, and a glimmer of hope was left – perhaps nothing had been discovered; perhaps, even if it had, he might put things right by brazenness and trickery, by which alone he could survive.

Armed with these vain hopes he came into the palace without his Gentlemen, who had been rudely turned back at the outer gate. It happened that inside was Varus, legate of Syria. Antipater went in to his father and in an attempt to brazen it out went up to him as if to embrace him. Herod put his hands in front of him and turned away his head, crying: 'How like a parricide, to want to put his arms round me with so much on his conscience! To hell with you, disgusting wretch! Don't touch me till you have disproved the accusations! You shall have a fair trial, and Varus has come at the right time to be your judge. Go and think out your defence for tomorrow; I will give you a chance to prepare some of your little tricks.' Too taken aback to answer a word Antipater turned and went, and his wife and mother came to him with full details of the charges. Then having recovered his composure he got to work on his defence.

Next day the king summoned a court consisting of his Counsellors and Gentlemen, inviting Antipater's Gentlemen to come too. Presiding jointly with Varus, he had all the witnesses brought in. These included some servants of the accused's mother who shortly before had been caught carrying a note from her to her son as follows: 'Your father has found out everything, so don't go near him unless you can count on help from Caesar.' When these had been brought in with the rest, Antipater entered and fell on his face at his father's feet. 'I beg you, father,' he began, 'not to condemn me in advance but to lend an unbiased ear to my defence: I shall prove my innocence, if you will let me.'

Interrupting him with a peremptory call for silence, Herod turned to Varus. 'That you, Varus, and every upright judge will condemn Antipater as a hopeless scoundrel I am quite certain. But I am afraid my own wretchedness will disgust you, and you will judge me worthy of every calamity for having fathered such sons. Yet for that very reason you ought to feel the more sorry for me, because I have been the most affectionate of parents to such foul wretches. My other sons I named kings when they were quite young, and in addition to having them educated in Rome I made them Caesar's friends, the envy of other kings – and I found them plotting against me! They are dead, chiefly for Antipater's sake; for he was young and he was the heir, so that his safety was my principal concern. And this filthy beast, gorged with my indulgence, has poured out his swollen insolence on me! He thought I lived too long; he was bored with my old age; he could not bear to become king except by parricide! It serves me right for bringing him back to the City after throwing him out, and thrusting aside the sons of a princess to make *him* heir to my throne! I freely admit, Varus, that I have been an utter fool: I provoked those other sons against me, robbing them of their just expectations for Antipater's sake. When did I ever show them the kindness I showed him? I very nearly abdicated in his favour; I openly named him in my will as heir to my throne with a yearly allowance of 50 talents; I showered gifts upon him from my privy purse; when he recently sailed for Rome I gave him 300 talents, and commended him, alone of all my family, to Caesar, as his father's preserver! What crime did the others commit to compare with Antipater's? What evidence was brought against them as strong as that which reveals this fellow's conspiracy?

'And now this parricide has dared to speak, and hopes to cover up the truth again with his tricks! Varus, be on the look-out! I know the little beast; and I can guess what specious pleas and crocodile tears he will produce! This is the man who in the days when Alexander was alive warned me to beware of him and not to trust my person to all and sundry; this is the man who escorted me to my bed and searched the room for any lurking assassin; this was the guardian of my sleep, my protector from anxiety, my comforter when I grieved for my dead sons, my surety for the loyalty of his surviving brothers, my shield, my bodyguard! When I remember, Varus, his cunning hypocrisy on every occasion, I can hardly believe I am alive and wonder how I escaped so deep a conspirator. But since some evil genius desolates my house and makes my dearest ones rise against me one by one, I shall indeed lament my cruel fate and inwardly grieve for my loneliness, but I will let no one escape who thirsts for my blood, not even if judgement finds every one of my children guilty!'

Overcome by emotion he could say no more, so he beckoned to Nicolaus, one of his Gentlemen, to repeat the depositions. But at this point Antipater, who had remained prone at his father's feet, raised his head and cried; 'You, father, have made my defence for me. How can I be a parricide if, as you agree, I have been your protector through thick and thin? You call my devotion to my father a hypocritical defence: how could I, so cunning in other ways, have been such a fool as not to realize that it was hard enough to hide from human eyes the preparation of so hideous a crime, and quite impossible to hide it from the Judge above, who sees everything and is everywhere present? Was I unaware of my brothers' end, and the terrible punishment they received from God for their evil designs against you? and what provoked me to injure you? the hope of being king? but I *was* a king! suspicion of your hate? but wasn't I most tenderly loved? fear of you on some other ground? but my care of you made others fear me! shortage of money? and who had more to spend than I? Suppose I had been the most degraded of men with the soul of a savage beast, father, should I not have been tamed by your kindness when you brought me back from exile, as you yourself said, and preferred me to your many sons, and proclaimed me king in your own lifetime, and by showering on me honours of all kinds made everyone envy me?

'Oh, what a pity I went abroad, opening the doors wide to envy and playing into the hands of intriguers! Yet it was for your sake, father, I went abroad; I went to fight your battles, so that Syllaeus should not treat your old age as a joke. Rome can bear witness to my love of my father; and so can the ruler of the whole world, Caesar, who often called me a devoted son. Here is the letter he has sent you. This is more trustworthy than local slander; this is my sole defence; this I put forward as testimony to my warm affection for you. Remember that I undertook the voyage against my will, knowing only too well the enmity against me lurking in this kingdom. It was you, father, who unintentionally ruined me by forcing me to give envy an opportunity for slander. However, here I am to face the charges; I have travelled over land and sea, nowhere coming to grief as a parricide should! But do not take me back into favour now because of *that* evidence; for I am convicted in God's eyes and in yours, father. But convicted as I am, I beg you not to base your beliefs on what others have admitted on the rack. Let the fire be used against me; let the instruments of torture pass right through my entrails; do not spare this foul body! If I am a parricide, I must not die unracked!'

At these cries, laments, and tears Varus and all the rest were overcome with emotion. Herod alone was too angry to weep – he knew that the charges were true.

Then Nicolaus rose, and on the king's instructions began with a thoroughgoing exposure of Antipater's duplicity, scattering all sympathy for him to the winds. Next he poured out a torrent of bitter accusations, holding him responsible for all the crime in the kingdom, and especially the murder of his brothers, proving that their deaths were due to his slanders. He further charged him with conspiring against the survivors in the line of succession. Was it likely that one who had prepared poison for his father would spare his brothers? Dealing next with the poisoning charge he gave an orderly exposition of the sworn statements; on the subject of Pheroras he could hardly contain himself – to think that Antipater should have turned him of all people into a fractricide, and by bribing the king's nearest and dearest filled the whole palace with corruption! After putting forward many other arguments and demonstrating their truth, Nicolaus resumed his seat.

Varus now called on Antipater to make his defence; but he only said 'God is witness of my complete innocence', and remained prone and silent. So Varus sent for the poison, gave it to a prisoner sentenced to death, and made him drink it. Death was instantaneous. He then conferred with Herod in private, wrote a report of the proceedings for Caesar, and left Jerusalem next day. The king threw Antipater into prison and dispatched messengers to Caesar to inform him of these calamitous events.

Shortly afterwards it was discovered that Antipater had plotted against Salome too. One of Antiphilus' manservants arrived from Rome with letters from a maidservant of Julia, Acme by name. From her the king learnt that she had found among Julia's papers letters from Salome and was sending them to him as she wished to help him. These letters, containing the most bitter abuse of the king and the most vehement accusations, had been forged by Antipater, who had bribed Acme to send them to Herod. His guilt was proved by her letter to him; for the woman had written to him too. 'In accordance with your wishes I have sent those letters to your father with a covering note; I am certain he will not spare his sister when he reads them. When it is all over, kindly remember your promise.'

When this letter was discovered along with those forged to ruin Salome, it occurred to the king that perhaps the documents inculpating Alexander were not genuine either, and his emotions were painful indeed when he thought how near he had been to executing his sister too through Antipater's machinations. So he decided to lose no time in punishing him for all his crimes. But as he was taking action against Antipater he was crippled by a severe illness; however, he sent word to Caesar about Acme and the crooked attempt to involve Salome. He also sent for his will and altered it; as his successor he nominated Antipas, cutting out the two eldest, Archelaus and Philip, both of whom had been slandered by Antipater. To Caesar, in addition to gifts other than money, he bequeathed 1,000 talents; to the emperor's wife, his children, Gentlemen, and freedmen about 500 talents; to the rest of his own children generous legacies in land and money. He set aside most splendid gifts as a special honour to his sister Salome. These were the amendments he made to his will. His illness was getting steadily worse, the disease having attacked him when old and despondent. He was now nearly seventy, and his spirit had been broken by the dreadful troubles with his children, so that even in health the good things of life meant nothing to him. His sickness was intensified by bitterness that Antipater was still alive: he was determined that the execution should be no hole and corner affair, so must wait for his own recovery.

In the midst of his troubles there occurred a popular rising. There were two rabbis in the City with a great reputation as exponents of national tradition, and for that reason held in the highest esteem by the whole nation – Judas the son of Sepphoraeus and Matthias the son of Margalus. Many young students came to them for instruction in the laws; in fact they daily attracted a host of men in their prime. When they learnt that the king was succumbing to his sickness of body and mind, they dropped a hint to their acquaintances that here was a wonderful chance to strike a blow for God and to pull down the works erected contrary to the laws of their fathers. Although it was unlawful to have in the Sanctuary images or portrait-busts or the likeness of any living thing, the king had put up over the Great Gate a golden eagle. This the rabbis now urged them to cut down, saying that even if danger was involved it was a glorious thing to die for the laws of their fathers: for those who came to such an end there was a sure hope of immortality and the eternal enjoyment of blessings, whereas the poor-spirited, knowing nothing of the rabbinical wisdom, through ignorance clung to life and chose death by disease rather than death in a righteous cause.

While they were preaching thus it was rumoured that the king was actually dying, so that the young men undertook the task with more confidence. At mid-day, when masses of people were walking about the Temple courts, they lowered themselves by stout ropes from the roof and began to cut down the golden eagle with axes. The news quickly reached the king's officer, who hurried to the spot with a large force, seized about forty young men and took them before the king. He began by asking them whether they had dared to cut down the golden eagle. They said they had. Who told them to do it? The law of their fathers. What made them so cheerful when they were about to be executed? The knowledge that they would enjoy greater blessings after their death. At this the king exploded with rage, and forgetting his sickness went out to address a public meeting. He attacked the men at great length as temple-robbers, who pleading the Law as an excuse had some ulterior purpose, and demanded their punishment for sacrilege. The people, fearing punitive measures on a wide front, begged him to punish first those who had suggested the attempt, then those who had been caught in the act, and to take no action against the rest. The king reluctantly agreed: those who had lowered themselves from the roof together with the rabbis he burnt alive; the rest of the men seized he handed over to his attendants for execution.

From then on the sickness spread through his entire body, accompanied by a variety of painful symptoms. He had a slight fever, an unbearable itching all over his body, constant pains in the lower bowel, swellings on the feet as in dropsy, inflammation of the abdomen, and mortification of the genitals, producing worms; as well as difficulty in breathing, especially when lying down, and spasms in all his limbs. The diviners said that his many diseases were a punishment for what he had done to the rabbis. But though he was wrestling with so many disorders he hung on to life, hoped for recovery, and planned his own treatment. He crossed the Jordan and tried the hot baths at Callirrhoe, which empty their water into the Dead Sea, water sweet enough to drink. The doctors there decided to warm his whole body with hot oil by lowering him into a full bath; but he fainted and turned up his eyes as if dead. The loud cries of his attendants brought him back to consciousness, but having no further hope of recovery he ordered the distribution of 50 drachmas a head to the soldiers and large gratuities to the officers and to his Gentlemen.

By the time he arrived at Jericho on the return journey he was melancholy-mad, and in a virtual challenge to death itself he proceeded to devise a monstrous outrage. He brought together the most eminent men of every village in the whole of Judaea and had them locked up in the Hippodrome. Then he sent for his sister Salome and her husband Alexas and said: 'I know the Jews will greet my death with wild rejoicings; but I can be mourned on other people's account and make sure of a magnificent funeral if you will do as I tell you. These men under guard – as soon as I die, kill them all – let loose the soldiers amongst them; then all Judaea and every family will weep for me – they can't help it.'

While he was giving these instructions a dispatch arrived from his ambassadors at Rome to notify him that at Caesar's command Acme had been executed and Antipater condemned to death; it went on to say that if his father preferred merely to banish him, Caesar had no objection. For a while Herod felt rather more cheerful, but later he was so tormented by lack of food and a racking cough that his sufferings mastered him and he made an effort to anticipate his appointed end. He took an apple and asked for a knife, it being his habit to cut up apples when he ate them; then looking round to make sure there was no one to stop him he raised his hand to stab himself. But his cousin Achiab dashed up and stopped him by grasping his wrist. At once loud cries went up in the palace as if the king had gone. Antipater soon heard the cheering news, and in his delight offered his jailers a handsome bribe to loose him and let him go. But the prison governor not only put a stop to this but ran and told the king of his attempt. Herod uttered a shout louder than seemed possible in so sick a man, and at once sent his body-guard to put Antipater to death. After ordering his body to be interred at Hyrcania he again modified his will, naming as heir Archelaus, his eldest son, and as tetrarch Archelaus' brother Antipas. He survived his son's execution by only five days. Reckoning from the date when he put Antigonus to death and became master of the state his reign had lasted thirty-three years; reckoning from his proclamation by the Romans as king, thirty-six.[1] In most respects he enjoyed good fortune if ever a man did: he came to the throne though he was a commoner, occupied it a very long time, and left it to his own children; but in his family life he was the most unfortunate of men.

Before the military knew that Herod was dead, Salome went out with her husband and freed the prisoners whom the king had ordered to be murdered. She told them the king had changed his mind and was permitting them all to go home again. When they were safely out of the way she informed the soldiers of the true situation, and summoned them to a joint meeting with the civilian population in the Amphitheatre at Jericho. Here Ptolemy came forward, displaying the signet-ring entrusted to him by the king, to whom he paid the warmest tribute, followed by words of advice to the civilians present. Next he read aloud the letter Herod had left for the troops, in which he made a lengthy appeal for loyalty to his successor. After the letter he opened and read the final will, in which Philip was named as heir to Trachonitis and the neighbouring districts, Antipas as tetrarch, as explained above, and Archelaus as king. Archelaus was to take Herod's ring to Caesar, with the state documents under seal, as Caesar was in sole charge of all his dispositions and executor of his will. All other provisions of the earlier will remained valid.

Vociferous congratulations were at once heaped upon Archelaus, and the soldiers came forward in companies with the civilians, pledged

1. *From 40 to 4 B.C.*

their loyalty, and joined in prayers for the blessing of God. Then they turned to the task of the king's burial. Everything possible was done by Archelaus to add to the magnificence: he brought out all the royal ornaments to be carried in procession in honour of the dead monarch. There was a solid gold bier, adorned with precious stones and draped with the richest purple. On it lay the body wrapped in crimson, with a diadem resting on the head and above that a golden crown, and the sceptre by the right hand. The bier was escorted by Herod's sons and the whole body of his kinsmen, followed by his Spearmen and the Thracian Company, Germans and Gauls, all in full battle order. The rest of the army led the way, fully armed and in perfect order, headed by their commanders and all the officers, and followed by five hundred of the house slaves and freedmen carrying spices. The body was borne twenty-four miles to Herodium, where by the late king's command it was buried. So ends the story of Herod.

CHAPTER 6

The Rise and Fall of Archelaus

ARCHELAUS was involved in fresh disturbances by the necessity of visiting Rome. He had spent a week mourning his father, and had provided the funeral feast for the populace on the most lavish scale – a custom which is the ruin of many Jews: they are obliged to feed the populace to escape the charge of impiety. Now he changed into white garments and proceeded to the Temple, where the people received him with varied acclamations. In reply he waved to the crowd from a golden throne on a raised platform, and thanked them heartily for the great pains they had taken with his father's funeral, and the respect they had already shown to himself as if he was already established as king. However, for the present he was not going to assume the royal power or even the title until his succession was confirmed by Caesar, who by the terms of Herod's will was in supreme control. At Jericho also, when the army had tried to set the crown on his head he had refused it; however, for their enthusiastic loyalty he would render full payment to soldiers and people alike, as soon as the powers that were had established him as king; he would endeavour in every way to show himself kinder to them than did his father.

This promise delighted the crowd, who at once tested his sincerity by making large demands. Some clamoured for a lightening of direct taxation, some for the abolition of purchase-tax, others for the release of prisoners. He promptly said Yes to every demand in his anxiety to appease the mob. Then he offered sacrifices and sat down to a banquet with his Gentlemen. But in the afternoon a number of men with revolutionary ideas collected, and began lamentations of their own when the public mourning for the late king was over, bewailing those who had been executed by Herod for cutting down the golden eagle from the Temple gate. These were not secret lamentations but piercing wails, weeping in chorus, and beating of breasts, that resounded throughout the whole City, as they were for men who, they said, had died for the laws of their country and for the Temple. To avenge them they clamoured for the punishment of Herod's placemen, and above all the removal of the man he had appointed high priest; for it was their duty to choose a man of greater piety and with cleaner hands.

This infuriated Archelaus, but he held his hand in view of his anxiety to begin his journey, fearing that if he aroused the hostility of the populace the consequent disturbance might delay his departure. He therefore tried to quieten the rebels by persuasion rather than by force, and privately sent his commander-in-chief to ask them to desist. The officer came to them in the Temple, but before he could utter a word the rioters stoned him and drove him away, doing the same to many others whom Archelaus sent after him to secure quiet. To every appeal they made a furious response, and it was evident that if they received general support there would be no holding them. To make things worse the Feast of Unleavened Bread was approaching – known to the Jews as the Passover, and celebrated with sacrifices on a vast scale – and there was a huge influx from the country for the festival. Meanwhile those who were bewailing the dead rabbis massed in the Temple and so provided fuel for sedition. This frightened Archelaus, who, to prevent the disease infecting the whole population, sent a tribune with his cohort to restrain by force the leaders of the sedition. Their approach infuriated the huge mob, who pelted the cohort with stones and killed most of the men, wounding the tribune, who barely escaped with his life. Then as if nothing strange had occurred they turned to sacrifice. Archelaus realized that the crowd could no longer be restrained without bloodshed; so he sent his whole army against them, the infantry in a body through the City, the cavalry through the fields. As all the men were sacrificing the soldiers suddenly swooped on them, killing about 3,000, and scattered the remainder among the neighbouring hills. Archelaus' heralds then followed, ordering everyone to go home; and home they all went, abandoning the Feast.

Archelaus with his mother and three Gentlemen – Poplas, Ptolemy, and Nicolaus – went down to the sea, leaving Philip as governor of the palace and custodian of his property. He was accompanied by Salome and her children and by the late king's nephews and sons-in-law, who professed the intention of supporting his claim to the throne, but whose real purpose was to denounce him for his lawless actions in the Temple.

At Caesarea they were met by Sabinus the procurator of Syria, who was on his way to Judaea to take charge of Herod's estate but was prevented from going further by the arrival of Varus, whom Ptolemy on Archelaus' behalf had begged to come. So for the time being

Sabinus, in deference to Varus' wishes, neither hastened to the citadels nor locked Archelaus out of his father's treasuries, but promised to postpone any action until Caesar had reached a decision, and remained at Caesarea. But as soon as restraint was removed by the return of Varus to Antioch and the departure of Archelaus for Rome, he promptly set out for Jerusalem, where he took possession of the palace, and sending for the garrison commanders and comptrollers tried to sort out the property accounts and to take possession of the citadels. However, the officers were loyal to Archelaus' instructions and continued to guard everything in the name of Caesar rather than of Archelaus.

Meanwhile Antipas also was strenuously laying claim to the kingdom, insisting that Herod's earlier will, not the later one, was valid, and that this named him king. He had a promise of support from Salome and many of the relatives who were sailing with Archelaus. He tried also to win over his mother and Nicolaus' brother Ptolemy, who seemed a weighty supporter in view of the trust Herod had reposed in him; for he had been the most honoured of Herod's Gentlemen. But he placed most confidence in the extraordinary skill of Irenaeus the orator; he therefore disregarded those who advised him to give way to Archelaus as the elder brother, named in the later will. In Rome all the relatives, who detested Archelaus, transferred their allegiance to Antipas. Their first preference was for autonomy under the protection of a Roman official; failing that they were prepared to accept Antipas as king.

In these endeavours they were aided by Sabinus, who sent letters denouncing Archelaus to Caesar and lavishing praise on Antipas. Salome and her friends collected all the charges and put the file in Caesar's hands. Then Archelaus in his turn sent Ptolemy with a written summary of his own claims, his father's ring, and the official records. Caesar, having considered in private the rival dossiers, the size of the kingdom, the value of the revenue, and also the number of Herod's children, read the dispatches from Varus and Sabinus about the matter. Then he called a meeting of the Roman magistrates, giving a seat for the first time to Gaius – son of Agrippa and his own daughter Julia, and adopted by him – and invited the disputants to put their case.

Salome's son Antipater at once rose. The cleverest speaker among Archelaus' opponents, he pointed out that, though professedly Archelaus was only laying claim to the throne, actually he had been reigning for a long time, so that it was mockery now to seek an

audience of Caesar, whose decision on the succession he had anticipated. As soon as Herod was dead he had secretly bribed certain persons
to crown him; he had sat in state on the throne and given audience as a
king; he had altered the organization of the army and granted
promotions. Furthermore he had conceded to the people everything
for which they had petitioned him as king, and had released men whom
his father had imprisoned for shocking crimes. And now he had come
to ask his master for the shadow of that kingship of which he had himself snatched the substance, allowing Caesar control not of realities but
of names. Antipater also alleged that his mourning for his father was a
sham – that in the daytime he assumed an expression of grief and at
night indulged in drunken orgies, which by arousing men's indignation had caused the popular unrest. The speaker directed the whole
force of his argument to the number of persons killed around the
Sanctuary, who had come to the Feast only to be brutally murdered
alongside their own sacrifices; such a huge pile of corpses in the Temple
courts as one would scarcely have expected to see if a foreign invader
had descended upon them without warning. Recognizing this vein of
cruelty in his son, Herod had never given him the least hope of succeeding to the throne till his mind became more decayed than his body, and
he was incapable of logical thought and did not realize what sort of
man he was making his heir by his new will, though he had no fault to
find with the heir named in the earlier one, written when his health
was good and his mind quite unimpaired. If however anyone was
inclined to attach more weight to the decision made when his health
was failing, the answer was that Archelaus had proved himself unfit to
rule by his illegalities; what would he be like after receiving authority
from Caesar, when he had put so many to death before receiving it?

After continuing in this vein at considerable length and bringing
forward most of the relatives to witness the truth of each accusation,
Antipater sat down. Then Nicolaus rose to defend Archelaus and
argued that the slaughter in the Temple was unavoidable, for the
killed had been enemies not only of the crown but of Caesar who was
now awarding it. The other measures with which he was charged had
been taken on the advice of the accusers themselves! As for the later
will, he claimed that it was valid for this reason especially, that in it
Caesar was appointed executor; a man sensible enough to put the
management of his affairs into the hands of the supreme ruler was not
likely to choose the wrong man for his heir, and one who knew the

authority that made the appointment was likely to show good sense in choosing the person to be appointed.

When Nicolaus too had had his say, Archelaus came forward and fell down at Caesar's knees without saying a word. The emperor raised him up in the most gracious manner and declared that he deserved to succeed his father, but made no definite announcement. After dismissing those who had been his assessors that day he thought over in private what he had been told, considering whether to appoint one of those named in the wills to succeed Herod, or to divide the power among the whole family; for it seemed necessary to provide support for the mass of interested persons.

Before Caesar could reach a decision, Archelaus' mother Malthace died of an illness, and letters arrived from Varus in Syria about the revolt in Judaea. He had seen this coming, and so when Archelaus had sailed he had gone to Jerusalem to restrain the prime movers, as it was obvious that the populace would not remain quiet. Then, leaving in the City one of the three legions he had brought from Syria, he returned to Antioch. However, as soon as he had gone Sabinus arrived, and promptly gave the people an excuse for sedition. He tried to compel the garrison to hand over the forts and made a ruthless search for the king's money, employing not only the soldiers left by Varus but a gang of his own slaves, arming them all and using them as instruments of his avarice. On the eve of Pentecost – a Jewish feast which takes place after seven weeks: 'Pentecost' means 'fiftieth day' – the people assembled, not to conduct the usual rites but to vent their wrath. An enormous crowd gathered from Galilee and Idumaea, from Jericho and Peraea east of Jordan; but they could not equal in number and enthusiasm the swarm of natives from Judaea itself. The whole mass split up into three divisions which established themselves in separate camps, one to the north of the Temple, one to the south by the Hippodrome, and the third near the Palace to the west. Thus they surrounded the Romans and began to blockade them.

Their numbers and determination alarmed Sabinus, who sent a stream of messengers to Varus to request immediate assistance: if it was delayed the legion would be cut to pieces. He himself went up to the highest tower of the fortress, the one called Phasael after Herod's brother who had died at the hands of the Parthians. From there he signalled to the legionaries to attack the enemy, for he was too panic-stricken even to go down to his own men. Doing as they were told, the soldiers dashed into the Temple and engaged in a fierce combat with the Jews, in which, as long as no one shot at them from above, their experience of war gave them the advantage. But when many of the Jews climbed on to the top of the colonnades and threw their missiles on to their heads, casualties were heavy, and it was difficult either to reply to this attack from above or to resist those who fought them hand to hand.

Hard pressed from both directions they set fire to the colonnades, works remarkable for both size and magnificence. The men on top were suddenly hemmed in by the flames: many of them were burnt to death; many others jumped down among the enemy and were destroyed by them; some turned about and flung themselves from the wall; a few, seeing no way of escape, fell on their own swords and cheated the flames; a number who crept down from the walls and rushed in among the Romans were easily overpowered in their confused state. As the survivors fled in terror the soldiers swooped on the unguarded treasury of God and carried off about 400 talents; what they did not steal Sabinus collected.

The effect on the Jews of this loss of life and property was to bring together a far bigger and better equipped force to oppose the Romans. They surrounded the Palace and threatened to destroy all its occupants unless they withdrew forthwith, but promised safe conduct to Sabinus if he was prepared to take his legion away. They were reinforced by the bulk of the royal troops, who deserted to them. But the most warlike section, 3,000 men from Sebaste with their officers, Rufus and Gratus, attached themselves to the Romans. Gratus commanded the royal infantry, Rufus the cavalry; each of them, even without the men under him, was brave and intelligent enough to turn the scales in war. The Jews conducted a vigorous siege, assaulting the walls of the fortress and at the same time vociferously urging Sabinus and his soldiers to withdraw, and not to hinder the Jews, now that at long last they were recovering their traditional independence. Sabinus would have been only too glad to withdraw quietly, but he distrusted their promises and suspected that their soft words were a bait to catch him. As he was also expecting Varus' reinforcements, he continued to hold out.

Meanwhile in the country districts also there were widespread disturbances and many seized the opportunity to claim the throne. In Idumaea 2,000 of Herod's veterans reassembled with their arms and proceeded to fight the royal troops. They were opposed by Achiab, a cousin of the late king; he sheltered behind the strongest fortifications and would not risk a battle in the open. At Sepphoris in Galilee Judas, son of Hezekiah – a robber chief who once overran the country and was suppressed by King Herod – collected a considerable force, broke into the royal armoury, equipped his followers, and attacked the other seekers after power. In Peraea Simon, one of the royal slaves, considered that his good looks and great stature entitled him to set a crown on his own head. Then he went round with a band of robbers and burnt down the palace at Jericho and many magnificent country residences, securing easy plunder for himself out of the flames. He would indeed have reduced every notable building to ashes had not Gratus, commander of the royal infantry, taken the archers from Trachonitis and the best troops from Sebaste and gone to meet the adventurer. The Peraeans suffered heavy losses in the battle: Simon himself fled up a ravine but was cut off by Gratus, and as he fled a blow from the side broke his neck. The palace at Betharamatha near the Jordan was burnt down by another gang from Peraea.

A third claimant to the throne was a shepherd called Athrongaeus, whose hopes were based on his physical strength and contempt of death, and on the support of four brothers like himself. Each of these he put in charge of an armed band, employing them as generals and satraps on his raids, and reserving to himself as king the settlement of major problems. He set a crown on his own head, but continued for a considerable time to raid the country with his brothers. Their principal purpose was to kill Romans and the royal troops; but not even a Jew could escape if he fell into their hands with anything valuable on him. Once they ventured to surround an entire century of Romans near Emmaus,[1] when they were conveying food and munitions to their legion. Hurling their spears they killed the centurion Arius and forty of his best men; the rest were in danger of meeting the same fate until the arrival of Gratus with the men of Sebaste enabled them to escape. Such was the treatment that throughout the war they meted out to natives and foreigners alike; but after a while three of them were defeated, the eldest by Archelaus, the next two in an encounter with Gratus and Ptolemy: the fourth submitted to Archelaus on terms. It was of course later that their career came thus to an end: at the time we are describing they were harassing all Judaea with their brigandage.

When Varus received the dispatches of Sabinus and the officers, he

1. *Not the Emmaus of Luke xxiv 13, which is mentioned on p. 378 only.*

was naturally afraid for the whole legion and hurried to the rescue. He picked up the other two legions and the four troops of horse attached to them and marched to Ptolemais, giving instructions that the auxiliaries provided by kings and local potentates should meet him there. In addition he collected 1,500 heavy infantry as he passed through the city of Beirut. At Ptolemais he was joined by a great number of allies. Prominent among these was Aretas the Arab, who because he had hated Herod brought a considerable force of infantry and cavalry. Varus at once dispatched a portion of his army to the part of Galilee near Ptolemais, under the command of his friend Gaius. Gaius routed those who blocked his way, captured the city of Sepphoris and burnt it, enslaving the inhabitants. With the rest of his forces Varus himself marched into Samaria, but kept his hands off the city as he learnt that when the whole country was in a ferment there had been complete quiet here. He encamped near a village called Arus, which belonged to Ptolemy and for that reason was plundered by the Arabs, who were angry with Herod and his friends too. From there he went on to Sappho, another fortified village, which they plundered in the same way, seizing all the revenues they found there. Fire and bloodshed were on every side, and nothing could check the depredations of the Arabs. Emmaus too, abandoned by its inhabitants, was destroyed by fire at the command of Varus to avenge Arius and those who had perished with him.

Then he marched on to Jerusalem where at the first sight of him and his forces the Jewish armies melted away, the fugitives disappearing into the countryside. The citizens however welcomed Varus and disclaimed all responsibility for the revolt, declaring that they had not lifted a finger but had been forced by the occurrence of the Feast to receive the swarm of visitors, so that far from joining in the attack they had, like the Romans, been besieged. Before this he had been met by Joseph, the cousin of Archelaus; by Rufus and Gratus, at the head of the men from Sebaste as well as the royal army; and by the members of the Roman legion with the normal arms and equipment – for Sabinus, not daring to come into Varus' sight, had already left the City for the sea. Varus sent portions of his army about the countryside in pursuit of those responsible for the upheaval, and great numbers were brought in: those who seemed to have taken a less active part he kept in custody, while the ringleaders were crucified – about two thousand.

Information reached him that in Idumaea there still remained a concentration of 10,000 men, heavily armed. But he found that the Arabs were not behaving as allies but campaigning in accordance with their own ideas, and ravaging the countryside contrary to his wishes through their hatred of Herod. So he sent them away, and with his own legions hurried to meet the rebels. They, before a blow was struck, took the advice of Achiab and gave themselves up. Varus acquitted the rank and file of any responsibility, but sent the leaders to Caesar to be examined. Caesar pardoned most of them, but some of the king's relatives – a few of the prisoners being connected with Herod by birth – he sentenced to death for having fought against a king of their own blood. Varus, having thus settled matters in Jerusalem, left as garrison the same legion as before and returned to Antioch.

At Rome Archelaus was involved in a new dispute with the Jews who before the revolt had been permitted by Varus to come as ambassadors and plead for racial autonomy. These numbered fifty and were backed by more than 8,000 of the Jews at Rome. Caesar summoned a meeting of the Roman magistrates and his own friends in the temple of Apollo which he himself had built on the Palatine and decorated regardless of expense. The Jewish mob stood with the ambassadors facing Archelaus and his friends: his relatives' friends stood apart from both; for hatred and envy made them unwilling to be associated with Archelaus, while they did not wish Caesar to see them with his accusers. They had also the support of Philip the brother of Archelaus, who had been sent by the kindness of Varus for two purposes – he was to co-operate with Archelaus, and if Caesar divided Herod's estate among all his descendants he was to secure a share of it.

When the accusers were called upon they first went through Herod's crimes, declaring that it was not to a king that they had submitted but to the most savage tyrant that had ever lived. Vast numbers had been executed by him, and the survivors had suffered so horribly that they envied the dead. He had tortured not only individual subjects but whole cities; for he had pillaged his own to adorn those of other races, and had shed Jewish blood to gratify foreigners. Depriving them of their old prosperity and their ancestral laws he had reduced his people to poverty and utter lawlessness. In fact the Jews had endured more calamities at Herod's hands in a few years than their ancestors had endured in all the time since they left Babylon in the reign of Xerxes[1]

1. According to Ezra, Artaxerxes.

and returned home. But they had become so subservient and inured to misery that they had submitted without a struggle to the continuance of their appalling slavery under Herod's successor. Archelaus, the son of that cruel tyrant, they readily acclaimed as king on the death of his father: they joined with him in mourning Herod's death and in praying for the success of his own reign. He, as though anxious to prove himself the true son of his father, inaugurated his reign by putting 3,000 citizens to death, offering to God that number of sacrifices for his enthronement, and filling the Temple with that number of dead bodies during a Feast! Those who survived such a succession of calamities had naturally reflected now on their sufferings and chosen like soldiers to receive their blows in front; they begged the Romans to pity the remnant of the Jews, and not to throw what was left of them to the savage beasts who would tear them to pieces, but unite their country with Syria and administer it through their own officials. This would show that men now falsely accused of sedition and aggression knew how to submit to reasonable authority.

With this request the Jews brought their accusation to an end. Nicolaus then rose and refuted the charges brought against the kings, accusing the populace of anarchic tendencies and habitual disloyalty to their kings. Lastly he abused those of Archelaus' relatives who had gone over to the accusers.

After hearing both sides Caesar adjourned the meeting; but a few days later he gave half the kingdom to Archelaus, with the title of ethnarch and the promise that he should be king if he showed that he deserved it: the other half he divided into two tetrarchies which he bestowed on two other sons of Herod, one on Philip, the other on Antipas who was disputing the kingship with Archelaus. Under Antipas were placed Peraea and Galilee with a revenue of 200 talents, while Batanaea, Trachonitis, Auranitis, and some parts of Zeno's domain round Innano,[1] with a revenue of 100 talents, were put under Philip. Archelaus' ethnarchy comprised Idumaea, all Judaea, and Samaria, Samaria being excused a quarter of its taxes as a reward for not joining in the revolt. The cities placed under his rule were Strato's Tower, Sebaste, Joppa, and Jerusalem: the Greek cities of Gaza, Gadara, and Hippos were detached from the kingdom and added to Syria. The revenue from the territory assigned to Archelaus amounted to 400 talents. Salome, in addition to what the king had left her in his

1. *Probably a copyist's mistake for Panias.*

II, 108 RISE AND FALL OF ARCHELAUS 123

will, was appointed mistress of Jamnia, Azotus, and Phasaelis, and as a gift from Caesar she received the palace at Ascalon. From all these she collected a revenue of 60 talents; but her domain came under the general control of Archelaus. Each of Herod's other descendants received what had been left to him in the will. On the two unmarried daughters Caesar bestowed in addition 500,000 silver drachmas, and arranged that they should marry the sons of Pheroras. After dividing up Herod's estate he also shared out among them all the legacy bequeathed to him by Herod – the sum of 1,000 talents – after picking out a few treasures of no intrinsic value in memory of the departed.

At this period a young man, Jewish by birth but brought up at Sidon by a Roman freedman, took advantage of his physical resemblance to pass himself off as Alexander whom Herod had executed, and thinking himself safe from detection came to Rome. Assisting him was a fellow-countryman who knew all that went on in royal circles, and who instructed him to say that the men detailed to execute him and Aristobulus had been moved by pity to smuggle them away, leaving instead bodies resembling theirs. With this pretence he deceived the Jews in Crete, who provided him with the means to travel in luxury to Melos. There by his amazing plausibility he collected a much greater sum, and induced his backers to sail with him to Rome. Landing at Puteoli he obtained very large contributions from the Jews there, and was escorted on his way like a king by his 'father's' friends. So convincing was the physical likeness that men who had seen Alexander and remembered him well swore it was he. The whole Jewish community in Rome poured out to see him, and an enormous crowd gathered in the narrow streets through which he was carried; for so completely had the Melians lost their wits that they carried him in a litter and furnished him with royal splendour at their own expense.

Caesar, acquainted with Alexander's features since he was accused by Herod before him, realized even before seeing the man that it was a case of impersonation; but on the chance that there was something behind these sanguine hopes he sent one Celadus, who remembered Alexander well, with orders to bring the young man to him. As soon as Celadus set eyes on him he observed the differences in his face, and noticing that his whole body was tougher and more like a slave's he saw through the whole plot, and was most indignant at the impudence of the fellow's story; for when asked about Aristobulus he insisted that he too was alive, but had been left in Cyprus on purpose for fear of treachery: they were safer apart. Celadus took him aside and said: 'Caesar will spare your life in return for the name of the man who persuaded you to tell such monstrous lies.' The youth replied that he would give him the required information and accompanied him into Caesar's presence, where he pointed to the Jew who had made use of his likeness to Alexander for profit: he himself had received more gifts in every city than Alexander received in his whole lifetime. Caesar was highly amused, and in view of his splendid physique sent the pseudo-Alexander to join his galley-slaves, but ordered the man who led him astray to be put to death. The Melians were sufficiently punished for their folly by the loss of their money!

Established as ethnarch Archelaus, unable to forget the old quarrels, treated not only Jews but even Samaritans so brutally that both peoples sent embassies to accuse him before Caesar, with the result that in the ninth[1] year of his rule he was banished to Vienne in Gaul, and his property transferred to Caesar's treasury. Before he was summoned by Caesar, so we are told, he dreamt that he saw nine large, full ears of corn devoured by oxen. He sent for the seers and some of the Chaldaeans and asked what they thought this foretold. Various interpretations were given, Simon, one of the Essenes, suggesting that the ears denoted years and the oxen a political upheaval, because by ploughing they overturned the soil. Archelaus would rule one year for every ear, and would pass through various political upheavals before he died. Five days after hearing this the dreamer was called to his trial.

I think I might also mention the dream of his wife Glaphyra, daughter of Archelaus, king of Cappadocia. She had first married Alexander, the brother of Archelaus about whom I have been writing, and son of King Herod, who put him to death as already explained. When he died she married Juba, king of Libya, and when he too died she returned home and lived as a widow in her father's house until the ethnarch Archelaus saw her, and fell so deeply in love with her that he instantly divorced his wife Mariamme and married her. Shortly after her arrival in Judaea she dreamt that Alexander stood over her and said: 'Your Libyan marriage was quite enough; but you were not satisfied with it; you came back again to my home after choosing a third husband and, you impudent woman, my own brother at that! I shall not overlook the insult; I will fetch you back to me whether you like it or not.' She related this dream, and in less than two days she was dead.

1. *Actually the tenth, as Josephus later realized.*

CHAPTER 7

Antipas and the two Agrippas

THE territory of Archelaus was brought under direct Roman rule, and a man of equestrian rank at Rome, Coponius, was sent as procurator with authority from Caesar to inflict the death penalty. In his time a Galilaean named Judas[1] tried to stir the natives to revolt, saying that they would be cowards if they submitted to paying taxes to the Romans, and after serving God alone accepted human masters. This man was a rabbi with a sect of his own, and was quite unlike the others.

Among the Jews there are three schools of thought, whose adherents are called Pharisees, Sadducees, and Essenes respectively. The Essenes profess a severer discipline: they are Jews by birth and are peculiarly attached to each other. They eschew pleasure-seeking as a vice and regard temperance and mastery of the passions as virtue. Scorning wedlock, they select other men's children while still pliable and teachable, and fashion them after their own pattern – not that they wish to do away with marriage as a means of continuing the race, but they are afraid of the promiscuity of women and convinced that none of the sex remains faithful to one man. Contemptuous of wealth, they are communists to perfection, and none of them will be found to be better off than the rest: their rule is that novices admitted to the sect must surrender their property to the order, so that among them all neither humiliating poverty nor excessive wealth is ever seen, but each man's possessions go into the pool and as with brothers their entire property belongs to them all. Oil they regard as polluting, and if a man is unintentionally smeared with it he scrubs himself clean; for they think it desirable to keep the skin dry and always to wear white. Men to supervise the community's affairs are elected by show of hands, chosen for their tasks by universal suffrage.

They possess no one city but everywhere have large colonies. When adherents arrive from elsewhere, all local resources are put at their disposal as if they were their own, and men they have never seen

---

1. *This is the Judas of Acts v 37.*

before entertain them like old friends. And so when they travel they carry no baggage at all, but only weapons to keep off bandits. In every town one of the order is appointed specially to look after strangers and issue clothing and provisions. In dress and personal appearance they are like children in the care of a stern tutor. Neither garments nor shoes are changed till they are dropping to pieces or worn out with age. Among themselves nothing is bought or sold: everyone gives what he has to anybody in need and receives from him in return something he himself can use; and even without giving anything in return they are free to share the possessions of anyone they choose.

They show devotion to the Deity in a way all their own. Before the sun rises they do not utter a word on secular affairs, but offer to Him some traditional prayers as if beseeching Him to appear. After this their supervisors send every man to the craft he understands best, and they work assiduously till an hour before noon, when they again meet in one place and donning linen loincloths wash all over with cold water. Thus purified they assemble in a building of their own which no one outside their community is allowed to enter: clean themselves they go into the refectory as if it was a holy temple and sit down in silence. Then the baker gives them their loaves in turn, and the cook sets before each man one plateful of one kind of food. The priest says grace before meat: to taste the food before this prayer is forbidden. After breakfast he offers a second prayer; for at beginning and end they give thanks to God as the Giver of life. Then removing their garments as sacred they go back to their work till evening. Returning once more they take supper in the same way, seating their guests beside them if any have arrived. Neither shouting nor disorder ever desecrates the house: in conversation each gives way to his neighbour in turn. To people outside the silence within seems like some dread mystery; it is the natural result of their unfailing sobriety and the restriction of their food and drink to a simple sufficiency.

In general they take no action without orders from the supervisors, but two things are left entirely to them – personal aid, and charity; they may of their own accord help any deserving person in need or supply the penniless with food. But gifts to their own kinsfolk require official sanction. Showing indignation only when justified, they keep their tempers under control; they champion good faith and serve the cause of peace. Every word they speak is more binding than an oath; swearing they reject as something worse than perjury, for they say a man is already condemned if he cannot be believed without God being named.[1] They are wonderfully devoted to the work of ancient writers, choosing mostly books that can help soul and body; from them in their anxiety to cure disease they learn all about medicinal roots and the properties of stones.[2]

Persons desirous of joining the sect are not immediately admitted. Excluded for a whole year a man is required to observe the same rule of life as the members, receiving from them a hatchet, the loin-cloth mentioned above, and white garments. When in this period he has given proof of his temperance, he is associated more closely with the rule and permitted to share the purer waters of sanctification, though not yet admitted to the communal life. He has demonstrated his strength of purpose, but for two more years his character is tested, and if then he is seen to be worthy he is accepted into the society. But before touching the communal food he must swear terrible oaths, first that he will revere the Godhead, secondly that he will deal justly with men, will injure no one either of his own accord or at another's bidding, will ever hate the wicked and co-operate with the good, will keep faith at all times and with all men – especially with rulers, since all power is conferred by God.[3] If he himself receives power, he will never abuse his authority, never by dress or additional ornament out-shine those under him; he will ever love truth and seek to convict liars, will keep his hands from stealing, his soul innocent of unholy gain, will never hide anything from members of the sect or reveal any of their secrets to others, even if brought by violence to the point of death. He further swears to impart their teaching to no man otherwise than as he himself received it, to take no part in armed robbery, and to preserve the books of the sect and in the same way the names of the angels. Such are the oaths by which they make sure of their converts.

Men convicted of major offences are expelled from the order, and the outcast often comes to a most miserable end; for bound as he is by oaths and customs he cannot share the diet of non-members, so is forced to eat grass till his starved body wastes away and he dies. Charity compels them to take many offenders back when at their last gasp, since they feel that men tortured to the point of death have paid a

1. *The same point as is made in the Sermon on the Mount.*
2. *Charms, no doubt.*
3. *Compare* St John xix 11 *and* Romans xiii 1.

sufficient penalty for their offences. In trying cases they are most careful and quite impartial, and the verdict is given by a jury of not less than a hundred: when they reach a decision there is no appeal. What they reverence most after God is the Lawgiver, and blasphemy against him is a capital offence. Obedience to older men and to the majority is a matter of principle: if ten sit down together one will not speak against the wish of the nine.

They are careful not to spit into the middle of other people or to the right, and they abstain from seventh-day work more rigidly than any other Jews; for not only do they prepare their meals the previous day so as to avoid lighting a fire on the Sabbath, but they do not venture to remove any utensil or to go and ease themselves. On other days they dig a hole a foot deep with their trenching-tool (for such is the hatchet they give to the novices) and draping their cloak round them so as not to affront the rays of the god, they squat over it; then they put the excavated soil back in the hole. On these occasions they choose the more secluded spots; and though emptying the bowels is quite natural they are taught to wash after it, as if it defiled them.

They are divided into four grades, according to the stage they have reached in their preparation; and so far are the juniors inferior to the seniors that if they touch them the persons touched must wash as though contaminated by an alien. They are long-lived, most of them passing the century, owing to the simplicity of their daily life, I suppose, and the regular routine. They despise danger and conquer pain by sheer will-power: death, if it comes with honour, they value more than life without end. Their spirit was tested to the utmost by the war with the Romans, who racked and twisted, burnt and broke them, subjecting them to every torture yet invented in order to make them blaspheme the Lawgiver or eat some forbidden food, but could not make them do either, or ever once fawn on their tormentors or shed a tear. Smiling in their agony and gently mocking those who put them on the rack, they resigned their souls in the joyous certainty that they would receive them back.

It is indeed their unshakable conviction that bodies are corruptible and the material composing them impermanent, whereas souls remain immortal for ever. Coming forth from the most rarefied ether they are trapped in the prison-house of the body as if drawn down by one of nature's spells; but once freed from the bonds of the flesh, as if released after years of slavery, they rejoice and soar aloft. Teaching the same doctrine as the sons of Greece, they declare that for the good souls there waits a home beyond the ocean, a place troubled by neither rain nor snow nor heat, but refreshed by the zephyr that blows ever gentle from the ocean. Bad souls they consign to a darksome, stormy abyss, full of punishments that know no end. I think the Greeks had the same notion when they assigned to their brave men, whom they call heroes or demigods, the Islands of the Blest, and to the souls of the wicked the place of the impious in Hades, where according to their stories certain people undergo punishment – Sisyphus and Tantalus, Ixion and Tityus, and the like. They tell these tales firstly because they believe souls to be immortal, and secondly in the hope of encouraging virtue and discouraging vice, since the good become better in their lifetime through the hope of a reward after death, and the propensities of the bad are restained by the fear that, even if they are not caught in this life, after their dissolution they will undergo eternal punishment. This then is the religious teaching of the Essenes about the soul, providing an inescapable inducement to those who have once tasted their wisdom.

Some of them claim to foretell the future, after a lifelong study of sacred literature, purifications of different kinds, and the aphorisms of prophets; rarely if ever do their predictions prove wrong.

There is a second order of Essenes, which agrees with the other in its way of life, customs, and rules, and differs only in its views on marriage. They think that the biggest thing in life – the continuance of the race – is forfeited by men who do not marry, and further, if everyone followed their example mankind would rapidly disappear. However, they put their brides on probation for three years, and do not marry them till the regularity[1] of their periods proves them capable of child-bearing. When conception has taken place intercourse ceases – proof that the object of the marriage was not pleasure but the begetting of children. When women bathe they wear a dress just as the men wear a loincloth. Such are the customs of the order.

Of the two schools named first, the Pharisees are held to be the most authoritative exponents of the Law and count as the leading sect. They ascribe everything to Fate or to God: the decision whether or not to do right rests mainly with men, but in every action Fate takes some part. Every soul is incorruptible, but only the souls of good men pass into other bodies, the souls of bad men being subjected to eternal

1. *So the Latin: the Greek text is unintelligible.*

punishment. The Sadducees, the second order, deny Fate altogether and hold that God is incapable of either committing sin or seeing it; they say that men are free to choose between good and evil, and each individual must decide which he will follow. The permanence of the soul, punishments in Hades, and rewards they deny utterly. Again, Pharisees are friendly to one another and seek to promote concord with the general public, but Sadducees, even towards each other, show a more disagreeable spirit, and in their relations with men like themselves they are as harsh as they might be to foreigners.

This is all I wish to say about the Jewish schools of thought.

When the ethnarchy of Archelaus came under Roman rule his brothers, Philip and Herod Antipas, continued to rule their respective tetrarchies. (Salome had died, leaving to Julia, Augustus' consort, her toparchy, with Jamnia and the palmgroves at Phasaelis.) Later, when on the death of Augustus, who had been in supreme control 57 years, 6 months and 2 days,[1] the empire passed to Tiberius, the son of Julia, these two remained undisturbed, and Philip founded the city of Caesarea near the sources of the Jordan in Paneas and Julias in Lower Gaulonitis, Antipas Tiberias in Galilee and a city called after Julia in Peraea.

As procurator of Judaea Tiberius sent Pilate, who during the night, secretly and under cover, conveyed to Jerusalem the images of Caesar known as *signa*. When day dawned this caused great excitement among the Jews; for those who were near were amazed at the sight, which meant that their laws had been trampled on – they do not permit any graven image to be set up in the City – and the angry City mob were joined by a huge influx of people from the country. They rushed off to Pilate in Caesarea, and begged him to remove the *signa* from Jerusalem and to respect their ancient customs. When Pilate refused, they fell prone all round his house and remained motionless for five days and nights.

The next day Pilate took his seat on the tribunal in the Great Stadium and summoned the mob on the pretext that he was ready to give them an answer. Instead he gave a pre-arranged signal to the soldiers to surround the Jews in full armour, and the troops formed a ring three deep. The Jews were dumbfounded at the unexpected sight, but Pilate, declaring that he would cut them to pieces unless they accepted the

1. *Reckoned from the death of Julius in 44 B.C. According to Suetonius 5 months, 4 days.*

images of Caesar, nodded to the soldiers to bare their swords. At this the Jews as though by agreement fell to the ground in a body and bent their necks, shouting that they were ready to be killed rather than transgress the Law. Amazed at the intensity of their religious fervour, Pilate ordered the *signa* to be removed from Jerusalem forthwith.

After this he stirred up further trouble by expending the sacred treasure known as Corban on an aqueduct 50 miles long. This roused the populace to fury, and when Pilate visited Jerusalem they surrounded the tribunal and shouted him down. But he had foreseen this disturbance, and had made the soldiers mix with the mob, wearing civilian clothing over their armour, and with orders not to draw their swords but to use clubs on the obstreperous. He now gave the signal from the tribunal and the Jews were cudgelled, so that many died from the blows, and many as they fled were trampled to death by their friends. The fate of those who perished horrified the crowd into silence.

At about this time Agrippa, son of that Aristobulus who had been put to death by his father Herod, sought an audience of Tiberius in order to accuse Herod the Tetrarch. When the accusation was not accepted he remained in Rome and made approaches to many eminent men, and particularly to Germanicus' son Gaius, as yet a private citizen. One day he invited him to dinner and, after entertaining him lavishly, finished by stretching out his hands and openly praying that Tiberius might die soon, so that he could see Gaius lord of the world. One of his domestics passed this on to Tiberius, who was enraged and had Agrippa locked up, keeping him in rigorous confinement for six months until his own death. He had reigned twenty-two years, six months, and three days.

Proclaimed Caesar, Gaius released Agrippa and set him over the tetrarchy of Philip, recently deceased, as king. Agrippa's acquisition of this title awoke jealous ambitions in Herod the Tetrarch. Herod's hopes of a crown were inspired chiefly by his wife Herodias, who kept nagging him for his inertia and declared that only his unwillingness to make the journey to Caesar prevented his acquiring a better title. Having promoted Agrippa from private citizen to king, the emperor would surely not hesitate to promote Herod from tetrarch. Yielding to this pressure Herod came to Gaius, who punished his ambition by banishing him to Spain. For he had been followed by Agrippa, who brought accusations against him and was rewarded by Gaius with the addition of Herod's tetrarchy. Herod, whose wife shared his exile in Spain, died there.

Gaius Caesar's accession to power so completely turned his head that he wished to be thought of and addressed as a god, stripped his country of its noblest men, and proceeded to lay sacrilegious hands on Judaea. He ordered Petronius to march with an army to Jerusalem and erect his statues in the Temple: if the Jews refused them he was to execute the objectors and enslave all the rest of the population. But God evidently took note of these instructions. Petronius, with three legions and a large body of Syrian allies, began a swift march from Antioch to Judaea. Some of the Jews disbelieved the rumours of war; others who did believe were at a loss how to defend themselves. But soon a shudder ran through them all; for the army was already at Ptolemais. This is a seaside town of Galilee, built on the edge of the great plain and shut in by mountains. To the east, seven miles away, is the Galilaean range; to the south is Carmel, fifteen miles distant; to the north is the highest range, called 'The Ladder of Tyre' by the natives: the distance in this case is twelve miles. About a quarter of a mile from the town flows the Beleus, a very tiny stream on whose banks is the Tomb of Memnon. Near this is an area fifty yards wide which is of great interest; it is a round hollow which yields crystalline sand. A large number of ships put in and clear this out; but the place fills up again thanks to the winds, which as if on purpose blow into it common sand from outside. This is at once converted by the mine into crystal. Still more wonderful, I think, is the fact that crystal which overflows from the basin reverts to ordinary sand. A most unusual spot.

The Jews with their wives and children massed on the plain near the city, and appealed to Petronius first for their ancestral laws and then for themselves. He yielded to the demands of such a formidable crowd, and left the army and the statues in Ptolemais. Then he advanced into Galilee, and summoning the populace with all the notables to Tiberias he enlarged on the power of Rome and the threats of Caesar. He demonstrated too the unreasonableness of their demands; for when all the subject races had set up the images of Caesar in their cities among the other gods, for Jews alone to object was tantamount to rebellion and deliberate disloyalty. When they pleaded their Law and ancestral customs and explained that it was not permissible for a graven image of God, much less of a man, to be placed in the Temple or even in some ordinary place in their country, Petronius retorted: 'Quite so; but I too am bound to keep the law of my sovereign lord: If I break it and spare you I shall perish as I deserve. It will be the Emperor himself who will make war on you, not I. I am subject to authority just as you are.' In reply the crowd roared that they were ready to suffer anything for their Law. When he had secured silence Petronius asked: 'Will you then go to war with Caesar?' The Jews replied that for Caesar and the people of Rome they sacrificed twice a day. But if he wished to set up the images in their midst he must first sacrifice the whole Jewish race: they were ready to offer themselves as victims with their wives and children. This reply filled Petronius with wonder and pity for the unparalleled religious fervour of these brave men and the courage that made them so ready to die. So for the time being they were dismissed with nothing settled.

During the next few days he got the leading men together privately and assembled the people publicly, and tried first persuasion and then advice. But for the most part he relied on threats, emphasizing the strength of the Romans, the fury of Gaius, and the necessity imposed on himself. Nothing that he could think of had any effect, and he saw that the land was in danger of remaining unsown; for it was at seed-time that the crowds had wasted seven weeks in idleness. So at last he got them together and said: 'It is better for me to take the risk. With God's help I shall convince Caesar and we can all breathe again: if he is exasperated I will gladly give my life to save so many.' Then he dismissed the throng, who offered many prayers on his behalf, withdrew the army from Ptolemais, and returned to Antioch. From there he at once sent a dispatch to Caesar, informing him of his invasion of Judaea and the appeals of the nation, and adding that unless he wished to destroy both the men and the land they tilled he must let them keep their law and withdraw his instructions. To this dispatch Gaius replied in no gentle terms, threatening Petronius with death for his slowness in carrying out his orders. But as it happened the messengers who carried this reply were held up for three months by storms at sea, while others who brought news of Gaius' death had a good voyage, so that Petronius received intimation of this event four weeks earlier than the denunciation of himself.

When after a reign of three years eight months Gaius was treacherously murdered, the armies in Rome forced the empire on Claudius. The Senate however, on the motion of the consuls Sextus Saturninus and Pomponius Secundus, ordered the three remaining cohorts to protect the City and assembled in the Capitol, where in view of the savagery of Gaius they voted to take military action against Claudius. They resolved to restore the aristocracy that had ruled the country in olden days, or else to choose by vote a man worthy to be emperor.

As it happened that Agrippa was then on a visit to Rome, the Senate sent and invited him to discuss the situation with them, and at the same time Claudius summoned him to his camp to assist him as occasion arose. Realizing that he was virtually Caesar already Agrippa went to Claudius, who dispatched him as ambassador to the Senate to explain his intentions. In the first place his hand had been forced by the soldiers, but he felt that to disregard their enthusiasm would be unfair, and to disregard his own future most unsafe; for the fact that he had been summoned to the Imperial Throne placed him in great danger. He added that he would carry on the government like a good popular leader, not like a dictator; for he was satisfied with the honour of the imperial title, and on every matter at issue he would follow the wishes of the people. Indeed, if he had not been a moderate man by inclination, he would have had a sufficient inducement to self-restraint in Gaius' death.

This message was delivered by Agrippa. The Senate answered that they relied on the army and on wise counsels and would not voluntarily submit to slavery. When Claudius heard this answer, he sent Agrippa back to inform them that he would never consent to betray those who had given him unanimous support, and must therefore fight, though most unwillingly, against those who should have been his best friends. However, they must choose a battlefield outside the City; for it would be sacrilege if by their folly they polluted their ancestral shrines with the blood of their countrymen. This message Agrippa conveyed to the Senate.

Meanwhile one of the soldiers with the Senate drew his sword and cried: 'Look here, you fellows; why should we think of killing our friends and attacking men just like ourselves who happen to be with Claudius? We have an emperor with nothing against him, and the closest ties with those we are proposing to march against.' With these words he strode through the middle of the Senate with his entire unit behind him. Left in the lurch the patricians immediately panicked; and as they could find no means of escape they went the way of the soldiers and hurried off to join Claudius. But before the walls they were met by the naked swords of those who had been quicker

than they to back the winning side; and the men who led the way
might have been in danger before Claudius was aware of the soldiers'
violent intentions, had not Agrippa run to him and shown him how
dangerous the situation was, pointing out that, unless he restrained the
violence of his men who were furious with the patricians, he would
lose the very people who could make his reign glorious, and find himself ruler of a desert.

When Claudius heard this, he put a stop to the violent behaviour of
the soldiery and received the Senate into the camp, making them welcome and then immediately going out with them to present to God
thankofferings for his accession. On Agrippa he at once bestowed the
entire kingdom of his forbears, adding the outer districts given by
Augustus to Herod, Trachonitis, and Auranitis, and also another
kingdom called that of Lysanias. The people he informed of this
bestowal by an edict; the magistrates he ordered to engrave the award
on bronze tablets to be set up in the Capitol. He then bestowed on
Agrippa's brother Herod – who was also his son-in-law, having married Bernice – the kingdom of Chalcis.

From such wide dominions wealth poured into Agrippa's treasury,
which he very quickly emptied; for he began to surround Jerusalem
with fortifications so huge that had they been finished they would
have made it futile for the Romans to attempt a siege. But before the
wall reached its full height he died in Caesarea, after three years as king
following three as tetrarch. He left three daughters born to him by
Cypros (Bernice, Mariamme, and Drusilla) and one son by the same
wife (Agrippa). As Agrippa was quite a child Claudius brought the
kingdom under direct rule again, dispatching as procurator Cuspius
Fadus, followed by Tiberius Alexander. These two left native customs
severely alone and kept the nation at peace. After this Herod King of
Chalcis died leaving two sons, children of his niece Bernice (Bernicianus
and Hyrcanus), and one son, the child of his former wife Mariamme
(Aristobulus). A third brother, Aristobulus, a private citizen, also died,
leaving a daughter Jotape. The three brothers, as I said before, were
sons of Aristobulus and grandsons of Herod; Aristobulus and Alexander were born to Herod by Mariamme and put to death by their
father. Alexander's descendants established a dynasty in Greater
Armenia.

After the death of Herod, King of Chalcis, Claudius gave the
throne to his nephew Agrippa, son of the first Agrippa. In the other

districts, which were under direct rule, the procurator Alexander was succeeded by Cumanus, whose governorship was marked by disturbances and further disaster to the Jews. The people had assembled in Jerusalem for the Feast of Unleavened Bread, and the Roman cohort stood on guard over the Temple colonnade, armed men always being on duty at the feasts to forestall any rioting by the vast crowds. One of the soldiers pulled up his garment and bent over indecently, turning his backside towards the Jews and making a noise as indecent as his attitude. This infuriated the whole crowd, who noisily appealed to Cumanus to punish the soldier, while the less restrained of the young men and the naturally tumultuous section of the people rushed into battle, and snatching up stones hurled them at the soldiers. Cumanus, fearing the whole population would rush at him, sent for more heavy infantry. When these poured into the colonnades the Jews were seized with uncontrollable panic, turned tail and fled from the Temple into the City. So violently did the dense mass struggle to escape that they trod on each other, and more than 30,000 were crushed to death. Thus the Feast ended in distress to the whole nation and bereavement to every household.

This disaster was followed by a further disturbance, the work of bandits. On the Beth-horon highroad Stephen, a slave of Caesar, was conveying some furniture when bandits swooped and seized the plunder. Cumanus sent out men with orders to bring the inhabitants of the neighbouring villages in chains to his headquarters, blaming them for their failure to pursue and capture the bandits. In one village a soldier found the sacred Law, tore the book in two and threw it on the fire. The Jews, as if their whole country was in flames, assembled in frantic haste, religious fervour drawing them together irresistibly, and on a single summons ran in their thousands from all directions to Caesarea, where they besought Cumanus not to let the man who had thus insulted God and His Law go unpunished. Cumanus, seeing that the mob could only be appeased by a conciliatory answer, agreed that the soldier should be produced, and ordered him to be led between the lines of his accusers to execution. Then the Jews went home.

Next came a clash between Galilaeans and Samaritans. In the village of Gema, situated in the great plain of Samaria, when numbers of Jews were going up to the Feast a Galilaean was murdered. This brought swarms of Galilaeans to the spot to attack the Samaritans; but their leading men came to Cumanus and begged that before the situation got beyond control he would cross into Galilee and punish those responsible for the crime: in no other way could the mass of men be dispersed and war avoided. Cumanus however made their petitions take second place to matters then in hand, and promised the petitioners nothing.

When news of the murder reached Jerusalem the crowds were infuriated, and abandoning the Feast they instantly set out for Samaria without generals, paying no heed to the appeals of their magistrates. The bandit and revolutionary element among them was led by one Eleazar, son of Dinaeus, and Alexander. These men swooped on their neighbours in the toparchy of Acrabatene and slaughtered them, sparing neither infants nor the aged, and setting fire to the villages.

Cumanus, taking from Caesarea one troop of horse, called the Augustans, went to the rescue of those who were being plundered, and rounded up many of Eleazar's followers, killing still more. The rest of the crowd that had set out to fight the Samaritans the Jerusalem magistrates, rushing out clad in sackcloth and with ashes poured on their heads, besought to return and not by their vengeful action against Samaria provoke the Romans to attack Jerusalem: they must spare their country and the Temple, and their own wives and children, who for the sake of avenging one Galilaean were all in danger of being destroyed. These appeals induced the Jews to disperse; but many turned to banditry as there was no one to stop them, and all over the country plundering went on and the bolder spirits rose in revolt. On the Samaritan side the leading men went to Numidius Quadratus, legate of Syria, at Tyre, and demanded the punishment of those who had ravaged their land. On the other hand prominent Jews, among them the high priest Jonathan son of Ananus, presented themselves and declared that it was the Samaritans who had begun the disturbance by the murder, but blame for what had followed lay at Cumanus' door, since he had refused to take action against the actual killers.

Quadratus for the time being put off both delegations with the promise that when he visited the area he would enquire into all the circumstances. But he went to Caesarea, and finding there those whom Cumanus had taken alive he crucified them all. From there he went on to Lydda, where he heard the Samaritan version again; then he sent for eighteen Jews who were reported to have taken part in the fighting and cut off their heads. Besides two other men in important positions, the chief priests Jonathan and Ananias, with the latter's son Ananus and several other leading Jews, were sent to Caesar, as were the most eminent of the Samaritans. He further instructed Cumanus, with Celer the military tribune, to sail for Rome and report to Claudius what had occurred. After making these arrangements he went from Lydda to Jerusalem, and finding that the people were celebrating the Feast of Unleavened Bread in an orderly manner, he returned to Antioch.

At Rome Caesar heard what Cumanus and the Samaritans had to say. Agrippa was there too, enthusiastically supporting the Jews while Cumanus too had many powerful advocates. Claudius found the Samaritans guilty and ordered their three most powerful men to be executed; Cumanus he banished, and Celer he sent in chains to Jerusalem with orders that he should be handed over to the Jews for torture, dragged round the City and finally beheaded.

After this he sent as procurator of Judaea Felix, the brother of Pallas, with the addition of Samaria, Galilee, and Peraea. From Chalcis he transferred Agrippa to a larger kingdom, giving him Philip's old province of Trachonitis, Batanea, and Gaulonitis, together with the kingdom of Lysanias and the old tetrarchy of Varus. He himself, having ruled the Empire for 13 years, 8 months, and 20 days, died, leaving his throne to Nero. His wife Agrippina had tricked him into adopting Nero as his heir, though he had a son of his own (Britannicus) by Messalina his former wife, and a daughter (Octavia) whom he had married to Nero. He also had by Petina a daughter Antonia.

Through excess of prosperity and wealth Nero lost his balance and abused his good fortune outrageously. He put to death in succession his brother, wife, and mother, turning his savage attention next to his most eminent subjects. The final degree of his madness landed him on the stage of a theatre. But so many writers have recorded these things that I will pass over them and turn to what happened to the Jews in his time.

Little Armenia Nero gave to Herod's son Aristobulus, with the title of King, while to Agrippa's kingdom he added four cities with their toparchies, Abila and Julias in Peraea, Tarichaeae and Tiberias in Galilee. Over the rest of Judaea he appointed Felix procurator. Felix captured the bandit chief Eleazar, who had been plundering the country for twenty years, with many of his men, and sent them as prisoners to Rome; the bandits whom he crucified, and the local inhabitants in league with them whom he caught and punished, were too many to count. When the countryside had been cleared of bandits another type sprang up in Jerusalem, known as *sicarii*. These in broad daylight and in the middle of the City committed numerous murders. Their favourite trick was to mingle with festival crowds, concealing under their garments small daggers with which they stabbed their opponents. When their victims fell the assassins melted into the indignant crowd, and through their plausibility entirely defied detection. First to have his throat cut by them was Jonathan the high priest, and after him many were murdered every day. More terrible than the crimes themselves was the fear they aroused, every man as in war hourly expecting death. They watched at a distance for their enemies, and not even when their friends came near did they trust them; yet in spite of their suspicions and precautions they were done to death; such was the suddenness of the conspirators' attack and their skill in avoiding detection.

In addition to these there was formed another group of scoundrels, in act less criminal but in intention more evil, who did as much damage as the murderers to the well-being of the City. Cheats and deceivers claiming inspiration, they schemed to bring about revolutionary changes by inducing the mob to act as if possessed, and by leading them out into the wild country on the pretence that there God would show them signs of approaching freedom. Thereupon Felix, regarding this as the first stage of revolt, sent cavalry and heavy infantry who cut the mob to pieces.

A greater blow than this was inflicted on the Jews by the Egyptian false prophet. Arriving in the country this man, a fraud who posed as a seer, collected about 30,000[1] dupes, led them round by the wild country to the Mount of Olives, and from there was ready to force an entry into Jerusalem, overwhelm the Roman garrison, and seize supreme power with his fellow-raiders as bodyguard. But Felix anticipated his attempt by meeting him with the Roman heavy infantry, the whole population rallying to the defence, so that when the clash occurred the Egyptian fled with a handful of men and most of his followers were killed or captured; the rest of the mob scattered and stole away to their respective homes.

When this fever too had died down, another festering sore appeared in the body politic. The religious frauds and bandit chiefs joined forces and drove numbers to revolt, inciting them to strike a blow for freedom and threatening with death those who submitted to Roman rule; men who willingly chose slavery would be forcibly freed. Then

1. *According to Acts xxi 38 only 4000; another Josephan exaggeration?*

splitting up into groups they ranged over the countryside, plundering the houses of the well-to-do, killing the occupants, and setting fire to the villages, till their raging madness penetrated every corner of Judaea. Day by day the fighting blazed more fiercely.

Another disturbance broke out round Caesarea, the Jewish settlers coming to blows with the Syrian inhabitants. The Jews claimed the city as their own on the ground that it had been built by a Jew, King Herod. The Syrians agreed that the founder was a Jew, but declared that the city belonged to the Greeks; Herod would not have set up statues and temples in it if he had meant it for the Jews. These were the arguments put forward by the two sides, and the dispute led to blows, the bolder spirits on both sides daily rushing forth to battle; for the elder Jews were unable to restrain their own partisans, and the Greeks could not bear to be worsted by Jews. The Jews had the advantage in material resources and bodily prowess: the Greeks enjoyed the help of the soldiers; for the greater part of the Roman force there had been raised in Syria, and they were ready to help their own flesh and blood. The Roman prefects, anxious to quell the disturbance, constantly arrested the more pugnacious and punished them with whipping and imprisonment. However, the pains of those arrested failed to check or frighten the remainder, who plunged still more furiously into the rioting. One day the Jews were victorious, and Felix came into the forum and ordered them with threats to retire. When they refused he sent his soldiers against them and killed a large number, whose property was promptly plundered. As however the rioting continued, he picked out the leading men of both communities and sent them as ambassadors to Nero, to argue the merits of the case.

CHAPTER 8

Florus and Agrippa II

THE next procurator, Festus, tackled the chief curse of the country;
he killed a considerable number of the bandits and captured
many more. Albinus, who followed him, acted very differently,
being guilty of every possible misdemeanour. Not content with
official actions that meant widespread robbery and looting of private
property, or with taxes that crippled the whole nation, he allowed
those imprisoned for banditry by local courts or his own predecessors
to be bought out by their relatives, and only the man who failed to pay
was left in jail to serve his sentence. Now too the revolutionary party in
Jerusalem cast off all restraint, and its leaders bribed Albinus to shut his
eyes to their subversive activities, whilst any of the common people
who did not care for peace and quiet joined forces with the procurator's associates. Every scoundrel, surrounded by his own gang, stood
out from his followers like a bandit chief or dictator and used his
henchmen to rob respectable citizens. The result was that the victims
kept their wrongs to themselves while those still immune, through
fear of the same fate, *flattered* those they should have *battered*. In short,
free speech was completely suppressed and tyranny reigned everywhere; from then on the seeds of the coming destruction were being
sown in the City.

Such a man was Albinus, but his successor Gessius Florus made
him appear an angel by comparison. Albinus for the most part did his
mischief with secrecy and dissimulation; Gessius boasted of the wrongs
he did to the nation and, as if sent as public executioner to punish
condemned criminals, indulged in every kind of robbery and violence.
When pitiable things happened, he showed himself the most heartless
of men; when disgraceful things, the most disgusting. No one ever
had less use for truth or thought out more subtle methods of crime.
Making a profit out of individuals he considered poor sport: he stripped
whole cities, ruined complete communities, and virtually announced to
the entire country that everyone might be a bandit if he chose, so long
as he himself received a rake-off. The result of his avarice was that

every district was denuded, and many people left their old homes and fled to foreign provinces.

As long as Cestius Gallus administered the province from his headquarters in Syria, no one dared even to inform against Florus; but when he appeared in Jerusalem on the eve of the Passover the people crowded round – at least 3,000,000 of them[1] – imploring him to pity the nation in its distress and shouting against Florus, the ruin of their country. Florus, who was present and stood at Cestius' side, laughed at their protests. Cestius, however, quieted the excited crowd by assuring them that he would guarantee more reasonable conduct on Florus' part in the future. Then he returned to Antioch. But Florus accompanied him as far as Caesarea, disguising the intention he had already formed of making war on the nation, his only hope of diverting attention from his own crimes; for if peace lasted he foresaw that he would have the Jews accusing him to Caesar, but if he contrived to make them revolt the greater outrage would forestall any enquiry into lesser ones. So to ensure a nation-wide revolt he daily added to the general distress.

Meanwhile the Greeks of Caesarea secured from Nero control of the city and returned with the decision in writing. War broke out in the twelfth year of Nero's reign and the seventeenth of Agrippa's, in the month of May. In comparison with the fearful disasters to which it led its pretext was insignificant. The Jews in Caesarea had a synagogue alongside a piece of ground belonging to a Greek citizen. This they had repeatedly tried to acquire, offering many times the real value. Scorning their requests, the Greek further insulted them by beginning to build a factory right up to the dividing line, leaving them a narrow and utterly inadequate passage. The immediate result was that the more hot-headed of the young men jumped in and interfered with the builders. When this display of force was suppressed by Florus, the leading Jews, among them John the tax-collector, having no other way out, gave Florus a bribe of 8 silver talents to put a stop to the work. As nothing mattered to him but money, he promised full co-operation; but as soon as the money was his he left Caesarea for Sebaste, allowing party strife to take its course as if he had sold the Jews permission to fight it out!

The next day was a sabbath, and when the Jews gathered in the synagogue a Caesarean partisan had placed a large earthen vessel upside down at the entrance and was sacrificing birds on it. This

1. *Josephus has surpassed himself this time!*

infuriated the Jews, who felt that their Law had been violated and the site desecrated. The steadier, gentler people advised an appeal to the authorities; the quarrelsome element and youthful hotheads burned for a fight. The Caesarean partisans stood waiting for them, for they had sent the men to sacrifice by prearrangement, and the clash soon came. Jucundus, the cavalry officer detailed to prevent it, stepped forward, picked up the vessel, and attempted to end the strife. But he was no match for the violence of the Caesareans, so the Jews seized their Law-book and retired to Narbata, a Jewish area seven miles from Caesarea. John and twelve other influential citizens followed Florus to Sebaste, where they complained bitterly of what had happened and implored him to help, tactfully reminding him of the 8 talents. He actually arrested these men and put them in prison, on the ground that they had removed the Law-book from Caesarea !

This new outrage caused anger in Jerusalem, but passions were still kept under control. Florus, however, as if he had contracted to fan the war into flame, sent to the Temple treasury and removed 17 talents on the pretext that Caesar required it. Uproar followed at once and the people rushed in a body into the Temple, where with piercing yells they called on the name of Caesar, imploring him to free them from Florus' misrule. Some of the rioters shouted the most scandalous abuse at the latter, and going round with a hat begged coppers for the poor starveling ! This did not cure his avarice but increased his determination to get rich quick. So instead of going to Caesarea to extinguish the conflagration that was breaking out there and to remove the causes of the trouble – as he had been paid to do – he dashed off to Jerusalem with an army of horse and foot, in order that by Roman arms he might get what he wanted and by intimidation skin the City. The people, anxious to make him ashamed of his attempt, met the soldiers with friendly greetings and prepared to receive Florus submissively. He, however, sent ahead fifty horsemen commanded by Capito, and ordered them to retire and not to mock with new-found cordiality the man they had abused so scandalously. If they were fearless and outspoken they ought to make fun of him to his face, and show by force of arms as well as words that they loved liberty. This took the crowd aback, and when Capito's troops charged into their midst they scattered before they could salute Florus or convince the soldiers of their readiness to obey. Returning to their homes they passed the night in fear and dejection.

Florus slept in the Palace, and the next day had a dais erected outside and took his seat. The chief priests, political leaders, and eminent citizens lined up before this tribunal. Florus ordered them to give up the men who had abused him, declaring that they themselves would feel the weight of his hand if the culprits were not forthcoming. The Jewish leaders insisted that the people were peacefully disposed and apologized for the offending remarks; in such a mass of people there were bound to be some impudent juveniles, and it was impossible to identify the miscreants when everyone was conscience-stricken and afraid to confess his guilt. If the procurator cared anything about the peaceful state of the nation and wished to save the City for the Romans, it would be better for the sake of the many innocent to pardon the few guilty than because of a few scamps to wreck the lives of so many loyal subjects.

This plea made Florus still more furious, and he shouted to the soldiers to sack the Upper Marketplace and kill all they met. Their acquisitiveness thus stimulated by their general's encouragement, they not only sacked the area to which they had been sent but burst into all the houses and murdered the occupants. There followed a flight through the narrow streets, the slaughter of those who were caught, and rapine in all its horror. Many peaceful citizens were seized and taken before Florus, who had them scourged and then crucified. The total number that perished that day, including women and children – for not even infants were spared – came to about 3,600. The disaster was made the more crushing by the unheard-of character of the Roman brutality. No one had ever before dared to do what Florus did then – to scourge men of equestrian rank before the judgement-seat and nail them to the cross, men who were indeed Jews, but yet enjoyed Roman status.

At this time it happened that King Agrippa had travelled to Alexandria to congratulate Alexander, who had been entrusted with Egypt by Nero and sent there as governor. However, his sister Bernice was in Jerusalem, and seeing the criminal conduct of the soldiers she was cut to the heart, and repeatedly sent her cavalry commanders and bodyguards to Florus to beg him to stop the slaughter. He, caring nothing for the number of the victims or the high rank of the petitioner, but only for the profit he made out of the loot, was deaf to her appeals; and the mad fury of the soldiers did not even spare the queen – not only did they torture their prisoners to death before her eyes; they would actually have killed her if she had not escaped in time into the royal palace and spent the night there with her guards, in fear that the soldiers would attack. She was staying in Jerusalem to perform a vow to God; it is usual for those who are sick or in distress to vow that for thirty days before they intend to sacrifice they will abstain from wine and shave their heads. These vows Bernice was then performing, and she stood barefoot before the judgement-seat appealing to Florus, but no respect was paid to her and she went in danger of her life.

These events occurred on the 16th of Artemisios. The next day the crowd in great distress swarmed into the Upper Marketplace, shrieking and lamenting for the dead and still more vociferously calling down curses on Florus. This alarmed the influential citizens and chief priests, who rent their clothes and falling down before one man after another begged them to desist and not, after all they had suffered, provoke Florus to commit some irreparable outrage. The crowd at once complied out of respect for the petitioners and in the hope that Florus would commit no more crimes against them.

The extinction of the disturbance annoyed the procurator, who in order to rekindle the flames summoned the chief priests and prominent citizens, and said that the only way of proving that the people would not revolt again was to go out and meet the troops approaching from Caesarea – two cohorts were on the way. While the people were still being collected he sent orders to the centurions of the cohorts to instruct their men not to return the Jews' salutes, and if they uttered a word against him to use their weapons. The chief priests assembled great numbers in the Temple and urged them to meet the Romans and to avert irreparable disaster by welcoming the cohorts. This appeal failed to influence the insurgent element, and the thought of the fallen swung the majority to the side of the bolder spirits.

Thereupon every priest and every minister of God brought out the sacred vessels and put on the robes they always wore when officiating, the harpers and singers appeared with their instruments, and they all fell down and implored the people to preserve their sacred ornaments and not provoke the Romans to plunder the treasures of God. The chief priests themselves could be seen heaping dust on their heads, their clothes rent and their breasts bared. They appealed by name to each of the prominent citizens and collectively to the crowd not by some trifling offence to betray their country to men who were anxious to sack it. What advantage would it be to the soldiers to be saluted by the Jews? What compensation for past wrongs not to go out now? If they gave them the usual welcome, Florus would be deprived of all pretext for war, and they themselves would enjoy their country and immunity from further wrong. Again, to give way to a handful of insurgents, when with their overwhelming numbers they could compel even them to behave sensibly, would be feeble in the extreme.

With these arguments they quietened the crowd while the insurgents yielded, some to threats, others to authority. Then leading the way they went quietly and in good order to meet the column, and when the soldiers came near saluted them; but when they met with no response they began to vilify Florus. This was the agreed signal to attack them. In a flash the soldiers had surrounded and begun to club them; when they fled the cavalry pursued them and trampled them down. Many fell under the blows of the Romans, more were crushed by their friends. Round the gates there was frightful congestion; as everyone raced to get in first the flight was slowed down for them all, and those who stumbled met a horrible end; suffocated and crushed to pulp beneath countless feet, they were unrecognizable when their kinsfolk came to bury them. The soldiers poured in with the fugitives, raining blows on any they caught, and drove the crowd through Bezetha,[1] in an effort to force their way through and seize the Temple and Antonia. For the same purpose Florus led his own men out of the royal palace and endeavoured to reach the fortress. But the attempt failed; for the people swung round to face him and blocked his advance, then lined up on the roofs and pelted the Romans. Suffering severely from the falling missiles and too weak to hack a way through the crowds that blocked the narrow streets, they retreated to their camp near the Palace.

The insurgents, afraid that Florus would come on again and seize the Temple by way of Antonia, climbed up at once and cut a gap in the colonnades that linked Antonia with the Temple. This cooled the avarice of Florus; for it was the treasures of God he was after, and for this reason he was anxious to get into Antonia, so that when the colonnades were broken down he was diverted from his attempt. He sent for the chief priests and the Sanhedrin, and told them that he was going to quit the City but would leave them as big a garrison as they wanted. In reply they solemnly promised to maintain order and prevent any rising, if he left them one cohort, but not the one that had been engaged, as the people hated it because of what it had done to

1. *The area inside the new north wall.*

them. So he changed the cohort as requested, and with the rest of his forces went back to Caesarea.

As a further inducement to hostilities he sent Cestius a false report of a Jewish revolt, alleging that they had started the recent fighting and charging them with violence of which they had in reality been the victims. The Jerusalem magistrates did not take this lying down; they and Bernice too wrote more than one letter to Cestius about the crimes which Florus had committed against the City. Cestius read the communications from both parties and consulted his staff. They advised him to go at once to Jerusalem at the head of an army, and either punish the revolt, if real, or strengthen the allegiance of the Jews if they were indeed loyal; but he thought it better to send one of his colleagues first to examine the position and to bring a reliable report of the state of Jewish feeling. So he sent the tribune Neapolitanus, who at Jamnia met King Agrippa on his way home from Alexandria, and told him who had sent him and why.

There too the Jews' chief priests, with influential citizens and the Sanhedrin, arrived to welcome the king. After paying homage they began to bewail their own calamities and to describe the savagery of Florus. This shocked Agrippa, but he discreetly turned his indignation on the Jews he inwardly pitied, wishing to humble their pride and by refusing to see that they had suffered any wrong to damp their ardour for revenge. They, being men of parts and property-owners with a personal interest in peace, realized that the king's rebuke was kindly meant. But the people came seven miles out of Jerusalem to welcome Agrippa and Neapolitanus, with the widows of the slain running in front and wailing, and the people replying to their groans with lamentations. They implored Agrippa to help them, and dinned into the ears of Neapolitanus all that Florus had done to them. When they entered the City the Jews pointed to the desolate Marketplace and sacked houses. Then with Agrippa's help they persuaded Neapolitanus with one attendant to walk round the City as far as Siloam, and see for himself that the Jews were submissive to all other Romans and only bitter against Florus because of his appalling savagery. Going through the City Neapolitanus found proof enough of their docility; so he went up into the Temple. There he assembled the people, praised them highly for their loyalty to Rome, and urged them strongly to keep the peace. Then from the Outer Court he made obeisance to the Sanctuary of God, after which he returned to Cestius.

The Jewish crowd now turned to the king and the chief priests, begging them to send envoys to Nero to denounce Florus, and by protesting against his wholesale massacres to end suspicions of a Jewish revolt. For they would be thought to have started hostilities if they were not quick to point out the real aggressor. It was evident that they would not take it quietly if anyone tried to block the embassy. Agrippa realized that to choose men to accuse Florus would be to ask for trouble, but that to stand by till Jewish fury flared up into actual hostilities was dangerous even for himself. So he summoned the crowd into the Gymnasium and placed his sister Bernice conspicuously on the roof of the Hasmonaean palace. This was above the Gymnasium on the other side of the Upper City; the Gymnasium was linked with the Temple by a bridge. Then he began:

'If I had found you all eager for war with the Romans, whereas in fact the most honest and sincere section of the people are bent on keeping the peace, I should not have come forward to address you or ventured to give advice, for it is a waste of breath to say anything in favour of a wise course when the audience is unanimously in favour of a foolish one. But some of you are young men with no experience of the horrors of war, others are too sanguine about the prospects of independence, others are led on by selfish ambition and the profit to be made out of weaker men if the explosion occurs. So in the hope that these men may learn sense and change their ways, and that the folly of a few may not be visited on good citizens, I felt obliged to call you all together and tell you what I think is best. Please do not interrupt me if you disapprove of what I say; for those who have absolutely made up their mind to revolt will be free to feel the same after hearing my views, but my words will be lost even on those who want to listen unless everyone keeps quiet.

'Now I am aware that many orate against the insolence of the procurators and rhapsodize about the wonders of liberty; but before I go into the question of who you are and whom you are planning to fight, I must first sort out your jumble of pretexts. If you are trying to avenge your wrongs, why do you prate about liberty? if on the other hand slavery seems unbearable, it is a waste of time to blame your rulers; if they were the mildest of men, it would still be disgraceful to be slaves.

'Consider these pretexts one at a time, and see how feeble are your grounds for war. First, the charges against the procurators. You should flatter, not provoke, the authorities; when for trifling errors you pile on reproaches, it is yourselves you hurt by your denunciation of the offenders; instead of injuring you secretly and shamefacedly they plunder you openly. Nothing damps an aggressor like patient submission, and the meekness of the persecuted puts the persecutor to shame. I grant that the ministers of Rome are unbearably harsh; does it follow that all the Romans are persecuting you, including Caesar? Yet it is on them that you are going to make war! It is not by their wish that an unscrupulous governor comes from Rome, nor can western eyes see the goings-on in the east; it is not easy in Rome even to get up-to-date news of what happens here. It would be absurd because of the trifling misdemeanours of one man to go to war with a whole nation, and such a nation – a nation that does not even know what it is all about! Our grievances can be quickly put right; the same procurator will not be here for ever, and his successors are almost sure to be more reasonable. But once set on foot, war cannot easily be either broken off or fought to a conclusion without disaster.

'As for your new passion for liberty, it comes too late; you ought to have made a supreme effort to retain it long ago. For the experience of slavery is a painful one, and to escape it altogether any effort is justified; but the man who has once submitted and then revolts is a refractory slave, not a lover of liberty. Thus the time when we ought to have done everything possible to keep the Romans out was when the country was invaded by Pompey. But our ancestors and their kings, with material, physical, and mental resources far superior to yours, faced a mere fraction of the Roman army and put up no resistance; will you, who have learnt submission from your fathers and are so ill provided compared with those who first submitted, stand up to the whole Roman Empire?

'Think of the Athenians. To preserve the liberty of Greece they once consigned their city to the flames. When proud Xerxes sailed across land and marched across water[1] and counting the seas no barrier led an army too big for Europe to hold, they chased him away in a single ship like a runaway slave. Near little Salamis they broke the might of Asia – and today they are slaves of Rome, and the city that once lorded it over Greece takes her orders from Italy! Think of the Spartans; after Thermopylae and Plataea, after Agesilaus who swept

---

1. *Xerxes cut a canal through the isthmus of Mt Athos and crossed the Dardanelles by a bridge of boats.*

across Asia, they are happy under the same masters. Think of the Macedonians. They still dream of Philip and see visions of the goddess who with Alexander sowed for them the seeds of world-empire; yet they endure this complete transformation and loyally serve the new recipients of Fortune's favours. Other nations by the thousand, bursting with greater determination to assert their liberty, no longer resist. Will you alone refuse to serve the masters of the whole world?

'Where are the men, where are the weapons you count on? Where is the fleet that is to sweep the Roman seas? Where are the funds to pay for your expeditions? Do you think you are going to war with Egyptians and Arabs? Look at the far-flung empire of Rome and contrast your own impotence. Why, our forces have been worsted even by our neighbours again and again, while their arms have triumphed over the whole world! And even the world is not big enough to satisfy them; Euphrates is not far enough to the east, or Danube to the north, or Libya and the desert beyond to the south, or Cadiz to the west; but beyond the Ocean they have sought a new world, carrying their arms as far as Britain, that land of mystery. Why not face facts? Are you richer than the Gauls, stronger than the Germans, cleverer than the Greeks, more numerous than all the nations of the world? What gives you confidence to defy the power of Rome?

'It is terrible to be enslaved, it will be said. How much worse for Greeks, who surpass every nation under the sun in nobility and fill such a wide domain, and yet bow before the fasces of a Roman governor, as do the Macedonians, who have a better right than you to demand their liberty! And what of the five hundred cities of Asia? Do they not without a garrison bow before one governor and the consular fasces? Need I mention the Heniochi, the Colchians, and the Tauric race, the peoples near the Bosporus, the Black Sea, and the Sea of Azov? At one time they recognized not even a native ruler, and now they submit to 3,000 legionaries, while forty warships keep the peace on the sea where before none but pirates sailed. How justly Bithynia, Cappadocia, Pamphylia, Lycia, and Cilicia might demand liberty! Yet without armed pressure they pay their dues.

'Then there are the Thracians, spread over a country five days' march in width and seven in length, more rugged and much more defensible than yours, a country whose icy blasts are enough to halt an invader. Yet 2,000 Roman guards suffice to maintain order. Their neighbours the Illyrians, whose land extends from Dalmatia to the

Danube frontier, need only two legions to keep them quiet; in fact Illyrians unite with Romans to halt Dacian raids. The Dalmatians again, who have so often tried to shake off the yoke and have always been driven by defeat to rally their forces and revolt again, now live peaceably under one Roman legion!

'But if any people might reasonably be tempted to rebel by its peculiar advantages, that people is the Gauls, provided as they are with such marvellous natural defences, on the east the Alps, on the north the Rhine, on the south the Pyrenees, on the west the Ocean. Yet in spite of these immense obstacles, in spite of the huge total of 305 nations, in spite of the prosperity that wells up from their soil and enables them to flood the whole world with their goods, they submit to being the milch cow of Rome and receiving from her hands what they themselves have produced! And this they tolerate, not from effeminacy or racial inferiority – they fought for eighty years to save their liberty – but because they are overawed by the might of Rome and still more by her destiny, which wins her more victories than do her arms. So Gaul is kept in order by 1,200 soldiers – hardly more men than she has cities!

'Then Spain – in the fight for independence the gold from her soil could not save her, nor could the vast stretch of land and sea that separates her from Rome, nor the tribes of Lusitania and Cantabria with their passion for fighting, nor the neighbouring Ocean that terrifies even the natives with its tides. Crossing the cloud-capped Pyrenees and advancing their arms beyond the Pillars of Hercules the Romans enslaved Spain too. Yet to guard this remote and almost invincible nation requires but one legion!

'Which of you has not heard of the Germans, with their inexhaustible manpower? You have, I am sure, seen their magnificent physique on many occasions, for on every side Roman masters have German slaves; yet this people occupies an immense area, their physique is surpassed by their pride, from the bottom of their hearts they despise death, and when enraged they are more dangerous than the fiercest of wild beasts. Yet the Rhine is the limit of their aggression and the Romans with eight legions have tamed them, enslaving the prisoners and driving the entire nation to seek refuge in flight.

'Consider the defences of the Britons, you who feel so sure of the defences of Jerusalem. They are surrounded by the Ocean and inhabit an island as big as this continent; yet the Romans crossed the sea and enslaved them, and four legions keep that huge island quiet, But why should I say more about that, when even the Parthians, the most warlike race of all, rulers of so many nations and protected by such vast forces, send hostages to Rome, and on Italian soil may be seen, humbly submitting for the sake of peace, the aristocrats of the east.   ,

'Almost every nation under the sun bows down before the might of Rome; and will you alone go to war, not even considering the fate of the Carthaginians, who boasted of great Hannibal and their glorious Phoenician ancestors, but fell beneath Scipio's hand? The Cyrenians (Spartans by descent), the Marmaridae (a race that extends to the waterless desert), Syrtes, whose very mention terrifies, Nasamonians, Moors, Numidians with their vast numbers – none of them could resist Roman skill at arms. This third of the whole world, whose nations could hardly be counted, bounded by the Atlantic and the Pillars of Hercules, and supporting the millions of Ethiopia as far as the Indian Ocean, is subdued in its entirety; and apart from the regular crops which for eight months of the year feed the whole population of Rome, these peoples pay tribute of every kind, and for the needs of the Empire willingly submit to taxation; and unlike you they take no offence when given orders, though only a single legion is quartered in their midst.

'But why should we go so far for evidence of the Roman power when we can find it in Egypt, our nearest neighbour? She stretches as far as Ethiopia and Arabia Felix; she is the port for India; she has a population of 7,500,000 (excluding the citizens of Alexandria), as is shown by the poll-tax returns. But she does not repudiate the rule of Rome – yet what a stimulus to revolt she has in Alexandria with its size, its population, its wealth! a city three and a half miles long and over a mile wide, which pays Rome every month more tribute than you pay in a year, and apart from money sends her corn for four months, and which is protected on every side by trackless deserts or harbourless seas or rivers or marshes. Yet none of these things proved equal to the fortune of Rome, and two legions stationed in the city curb the remotest parts of Egypt and the nobility of Macedon as well.

'Whom, I ask you, will you find in the uninhabited wilds to be your allies in this war? for in the inhabited world all are Romans – unless you extend your hopes beyond the Euphrates and imagine that your kinsmen even beyond the Tigris will come to your aid! But they will not without good reason get involved in a full-scale war, and if they should decide on anything so foolish the Parthian king would put a stop to it; for he is anxious to preserve his armistice with the Romans, and will consider it a breach of the truce if any of his tributaries takes the field against them.

'So there is no refuge left except to make God your ally. But He too is ranged on the Roman side, for without His help so vast an empire could never have been built up. Think too how difficult it would be, even if you were fighting feeble opponents, to preserve the purity of your religion, and how you will be forced to transgress the very laws which furnish your chief hope of making God your ally, and so will alienate Him. If you observe the custom of the Sabbath with its complete cessation of activity, you will promptly be crushed, as were your ancestors by Pompey, who was most active in pressing the siege on the days when the besieged were passive. But if in the war you transgress your ancestral Law I don't see what you have left to fight for, since your one desire is that none of your ancestral customs should be broken. How will you be able to call the Deity to your aid if you deliberately deny Him the service that is due?

'Everyone who engages in war relies on either divine or human help; but when, as is probable, both are denied, the aggressor is bringing certain destruction on himself. What prevents you from killing your wives and children with your own hands and from consigning your ancestral home, the most beautiful in the world, to the flames? By such madness you will at least avoid the shame of defeat! It is wise, my friends, it is wise, while the vessel is still in harbour, to foresee the approaching storm, and not to sail out into the middle of the hurricane to sure destruction. For those on whom disaster falls out of the blue are at least entitled to pity, but a man who plunges into destruction with his eyes open earns only contempt.

'Possibly some of you suppose that you are making war in accordance with agreed rules, and that when the Romans have won they will be kind to you, and will not think of making you an example to other nations by burning down your Holy City and destroying your entire race. I tell you, not even if you survive will you find a place of refuge, since every people recognizes the lordship of Rome or fears that it will have to do so. Again, the danger threatens not only ourselves here but also those who live in other cities; for there is not a region in the world without its Jewish colony. All these, if you go to war, will be massacred by your opponents, and through the folly of a few men every city will run with Jewish blood. There would be an excuse for such a massacre;

but if it did not take place, think how wicked it would be to take up arms against such kindly people! Pity your wives and children, or at least pity your mother city and its sacred precincts. Spare the Temple and preserve for your use the Sanctuary with its sacred treasures. For the Romans will no longer keep their hands off when they have captured these, since for sparing them hitherto they have received no thanks at all. I call to witness all you hold sacred, the holy angels of God, and the Fatherland we all share, that I have not kept back anything that is for your safety; if you make a right decision you will share with me the blessings of peace, but if you are carried away by your passions you will go without me to your doom.'

At the end of his speech he burst into tears as did his sister, and with his tears considerably damped the ardour of his hearers. But they shouted that it was not Rome they were fighting, it was Florus – the man who had done them such wrong. To this King Agrippa replied: 'But you have acted as if you were already at war with Rome; you have paid no tribute to Caesar and you have cut down the colonnades leading to Antonia. You can refute the charges of insurrection by joining up the colonnades again and paying the tax; for, you know, Florus doesn't own the fortress, and Florus will not receive your money.'

Accepting this advice, the people with the king and Bernice went up into the Temple and began to rebuild the colonnades, while the magistrates and councillors went to the various villages and collected the tribute, quickly getting together the 40 talents due. In this way Agrippa delayed for the moment the threatened war; but when he tried further to persuade the mob to obey Florus until Caesar sent a successor to replace him, they were furious and abused the king and announced his banishment from the City. Some of the insurgents even dared to throw stones at him. The king saw that the passions of the revolutionaries could no longer be controlled, and wounded by the insults he had received he sent their magistrates and influential citizens to Florus at Caesarea, in order that he might choose some of them to collect the tribute from the countryside. Then he retired to his own kingdom.

CHAPTER 9

The Outbreak of War

MEANWHILE some of those most anxious for war made a united attack on a fort called Masada, captured it by stealth, and exterminated the Roman garrison, putting one of their own in its place. At the same time in the Temple courts Eleazar, son of Ananias the high priest and a very confident young man, who was Temple Captain, persuaded the ministers of the Temple to accept no gift or offering from a foreigner. This it was that made war with Rome inevitable; for they abolished the sacrifices offered for Rome and Caesar himself, and in spite of the earnest appeals of the chief priests and prominent citizens not to cancel the customary offerings for the government they would not give in. Their numbers made them supremely confident, backed as they were by the toughest of the revolutionaries, but chiefly they pinned their faith to Eleazar, the Temple Captain.

The prospect of irreparable disaster brought together the leading citizens, the chief priests, and the most prominent Pharisees to discuss the crisis. They decided to try an appeal to the insurgents and summoned a public meeting in front of the Bronze Gate,[1] the eastern entrance to the Inner Temple. They began by vehemently denouncing the folly of a revolt which would involve their country in total war, and went on to ridicule the pretext. Their ancestors had adorned the Sanctuary at foreign expense for the most part, never refusing a Gentile gift, and so far from debarring any man from sacrifice, a most irreligious thing to do, had set up votive offerings all round the Temple in conspicuous and prominent positions. And now these men were inviting the Romans to intervene and courting disaster at their hands by an alien innovation in their religion, and apart from the danger were condemning the City as irreligious, if among the Jews alone no foreigner might sacrifice or worship. If this law was brought in to debar a single individual, they would be indignant at such organized inhumanity, but they cared nothing when the Romans and even Caesar were shut out! But there was a danger that if they

1. Probably the 'Beautiful Gate' of Acts iii 2.

abolished the sacrifices offered for Rome they might be forbidden to sacrifice even for themselves, and that the City would be shut out of the Empire – unless they quickly recovered their common sense, restored the sacrifices, and wiped out the insult before it was reported to those they had insulted.

While they pleaded thus they brought forward priests with expert knowledge of the traditions, who testified that all their ancestors had accepted offerings from aliens. But none of the revolutionaries would listen and not even the Temple ministers came forward – they were too busy making war inevitable. So seeing that the insurrection was now beyond their control and that the vengeance of Rome would fall upon them first, the most influential citizens determined to establish their own innocence and sent delegations to Florus and Agrippa, the former led by Simon the son of Ananias, the other distinguished by the inclusion of Saul, Antipas, and Costobar, kinsmen of the king. They begged both to come with large forces to the City and suppress the insurrection before it got beyond control. Florus was delighted with the news, and in his eagerness to start the conflagration gave no answer to the delegates. But Agrippa, equally concerned for the rebels and their opponents, anxious to preserve the Jews for the Romans, and the Temple and Capital for the Jews, and aware that he himself stood to lose by the strife, sent to the help of the people 2,000 horsemen from Auranitis, Batanaea, and Trachonitis under Darius the cavalry commander and Philip, son of Jacimus, the general.

Thus encouraged the leading citizens, the chief priests, and all the peace-loving section of the populace occupied the Upper City, the Lower City with the Temple being in the hands of the insurgents. There followed an all-day exchange of stones from hand and sling, a continuous stream of missiles from both quarters. Sometimes they even sallied forth in company strength and fought hand to hand, the insurgents showing the greater courage, the king's troops the greater skill. The latter fought chiefly to get possession of the Temple and to drive out those who were polluting the Sanctuary, Eleazar and the insurgents to hold what they had and capture the Upper City in addition. The result was seven days of mutual slaughter, without either side being dislodged from its original position.

The next day was the Feast of Wood-carrying, on which the custom was that everyone should bring wood for the altar, so that there should never be a lack of fuel for the fire which is always kept alight. The

Jews excluded their opponents from this ceremony; but when an unarmed crowd poured in and with them numbers of the Sicarii – brigands who took their name from a dagger carried in their bosoms – they joined forces with these ruffians and pressed their attacks more confidently. The king's troops, inferior now in numbers as well as courage, were driven out of the Upper City. Their opponents rushed in and burnt down the house of Ananias the high priest and the palaces of Agrippa and Bernice; then they took their fire to the Record Office, eager to destroy the money-lenders' bonds and so make impossible the recovery of debts, in order to secure the support of an army of debtors and enable the poor to rise with impunity against the rich. The keepers of the records fled and the building was set on fire. When the nerve-centre of the City had gone up in flames, the insurgents went after their foes. Some of the leading citizens and chief priests plunged into the sewers and disappeared from view, others with the king's troops fled to the Upper Palace and lost no time in bolting the doors. Among these were Ananias the high priest, his brother Hezekiah, and those who had gone as delegates to Agrippa. So for the moment, satisfied with their victory and with the destruction they had wrought, the enemy called off the pursuit.

The next day however, the 15th of Loös, they assaulted Antonia, and after a two day siege captured and killed the garrison and set fire to the fortress. Then they went off to the Palace where the king's men had taken refuge, and breaking up into four bodies began to assail the walls. None of the defenders dared attempt a sortie in face of the swarm of attackers; but they lined the breastworks and towers and pelted all who approached, so that many of the bandits fell at the foot of the walls. Night and day the struggle continued without a break, the insurgents hoping to starve out the defenders, the defenders to wear down the besiegers.

Meanwhile one Menahem, son of Judas the Galilaean, the very clever rabbi who in the time of Quirinius had once reproached the Jews for submitting to the Romans after serving God alone, took his friends with him and went off to Masada, where he broke open King Herod's armoury and distributed weapons to his fellow-townsmen and other bandits. With these as bodyguard he returned like a king to Jerusalem, put himself at the head of the insurgents, and took charge of the siege. But they had no engines, and to undermine the wall under the enemy's eyes was impossible while they were pelted from above.

So starting at a distance they dug a mine as far as one of the towers, transferred the weight of the tower to wooden props, set the props on fire and withdrew. When the supports were burnt through the tower suddenly collapsed, only to reveal another wall built further back; for the defenders had detected the stratagem in good time – possibly the tower had moved while it was being undermined – and had furnished themselves with a second barrier. This unexpected sight was a bitter blow to the assailants, who had felt sure that victory was theirs already. However, the defenders sent to Menahem and the leaders of the insurrection, requesting leave to come out under an armistice. This was granted only to the king's troops and Jewish nationals, who then came out. Left unsupported, the Romans lost heart; they could not force their way through such a host, and were ashamed to ask for terms – besides, they might not be kept, even if granted. So they evacuated their camp as indefensible and fled to the King's Towers, Hippicus, Phasael, and Mariamme. Menahem and his men charged into the position thus deserted, caught and killed all who had not been quick enough to escape, looted the baggage, and fired the camp. This happened on the 6th of Gorpiaios.

On the next day the high priest Ananias was caught hiding near the Palace canal, and murdered by the bandits along with his brother Hezekiah. Then the insurgents invested the towers and kept guard so that no soldier should escape. But Menahem, his head swelled by the overthrow of such strong positions and by the high priest's death, turned to savagery, and thinking he had no rival in the conduct of affairs became unbearably tyrannical. Eleazar and his men rose against him, agreeing that it was absurd to revolt from Rome for love of liberty and then hand over that liberty to a Jewish executioner and submit to a master who, even if not violent, was certainly inferior to themselves. If they must put everything in one man's hands, anyone would be preferable to this fellow! So they formed their plans and attacked him in the Temple when he entered in pomp to worship, decked with kingly robes, and followed by a train of armed zealots. Eleazar and his men rushed at him while the rest of the people seized stones and began to pelt the rabbi, thinking that his overthrow would put a final end to the revolt. Menahem and his men held out for a while, but when they saw the whole populace rushing towards them they fled in all directions. Those who were caught were massacred, those who hid were ferreted out. A very few escaped by slipping away to Masada, among them Eleazar son of Jairus who was related to Menahem and later became autocrat of Masada. Menahem himself fled to Ophales and while hiding ignominiously there was taken alive, dragged into the open, and put to death by prolonged torture. A like fate befell his lieutenants, including the chief instrument of his domination, Absalom.

The people, as I said, took part in this massacre, in the hope of suppressing the insurrection altogether; the conspirators were in no hurry to end hostilities – it was for the sake of a free hand in the campaign that they had put Menahem to death. In fact the more the people urged them to abandon the siege of the soldiers, the more vigorously they pressed it, until unable to hold out any longer Metilius, the Roman commander, sent officers to Eleazar to ask only that their lives should be guaranteed, as they were ready to surrender their arms and all their possessions. The Jews jumped at the proposal and sent to them Gorion the son of Nicomedes, Ananias the son of Zadok, and Judas the son of Jonathan to promise them safety on oath. On this Metilius marched the soldiers down. As long as they were armed the insurgents left them alone and gave no sign of treachery; but when as agreed they laid down their shields and swords, and without a suspicion in their minds were marching away, Eleazar and his men rushed at them, surrounded them and cut them down, while they neither resisted nor begged for mercy, but merely appealed loudly to the agreement and the oaths. Thus brutally were they all murdered except Metilius, who begged for mercy and by promising to turn Jew and even be circumcised managed to save himself alone. This setback meant little to the Romans, whose immense numbers were unaffected by so trifling a loss, but to the Jews it seemed the prelude to their destruction. They saw no way to undo the provocation they had given for war; and the City was stained by such guilt that they must expect a visitation from heaven if not the vengeance of Rome. So there was universal lamentation and the streets were full of long faces, every decent citizen being terrified at the prospect of paying for the misdeeds of the insurgents. For it so happened that the massacre was carried out on the Sabbath, on which for religious reasons not even right deeds may be done.

On the same day and at the same hour, as if divinely ordained, the people of Caesarea had massacred the Jewish colony, in less than an hour slaughtering more than 20,000 and emptying Caesarea of the last

Jew; for those who might have escaped were seized by Florus and sent in chains to the dockyards. This blow made the whole nation wild with anger, and parties sacked the Syrian villages and the neighbouring cities, Philadelphia, Sebonitis, Gerasa, Pella, and Scythopolis. Next they swooped on Gadara, Hippos, and Gaulanitis, destroying some places and firing others. Then on to Kedasa near Tyre, Ptolemais, Gaba, and Caesarea. There was no resistance to their onslaughts in either Sebaste or Ascalon, both of which they burnt to the ground, going on to demolish Anthedon and Gaza. Round each of these cities a number of villages were looted, and the adult captives mercilessly slaughtered.

The Syrians on their side killed just as many Jews; they too slaughtered those they caught in the cities, not only through hatred as before, but now to avert their own peril. The whole of Syria was filled with hopeless confusion, and every city was divided into two camps, the survival of the one depending on the destruction of the other. The days were spent in bloodshed, the nights – still more terrible – in fear. For though they thought they were rid of the Jews, every community was suspicious of Jewish sympathizers, and while they hesitated to exterminate on the spot the doubtful element in their midst, they feared these nondescripts as much as complete foreigners. To the slaughter of their opponents even those who had always been deemed the most harmless of men were tempted by avarice; for they plundered with impunity the property of their victims, and as if from a battlefield carried off the spoils of the slain to their own homes, special honour being paid to the man who grasped the most, as if he had overcome more powerful enemies. The cities could be seen full of unburied corpses, the dead bodies of the aged flung down alongside those of infants, women without a rag to conceal their nakedness, the whole province full of indescribable horrors. Even worse than the atrocities continually committed were the threats of terrors to come.

So far the Jews had been attacking foreigners, but when they raided Scythopolis they found the Jews there opposed to them; for they lined up with the Scythopolitans, and treating their own safety as of more importance than the ties of blood they joined battle with their countrymen. But suspicion was aroused by this excess of zeal – the citizens feared that these men would attack the city in the night and bring a great disaster upon them, in order to compensate their fellow-Jews for their failure to support them. So they ordered them, if they wished to prove their loyalty and demonstrate their fidelity to their foreign neighbours, to go with their families into the Grove. The Jews carried out the order, suspecting nothing, and for two days the Scythopolitans made no move, thus deceiving them into thinking themselves safe; but on the third night they watched their opportunity when some were off their guard and others asleep, slaughtered them all – more than 13,000 of them – and looted the property of the whole colony.

An account must be given of the fate of Simon, son of a not undistinguished father, Saul. His bodily strength and personal courage were exceptional, but to the injury of his countrymen he abused both. He went out every day and killed many of the Jews before Scythopolis; often he routed their whole army and won the battle almost unaided. But he was overtaken by the punishment he had deserved by the slaughter of his own flesh and blood. When the men of Scythopolis surrounded the Grove and began to shoot down the men inside, he drew his sword but made no move towards the enemy as he saw their overwhelming numbers. Instead he exclaimed with great emotion: 'It serves me right for what I have done – I and the rest who have murdered so many of our own kith and kin to prove our loyalty to you Scythopolitans. Small wonder we have found foreigners treacherous when we have utterly betrayed our own nation; so let us die in disgrace by our own hands; we are not fit to die by those of the enemy. The same act can be the punishment my foul deeds deserve and the proof of my courage, so none of my foes shall boast of my death or gloat over my body.' So saying he glanced round with a look of mingled pity and rage at his own family – wife, children, and aged parents. Then first seizing his father by his grey hairs he ran him through with his sword; next he killed his unresisting mother, finally his wife and children, each of them almost falling on the sword, so eager were they to forestall the enemy. Then Simon, having gone through all his family, stood over the bodies in view of everyone, and raising his right hand aloft for all to see plunged the whole length of the blade into his own throat. We may well feel pity for the young man in view of his prowess and courage; but his trust in foreigners made his tragic end inevitable.

The wholesale slaughter at Scythopolis caused all the other cities to take arms against their Jewish colonies. In Ascalon 2,500 were put to death, in Ptolemais 2,000, and many were thrown into prison. At Tyre large numbers were killed and still more put under lock and key. A

Hippos and Gadara the same thing happened, the bolder spirits being destroyed and the timid kept in custody, and so with the other cities of Syria, according to the hate or fear with which each regarded the Jewish race. Only in Antioch, Sidon, and Apamea were the settlers spared, there being no inclination to kill or imprison any of the Jews. Perhaps their vast populations made them indifferent to the possibility of a Jewish rising, but the chief reason as it seems to me was pity for men in whom they detected no sign of revolution. At Gerasa not only were those who remained left unmolested, but those who wished to leave were escorted to the frontiers.

There was formed even in Agrippa's kingdom a plot against the Jews. He himself had gone to see Cestius Gallus at Antioch, leaving in charge of affairs a friend of his called Noarus, a blood-relation of King Soaemus. From Batanaea came seventy men, citizens outstanding in birth and ability, to ask for an army so that, if there should be any disturbance in their district, they would have adequate forces to suppress the rising. Noarus sent out by night some of the king's heavy infantry and massacred all seventy, committing this dastardly crime without reference to Agrippa, and through his unlimited avarice deliberately playing the traitor to his countrymen, with calamitous effect on the kingdom. He continued to outrage the nation cruelly till Agrippa heard of his conduct, and though unwilling to hurt Soaemus' feelings by putting him to death deprived him of his regency.

The insurgents seized a fortress called Cypros overlooking Jericho, exterminating the garrison and razing the defences to the ground. At about the same date the mass of Jews at Machaerus urged the Roman garrison to leave the fortress and hand it over to them. The Romans, afraid that it would be taken away from them by force, agreed to withdraw under a truce, and accepting the guarantees provided handed over the fortress, which was promptly occupied and garrisoned by the citizens.

At Alexandria there had been constant strife between the natives and the Jewish colony ever since Alexander, finding the Jews very ready to help against the Egyptians, rewarded their active support with permission to reside in the city with the same rights as the Greeks. They retained this privilege under his successors who in addition assigned them a quarter for their exclusive use, so that they could preserve their own way of life uncorrupted by needless contact with other races, and allowed them to call themselves Macedonians. When the Romans became masters of Egypt, neither the first Caesar nor any of his successors allowed the privileges granted to the Jews from Alexander's time onwards to be diminished. But there were continual clashes between Jews and Greeks, and as the authorities punished many of both sides the strife became ever more acute. At this time, when everywhere else confusion reigned, the fires were fanned into flame in Alexandria too. It happened that the citizens were holding a public meeting to consider a proposal to send an embassy to Nero, when there poured into the amphitheatre along with the Greeks a great stream of Jews. As soon as they caught sight of them their opponents yelled: 'Enemy spies!' Then they sprang up and went for them tooth and nail. Most of them fled and dispersed, but three men were seized and hauled off to be burnt alive. The whole Jewish colony sprang to their defence; first they pelted the Greeks with stones; then they snatched up torches and rushed to the amphitheatre, threatening to burn to death every single person there. And they would actually have done it had their ardour not been checked by Tiberius Alexander, the governor of the city. He employed no force in his first attempt to teach them sense, but unobtrusively sent respected figures among them to appeal to them to desist and not provoke the Roman army to attack them. But treating this appeal with contempt the insurgents heaped abuse on Tiberius.

He, realizing that nothing less than a major calamity would halt the rebels, let loose among them the two Roman legions, and with them 2,000 soldiers who happened to have come from Libya, with fearful consequences for the Jews. He gave the men leave not merely to kill them but also to plunder their property and burn down their houses. The soldiers rushed into the area called Delta where the Jews were concentrated, and proceeded to carry out their orders, but not without bloodshed on their own side; for the Jews stood shoulder to shoulder with their most heavily armed men in front and held their ground magnificently, but when once the line gave they were destroyed wholesale. Death came upon them in every form; some were overtaken in the open, others driven into their houses, which the Romans first looted and then burnt down. They felt no pity for infants, no respect for the aged; old and young were slaughtered right and left, so that the whole district was deluged with blood and 50,000 corpses were heaped up; nor would the remnant have survived had they not begged for mercy till Alexander, pitying them, ordered the Romans to retire. They with their habitual obedience broke off the massacre on the instant, but the populace of Alexandria through the bitterness of their hate were disinclined to obey and could hardly be dragged away from the bodies.

Such was the calamity that befell the colony at Alexandria. Cestius felt the necessity of action now that on every side the Jews were involved in war. He set out from Antioch at the head of the Twelfth Legion at full strength, 2,000 picked men from each of the others, six infantry cohorts, and four troops of cavalry, reinforced by contingents sent by the kings, Antiochus[1] furnishing 2,000 horse and 3,000 foot, all bowmen, Agrippa the same number of foot and nearly 2,000 horse, while Soaemus followed with 4,000 men, of whom a third were mounted and the majority bowmen. With this force Cestius advanced towards Ptolemais. Very large reinforcements were collected from the cities. Their skill was inferior to that of the soldiers, but their enthusiastic hatred of the Jews made up for their lack of training. Agrippa was there in person to guide and advise Cestius. At the head of a portion of his troops Cestius marched against a stronghold in Galilee called Zebulon, a frontier town between Jewish territory and Ptolemais. This he found deserted, as the population had fled to the mountains; but it was full of valuables of every kind, which he allowed the soldiers to loot. The town, as he realized, was very beautiful, the architecture being similar to that of Tyre, Sidon, and Beirut, but he set fire to it nevertheless. Then he overran the district, looted everything he came across, burnt down the surrounding villages, and returned to Ptolemais. But while the Syrians, especially the men from Beirut, were busy looting, the Jews plucked up courage on learning that Cestius had gone, and swooping without warning on the units he had left behind destroyed about 2,000 men.

Cestius left Ptolemais and marched to Caesarea, sending part of his army ahead to Joppa. If they could surprise the city they were to garrison it; if their approach was observed they were to wait for him to bring up the rest of the army. However, they divided into two parties, and advancing rapidly by sea and land attacked from both directions and easily captured the city: the inhabitants had no time to escape, much less to prepare for battle, so the Romans burst in and slaughtered them all with their families, and looted and burnt the city. The number killed was 8,400. In the same way Cestius sent into the toparchy of Narbatene[2] a large force of cavalry, who ravaged the land and

1. *King of Commagene in N. Syria.*   2. *Near Caesarea.*

destroyed a great number of the inhabitants, looting their property and burning down their villages.

Into Galilee he dispatched Caesennius Gallus, commander of the Twelfth Legion, giving him such forces as he thought sufficient to deal with that part of the country. He had an enthusiastic reception in Sepphoris, the strongest city in Galilee, and the good sense shown there caused the other towns to remain quiet. The insurgents and bandits all fled to the mountain in the very middle of Galilee situated opposite Sepphoris and known as Asamon. Against these Gallus led his troops. As long as the Galilaeans held a position of advantage they easily repulsed the advancing Romans, killing some 200 of them; but when the Romans by a turning movement reached higher ground still they were quickly worsted; men lightly armed could not withstand heavy infantry in a hand-to-hand struggle, nor could they in the rout escape the cavalry, so that while a few took advantage of the difficult ground to elude capture, the killed numbered 2,000.

Gallus saw no further signs of revolt in Galilee, so he led his army back to Caesarea. Cestius then set out with his whole force and entered Antipatris. There he learnt that in a town called Aphek a large force of Jews had collected; so he sent on a detachment to attack it. But before a blow was struck the Jews scattered in panic, leaving their camp open to the attackers, who burnt it with the surrounding villages. From Antipatris Cestius went on to Lydda, which he found empty; to keep the Feast of Tabernacles the whole population had gone to Jerusalem. Fifty of those who did appear were killed and the town burnt down; then Cestius continued his advance, climbed up through Beth-horon and encamped in a place called Gibeon, six miles from Jerusalem.

The Jews, seeing that war was now approaching the Capital, abandoned the Feast and rushed to arms; and with complete confidence in their numbers but without any organization they leapt boisterously into the fray, utterly disregarding the seventh day's rest, although this was the Sabbath they usually observed most carefully. But the passion that shook them out of their piety carried them to victory in the battle; they fell upon the Romans with such fury that they drove a wedge into their ranks and charged through the gap, inflicting heavy casualties. Had not the cavalry, with those infantry units that were not too involved, made a detour and come to the aid of the broken line, the whole of Cestius' army would have been in peril. The Romans lost 515 killed – 400 infantry and the rest cavalry; the Jews 22, of whom the most splendidly courageous were two kinsmen of Monobazus the king of Adiabene,[1] Monobazus and Cenedaeus, closely followed by the Peraean Niger and Silas the Babylonian; the latter had deserted to the Jews from King Agrippa, in whose army he had served. Their frontal attack halted, the Jews turned back to the City, but as the Romans went up the slope to Beth-horon Simon, son of Gioras, fell upon them from behind, severely mauled their rearguard, and carried off numbers of their baggage-animals, which he then drove into the City. Cestius remained immobile for three days; meanwhile the Jews seized the heights and kept watch on the approaches, making it clear that they would react promptly if the Romans began to march.

At this point Agrippa, seeing that not even a Roman army was safe when such a huge enemy force occupied the hills around, decided to try an appeal to the Jews – either he would persuade them all to cease hostilities or he would detach the peace party from their opponents. He therefore chose from his staff the two men best known to the Jews, Borcius and Phoebus, and sent them to promise that Cestius would grant them a treaty, and to guarantee that the Romans would overlook their offences if they threw away their arms and made their submission. But the insurgents, fearing that in the hope of indemnity the entire host would accept Agrippa's terms, violently assaulted his emissaries. Before he had uttered a word, Phoebus was murdered: Borcius was wounded but managed to escape. Those citizens who protested at this outrage were attacked with stones and clubs and chased into the City.

Cestius, seeing that their internal divisions invited attack, brought up his entire army, routed the Jews, and pursued them to Jerusalem. He pitched his camp on Look-Out Hill,[2] three quarters of a mile from the City, but for three days he launched no attack, perhaps expecting that the occupants would move towards surrender. Meanwhile he sent out many of his soldiers to seize corn in the surrounding villages. On the fourth day, the 30th October, he formed up his army and marched into the City. The people were under the thumb of the insurgents, and the insurgents, demoralized by the discipline of the Romans, withdrew from the outskirts of the City and retreated into the Inner City and the Temple. Cestius on arrival set fire to Bezetha (also known as 'The New City') and the Timber Market, and then went on to the Upper City and encamped in front of the Royal Palace.

1. *Near the Upper Tigris.*
2. *Mt Scopus.*

If he had chosen at that very hour to force his way inside the walls, the City would have been his immediately and the war brought to an end. But his chief-of-staff Tyrannius Priscus and most of the cavalry officers had been bribed by Florus to turn him from the attempt; thus it came about that the war lasted so long and the Jews were overwhelmed by irretrievable disasters.

At this juncture many of the prominent citizens, at the suggestion of Ananus the son of Jonathan, sent invitations to Cestius, assuring him that they would open the gates to him. He however, filled with anger, contempt, and incredulity, played for time until the insurgents, finding themselves betrayed, threw Ananus and his associates down from the wall, pelted them with stones and drove them into their houses, then formed a long line and showered missiles from the towers on those who were trying to climb the wall. For five days the Romans kept up their attacks from all directions and made no progress; on the next day Cestius, at the head of a large force of picked men and all the archers, began to assault the Temple from the north. The Jews resisted from the roof of the colonnade, and repeatedly drove back those who approached the wall, but at length they were overwhelmed by the hail of missiles and withdrew. The front rank of the Romans then rested their shields against the wall, and on these the second row rested theirs and so on, till they formed a protective covering known to them as the Tortoise. When the missiles fell on this they glanced off harmlessly, so that the soldiers received no hurt as they undermined the wall and prepared to set the Temple gate on fire. Utter panic seized the insurgents, and many now began to run from the City in the expectation that it would fall at any moment. This served to revive the people's hopes, and as the scoundrels retreated better men went forward to open the gates and welcome Cestius as a benefactor. If only he had persevered with the siege a little longer he would have captured the City at once; but I think that because of those scoundrels God had already turned His back even on the Sanctuary, and would not permit that day to witness the end of the war.

At any rate Cestius, aware of neither the despair of the besieged nor the feelings of the people, suddenly called off his men, abandoned hope though he had suffered no reverse, and flying in the face of all reason retired from the City. In view of this change of plan the bandits' hopes revived, and dashing out to attack his rearguard they destroyed numbers of cavalry and infantry. That night Cestius passed in his camp on

Look-Out Hill; the next day by retreating still further he invited fresh attacks, and the enemy pursuing relentlessly inflicted many casualties on his rearguard. They also pushed ahead on both sides of the road and hurled their spears at both flanks of the column. The rear files dared not turn and face those who were striking them down from behind, as they thought an enormous army was pursuing them; and those who were attacking them from the flanks they did not venture to drive back, as they themselves were heavily armed and afraid to open their ranks, while they saw that the Jews were lightly armed and adapted for sudden swoops. This meant that they suffered severely without any corresponding damage to the other side. Throughout the march the battering continued, and men who lost their places in the column were killed. At last when many were dead, among them Priscus the commander of the Sixth Legion, Longinus the tribune, and a cavalry officer named Aemilius Jucundus, they managed to reach their old camp at Gibeon, after abandoning the bulk of their baggage. There Cestius remained two days at a loss what to do; on the third, seeing the numbers of the enemy greatly swelled and all the ground on every side swarming with Jews, he realized that he had lost by the delay and that if he remained any longer he would have more enemies still.

To speed his flight he ordered everything that slowed down the column to be reduced to a minimum. The mules and asses were slaughtered and even the wagon-horses, except those conveying missiles and artillery; these they determined to keep for their own use, especially as they feared the Jews would capture them and turn them against themselves. Then Cestius led his army on towards Beth-horon. In the wide spaces the Jews pressed them less vigorously, but when they were crowded together in the defiles of the descending road, one group got in front of them and barred their egress, others pushed the rearmost down into the ravine, and the main body lined the high ground overlooking the waist of the pass and showered missiles on the massed Romans. At this point the infantry were unable to defend themselves, and the danger to the cavalry was still greater; for they could not keep their formation and march down the road while being pelted, and the steep slope made it impossible for mounted men to charge the enemy; on both sides there were cliffs and ravines into which they fell to destruction. No one could find a way to flee or a means to defend himself; in their helplessness they turned to lamentation and despairing groans. The Jews retorted with cheers and shouts of mingled joy and rage; and they would certainly have captured Cestius and his whole army had not darkness descended, enabling the Romans to take refuge in Beth-horon, while the Jews ringed them in and waited for them to come out.

Despairing now of openly continuing the march, Cestius decided on ignominious flight. He picked out some 400 of his most courageous soldiers and posted them on the roofs, instructing them to shout the watchwords of the camp sentries so that the Jews would believe the entire force to be still in position. He himself with the rest of his men advanced without a sound three and a half miles. At stand-to the Jews observed that the Roman quarters were empty, and rushing at the 400 who had tricked them quickly disposed of them with javelins, then set off in pursuit of Cestius. He had gained a long lead in the night, and as soon as it was light put on such a turn of speed that the soldiers in utter panic dumped the Batterers and Quick-loaders and most of the other engines. These the Jews promptly seized, later using them against their original owners. They pursued the Romans all the way to Antipatris but failed to catch them; so turning back they carried off the machines and despoiled the dead, collected the booty that had been left behind, and with hymns of victory marched back to the Capital. Their own casualties were negligible, but the Romans and their allies had lost 5,300 infantrymen and 480 cavalrymen killed. This action was fought on the 8th of Dios in the twelfth year of Nero's reign.[1]

---

1. *Josephus apparently means November of 66 A.D.; but Nero's twelfth year had ended in October.*

CHAPTER 10

Josephus Governor of Galilee

AFTER the disastrous defeat of Cestius many prominent Jews fled from the City like swimmers from a sinking ship. Costobar with his brother Saul and Philip, son of Jacimus, the commander of King Agrippa's army, slipped out of the City and went over to Cestius. But their companion in the siege of the Royal Palace, Antipas, declined to flee and was put to death by the insurgents, as I shall describe later. Cestius sent Saul and his friends at their own wish to Nero in Achaia, to acquaint him with their own plight and to lay the blame for the war on Florus; Nero's anger against Florus would, he hoped, lessen the danger to himself.

At this time the people of Damascus, learning of the destruction of the Roman force, were eager to exterminate the Jews in their midst. As they had had them cooped up in the Gymnasium for a long time now, taking this precaution as a result of suspicion, the task appeared perfectly simple; but they were afraid of their own wives, who had almost all gone over to the Jewish religion, so that their chief anxiety was to keep them in the dark. Accordingly they fell upon the Jews, crowded together and unarmed, and though they numbered 10,500 they slaughtered them all in one hour without any trouble.

Those who had pursued Cestius returned to Jerusalem, where by force or persuasion they won over those who still favoured Rome, and at a mass meeting in the Temple appointed additional generals for the army. They chose Joseph the son of Gorion and the high priest Ananus to take full charge of all arrangements in the City, with special responsibility for increasing the height of the walls. Simon's son Eleazar had in his possession the Roman booty and the money captured from Cestius, together with vast public funds; but they did not put him in charge of affairs as they saw that he had dictatorial tendencies, and that his devoted followers were behaving like an armed bodyguard. Gradually, however, the shortage of money and Eleazar's jugglery induced the people to submit to him completely. For Idumaea they chose two other generals, Jeshua (son of Sapphas) one of the chief priests, and Eleazar (son of the high priest Neus); the then governor of

II, 577 GOVERNOR OF GALILEE

Idumaea, Niger, a native of Peraea, east of Jordan, and therefore known as the Peraean, was instructed to accept orders from these two. Nor did they neglect the rest of the country; Joseph son of Simon was sent to take command at Jericho, Manasseh in Peraea, John the Essene in the toparchy of Thamna, to which were attached Lydda, Joppa, and Emmaus. The districts of Gophna and Acrabetta were put under the command of John, son of Ananias; while both parts of Galilee were assigned to Josephus, son of Matthias, together with Gamala, the strongest city in that area.

Each of these generals carried out the task assigned to him with all the energy and ability he possessed. Josephus on arriving in Galilee gave first priority to securing the good-will of the inhabitants, knowing that this would serve him in very good stead even if some things went wrong. He saw that he would win the support of the leading men if he shared his authority with them, and of the people in general if he issued his instructions mainly through the channel of well-known residents. So he chose seventy elderly men, the most sensible he could find in the country, and put them in charge of the whole of Galilee, appointing also seven magistrates in every town to settle petty quarrels, on the understanding that major disputes and cases of homicide should be referred to himself and the seventy. When he had made these rules for settling the internal problems of the cities, he turned his attention to their safety from external foes. Realizing that the Romans would invade Galilee first, he fortified the most defensible positions, Jotapata, Bersabe and Selame, Caphareccho, Japha and Sigoph, Mt Tabor, Tarichaeae and Tiberias, next fortifying the caverns near Lake Gennesareth in Lower Galilee, and in Upper Galilee the rock called Acchabaron, Seph, Jamnith, and Mero. In Gaulonitis he strengthened the defences of Seleucia, Soganaea, and Gamala. Only in Sepphoris were the citizens invited to build a wall on their own responsibility: Josephus saw that they had ample means and that their enthusiasm for the war needed no stimulus. In the same way Gischala was fortified by John, son of Levi, on his own responsibility at the request of Josephus. The building of all the other strongholds was personally supervised by Josephus, who directed the work and himself lent a hand. He also raised in Galilee a force of over 100,000 young men, equipping them all with old weapons that he had got together.

Josephus knew that the invincible might of Rome was chiefly due to unhesitating obedience and to practice in arms. He despaired of pro-

viding similar instruction, demanding as it did a long period of training; but he saw that the habit of obedience resulted from the number of
their officers and he now reorganized his army on the Roman model,
appointing more junior commanders than before. He divided the soldiers into different classes, and put them under decurions and centurions, those being subordinate to tribunes, and the tribunes to commanders of larger units. He taught them how to pass on signals, how to
sound the advance and the retreat, how to make flank attacks and
encircling movements, and how a victorious unit could relieve one in
difficulties and assist any who were hard pressed. He explained all that
contributed to toughness of body or fortitude of spirit. Above all he
trained them for war by stressing Roman discipline at every turn: they
would be facing men who by physical prowess and unshakable
determination had conquered almost the entire world. He would feel
certain of their soldierly qualities even before they went into action,
if they refrained from their besetting sins of theft, banditry, and looting,
from defrauding their countrymen, and from regarding as personal
gain the misfortunes of their closest friends. For if those who went to
war had a clear conscience, victory was certain; but men whose private
life was smirched had not only human enemies but God to contend
with. To this effect he exhorted them continually. The army he
had raised and trained for battle numbered 60,000 foot and 250 horse,
together with the troops he trusted most, about 4,500 professional
soldiers. He had also 600 picked men as a personal bodyguard. Maintenance for all except the professionals was easily obtained from the
towns, as only half the conscripts from each town served with the
colours, the rest staying behind to supply them with rations; thus one
party was detailed for combatant duty, the other for fatigues, and those
who provided the food were repaid by the combatants with security.

While Josephus was busy organizing the defence of Galilee, there
appeared on the scene a plotter from Gischala, the son of Levi, John by
name, the most unprincipled trickster that ever won ill fame by such
vicious habits. He began as a poor man and for a long time his propensities were held in check by lack of means; but being a ready liar and
clever at winning the trust of his victims, he made a virtue of deceit and
practised it on his closest friends, and while parading his humanity was
prepared to murder anybody for his money; there was no limit to his
ambitions, but his hopes were nourished by contemptible misdemeanours. He started as a solitary bandit but later found associates

for his ventures, a handful at first but more and more numerous as he grew more successful. He was careful to accept no one who would give in easily, and chose men for their physique, sticking-power, and military experience, till he got together a gang 400 strong, consisting mainly of outlaws from Tyre and the neighbouring villages. With their help he plundered all Galilee and preyed upon the masses, distracted as they were by the imminence of war.

He already pictured himself as general or something greater still, and only shortage of money kept him down. When he saw that Josephus was delighted with his energy, he first persuaded him to entrust him with the rebuilding of the walls of his home-town, thereby enriching himself at the expense of the well-to-do. Next he contrived a remarkable piece of roguery. Pretending that he wished to save all the Jews in Syria from using oil from non-Jewish sources, he obtained leave to deliver it to them at the frontier. Then he cornered the available supplies, paying Tyrian currency worth 4 Attic drachmas for 35 gallons and reselling at eight times that price. As Galilee is renowned for its olives and the harvest had been exceptional, John, by exploiting his monopoly and supplying large quantities wherever there was a shortage, amassed untold wealth, which he promptly used to injure the man who had put this commerce in his hands. Supposing that if he brought Josephus down he would himself become master of Galilee, he ordered the members of his gang to put still more vigour into their raids; in the general turmoil that would follow, if the governor went to the rescue he could be ambushed and finished off; if he failed to deal with the gang he could be slandered to the people of the country. Finally he had long been spreading a rumour that Josephus was betraying the country to the Romans, and devising many similar expedients to bring him down.

At this time some young men from the village of Dabarittha, members of the guard stationed in the Great Plain, waylaid Ptolemy, chief minister of Agrippa and Bernice, and robbed him of all his baggage, which included a large quantity of expensive clothing, a number of silver goblets and 600 gold coins. Unable to dispose of the loot secretly they brought it all to Josephus at Tarichaeae. He condemned their violence to the king's servants, and deposited the stolen goods with the chief citizen of Tarichaeae, Annaeus, intending to take the first opportunity of restoring them to their owners. This was a most dangerous thing to do; for the robbers were furious at receiving no share of the loot, and realizing that Josephus meant to present the king and queen with the fruits of their labours, they hurried off to the villages at night and everywhere denounced Josephus as a traitor. They further put the neighbouring cities in an uproar, so that when day broke 100,000 armed men gathered to attack him. The crowd packed the Hippodrome at Tarichaeae and filled the air with yells of rage, some clamouring to stone the 'traitor', others to burn him alive. The fury of the mob was whipped up by John, backed by Jeshua son of Sapphias, then governor of Tiberias. The friends and bodyguard of Josephus, terrified by the huge crowd out for blood, fled with the exception of four men. He himself was asleep and did not wake till the house was on the point of being set on fire. The four who had remained urged him to fly, but he, though he saw himself alone in the midst of a howling mob, showed no trace of fear. He sprang forward, his clothes rent and his head sprinkled with ashes, his hands behind him and his sword dangling from his neck. Seeing this his friends, especially the Tarichaeans, were sorry for him, but the country-folk and those from the neighbourhood who resented his rule heaped abuse on him, insisting that he should instantly produce the public money and admit his compact to betray them. For they had gathered from his appearance that he would not deny any of the things they suspected, and that it was in order to obtain pardon that he had grovelled thus abjectly.

But the real purpose of this self-abasement was to prepare the way for a stratagem by which he would induce his enraged critics to quarrel among themselves. He promised to give a full explanation of the actions that had angered them, and when he was given leave to speak he began: 'I had no intention of either returning this money to Agrippa or of lining my own pockets. I trust I shall never treat your enemy as my friend or turn the country's loss to private gain. But I saw that your city of Tarichaeae stood more in need of defence than other cities and that it could not build walls for lack of funds; and fearing that in Tiberias and other places people had their eyes on these spoils, I intended to keep the money and say nothing till I had given you the protection of a wall. If you are not satisfied, I will produce what was brought to me and give it you to share out. But if I have acted in your interest, why punish your benefactor?'

On hearing this the Tarichaeans expressed their approval, but the people of Tiberias and elsewhere yelled abuse and threats. Then both parties let Josephus alone and turned to each other. He, confident of his new supporters – nearly 40,000 Tarichaeans – proceeded to address the whole throng in bolder terms. He condemned their headstrong behaviour in no uncertain fashion, and then declared that with the money in hand he would fortify Tarichaeae and provide equal security for the other cities as well. There would be no lack of funds if only they made up their minds who they were going to fight, instead of letting fly at the man who provided the means.

At this the bulk of the deluded crowd withdrew, though still very angry; but 2,000 men rushed at him, weapons in hand, and though he got back into the house in time they besieged the doors and shouted threats. In this crisis Josephus resorted to a second trick. He went up on the roof, silenced them with a gesture and declared that he had no idea what they wanted, as he could not hear when they all shouted at once. But he would do whatever they demanded if they would send in a delegation to talk things over with him quietly. On hearing this the leading men and the magistrates came in. Josephus then dragged them into the inmost recesses of the house, shut the outer door and flogged them all till he had torn their flesh to ribbons. Meanwhile the mob waited outside thinking the delegates were arguing their case at length. But Josephus suddenly flung open the doors and pushed the men out covered with blood, striking such terror into the threatening crowd that they threw down their weapons and fled.

This triumph made John more jealous still, and he framed a second plot against Josephus. Feigning sickness, he sent a letter begging his permission to seek a cure by taking the hot baths at Tiberias. Not yet suspecting a plot. Josephus wrote to his representatives in the city to accommodate John and provide everything necessary. John made himself comfortable, and two days later got his scheme under way. Deceiving some, bribing others, he strove to induce the citizens to revolt from Josephus. When this came to his ears, Silas, the appointed guardian of the city, reported the plot to his superior without a moment's delay. Josephus, on receiving this dispatch, set off on a swift night march which brought him at dawn to Tiberias, where he was met by the whole population except John. John had little doubt that this visit was directed against him; nevertheless he sent one of his friends to make the excuse that he was unwell and confined to bed, and so could not pay his respects. But when Josephus had collected the citizens in the Stadium and was trying to tell them about the report he had received, John quietly sent armed men with orders to assassinate him.

These men drew their swords, but the people saw what was coming and gave a shout. Hearing the noise Josephus swung round, and seeing the bare steel within inches of his throat took a flying leap on to the beach – while addressing the people he had been standing on a mound nine feet high – and jumping into a boat moored near by with two members of his bodyguard made a dash for the middle of the lake.

His soldiers instantly seized their weapons and charged the conspirators. Then Josephus, fearing that if civil war broke out through the jealousy of a few the city would be ruined, sent a message to his men that they were only to see to their own safety, and neither kill anybody nor bring the guilty to trial. In obedience to this injunction the soldiers refrained from action; but the people of the neighbourhood, when they learnt of the plot and of the person responsible, massed together to deal with John. He however slipped away in time and fled to Gischala, his home-town. From every city in Galilee the people streamed to the support of Josephus till the number swelled to thousands and thousands of armed men, who proclaimed that they had come to settle accounts with John, the enemy of the nation; they would burn him alive, and burn any city that received him. Josephus expressed his appreciation of their loyalty but restrained their fury, choosing to outwit his enemies rather than to kill them. He found out the names of those in every city who had revolted with John, their fellow-citizens being delighted to give the information, and made a public announcement that anyone who failed to sever connexion with John in the next five days would have his property seized and his house burnt together with his family. The immediate result was that 3,000 deserted John, came to Josephus and threw down their weapons at his feet, while with the rest, about 2,000 Syrian outlaws, John again took refuge in secret plots, abandoning open hostilities. He sent messengers to Jerusalem by stealth to allege that Josephus was growing too powerful, and to say that he might at any moment set himself up as dictator in the Capital itself, if his attempt was not forestalled.

The people were prepared for this story and took no notice; but leading citizens, including some of the magistrates, were moved by jealousy to send money secretly to John, so that he could raise a force of mercenaries and make war on Josephus. They further issued a decree on their own authority recalling him from his command; but as they doubted its validity they dispatched 2,500 armed men with four distinguished citizens, Joesdrus son of Nomicus, Ananias son of Zadok,

Simon and Jude sons of Jonathan, all gifted speakers, in order to deprive Josephus of popular support. If he came quietly, they were to let him give an account of himself; if he insisted on remaining, they must treat him as an enemy. Josephus had been warned by his friends that an army was on the way, but the reason was not explained as his enemies had taken their decision in secret. The result was that he took no countermeasures, and four towns promptly went over to the other side, Sepphoris, Gamala,[1] Gischala, and Tiberias. But he quickly recovered these without the use of force, and then by stratagems got the four commanders into his hands and sent them back with the most efficient of their soldiers to Jerusalem. They met with a most hostile reception from the people, who would have killed them and those who had sent them out, had they not immediately fled.

From that time on John was kept within the walls of Gischala by fear of Josephus. A few days later Tiberias again revolted, the citizens having called in King Agrippa. Agrippa failed to arrive on the date fixed, but a few Roman cavalry turned up unexpectedly that very day and the gates were shut against Josephus. He was at Tarichaeae, where he was promptly informed of this revolt; but he had sent out all his soldiers in search of food, and could neither take the field alone against the rebels nor stay where he was, for fear that this delay might enable the royal troops to slip into the city before him. Furthermore he would be unable to make any move on the next day owing to the Sabbath restrictions. However, he thought of a ruse to circumvent the rebels. He ordered the gates of Tarichaeae to be shut, to prevent any warning of his intentions from reaching those he was planning to attack; then he collected all the boats there were on the lake – 230, with not more than four sailors in each – and made at full speed for Tiberias. He kept far enough from the city to make clear vision impossible, ordering the vessels to ride in deep water unmanned, while he himself with only seven guards – unarmed[2] – went near enough to be seen. On sighting him from the walls his opponents, who had not ceased to vilify him, were so amazed that they assumed that all the craft were packed with armed men, flung down their weapons, and waving olive-branches begged him to spare the city.

Josephus gave vent to threats and reproaches. First, after taking up arms against Rome they were dissipating their strength beforehand

---

1. *Other readings* – Gadara *and* Gabara.
2. *So all MSS.: perhaps a mistake for* armed.

in civil strife and so playing into their enemies' hands; secondly, they were striving to get rid of their one bulwark against destruction, and were not ashamed to close their city to the architect of its defences. Nevertheless he declared his willingness to receive a delegation that would offer an apology and co-operate in making the city secure. Ten citizens at once came down, the most important men in Tiberias. These he took on board one of the vessels and carried out to sea; fifty others, leading members of the senate, he ordered to come forward, on the ground that he wished to obtain a pledge from them. Then, by inventing one pretext after another, he called out group after group as if to arrange terms. As the boats were filled he ordered the masters to make with all speed for Tarichaeae and to clap the men into prison. In this way the whole senate, 600 strong, and about 2,000 private citizens were arrested and conveyed in boats to Tarichaeae. The remainder shouted that the real author of the revolt was one Clitus, and urged Josephus to vent his wrath on him. Josephus was anxious to put no one to death; so he ordered Levi, one of his guards, to step ashore and cut off Clitus' hands. The soldier, taking fright, refused to go alone into the hostile crowd. At this Josephus boiled with rage and was on the point of jumping overboard to carry out the sentence himself when Clitus, watching from the beach, besought him to leave him one of his hands. Josephus agreed, on condition that he cut off the other himself, whereupon Clitus drew his sword with his right hand and cut off his left; so completely had Josephus terrified him. Thus with unmanned boats and seven guards the whole population was made prisoner and Tiberias brought back to its allegiance. But a few days later Josephus found that the city had revolted again in conjunction with Sepphoris, so he handed it over to the soldiers to pillage. However, he collected all the plunder and gave it back to the townspeople. He did the same at Sepphoris; for he subdued that town as well and decided to give the citizens a sharp lesson by pillaging it, and then by giving back their possessions to recover their good-will.

In Galilee all was now quiet, and abandoning internal dissension the people turned to preparations for war with Rome. In Jerusalem Ananus the high priest and all the leading men who did not favour Rome were repairing the walls and piling up munitions. All over the City they were forging missiles and suits of armour, most of the young men were receiving haphazard training, and there was tumult everywhere. Among the more stable, however, there was utter dejection;

many saw only too well the approaching calamity and openly lamented. There were omens too, which to the peace-lovers portended disaster, but for which those who had lit the fires of war could easily invent a happy interpretation. In fact the whole condition of the City before the arrival of the Romans proclaimed the coming destruction. Ananus, indeed, nourished the hope that, if he gradually abandoned the preparations for war, he would incline the insurgents and the crazy 'Zealots' to take a wiser course; but he yielded to their violence, and in a later chapter[1] his tragic end will be related.

Finally, in the toparchy of Acrabatene Simon, son of Gioras, collected a large band of revolutionaries and gave himself up to pillage. He not only looted the houses of the rich, he ill-used them personally; and it was evident from the start that his aim was despotism. When a force was sent against him by Ananus and the magistrates, he fled with his followers to the bandits at Masada, and there till the death of Ananus and his other enemies he remained, joining in the pillage of Idumaea and forcing the authorities there, in view of the number murdered and the constant raids, to muster an army and garrison the villages. So much for events in Idumaea.

1. *Chapter 15.*

CHAPTER II

The Coming of Vespasian and Titus

WHEN Nero was informed of the reverses in Judaea he was naturally filled with consternation and alarm. This he was careful to conceal, treating the matter in public with anger and contempt: it was the commander's negligence, he said, not the enemy's prowess, that had caused the trouble. No doubt he felt that the majesty of empire obliged him to treat bad news with lordly disdain and to show himself superior to all eventualities. Nevertheless the turmoil of his spirit was betrayed by his furrowed brow. He was wondering to whom he could entrust the East in its disturbed state, with responsibility for punishing the Jewish upheaval and preventing the spread of the infection to the surrounding nations. He found no one but Vespasian equal to the task and capable of undertaking a war on such a tremendous scale. Vespasian had been a soldier all his life and was now a veteran;[1] years ago he had pacified the West and crushed the rebellion against Rome which the Germans had provoked; by force of arms he had added to the Empire Britain, till then unknown, so enabling Nero's father[2] Claudius, who had not lifted a finger himself, to celebrate a triumph.

Such a record was highly auspicious, and a man of Vespasian's age and experience could obviously be trusted. His sons moreover were hostages for his good faith, and being in the prime of life could provide the hands if their father provided the brains. Perhaps also God was already planning the future of the world. For whatever reason, Nero sent this man to assume command of the armies in Syria, paying him in view of the urgent situation every smooth compliment that necessity can suggest. From Achaia, where he was on Nero's staff, Vespasian dispatched his son Titus to Alexandria to fetch the Fifteenth Legion from there; he himself crossed the Dardanelles and travelled overland to Syria. There he concentrated the Roman forces and large allied contingents provided by the neighbouring kings.

After the defeat of Cestius the Jews were so elated by their unexpected success that they were wild with excitement, and as if carried

1. *He was 57.*   2. *By adoption.*

off their feet by this stroke of luck they determined to send their armies further afield. Without loss of time all their most warlike elements joined forces and marched to Ascalon. This is an old town 60 miles from Jerusalem, though the Jews hated it so bitterly that when they made it the object of their first attack it seemed much nearer than that! The expedition was led by three men of unequalled prowess and ability, Niger from Peraea, Silas the Babylonian, and John the Essene. Ascalon was strongly fortified, but the defenders were miserably few; it was garrisoned by a cohort of foot and one troop of horse, commanded by Antonius.

The Jews in their fury marched at a most unusual pace, and as if their starting-point had been quite near they suddenly appeared before the city. Antonius however had been well aware of their approach: he led out his cavalry, and in utter disregard of the numbers and determination of the enemy stood up manfully to their first onslaught and beat off an attack on the wall. When raw levies were confronted by veteran troops, infantry by cavalry, undisciplined individuals by regulars who fought as one, men with nondescript weapons by fully armed legionaries, men guided by passion rather than reason by men who instantly responded to every signal, the issue could never be in doubt. When once the front ranks of the attackers were broken they were routed by the cavalry, and collided with units pushing forward from behind to assault the wall. Thus Jew fought Jew till the entire mass gave way before the cavalry charges, and scattered all over the plain. This was very large and ideal for cavalry tactics, a fact which weighted the scales in favour of the Romans and led to frightful carnage on the Jewish side; for the fugitives were headed off and turned back, and when they were herded together in their flight the horsemen charged right through and slaughtered them by the hundred. Whichever way they turned the Romans encircled them, group by group, and as they galloped round struck them down with javelins that could not miss.

In spite of their vast numbers, the Jews felt in their helpless state that they were terribly alone; the Romans were succeeding so wonderfully that few as they were they never doubted that they actually outnumbered the enemy. The Jews battled against their reverses, ashamed of their swift defeat and hoping for a change of fortune; the Romans relentlessly followed up their success. So the struggle continued till dusk, by which time 10,000 Jewish soldiers had fallen with two of their commanders, John and Silas. The survivors, wounded for the most part, with the one general left, Niger, fled to a little town in Idumaea called Chaallis. Roman casualties in this encounter amounted to a few men wounded.

So far from being broken-hearted by this fearful disaster, the Jews were stimulated by defeat to still greater determination, and disregarding the dead bodies at their feet they were lured by their earlier successes to a second disaster. Without even waiting for their wounds to heal they mustered all their forces and with greater fury than before, and much greater numbers, tore back to Ascalon. But together with their inexperience and other military deficiencies their old ill luck went with them. For Antonius laid ambushes in the passes, and taking no precautions they fell into these traps. Before they could take up battle stations they were encircled by the cavalry and again lost over 8,000. The survivors all fled, including Niger, who during the flight gave many proofs of his heroism. In the end the enemy pressure drove them into a strong fort in a village called Belzedek. Antonius and his men, to avoid wearing themselves out in an assault on this almost impregnable fort or else leaving the enemy's heroic commander alive, lit a fire at the foot of the wall, and the fort was soon ablaze. The Romans then withdrew, satisfied that Niger had perished with it, and blissfully unaware that he had leapt down from the fort and escaped into a cave in the very centre of the position. Three days later his friends were seeking his body in order to bury it and were lamenting aloud when they heard a muffled voice. Niger emerged, and joy undreamed-of filled every Jewish heart: had not the providence of God preserved him to lead them into battle again?

At Antioch, the capital of Syria, and by virtue of its size and prosperity undoubtedly the third city of the Roman Empire, Vespasian had found King Agrippa awaiting his arrival with the whole of his own army. He put himself at the head of all the available forces and advanced swiftly to Ptolemais. There he was met by the inhabitants of Sepphoris, the only people in Galilee who desired peace. With their own safety and Roman supremacy in mind, they had already before Vespasian arrived given guarantees to Caesennius Gallus, received his assurances, and admitted a garrison. Now they gave an enthusiastic reception to the supreme commander and pressed him to accept their help against their own countrymen. In response to their request he allotted them for the time being a defensive force of horse and foot, adequate in his opinion to defeat any incursions the Jews might choose to make; for he thought it would seriously endanger the campaign he was about to open if he lost Sepphoris, the biggest city in Galilee, ideally sited to be a bulwark against attack and to keep the whole area quiet.

There are two Galilees, known as Upper and Lower, shut in by Phoenicia and Syria. They are bounded on the west by Ptolemais with its border region and Carmel, a mountain that once belonged to Galilee but now belongs to Tyre; adjoining Carmel is Gaba, known as Cavalry Town because King Herod's cavalry settled there on their discharge. The southern limit is formed by Samaria and Scythopolis as far as the streams of Jordan, the eastern by the districts of Hippos, Gadara, and Gaulonitis, where Agrippa's kingdom begins. Beyond the northern frontier lie Tyre and the Tyrian lands. Lower Galilee stretches in length from Tiberias to Zebulon, the neighbour of Ptolemais on the coast, in breadth from the village of Xaloth in the Great Plain to Bersabe. Here begins Upper Galilee, which stretches in width as far as Baca, a village on the Tyrian frontier; in length it extends from Meroth to Thella, a village near Jordan.

Small as they are, and encircled by such powerful foreign neighbours, the two Galilees have invariably held out against enemy attack; for the Galilaeans are fighters from the cradle and at all times numerous, and never has cowardice afflicted the men or a declining population the country. The whole area is excellent for crops or cattle and rich in forests of every kind, so that by its adaptability it invites even those least inclined to work on the land. Consequently every inch has been cultivated by the inhabitants and not a corner goes to waste. It is thickly studded with towns, and thanks to the natural abundance the innumerable villages are so densely populated that the smallest has more than 15,000 inhabitants.[1]

In short, it may be true that Galilee is smaller in size than Peraea, but it takes the palm for productivity; for the whole country is cultivated, and fruitful from end to end, while Peraea though much greater in extent is mostly a stony desert, too wild to produce cultivated crops. Some parts however have workable soil that can bear crops of every kind, and in the plains grow trees of many species, those chiefly planted being the olive, vine, and palm. The country is watered by mountain torrents, and by perennial springs that suffice even in the dog-days when the torrents dry up. In length it stretches from Machaerus to

1. *Are we to believe this?*

Pella, in breadth from Philadelphia to the Jordan.[1] Pella, just mentioned, forms the northern boundary, Jordan the western; the southern limit is Moab, and on the east it shares a frontier with Arabia, Silbonitis, Philadelphia, and Gerasa.

Samaria lies between Galilee and Judaea; beginning at a village in the Great Plain called Ginaea, it ends at the toparchy of Acrabatene. In character it is exactly like Judaea: both are made up of hills and plains, with soil easily worked and amply repaying cultivation. They are well wooded and prolific in fruit, both wild and cultivated; for no-where is the soil arid by nature and rain is generally ample. All their streams are remarkably sweet, and lush grass is so plentiful that the milk-yield of their cows is exceptionally heavy. The final proof of their outstanding productivity is the swarming population of both countries.

On their common frontier lies the village of Anuath Borceos, the limit of Judaea on the north. The southern region, to go to the other end, terminates at a village close to the Arabian frontier known as Jardan to the Jews of the locality. Crosswise it stretches from the River Jordan to Joppa. Right in the middle lies the City of Jerusalem, so that some have quite appropriately called her the navel of the country. Nor is Judaea cut off from seaside delights, since it has a coastal strip that stretches all the way to Ptolemais. It is divided into eleven districts, of which the royal City, Jerusalem, has the primacy, raised above the whole neighbourhood as the head above the body. The other districts or toparchies are less highly esteemed. Gophna ranks second, followed by Acrabata, Thamna, Lydda, Emmaus, Pella, Idumaea, Engedi, Herodium, and Jericho. We must include also Jamnia and Joppa, which control their neighbourhood, and finally the Gamala district, Batanaea and Trachonitis, though they are in Agrippa's dominions. These begin at Mount Lebanon and the sources of the Jordan, and in width stretch to Lake Tiberias, in length from a village called Arpha to Julias. The population is a mixture of Jews and Syrians.

The foregoing must serve as the briefest possible description of Judaea and its neighbours.

The support that Vespasian sent to Sepphoris consisted of 1,000 horse and 6,000 foot, commanded by the tribune Placidus. After camping in the Great Plain the force divided, the foot moving into the city as a garrison and the horse remaining encamped outside. Both arms made a series of sorties, overrunning the whole district and doing

1. *Pella and Philadelphia were outside the frontiers of Peraea, in Decapolis.*

great damage to Josephus and his men. If they remained inactive in
their towns the surrounding country was plundered; whenever they
ventured to sally forth they were driven back. Josephus actually assailed
the city in the hope of capturing it, though before it seceded from the
Galilaeans he had himself fortified it so strongly that even the Romans
would have found it almost impregnable; and so the attempt failed, for
he proved too weak either by force or by persuasion to bring Sepphoris
over to his side. Moreover he provoked more vigorous attacks on his
country; night and day in retaliation for his attempt the Romans
ceaselessly ravaged the plains and plundered the villagers' belongings,
killing everyone fit to bear arms and enslaving those who could not
resist. From one end of Galilee to the other there was an orgy of fire
and bloodshed; no horror, no calamity was spared; the only safety
for the fugitive inhabitants was in the towns which Josephus had
fortified.

Titus meanwhile had sailed from Achaia to Alexandria in less time
than is usual for a winter crossing. There he took over the force for
which he had been sent, and marching at a great pace quickly reached
Ptolemais. There he found his father, and to the two legions that
accompanied him, the world-famous Fifth and Tenth, he united
his own Fifteenth. To these legions were attached 18 cohorts;
they were joined also by five cohorts and one troop of horse from
Caesarea, and five troops from Syria. Of the cohorts ten were 1,000
infantry strong, the other thirteen 600 infantry and 120 cavalry. A
large allied contingent was also contributed by the kings, Antiochus,
Agrippa, and Soaemus each providing 2,000 unmounted bowmen and
1,000 horse, while the Arab Malchus sent 1,000 horse as well as 5,000
foot, most of them bowmen. Thus the whole force, cavalry and infantry, including the men contributed by the kings, totalled 60,000[1],
apart from servants who followed in great numbers and in view of their
sharing the military training ought not to be distinguished from the
combatants – in peace they always took part in their masters' exercises,
in war they shared their dangers, so that in skill and prowess none but
their masters surpassed them.

The Romans showed remarkable foresight in making their domestic
staff useful to them not only in the services of everyday life but also in
war. Anyone who will take a look at the organization of their army in

---

1. *It seems hardly possible that the units listed contained so many; and like the figures
given above for Jewish losses at Ascalon the present figure seems too large for belief.*

general will recognize that they hold their wide-flung empire as the prize of valour, not the gift of fortune. They do not wait for war to begin before handling their arms, nor do they sit idle in peacetime and take action only when the emergency comes – but as if born ready armed they never have a truce from training or wait for war to be declared. Their battle-drills are no different from the real thing; every man works as hard at his daily training as if he was on active service. That is why they stand up so easily to the strain of battle: no indiscipline dislodges them from their regular formation, no panic incapacitates them, no toil wears them out; so that victory over men not so trained follows as a matter of course. It would not be far from the truth to call their drills bloodless battles, their battles bloody drills.

They never give the enemy a chance to catch them off their guard; for whenever they invade hostile territory they rigidly refuse battle till they have fortified their camp. This they do not construct haphazard or unevenly, nor do they tackle the job with all their manpower or without organized squads; if the ground is uneven it is thoroughly levelled, then the site is marked out as a rectangle. To this end the army is followed by a large number of engineers with all the tools needed for building. The inside is divided up ready for the huts. From outside the perimeter looks like a wall and is equipped with towers evenly spaced. In the gaps between the towers they mount quick-loaders, catapults, stone-throwers, and every type of ordnance, all ready to be discharged. Four gates are constructed, one in each length of wall, practicable for the entry of baggage-animals and wide enough for armed sorties, if called for. The camp is divided up by streets accurately marked out; in the middle are erected the officers' huts, and in the middle of these the commander's headquarters, which resembles a shrine. It all seems like a mushroom town, with market-place, workmen's quarters, and orderly-rooms where junior and senior officers can settle disputes as they arise. The erection of the outer wall and the buildings inside is accomplished faster than thought, thanks to the number and skill of the workers. If necessary a ditch is dug all round, six feet deep and the same width.

The fortifications completed, the men go to their quarters unit by unit in a quiet and orderly manner. All other duties are carried out with attention to discipline and security, wood, food, and water as required being brought in by the units detailed. They do not have supper or breakfast just when they fancy at individual discretion, but all together. Times for sleep, guard-duty, and reveille are announced by trumpet-calls, and nothing whatever is done without orders. At stand-to the private soldiers report by units to their centurions, the centurions go to their tribunes to salute them, and the tribunes accompany all their superior officers to Headquarters, where the commander-in-chief, in accordance with routine, gives them the password and other orders to communicate to their subordinates. They act in the same orderly way on the battle field, changing direction promptly as required, and whether attacking or retreating move as one man.

When camp is to be struck, the trumpet sounds and every man springs to his duty. Following the signal huts are instantly dismantled and all preparations made for departure. The trumpet then sounds 'Stand by to march!' At once they load the mules and wagons with the baggage and take their places like runners lined up and hardly able to wait for the starter's signal. Then they fire the camp, which they can easily reconstruct if required, and which might some day be useful to the enemy. For the third time the trumpets give the same signal for departure, to urge on those who for any reason have been loitering, so that not a man may be missing from his place. Then the announcer, standing on the right of the supreme commander, asks three times in their native language whether they are ready for war. They three times shout loudly and with enthusiasm 'Ready', hardly waiting for the question, and filled with a kind of martial fervour raise their right arms as they shout. Then they step off, all marching silently and in good order, as on active service every man keeping his place in the column.

The infantry are armed with breastplate and helmet and carry a blade on each side; of these by far the longer is the one on the left,[1] the other being no more than nine inches long. The general's bodyguard of picked infantry carry lance and buckler, the other units javelin and long shield, together with saw and basket, axe and pick, as well as strap, reaphook, chain, and three days' rations, so that there is not much difference between a foot-soldier and a pack-mule! The trooper carries a long sword on his right hip and an enormous pike in his hand, a shield slanted across his horse's flank, and in a quiver slung alongside three or more darts, broad-pointed and as big as spears. Helmets and breast-plates of infantry pattern are worn by all arms. Equipment is exactly the same for the general's mounted bodyguard as for the other cavalry units. Lots are always drawn for the legion that is to head the

1. *This statement contradicts all other evidence.*

column. So much for Roman routine on the march and in quarters, and for the variety of equipment.

In battle nothing is done without plan or on the spur of the moment; careful thought precedes action of any kind, and to the decisions reached all actions must conform. As a result they meet with very few setbacks, and if anything goes wrong the setbacks are easily cancelled out. They regard successes due to luck as less desirable than a planned but unsuccessful stroke, because victories that come of themselves tempt men to leave things to chance, but forethought, in spite of occasional failures, is good practice in avoiding the same mistake. Good things that come of themselves bring no credit to the recipient, but unfortunate accidents that upset calculations have at least this comfort in them, that plans were properly laid.

Military exercises give the Roman soldiers not only tough bodies but determined spirits too. Training methods are partly based on fear; for military law demands the death penalty not only for leaving a post but even for trivial misdemeanours; and the generals inspire more fear than the law, since by rewarding good soldiers they avoid seeming harsh towards the men they punish. So complete is their submission to their superiors that in peace they are a credit to Rome and in the field the whole army is a single body; so knit together are their ranks, so flexible their manoeuvres, so ready their ears for orders, their eyes for signals, their hands for the tasks to be done. Thus it is that they are as quick to act as they are slow to give way, and never was there an engagement in which they were worsted by numbers, tactical skill, or unfavourable ground – or even by fortune, which is less within their grasp than is victory. When planning goes before action, and the plans are followed by so effective an army, who can wonder that in the east the Euphrates, in the west the ocean, in the south the richest plains of Africa, in the north the Danube and the Rhine are the limits of the Empire? One might say with truth that the conquests are less remarkable than the conquerors.

The purpose of the foregoing account has been less to eulogize the Romans than to console their defeated enemies and to deter any who may be thinking of revolt; and possibly those of an enquiring frame of mind who have not studied the matter may find it useful to get an insight into the Roman military set-up. This is all that I propose to say on the subject.

While Vespasian with his son Titus spent some time at Ptolemais organizing his forces, Placidus swept through Galilee destroying great numbers of men who fell into his hands, these being the feebler members of the Galilaean community and the faint-hearted. Then seeing that the warlike spirits regularly took shelter in the towns that Josephus had fortified, he set out to attack the strongest of them, Jotapata, in the expectation that it would easily fall to a surprise assault. This would establish his reputation with his superiors and greatly improve their chances in the coming campaign; for the other towns would take fright and surrender once the most powerful had gone. But his hopes were completely dashed. As he approached Jotapata the citizens saw him in good time and laid an ambush before the town. Then they pounced upon the unsuspecting Romans. With superior numbers, ready for battle and eager to ward off the danger that menaced their homes, their wives, and their children, they routed them at once. Many Romans were wounded but only seven killed, thanks to the orderliness of their retreat, the superficial nature of their wounds (their bodies being completely protected), and the fact that the Jews launched their missiles at long range and dared not without armour close with heavy infantry. Jewish casualties did not exceed three killed and a handful wounded. So Placidus decided that to attack the town was beyond his strength, and took to his heels.

Vespasian, eager to invade Galilee himself, set out from Ptolemais with his army arranged in the usual Roman marching order. The light-armed auxiliaries and bowmen formed the vanguard, with orders to repel sudden enemy rushes and reconnoitre woods suspected of concealing ambushes. Next came a body of heavy-armed Roman troops, mounted and unmounted. These were followed by ten men from every century carrying, besides their own kit, the instruments for marking out the camp-site. After them came roadmakers to straighten out bends in the highway, level rough surfaces, and cut down obstructive woods, so that the army would not be exhausted by laborious marching. In the rear of these the personal baggage of the commander and his senior officers was concentrated under the protection of a strong cavalry force, behind which rode Vespasian himself with the cream of his horse and foot and a body of spearmen. Next came the legionary cavalry; for each legion has its own troops of 120 horse. These were followed by the mules that carried the Batterers and other mechanical devices. After them came the generals, cohort-commanders, and tribunes, with a bodyguard of picked troops; next the standards enclosing the Eagle which is at the head of every legion, as the king of birds and most fearless of all: this they regard as the symbol of empire and portent of victory, no matter who opposes them. The sacred emblems were followed by the trumpeters, and in their wake came the main body, shoulder to shoulder, six men abreast, accompanied as always by a centurion to maintain the formation. The servants of every legion marched in a body behind the infantry, looking after the soldiers' baggage carried by the mules and other beasts. In the rear of all the legions marched the bulk of the mercenaries, followed by a protective rearguard of light and heavy infantry with a strong body of cavalry.

Marching in this way Vespasian arrived with his army at the frontiers of Galilee. There he pitched his camp, and restraining his soldiers' ardour for battle he made a show of force to inspire terror in the enemy and give them time for second thoughts in the hope that before battle was joined they would change their minds; at the same time he got ready to besiege their strongholds. The sight of the commander-in-chief did indeed lead to second thoughts in many, and to terror in them all. The troops of Josephus who were in camp not far from Sepphoris, seeing the war approaching and the Romans on the point of swooping upon them, did not wait for a battle but even before seeing their opponents fled in all directions. Left behind with a handful of men, Josephus saw that he had not a force capable of stopping the enemy, that the morale of the Jews had collapsed, and that if they could get the Romans to trust them the majority would be only too pleased to ask for terms. He already saw disaster looming ahead, but for the time being he decided to keep as far away as possible from danger, and with those who had stuck to him sought shelter in Tiberias.

Vespasian descended on Gabara, and finding it almost without defenders took it at the first assault. He marched into the town and put to the sword all except small children, the Romans showing mercy to neither young nor old through hatred of the nation and the memory of the way they had treated Cestius. He burnt down not only the town itself but all the hamlets and villages around. Some of these he found completely abandoned; from others he carried off all the occupants as slaves.

Josephus by his hurried arrival produced panic in the city he had chosen as a refuge. The people of Tiberias concluded that if he had not completely written off the war he would never have taken to flight. In this they were perfectly right about his opinion; for he saw the in-evitable end awaiting the Jews, and knew that their one safety lay in a change of heart. He himself, he felt sure, would be pardoned if he went over to the Romans, but he would rather have died over and over again than betray his motherland and flout the trust reposed in him in order to make himself at home with those he had been sent to fight. So he determined to write for the Jerusalem authorities a detailed apprecia-tion of the situation, without either exaggerating the strength of the enemy and so later finding himself abused as a coward, or minimizing it and thereby reviving their hopes just when they were having second thoughts. He suggested that if they were ready to sue for terms they should write back at once; if they were determined to fight the Romans they must send him adequate forces. Having set down these proposals he dispatched the letter to Jerusalem by express messengers.

Vespasian was eager to destroy Jotapata; for he was informed that the biggest number of the enemy had taken refuge there, and that in addition it was a strong base for their activities. He therefore sent in-fantry and cavalry ahead to level the road, which was stony mountain track, difficult for infantry and for cavalry quite impossible. They took only four days to complete their task, opening a broad highway for the army. On the fifteenth day – the 21st of Artemisios – Josephus left Tiberias and slipped into Jotapata in time, awakening new courage in the sinking hearts of the Jews. Vespasian heard the good news of his arrival from a deserter, who urged him to attack the city with all speed, for when it submitted all Judaea would submit, provided Josephus fell into his hands. Vespasian seized on this news as a most marvellous piece of luck. It must be by divine providence that the man who was considered the most able of his enemies had put his own head in the noose. Without losing a moment he sent 1,000 horsemen under Placidus and the decurion Aebutius, a man with a reputation for energy and ability, with orders to put a ring round the town and pre-vent the secret escape of Josephus. Next day the general himself fol-lowed with his entire force, and after marching till dusk arrived before Jotapata. He led the army to the north of the town and pitched his camp on rising ground three quarters of a mile from the walls, trying to make himself as conspicuous as possible in order to demoralize the enemy. The effect was immediate, and so overwhelmed the Jews that no one dared to go outside the walls. The Romans did not feel inclined to make their onslaught at once, after marching all day, but they put a double line of infantry round the town, stationing a third line outside them, formed from the cavalry, so blocking all the enemy's means of egress. Thus robbed of all hope of escape, the Jews were stimulated to deeds of daring; for in war there is nothing like necessity to rouse the fighting spirit.

Next morning the assault began. At first the Jews stood their ground, remaining where they were encamped before the wall opposite the Romans. So Vespasian brought up against them his bowmen and slingers and all who were equipped with long-range weapons, with instructions to keep up a barrage while he himself with the infantry pushed up the slope where the wall was easy to surmount. Then Josephus, seeing disaster threaten the city, made a vigorous sortie at the head of the whole Jewish garrison. Falling in a body on the Romans they drove them back from the wall, performing many remarkable deeds of prowess and daring. However, the enemy's losses were equalled by their own; the Jews were spurred on by the hopelessness of their situation, the Romans just as effectively by a sense of shame; one side was armed with experience as well as prowess, the other had no weapon but animal courage, no captain but blind fury. All day long they were locked in battle till night parted them. Roman casualties were very heavy, and included thirteen killed: on the Jewish side the dead numbered seventeen and the wounded 600.[1]

On the next day the Romans attacked again, and the Jews, sallying out against them, met their advance with greatly increased determination, emboldened by their surprisingly effective resistance on the previous day. But they found the Romans too more aggressive than before; for shame put them into a blazing passion and they considered a failure to win quickly equivalent to a defeat. For five days the Roman attacks were incessant, and the sallies of the defenders and their fighting on the walls grew more and more determined; the Jews were not dismayed by the strength of the enemy, nor the Romans put off by the difficulty of capturing the town.

Jotapata is almost entirely perched on a precipice, cut off on three sides by ravines of such extraordinary depth that when people look down into them their sight cannot reach the bottom. The only access is from the north, where the town is built up to the lowest slope of the mountain. This slope Josephus had included when he built the walls, so that the enemy could not occupy the ridge which

1. *Surely an incredible proportion; but see page 203.*

commanded the town. This a ring of heights screened so effectively that until a man was actually inside it could not be seen at all. Such were the bastions of Jotapata.

Vespasian was not going to be defeated either by the natural strength of the place or by the daring resistance of the Jews; he determined to prosecute the siege more vigorously and called a meeting of senior officers to plan the assault. It was resolved to build a platform against the approachable section of the wall, so Vespasian sent out the whole army to collect material. The heights round the town were stripped of their trees, and along with the timber a mountain of stones was piled up. Then as a shelter from missiles descending from above a second party erected a line of hurdles supported by uprights and constructed the platform under their shelter, the bombardment from the walls causing few if any casualties. A third party tore up the hillocks near by and kept up a constant supply of earth to the builders. Thus with the men working in three groups nobody was idle. Meanwhile the Jews launched great rocks from the walls on to the enemy's screens, together with every kind of missile; even when they failed to reach their mark the noise was frightful and hindered the work.

Vespasian next set up his projectile-throwers in a ring – 160 engines in all – and gave instructions to bombard the men on the wall. In a synchronized barrage the catapults shot lances into the air, and stones weighing nearly a hundredweight were discharged from stone-throwers, together with firebrands and a dense shower of arrows, driving the Jews not only from the wall but also from the area inside traversed by the missiles; for a host of Arab bowmen with all the javelin-men and slingers let fly at the same time as the artillery. The defenders, however, though unable to retaliate from the ramparts were by no means idle. They made swift sallies in company strength guerrilla-fashion, tore away the screens that sheltered the working-party, and assailed them in their unprotected state; and whenever the Romans retired they broke up the platform and set light to the uprights and hurdles. This continued till Vespasian realized that the lack of continuity in the earthworks was the cause of the trouble, since the gaps provided the Jews with an avenue of attack. He then linked the screens together and at the same time concentrated his forces, bringing to an end the Jewish penetrations.

As the platform was now rising and had almost reached the battlements, Josephus, thinking it disgraceful if he failed to invent some counter-device to save the town, collected stone-masons and instructed them to raise the wall higher. When they declared that it was impossible to build under such a hail of missiles, he devised protection for them as follows. He ordered the men to fix railings to the wall and over these to stretch raw oxhides, so that when the stones hurled by the engines fell on them they would give without splitting; other types of missile would glance off them and firebrands would be quenched by their moisture. Thus protected the builders worked in safety day and night. They raised the wall to a height of thirty feet, built towers on it at short intervals, and completed it with a stout parapet. At this the Romans, who had fancied themselves already inside the town, were plunged into despondency; the resourcefulness of Josephus and the determination of the defenders amazed them. Vespasian was exasperated both by the cleverness of the stratagem and by the fearlessness of the townsmen, who, encouraged by the new fortifications, resumed their night sorties against the Romans and in the daytime engaged them at company strength. Every device of guerrilla war was brought into play, everything in their path was plundered, and the rest of the besiegers' works were set on fire. At length Vespasian recalled his troops from the battle and determined to blockade the town till starvation forced it to surrender; for the defenders would either be compelled by lack of provisions to beg for mercy, or if they held out to the bitter end would die of starvation. He was confident that he would overwhelm them much more easily on the battlefield if he waited awhile and made a fresh onslaught when they were exhausted. He therefore ordered watch to be kept on the sally-ports.

Inside there was plenty of corn and all other necessaries except salt, but the water-supply was inadequate as there was no spring within the walls and the townsfolk depended on rainwater – and little or no rain falls in the district during summer. As it was at that season that the siege took place they were terribly despondent at the prospect of having nothing to drink, and fretting already as if the water-supply had failed completely. For Josephus, seeing that the town had all other necessaries in abundance and that morale was high, and wishing to pin down the besiegers longer than they expected, had rationed his men's drink from the beginning. They, however, found this husbanding of resources harder to bear than actual shortage; unable to please themselves they felt the craving the more acutely, and as if they had already reached the last degree of thirst they began to flag. Their condition could not be hidden from the Romans. From the rising ground they looked over the wall and saw the Jews collecting in one spot to receive their water-ration; so they made this spot the target for their quick-loaders, causing very heavy losses. Vespasian hoped that before long the tanks would be empty and the surrender of the town would inevitably follow. But Josephus, determined to shatter this hope, ordered numbers of men to soak their outer garments and hang them round the battlements, so that the whole wall suddenly ran with water. The result was despondency and consternation in the Roman ranks, when they saw such a quantity of water thrown away in jest by men who were thought to have nothing to drink. The commander-in-chief himself despaired of capturing the town through shortage and reverted to armed onslaught. Nothing could have pleased the Jews better; for they had long despaired of saving the town or themselves, and dreaded hunger and thirst far more than death in battle.

Josephus, however, devised a second stratagem to obtain more supplies than he needed. Down a gully well-nigh impassable and consequently overlooked by the Roman guards, and along the western portion of the valley, he sent out messengers who delivered letters to Jews outside with whom he wished to make contact and brought back their answers, together with ample supplies of all necessaries that the town lacked. The messengers were instructed to crawl past the guard-posts as a rule, and to cover their backs with sheepskins so that if anyone did see them in the night they would be mistaken for dogs. But after a while the pickets detected the device and blocked the gully.

CHAPTER 12

Josephus the Prisoner of Vespasian

AT this point Josephus realized that the town could not hold out long and that his own survival was doubtful if he stayed, so he discussed with the leading citizens how they could escape. The people saw what was afoot and poured round him, imploring him not to forget that they depended on him alone. He was the one hope of survival for the town if he stayed; if it fell he would be their one comfort. It would be unforgivable in him to run away from his enemies and abandon his friends – to leap overboard when the ship on which he had embarked in a calm was tossed by a storm. For he would sink their town, as no one would venture to oppose the enemy any more, once their only source of confidence was gone. Josephus concealed his anxiety for his own safety and declared it was for their sakes he was arranging to leave. By staying in the town he could give them little help if they survived; if they fell into enemy hands he would be but one more victim. On the other hand by escaping from the siege he could send them help from outside on the greatest scale; he would at once assemble an army from the whole of Galilee, and by a diversionary campaign draw off the Romans from their town. He did not see how by staying with them he could be of any use to them in present conditions. The most likely result would be to drive the Romans to increase the vigour of the siege, as their chief desire was to capture him. If on the other hand they learnt that he had fled, they would greatly reduce the pressure on the town.

This appeal fell on deaf ears; it simply made the people more determined to hold on to him. Children, old men, women with infants in arms wept and fell down before him. They all grasped him by the feet and held him fast, imploring him with sobs to remain and share their lot – not through envy of his escape, I think, but in the hope of their own; for they felt perfectly safe so long as he remained. Josephus realized that if he yielded these appeals would be all, but if he refused he would be watched. Furthermore his determination to desert them was badly shaken by pity for their tears. So he made up his mind to stay, and turning the general despair into a weapon he exclaimed:

'Now is the time to begin the fight, when there is no hope of escape left. It is a glorious thing to win renown at the cost of one's life, and by some splendid deed to make oneself remembered by future generations.' Then he fell to work, and making a sortie with his toughest fighters he scattered the guards and dashed as far as the Roman camp, where he tore to pieces the skin tents which sheltered the troops on the platforms and set fire to their works. The next day and the day after that he repeated his exploit, and for many days and nights he fought on without rest.

Vespasian saw that the Romans were damaged by these sorties. They felt sore at being worsted by Jews, and when the Jews were worsted pursuit was hampered by the weight of their armour. Again, the enemy after striking their blow always got back to the town before the Romans could retaliate. He therefore ordered the legionaries to avoid Jewish attacks and not become involved with men who wanted to die. Nothing was so productive of heroism as despair, but like a fire without fuel their enthusiasm would fizzle out when there was no new target for their attacks. And even Romans should avoid needless risks in winning their victories, since they were fighting not for survival but to enlarge their dominions. He made the Arab bowmen and the Syrian slingers and stone throwers bear the brunt of the Jewish onslaughts, and kept most of his siege-guns constantly in action. These did such damage that the enemy had to give way, but once inside the minimum range of the far-flung missiles they assailed the Romans furiously without a thought for life or limb, exhausted units being constantly replaced by fresh waves of attackers.

As time dragged on and the sorties continued, Vespasian felt it was he who was being besieged, and as the platforms were now getting near the walls he decided to bring up the Ram. This is a huge baulk like the mast of a ship, fitted at the end with a great lump of iron in the shape of a ram's head, whence the name. It is supported at the middle, like the beam of a balance, by ropes passing over another baulk which rests on posts fixed on the ground on either side. The Ram is drawn back by a great number of men, who then with a gigantic united heave swing it forward again so that it strikes the wall with the projecting iron. The first blows may be ineffective, but no wall is so thick that it can stand up to a prolonged battering. This was the method the Roman commander resolved to adopt in his anxiety to take the town by storm; for the blockade was sapping the vigour of his army and the Jews had the initiative. So in order to bring within range the Jews on the wall who were trying to stop them, the Romans pushed forward their catapults and other engines and began to bombard them. The bowmen and slingers moved forward at the same time. As a result no one dared mount the rampart, and this enabled other troops to bring up the Ram under the protection of overlapping hurdles covered with skins to safeguard both men and machine. The very first blow rocked the wall, and piercing shrieks were raised by those within, as if the town had been captured already.

Under the relentless battering of the same spot, Josephus saw that at any moment the wall would be laid flat, so he devised a scheme to counter for a time the force of the machine. Sacks were to be filled with chaff and lowered by ropes to the spot where they saw that the next blow was coming, so that the head would be deflected and the blows cushioned into ineffectiveness. This tactic held up the Romans completely, for to whatever spot they directed the Ram the defenders above put their sacks in the way and intercepted the strokes, so that the impact did no damage to the wall – till the Romans retaliated by attaching reaphooks to the ends of long poles and cutting down the sacks. The effectiveness of the Batterer was thus restored, and the wall, so recently built, began to give way; so now Josephus and his helpers had recourse to fire. Setting light to all the dry wood they could lay their hands on, they rushed out in three columns and made a bonfire of the enemy's engines, hurdles, and platforms. The Romans made little effort to save them: they were paralysed by the Jews' astonishing courage and beaten by the flames in their race to the rescue. For the wood was dry, and mixed with bitumen, pitch, and even brimstone, so that the flames flew in every direction faster than thought, and what had cost the Romans many hours of toil was consumed in a single hour.

In this struggle one of the Jews distinguished himself in a way that calls for very special mention. His father's name was Samias, his own Eleazar, his birthplace Saba in Galilee. This man raised a huge stone and flung it from the wall at the Batterer with such tremendous force that he broke off the head of the Ram. Then he leapt down and seizing the head under the noses of the enemy carried it back to the wall without turning a hair. A target now for all his foes and with no armour to protect his body from the rain of missiles, he was pierced by five shafts; but paying not the slightest regard to these he climbed the wall and stood there for all to admire his daring, then writhing with the pain of his wounds fell to the ground with the Ram's head still in his grip. Most conspicuous for courage after him were two brothers, Neiras and Philip, from the village of Ruma, Galilaeans like Eleazar. They charged the ranks of the Tenth Legion, falling upon the Romans with such dash and fury that they broke through their lines and routed all who stood in their path.

Inspired by their example Josephus and the rest of the defenders again snatched up firebrands and set light to the engines, shelters, and constructions of the Fifth Legion and the routed Tenth. The other units were quick to cover their tackle and all their timber with earth. In the evening they again set up the Ram and brought it against the place where the earlier battering had weakened the wall. At this juncture one of the defenders on the battlements hit Vespasian with an arrow in the sole of his foot. The wound was superficial, as the impact of the shaft was weakened by the long range, but the occurrence produced the utmost consternation in the Roman ranks; for the sight of the blood badly shook those nearest to Vespasian, and the news ran through the whole army, with the result that most of the men forgot the siege and in dismay and terror came running towards their commander. First to arrive was Titus, in fear for his father's life, so that the rank and file were agitated both by their regard for their leader and by the evident distress of his son. However it was quite easy for the father to put an end to his son's fears and the consternation of the army. Rising superior to his pain and showing himself instantly to all who were alarmed on his behalf, he stimulated them to yet more furious onslaughts; every man in his eagerness to avenge his commander was anxious to be in the forefront of danger, and shouting encouragement to each other they dashed towards the wall.

Josephus and his men, although falling in heaps under the barrage of spears and stones, clung stubbornly to the battlements and with fire, steel, and stones continued to pelt those who under cover of their hurdles were swinging the Ram. But they accomplished little or nothing, and they themselves were continually falling because the enemy could see them without being seen; for their own fires lit them up from every side, making them as conspicuous a target for the enemy as in daylight, and since the engines were too far off to be visible it was difficult to avoid the missiles. The force of the quick-loaders and spear-throwers was such that a single projectile ran through a row of men, and the momentum of the stones hurled by the engine carried away battlements and knocked off corners of towers. There is in fact no body of men so strong that it cannot be laid low to the last rank by the impact of these huge stones. The effectiveness of such ordnance can be gathered from the events of that night. Getting in the line of fire, one of the men standing near Josephus on the rampart had his head knocked off by a stone, his skull being flung like a pebble from a sling more than 600 yards; and when a pregnant woman on leaving her house at day-break was struck in the belly, the unborn child was carried away 100 yards; so tremendous was the power of the stone-throwers. Even more terrifying than the siege-guns and their missiles was the rushing sound and the final crash. There was a constant thudding of dead bodies as they were thrown one after another from the rampart. Within the town rose the terrible shrieks of the women, echoed from without by the groans of dying men. The whole strip of ground that encircled the battlefield ran with blood, and it was possible to climb up the heap of corpses on to the battlements. The din was made more terrifying by the echoes from the mountains around, and on that night nothing was wanting that could horrify ear or eye. Hundreds of those engaged in Jotapata's death-struggle fell like heroes; hundreds were wounded. Not till the time of the morning watch did the wall yield to the con-tinual blows of the Ram; and then the Jews filled the breach with their bodies and their weapons to block the way before the Romans could rush the scaling-gangways into position.

At daybreak Vespasian assembled his army for the final assault, refreshed by a short rest after the toils of the night. As he wished to draw off the defenders from the breaches, he dismounted the pick of his horsemen and ranged them in three groups against the gaps in the wall, completely encased in armour and with long spears in rest, in order that as soon as the gangways were in position they might force the first entry. Behind them he ranged the flower of his infantry. The rest of the cavalry he extended opposite the wall across the whole slope to inter-cept any man who might escape when the town was captured. Still further back he stationed the bowmen in a curving line, ordering them to have their arrows ready to discharge; the slingers and artillerymen received similar instructions. Other men were to carry ladders and set them up against the undamaged portions of the wall, in the hope that some Jews in their efforts to hold them off would abandon the defence of the breaches, while the rest would be forced by the deluge of missiles to leave the way in unguarded.

Josephus, realizing what was afoot, stationed the older men and the battle-weary on the undamaged parts of the wall, where they were unlikely to suffer any hurt: where the wall had been broken through he posted the fittest of his men, each group headed by six officers, among whom he himself drew a place in order to be in the thick of the fight. He issued instructions that when the legions raised their battle-cry the men were to stop their ears to avoid panic, and when the hail of arrows fell they were to bend double under cover of their long shields and withdraw a little way, until the bowmen had emptied their quivers. But as the gangways fell into position they were to be the first to leap forward, hurling themselves at the enemy by means of their own instruments. Every man must fight to the death, not for a birthplace that could still be saved, but for one that was already lost yet must be avenged. 'Picture to yourselves,' he concluded, 'old men butchered, women and children slaughtered by the foe at any moment now; the fury which these impending disasters arouse in your breasts seize with both hands and hurl at those who will bring them upon you.'

Such were the arrangements Josephus made for the two classes of defenders. But when the useless section of the community, the women and children, saw the triple line that encircled the town – none of the guards posted earlier had been moved into the battle – and saw too before the fallen ramparts the enemy, sword in hand, and the slope above them flashing with arms, and above them again the arrows of the Arab bowmen, they raised a last united shriek at their capture, as if ruin was no longer a threat but a present reality. Josephus, for fear their lamentation might weaken the resolution of their menfolk, locked them in their homes, threatening them with punishment if they did not hold their tongues. Then he strode into the breach and took his stand where the lot had fallen to him. Of those who were bringing up the ladders elsewhere he took no notice, his thoughts intent on the coming rain of arrows.

At one and the same moment the trumpets of all the legions blared and a hair-raising battle-cry burst from ten thousand throats. This was the signal for a volley of arrows from every side that darkened the sky. Not forgetting Josephus' instructions the men under him stopped their ears against the shout and shielded their bodies from the volleys: as the gangways were dropped into position, they charged over them before the men who were dropping them could set foot on them. Then pouncing upon the enemy as they struggled up they gave a magnificent

display of prowess and fighting spirit, striving in the midst of utter ruin
to prove themselves the equals of those who with so much less at stake
showed such remarkable courage. No one broke off his struggle with
an opponent until one or the other was dead. But while the Jews were
being steadily worn out by the non-stop battle and were unable to
replace their front-line officers, on the Roman side exhausted units
were relieved by fresh troops and as soon as one group was forced back
another came forward; they cheered each other on, and standing shoulder to shoulder under cover of their long shields they formed an un-
breakable mass, which with the whole formation pushing as one man
forced the Jews up the slope and a minute later would have been on the
wall.

The situation was critical, and Josephus taught by necessity – always
quick to improvise when despair applies the spur – ordered boiling oil
to be poured on the soldiers under the shields. As his men had it ready,
numbers of them from every side poured quantities of it on the
Romans, followed by the vessels still hissing from the flames. Scalded
and burnt, the Romans broke up their formation and in agonizing pain
rolled down from the wall; for the oil instantly ran under their armour
and over their entire bodies from head to foot, consuming their flesh as
relentlessly as a fire, being by nature quick to grow hot and slow to
cool because of its fattiness. Imprisoned in their cuirasses and helmets
they could not escape from the scalding fluid. Leaping into the air and
contorted with pain they fell from the wooden bridges one after
another, while those who retired ran into their own men as they
pressed forward, making themselves an easy target for the enemy
shafts.

The Romans in their sorry plight displayed as much fortitude as
ever, the Jews as much resource. The Romans, though they saw the
pitiable sufferings of those who had been drenched with oil, continued
their relentless advance against those who had drenched them, everyone abusing the man in front for blocking his way. The Jews employed
a second ruse to trip them up as they advanced: they poured boiled
fenugreek on the boards of the gangways, so that the enemy slithered
and lost their footing. Whether retiring or advancing nobody could
stand upright; some fell on their backs while still on the gangways and
were trodden to death, many tumbled off on to the platform, and these
were at the mercy of the Jews; for as the Romans could not stand their
opponents were no longer involved in hand-to-hand fighting and so

could take careful aim. As they had been badly mauled in this assault, the commander towards evening called off his troops. Of the Romans many were dead and more were wounded; of the defenders of Jotapata only six had been killed, but over 300 wounded were brought back from the battle. This fighting took place on the 20th of Daisios.

Vespasian tried to console his army for its misfortunes, but when he saw that the men were angry and needed not exhortation but work to do, he ordered them to raise the platforms higher and to erect three towers, each 50 feet high, encased in iron on all four sides, so that they would be too heavy to overturn and almost proof against fire. These he pushed forward on to the platforms, placing on top spearmen, bowmen, and light artillery, and also the most powerful of the slingers. These men, concealed by the height of the towers and the breastworks, proceeded to pelt the defenders exposed on the ramparts. The Jews found it almost impossible to dodge the missiles launched at their heads or to retaliate on their invisible assailants, and seeing that the tops of the towers were beyond the reach of weapons thrown by hand, while the iron that encased them was proof against fire, they abandoned the wall and sallied out to meet any attack that might be attempted. In this way Jotapata held out, though every day many lost their lives and the survivors could do no damage to the enemy in return, but only at great risk block their advance.

While all this was happening, one of the towns in the neighbourhood, called Japha, revolted in the excitement aroused by the astonishing way that Jotapata held out. Vespasian therefore dispatched Trajan,[1] commander of the Tenth Legion, at the head of 1,000 horse and 2,000 foot. Trajan saw that the town would be difficult to capture; for beside the natural strength of its position it was surrounded by two separate walls. But the inhabitants came out to meet him in their eagerness for battle, and when he saw them he attacked, quickly broke their resistance and drove them back. They took refuge inside the outer wall, but the Romans followed on their heels and burst in with them. When they made a new dash for the inner wall they were shut out of the town by their own friends, who feared the enemy would charge in with them. It was God without a doubt who made the Romans a present of the unfortunate Galilaeans: it was God who at this moment allowed the population of the town to be shut out by the hands of their own kinsmen and handed over, every man of them, to

1. *His son later became emperor.*

their bloodthirsty foes for destruction. For hurling themselves in a body at the gates and frantically appealing to the keepers they were butchered in the midst of their supplications. The outer wall was closed to them by the enemy, the inner by their friends. Crushed between the two ramparts so that they could not move, many were impaled on their comrades' swords, many on their own: immense numbers were slaughtered by the Romans, having no mind even to defend themselves; for as well as being terrified by the enemy they were heartbroken at being abandoned by their friends. They died cursing not the Romans but their own people, till in the end they were all destroyed, 12,000 of them.

Assuming that there were no fighting men left in the town, and taking it for granted that even if there were a few inside they would be too frightened to make any resistance, Trajan reserved the actual capture for the commander-in-chief, and dispatched messengers to Vespasian inviting him to send his son Titus to put the finishing touches to the victory. Vespasian, suspecting that the struggle was not yet over, sent his son with a force of 500 horse and 1,000 foot. Titus marched to the town with all speed, drew up his forces with Trajan posted on the left wing and himself in command on the right, and led them to the attack. The soldiers brought up ladders to the wall on every side, and for a short while the Galilaeans on the battlements tried to fight them off; but they soon abandoned their defences, and at once Titus' men sprang on to the battlements and a moment later were in possession of the town. Those inside the wall, however, rallied to oppose them and a furious struggle broke out. In the narrow streets the men of action fell upon the legionaries; and from the house-tops the women pelted them with anything they could lay their hands on. For six hours they kept up their resistance; but when the fighting men had been expended the rest of the population were butchered in the open and in the houses, young and old together. For no male was left alive apart from infants in arms, who with the women were sold into slavery. Those who had been slaughtered, either in the town or in the preceding engagement, totalled 15,000, the slaves 2,130. This catastrophe befell the Galilaeans on 25th of Daisios.

Nor did the Samaritans remain immune from disaster. They assembled on Mt Gerizim, which they regard as sacred, and though they made no move there was a threat of war in this concentration of manpower and militant attitude. Not even the calamities of their neighbours could teach them sense; in face of the Roman successes they took an illogical pride in their own weakness and were thrilled at the prospect of a head-on collision. Vespasian thought it wisest to forestall the rising and nip their attempt in the bud; for though every corner of Samaria was garrisoned, the size and organization of the assembled host was alarming. So Cerealius, commanding the Fifth Legion, was sent at the head of 600 horse and 3,000 foot. In this officer's opinion it was unsafe to ascend the mountain and join battle, as so many of the enemy occupied still higher ground; so encircling with his troops the whole base of the mountain he kept the enemy under observation all day long. It happened that just when the Samaritans were growing short of water they were burnt up by a terrible heatwave – it was summertime, and the mass of men were without essential supplies. As a result some of them that very day died of thirst, and many, feeling that such a death was worse than slavery, deserted to the Romans. From their condition Cerealius inferred that those who still held together were broken by their sufferings, and proceeded to climb the mountain and post his men in a ring round the enemy. Then as a first step he invited them to come to terms, urging them to save their lives and guaranteeing their safety if they threw down their arms. When his proposals were rejected he fell upon them and slew them all to the number of 11,600. It was on the 27th of Daisios that the Samaritans suffered this terrible calamity.

In Jotapata the defenders still held out, bearing up under their sufferings longer than seemed possible. But on the forty-seventh day the Roman platforms overtopped the wall, and that very day a deserter informed Vespasian how few men were left in the city and how weak they were, and assured him that spent with total lack of sleep and constant fighting they could no longer withstand an assault and would fall to a ruse if one was attempted. In the last hour of the night, when they counted on some respite from their sufferings and when exhausted men are most easily overcome by morning sleep, the sentries, he said, used to drop off, so that was the best time for an assault. Vespasian mistrusted the deserter, knowing how loyal the Jews were to each other and how contemptuous of punishment; for earlier on when a man from Jotapata had been captured he had borne up in the face of the most horrible tortures, and even when the enemy used flames to extort information had refused to say a word about conditions in the town, finally going to death by crucifixion with a smile on his face. On the other hand the traitor's story was too convincing to be disbelieved, and thinking that possibly he was speaking the truth, and that even if he was laying a trap the consequences to the Romans would not be serious, the general ordered him to be closely guarded but got his army ready for the capture of the town.

At the hour indicated they moved forward noiselessly to the wall. First to climb up was Titus, accompanied by one of the tribunes, Domitius Sabinus, and followed by a handful of men from the Fifteenth Legion. Quickly disposing of the sentries they entered the town. In their rear Sextus Calvarius, a tribune, and Placidus introduced the units they commanded. Soon the citadel had been captured, the enemy were sweeping through the centre of the town, and it was broad daylight – and yet the vanquished defenders had no idea the town had fallen! For most of them were helpless with fatigue and fast asleep; if anyone did rouse himself he could not see for a dense mist which at the critical moment happened to envelop the town. At last, when the whole army had streamed in, they jumped up, only to discover that all was lost: they did not realize that the town had fallen till the massacre began.

The Romans, remembering what the siege had cost them, showed neither mercy nor pity for anyone. They drove the people down the slope from the citadel and slaughtered them. There even those still capable of resistance were deprived by the difficult ground of any chance to defend themselves. Jostling each other in the narrow streets and slipping down the steep face they were swamped by the wave of destruction sweeping down from the citadel. Many even of Josephus' picked soldiers were driven to suicide; for when they saw that they could not kill a single Roman, they made sure that at least they should not die at Roman hands, and collecting at the far edge of the town they killed themselves.

Some of the sentries on first realizing that the end had come had got away in time. These went up into one of the northern towers and held out there for a time; but when they were hemmed in by a large enemy force they at last put up their hands and offered their throats to their opponents without flinching. The Romans might well have claimed that the final stage of the siege was a bloodless victory, if one man had not fallen at the time of the capture – the centurion Antonius, victim of a trick. One Jew who with a great many others had taken refuge in the caves begged Antonius to give him his hand as a pledge of protection and to help him climb out. The Roman incautiously gave him his hand, and with a swift upward thrust the man stabbed him in the groin and killed him instantly.

On that day the Romans killed all who were in the open; on the next few days they searched the hiding-places, falling on all whom they found in the sewers and caves, and destroying them regardless of their age, except women and babes. 1,200 prisoners went into the cages, while the dead, including those killed in the battles preceding the capture, were reckoned at 40,000. Vespasian ordered the city to be demolished and set fire to all the guardposts. Such was the end of Jotapata, captured on the 1st of Panemos in the thirteenth year of Nero's reign.

The Romans sought everywhere for Josephus both because their blood was up and because it was their commander's express wish, since the war would be virtually over once Josephus was in his hands. So they combed the dead bodies and the men who had gone into hiding. But while the capture was taking place, Josephus, helped by some divine providence, had stolen away from the midst of the enemy and jumped into a deep pit communicating on one side with a wide cave which could not be seen from above. There he had found forty persons of importance concealed, and essential supplies that would last for many days. So in the daytime he lay hid as the enemy were everywhere, but at night he came out and looked for an escape route and scrutinized the sentry-posts; but as every avenue was blocked on his account and there was no possibility of escape he went down into his cave again. So for two days he escaped detection, but on the third a woman of his party was captured and gave him away. Vespasian without a moment's hesitation sent two tribunes, Paulinus and Gallicanus, with orders to offer Josephus safe conduct and persuade him to come out.

When these arrived they gave him a warm invitation and guaranteed his safety, but without avail. The probable fate of one who had struck so many blows blinded him to the habitual gentleness of those who invited him, and made him highly suspicious; and he continued to fear that they were summoning him to punishment until Vespasian sent a third tribune, Nicanor, known to Josephus – in fact an old friend. He came forward and enlarged on the habitual kindness of the Romans towards the vanquished. Josephus' prowess made him admired rather than hated by the generals, and the commander-in-chief was anxious to bring him out, not for punishment – he could inflict that even without Josephus coming forth – but because he preferred to save so excellent a man. He added that if Vespasian had been laying a trap he would not have sent a friend, hiding the foulest crime – perfidy – behind the fairest virtue – friendship; and if he himself had been required to deceive his friend, he would never have agreed to come.

While in spite of Nicanor's assurances Josephus still hesitated, the rank and file in their fury were eager to roast him out of the cave, but they were restrained by the tribune who was determined to take him alive. As Nicanor urged his appeals and the threatening attitude of the enemy masses became evident to Josephus, the memory came to him of those dreams in the night by which God had forewarned him both of the calamities coming to the Jews and of the fortunes of the Roman emperors. Moreover in the matter of interpreting dreams he was capable of divining the meaning of equivocal utterances of the Deity: he was familiar with the prophecies of Holy Scripture, being a priest himself and the descendant of priests. At this very moment he was inspired to understand them, and seizing on the terrifying images of his recent dreams he sent up a secret prayer to God: 'Inasmuch as it pleaseth Thee to visit Thy wrath on the Jewish people whom Thou didst create, and all prosperity hath passed to the Romans; and because Thou didst choose my spirit to make known the things to come, I yield myself willingly to the Romans that I may live, but I solemnly declare that I go, not as a traitor, but as Thy servant.'

With these words he was on the point of giving in to Nicanor. But the Jews who had taken refuge along with him realized that he was accepting the invitation and crowded round him shouting: 'Surely a cry would go up to heaven from the laws of our fathers, ordained by God Himself, who endowed our race with spirits that despise death! Are you so in love with life, Josephus, that you can bear to live as a slave? How quickly you have forgotten yourself! How many you have persuaded to lay down their lives for liberty! False, utterly false, was the reputation you won for courage and shrewdness, if you really expect to be spared by those you have hit so hard, and, even supposing their offer of pardon is genuine, you stoop to accept it! But if *you* have been dazzled by Roman success, *we* must take care of our country's good name. We will lend you a sword and a hand to wield it. If you die willingly, you will die as commander-in-chief of the Jews; if unwillingly, as a traitor.' As they said this, they pointed their swords at him and threatened to run him through if he gave in to the Romans.

Fearing the threatened assault and believing that it would be a betrayal of the commands of God if he died before imparting his message, Josephus in his critical situation began to philosophize. 'Why, my friends,' he began, 'are we so anxious to commit suicide? Why should we make those best of friends, body and soul, part company? It is suggested that I have changed. Well, the Romans know all about that. I am told it is a glorious thing to die in war. Quite so; but by the laws of war – that is, by the hands of the victors. If I am shrinking from the Roman swords, I fully deserve to die by my own hand; but if they are disposed to spare an enemy, how much more justified should we be in sparing ourselves? It would be absurd to do to ourselves what we are fighting to prevent their doing to us! You say it is glorious to die for freedom; I say so too, but on the battlefield and at the hands of those who are trying to take freedom from us. But now they are not coming to do battle with us or to kill us. The man who doesn't want to die when he ought is no more cowardly than the man who does want to when he ought not. What keeps us from going up to the Romans? Isn't it fear of death? Well, then, shall we, because we fear possible death at the hands of our foes, inflict certain death on ourselves? "No, it is fear of slavery," someone will say. As if we were free men now! "It is a brave act to kill oneself," another will suggest. Not at all! It is a most craven act. *I* think a pilot would be a most arrant coward, if through fear of bad weather he did not wait for the storm to break but sank his ship on purpose.

'Again, self-murder is contrary to the instincts shared by all living things, and towards the God who made us it is sheer impiety. Of all living things there is not one that dies on purpose or by its own act; it is an irresistible natural law that all should wish to live. For that reason if men openly attempt to rob us of life we treat them as enemies; if they lay a trap for us we punish them. And do you suppose God isn't angry when a man treats His gift with contempt? It is from Him we have received our being, and it is to Him we must leave the right to take it away. The bodies of all men are mortal and have been fashioned out of perishable matter; the soul is immortal for ever, a fragment of God dwelling in our bodies. If a man destroys something entrusted to him by another man or misuses it, he is judged a faithless rogue, is he not? then if a man throws away what God has entrusted to his personal keeping, does he think the One he has wronged is unaware? To punish runaway slaves is considered right, even if the masters they are leaving are rogues; if we ourselves run away from the best of masters, God, shan't we be judged impious? Don't you know that those who depart this life according to the law of nature, and repay the loan they received from God at such time as the Lender chooses to claim it back, win everlasting glory? that their homes and families are safe? and that their souls remain unspotted and obedient, having won the most holy place in heaven, from which when time's wheel has turned full circle they are again sent to dwell in unsullied bodies? But if men go mad and lay hands on themselves, Hades receives their souls into the shadows, and God their Father visits the sins of the fathers upon the children. For that reason self-murder is hateful in God's sight and the wisest of lawgivers has declared it a punishable offence. Those who destroy themselves must by our rules be exposed unburied till sundown, though even our enemies are thought to be entitled to burial. In other lands it is laid down that the right hands of those who die thus should be cut off, since they have made war on themselves, on the ground that as the body has been divorced from the soul, so the hand must be divorced from the body.

'It is our duty then, comrades, to choose the honourable course and not to add to our human sufferings impiety towards our Creator. If we think it right to accept life when it is offered, let us accept it; for an offer of life brings no discredit if it comes from those whom by our tremendous resistance we have convinced of our mettle; if we choose to die, how better than at the hands of our conquerors? I shall not go over to the Roman side in order to be a traitor to myself; if I did, I should be much sillier than those who desert to the enemy; for to them desertion means life, for me it means death, my own death. However, I pray that the Romans may prove traitors: if after giving me their word they put me to death, I shall die happy, finding in the broken faith of such liars a consolation greater than victory itself.'

On these lines Josephus argued at great length in his desire to avert mass suicide. But desperation made his hearers deaf; they had long ago devoted themselves to death, and now they were furious with him. Running at him from all directions sword in hand, they reviled him for cowardice, everyone appearing to be about to strike him. But he called one by name, glared like a general at another, shook hands with a third, pleaded with a fourth till he was ashamed, and distracted by conflicting emotions in his critical situation, he kept all their swords away from his throat, turning like an animal at bay to face each assailant in turn. Even when he was at his last gasp they still respected their commander; their arms were enfeebled, their blades glanced off him, and many while thrusting at him with their swords spontaneously lowered their points.

In this predicament his resourcefulness did not fail him. Putting his trust in divine protection he staked his life on one last throw. 'You have chosen to die,' he exclaimed; 'well then, let's draw lots and kill each other in turn. Whoever draws the first lot shall be dispatched by number two, and so on down the whole line as luck decides. In this way no one will die by his own hand – it would be unfair when the rest were gone if one man changed his mind and saved his life.' The audience swallowed the bait, and getting his way Josephus drew lots with the rest. Without hesitation each man in turn offered his throat for the next man to cut, in the belief that a moment later his commander would die too. Life was sweet, but not so sweet as death if Josephus died with them! But Josephus – shall we put it down to divine providence or just to luck?[1] – was left with one other man. He did not relish the thought either of being condemned by the lot or, if he was left till last, of staining his hand with the blood of a fellow Jew. So he used persuasion, they made a pact, and both remained alive.

Having thus come safely through two wars – one with the Romans and one with his own people – Josephus was brought by Nicanor before Vespasian. The Romans all rushed to see him, and as the noisy mob milled round their commander they raised conflicting cries, some exulting over the prisoner, some threatening him, some elbowing their way forward to get a nearer view. Those at the back clamoured for the execution of their enemy; those at the front remembered his exploits and were astounded at the change in his fortunes. As for the officers, the anger they had felt before was entirely forgotten now that they saw him. More than anyone else Titus was impressed by the courageous bearing of Josephus in his misfortunes and by pity for his youth.[2] When he remembered how he had fought in time past and saw him now a prisoner in enemy hands, he had occasion to reflect on the power of fortune, the sudden tilting of the scales in war, the absence of any certainty in human affairs. So at this time he led very many

1. Or to shameless trickery on Josephus' part? See the Slavonic Version quoted in the Appendix.
2. Josephus was thirty, Titus only twenty-six!

Romans to feel for Josephus the pity he felt himself, and he was chiefly responsible for his father's decision to spare the prisoner's life. However, Vespasian gave instructions that he should be kept in the closest custody, as he intended to send him as soon as possible to Nero. Hearing this, Josephus asked to say a word to him in private. Vespasian ordered everyone except his son Titus and two friends to withdraw, and Josephus began thus:

'You suppose, sir, that in capturing me you have merely secured a prisoner, but I come as a messenger of the greatness that awaits you. Had I not been sent by God Himself, I knew the Jewish law and how a general ought to die. Are you sending me to Nero? How so? Will Nero and those who succeed him before your turn comes remain on the throne? You, Vespasian, are Caesar and Emperor, you and your son here. So load me with your heaviest chains and keep me for yourself; for you are master not only of me, Caesar, but of land and sea and all the human race; and I ask to be kept in closer confinement as my penalty, if I am taking the name of God in vain.'

At the time Vespasian seemed unwilling to take these suggestions seriously, assuming that Josephus was lying to save his skin. But gradually he became convinced, for God was already awakening in him imperial ambitions and foreshowing the sceptre by other portents. Moreover he found that the prophecies of Josephus had proved correct on other occasions; for one of the friends present at the private interview expressed surprise that he had not warned the defenders of Jotapata that the town would fall or foreseen his own captivity – unless he was now talking nonsense to avert the anger he had brought on himself. But Josephus replied that he had predicted to the people of Jotapata that the town would fall after forty-seven days and that he himself would be taken alive by the Romans. Vespasian took the prisoners aside and questioned them about these claims; when he found they were true he began to take seriously the predictions about himself. So, although he kept Josephus locked up in prison, he presented him with clothing and other valuable gifts and treated him with kindness and consideration at all times, Titus showing the same eagerness to do him honour.

CHAPTER 13

Vespasian's Conquering Advance

ON the 4th of Panemos Vespasian marched his army to Ptolemais
and thence to the coastal city of Caesarea, one of the largest in
Judaea, with a predominantly Greek population. Army and generals
alike were received with loud applause and in the friendliest spirit,
partly through good will towards the Romans, but still more through
hatred of the vanquished, hatred which caused a howling mob to
clamour for Josephus to be executed. But this demand, proceeding as
it did from mass ignorance, Vespasian dismissed with contemptuous
silence. Two of the legions he settled for the winter at Caesarea, as he
found the city convenient; the Fifteenth he sent to Scythopolis, to
avoid burdening Caesarea with his whole army. That city too is as
mild in winter as it is suffocatingly hot in summer, being situated on
the plain and near the sea.

Meanwhile those who in faction fights had been expelled from
their towns joined with those who had survived the recent defeats,
forming a sizeable force, and proceeded to rebuild Joppa (recently
devastated by Cestius), to serve as their base. Then, as they were cut off
from the land which had been overrun, they decided to turn to the sea.
They built a large pirate fleet and began to raid the Syrian and Phoenician waters and the route to Egypt, making it impossible for anyone to
sail those seas. Vespasian, on hearing of this organization, sent horse and
foot to Joppa. As the town was unguarded, this force entered it at night.
The inhabitants were forewarned of the attack, but in their terror they
abandoned all hope of keeping out the Romans, and fleeing to their
ships spent the night out of range.

There is no natural harbour at Joppa, which ends in an uneven beach
straight for most of its length but curving gently at both ends. These
are formed by lofty cliffs and reefs running out into the sea, where the
marks of Andromeda's chair are still shown as proofs of the antiquity
of the legend. Beating full on this shore and dashing the waves high
against the opposing rocks, the north wind makes the anchorage more
dangerous than a landless sea. Here the men from Joppa were riding at
anchor when just before daylight they were struck by a violent gale,

known to sailors in those parts as the Black North. Some of the ships it dashed against the others then and there, others it drove on to the rocks. Many in the face of the oncoming surge forced their way into deeper waters, so great was the fear of this rocky shore and the enemy in possession of it; but even in the open sea the mountainous waves overwhelmed them. There was no way of escape, and no safety if they stayed: the power of the wind kept them from the sea, the power of the Romans from the land. There were agonizing shrieks as the vessels collided; when they broke up the noise was deafening. Of the men on board many were submerged by the waves and drowned, many lost their lives entangled in the wreckage, while some, thinking it less painful to die by the sword, cheated the sea by killing themselves. But most of them were cast up by the waves and dashed to pieces against the cliffs, so that a wide stretch of sea was stained with their blood and the beach was covered with corpses; for the Romans set upon those who were cast up on the shore and destroyed them. The number of bodies washed up was 4,200. The Romans captured the town without any fighting and demolished it.

Thus in a short period Joppa twice fell to the Romans. To prevent the pirates from again settling there Vespasian established a camp on the acropolis and left his cavalry in it along with a small infantry force. The latter were to stay where they were and guard the camp while the cavalry plundered the surrounding country and destroyed the villages and little towns in the neighbourhood of Joppa. These orders were duly executed: the countryside was overrun and devastated day after day till it was utterly desolate.

When Jerusalem received news of the catastrophe at Jotapata, at first very few believed it – the disaster was so overwhelming, and no eyewitness was available to confirm the report. No one had survived to relate what had happened, but a spontaneous rumour – for rumour delights in tragic news – announced the fall of the town. But by degrees the truth trickled through, and everyone knew that there was no longer room for doubt. Truth, however, was supplemented by invention; for instance, it was stated that among those killed when the town fell was Josephus himself. This report caused extreme distress in Jerusalem; whereas the lamentation for each of the dead was confined to his own household and kindred, the mourning for the commander was nationwide – some grieved for acquaintances, some for kinsmen, some for close friends, some for brothers, but the loss of Josephus distressed them all. For a whole month the wailing never stopped in the City, and a great many hired professional mourners to lead their lamentations. But before long the truth came to light, and what had really happened at Jotapata. When the people found out that the tragic fate of Josephus was an invention, and learnt that he was alive and with the Romans, and that he was receiving from the officers treatment no prisoner could expect, they were as furious with him living as they had been kind about him when believed dead. Some reviled him as a coward, some as a traitor; the City seethed with indignation and nothing was too bad to say about him. The people were maddened by the blows they had suffered and inflamed by their disasters. A setback, which with sensible people is an inducement to caution and to the avoiding of similar occurrences, with them was a spur to new calamities; and the end of one misery was invariably the beginning of another. So they were still more eager to get at the Romans in the hope that in damaging them they would requite Josephus. Such was the excitement that held Jerusalem in its grip.

Vespasian decided to acquaint himself with Agrippa's kingdom. He had been invited by the king himself, who was anxious to entertain the commander-in-chief and his army to the full extent of his privy purse, and at the same time to use them to settle the troubles within his borders. Starting therefore from Caesarea on the coast he marched to Caesarea Philippi. There he rested his troops for three weeks while he himself attended state banquets and offered sacrifices to God in gratitude for his successes. But when he was informed that Tiberias was in a rebellious state and Tarichaeae had revolted already, each being part of Agrippa's dominions, resolved as he was to crush the Jews everywhere he decided that this was the moment to march against the rebels, and to repay Agrippa's hospitality by subduing his cities for him. So he sent his son Titus to Caesarea to bring the forces still there to Scythopolis – the biggest city of Decapolis, not far from Tiberias – where he himself met him. Advancing at the head of three legions he encamped three and a half miles from Tiberias at a station well within view of the rebels, called Sennabris. Then he sent the decurion Valerian with a troop of horse to make proposals of peace to the townsfolk and induce them to give pledges; for he had heard that the people were anxious for peace, but were being driven into war by a powerful faction.

Valerian rode to Tiberias, and when he was near the wall

dismounted and made his men do the same, that they might not be thought to have come to skirmish. But before any words were exchanged the leading rebels sallied out against him weapons in hand, led by one Jeshua son of Shaphat, the supreme head of the terrorist gang. Valerian thought it unsafe to join battle against the general's orders even if victory was certain, and very dangerous indeed for a handful of men caught off their guard to engage a large force which had the initiative. Besides, he was disconcerted by the unexpected daring of the Jews. So he fled on foot, and five others similarly abandoned their horses, which Jeshua and his men brought back to the city as delighted as if they had captured them in battle, not by surprise. This so alarmed the elder citizens and acknowledged leaders that they fled to the Roman camp, and calling the king to their aid threw themselves at Vespasian's feet, entreating him not to reject their appeal, or impute the madness of a few to the entire city, but to spare the citizens, who had been friendly to the Romans at all times, and punish only those responsible for the revolt, but for whom they themselves would have been only too glad to make their submission long ago. To these entreaties the general yielded, though the seizure of his horses made him angry with the whole city; for Agrippa's concern for his subjects was evident. As the delegates had made their submission in the name of all the citizens, Jeshua and his supporters decided that Tiberias was no longer a healthy place to stay in, and made a dash for Tarichaeae.

Next day Vespasian sent forward a body of horse under Trajan as far as the ridge to find out whether the whole population was peaceminded. As soon as he felt sure that the citizens were unanimous in supporting their representatives, he marched his army to the city. The people opened their gates to him and met him with acclamations, calling him their saviour and benefactor. As the army was held up by the narrowness of the entrances, Vespasian ordered his men to break through the south wall, and thus made a wide passage for them. Plundering and violence, however, he ruled out in deference to the king, who induced him also to spare the walls by guaranteeing the future loyalty of the inhabitants. Thus after suffering grievously from its internal divisions the city received a new lease of life.

Then marching to a spot between Tiberias and Tarichaeae Vespasian pitched his camp, making it unusually strong, in case he was held up there by prolonged fighting; for into Tarichaeae was pouring an endless stream of insurgents, who relied on the strength of the town and the protection of the lake known locally as Gennesaret. The town was situated, like Tiberias, at the foot of the mountains, and except where it was washed by the lake it had been fortified all round by Josephus – strongly, but not as strongly as Tiberias; for there the rampart had been built in the early stages of the revolt when he had unlimited money and power, but Tarichaeae had only enjoyed the remnants of his munificence. The occupants had a large number of boats ready on the lake to evacuate them if defeated on land, and equipped for a sea fight if necessary. While the Romans were fortifying their camp, Jeshua and his supporters, fearless in the face of the numbers and perfect discipline of the enemy, made a sortie and at the first onset scattered the working-party and tore down a short length of the wall. But when they saw the legionaries forming up, they avoided all loss by a rapid withdrawal to their own lines. When the pursuing Romans forced them to take to their boats, they put out from shore but kept the Romans within bowshot, then dropped anchor with their vessels side by side like infantrymen standing shoulder to shoulder, and engaged in a sea fight with their enemy on land.

Meantime Vespasian, learning that the great bulk of them were formed up on the plain before the town, sent his son with 600 picked troopers. He, finding himself seriously outnumbered, sent a request to his father for reinforcements. In the meantime, seeing that while most of his troopers were eager to fight without waiting for help to arrive, some few could not hide their consternation at the Jews' advantage in numbers, he took his stand where all could hear him and began:

'Romans, I cannot begin better than by reminding you of the name you bear, that you may realize how different we are from the men we are going to fight. From our hands nothing in the wide world has hitherto escaped; the Jews, we must admit, have not yet shown any sign of lying down under defeat. It would be a shocking thing if, when they stand unbowed in the midst of disaster, we should flag in the midst of success. The enthusiasm you outwardly display I am delighted to see, but I fear the enemy's advantage in numbers may produce in a few of you a secret fear. If so, they should again ponder the difference between their opponents and themselves, and the fact that the Jews, though extremely bold and contemptuous of death, have neither discipline nor experience of war, and are nothing but a rabble, not fit to be called an army. Of our own experience and discipline nothing need be said. But our object in being the one people to undergo military training in peacetime is that in war we may not have to com-pare our numbers with our opponents'. What should we gain be being constantly on active service, if we needed equal numbers to oppose a mob of raw recruits?

'Remember again that you are fighting in full armour against men who have none, that you are horse and they are foot, that you have leaders and they are leaderless. These advantages make you in effect far more numerous than you are, while the enemy's dis-advantages make their numbers count for very little. Wars are won, not by the size of an army however skilful, but by courage however tiny the forces available. Small forces can be quickly deployed and can readily support each other, while swollen armies do themselves more damage than the enemy can do. The Jews are inspired by reckless audacity and desperation, emotions that invigorate while things go well but are extinguished by the smallest setback. We are inspired by disciplined courage and fortitude, which in prosperity reaches its greatest heights and in adversity endures to the end. And you will be fighting for a greater prize than the Jews; for though they face the dangers of war to defend the liberty of their country, what greater prize could you win than glory, and the assurance that after mastering the whole world we do not acknowledge the Jews as rivals? Observe too that there is no fear of our suffering any irretrievable disaster. Ample reinforcements are at hand; but we can snatch the victory our-selves, and we must not wait for the men my father is sending to support us: if no one shares it, our triumph will be the greater.

'My own feeling is that at this moment my father is on trial, so am I, and so are you. Does he deserve his past triumphs? Do I deserve to be his son, and you to be my soldiers? With *him* victory is a habit; *I* could not bear to return to him defeated; would *you* not be ashamed if your commander led the way into danger and you failed to follow? I *shall* lead the way, you may be sure, and shall be the first to charge the enemy. So don't you fail me, or doubt for a moment that with God at my side my efforts are bound to succeed. I tell you plainly in advance that in fighting here outside the walls we shall win a far-reaching triumph.'

As Titus delivered this address a sudden wave of enthusiasm swept the men off their feet; and when Trajan arrived before the battle with 400 horse they were vexed that the victory would bring them less credit through being shared. Vespasian also sent Antonius Silo with

2,000 bowmen, who were to seize the hill opposite the town and pin down the defenders on the wall. These orders were carried out, and every attempt to bring help from within was frustrated. Meanwhile Titus galloped to the front and charged the enemy; with loud hurrahs the rest followed, extending their line across the plain to the length of the enemy front, and so giving the impression of much greater numbers than they possessed. The Jews, though taken aback by their discipline and dash, for a time stood up to the onslaught; but pierced by lances and overborne by the momentum of horses and men they were trampled underfoot, and death reigned everywhere. The survivors scattered and fled to the town, every man as fast as he could run. Titus, hard on their heels, cut down the stragglers, drove through tight masses, rode past other groups and charged them from the front, pulverized many by leaping among them as they got in each other's way, headed them all off as they fled towards the walls, and turned them back towards the plain until by weight of numbers they forced their way through and sought safety in the town.

Once within the walls they were again involved in party strife. The residents clung to their possessions and their town, and had been opposed to the war from the first; now after the defeat they were still more opposed to it. But the newcomers, who were very numerous, insisted all the more, both sides lost their tempers, and the shouting and uproar made it evident that they would soon be at each other's throats. Hearing the commotion Titus, who was not far from the wall, exclaimed: 'Now is your chance, men; why hesitate, when the Jews are ours for the asking? Seize your opportunity! Do you not hear the row? The men who have slipped through our fingers are fighting each other! The town is ours if we make haste; but we will have to work hard and fight hard too. Great prizes cannot be won without taking risks. We must not wait for the enemy to make up their quarrel – necessity will reconcile them soon enough; and we must not wait for reinforcements either – we have beaten a whole army with a handful of men, and now we will capture the town by ourselves.'

With these words he leapt into the saddle and led the way to the lake. Riding through the water he entered the town at the head of his men. His audacity filled the defenders with terror, and not a man stayed to offer the least resistance. Abandoning their posts Jeshua and his supporters fled across country, while the rest rushed down to the lake where they ran into the enemy advancing to meet them. Some were killed as they got into their boats, others as they tried to swim to those who had put out before. In the town the streets ran with blood, the same fate befalling newcomers who had not escaped in time and now tried to resist and the residents who offered no resistance at all, as in the hope of their submission being accepted and the knowledge that they had opposed the war they refused to fight. At last Titus, having disposed of the culprits, took pity on the residents and put an end to the slaughter. Those who had taken refuge on the lake, when they saw that the town had fallen, put out as far from the enemy as they could.

Titus sent a dispatch-rider to give his father the good news of what had happened. Vespasian was naturally delighted at his son's prowess and at the resounding victory, thinking that a very important chapter of the war had been brought to a close. Going at once to the scene he ordered the town to be encircled by guards: if anyone slipped out he must be killed. The next day he went down to the lake and ordered rafts to be put together for the pursuit of the fugitives. These were soon ready, as there was abundance of wood and no lack of carpenters.

Lake Gennesareth takes its name from the region adjoining it. Though it measures 16 miles by 4½ its water is most delicious; for it is clearer than cloudy marsh water and quite pure, as on every side it ends in a sandy beach. When drawn it is pleasantly warm, more agreeable than river or spring water but always cooler than one would expect from a lake of that size. It is as cold as snow when exposed to the air – a regular practice of the local people on summer nights. The species of fish that live in the lake differ in taste and appearance from those found elsewhere. Right through the middle flows the Jordan. Jordan is believed to rise at Paneum: actually it flows there out of sight underground from the Bowl. Anyone going up into Trachonitis will find this pool 14 miles from Caesarea,[1] not very far to the right of the road. It is very aptly called the Bowl because of its shape, being as round as a wheel: the water always remains level with its brim, neither sinking nor running over. For a long time it was not known that the Jordan rose there, but the truth was established by the tetrarch of Trachonitis, Philip, who threw chaff into the Bowl and found it came to the surface at Paneum, which earlier generations had believed to be the source of the river. Paneum, naturally beautiful, has been further embellished by royal bounty, being adorned at Agrippa's expense. The visible

1. *Caesarea Philippi.*

course of the Jordan begins at this cavern, cuts through the still, marshy waters of Lake Semechonitis,[1] covers another 14 miles, and after passing the city of Julias goes straight through the middle of Lake Gennesareth, then after a long journey through desert country finishes up in the Dead Sea.

Alongside Lake Gennesareth is a stretch of country with the same name, wonderful in its characteristics and in its beauty. Thanks to the rich soil there is not a plant that does not flourish there, and the inhabitants grow everything: the air is so temperate that it suits the most diverse species. Walnuts, most winter-loving of trees, flourish in abundance, as do palms, which thrive on heat, side by side with figs and olives, for which a milder air is indicated. One might deem it nature's crowning achievement to force together into one spot natural enemies and to bring the seasons into healthy rivalry, each as it were laying claim to the region. For not only does it produce the most surprisingly diverse fruits; it maintains a continuous supply. Those royal fruits the grape and the fig it furnishes for ten months on end, the rest ripening on the trees all year round; for apart from the temperate atmosphere it is watered by a spring with great fertilizing power, known locally as Capernaum. Some have thought this an offshoot of the Nile, as it breeds a fish very like the perch caught in the lake of Alexandria. The length of the region measured along the shore of the lake that bears the same name is 3½ miles, the width 2½. Such is the character of the locality.

Preparations completed, he put on board as much of his force as he thought adequate to deal with their opponents in the boats, and the pursuit began. Thus encircled the Jews could neither escape to land, where the enemy were in full possession, nor fight it out on the water with any hope of success. Their boats were small and built for piracy, and were weak in comparison with the rafts, and the men on board each one were so few that they dared not come to grips with the Romans who attacked them in mass formation. However, they circled round the rafts and sometimes even approached, pelting the Romans with stones at long range, then scraping past and attacking them at close quarters. In either case they got the worst of it: their shower of stones merely rattled on the Roman armour while they themselves were targets for Roman arrows; and when they ventured to approach they had no time to do anything before disaster overtook them and

1. *Lake Huleh.*

they went down, boats and all. Some tried to break through, but the Romans were near enough to transfix many of them with their lances, killing others by leaping into the boats sword in hand. Some, as the rafts closed in, were caught in the middle and destroyed along with their craft. If any of those who had been plunged into the water came to the surface, they were dispatched with an arrow or caught by a raft. If in their extremity they attempted to climb on board, their heads or hands were severed by the Romans. Vast numbers of Jews perished in countless ways on every side, until the fleeing remnant were driven to the shore, their craft completely surrounded. As they poured out of them many were struck down while still in the water; many who had leapt clear were destroyed by the Romans on the beach. A fearful sight met the eyes – the entire lake stained with blood and crammed with corpses; for there was not a single survivor. During the days that followed a horrible stench hung over the region. The beaches were thick with wrecks and swollen bodies which, hot and steaming in the sun, made the air so foul that the calamity not only horrified the Jews but revolted even those who had brought it about. Such was the outcome of this naval engagement. The dead, including those who earlier perished in the town, totalled 6,700.

After the battle Vespasian held a court-martial in Tarichaeae. Making a distinction between the residents and the newcomers whom he considered responsible for the war, he put the question to his staff whether these too should be spared. The verdict was that it would be against the public interest to set them free: if released they would not keep the peace, being stateless refugees, in a position to induce those who sheltered them to take up arms. Vespasian decided that they did not deserve to be spared, and that if they were released they would injure those who had set them free, but he was not sure of the right way to get rid of them. If he killed them then and there he suspected that he would antagonize the residents, who would be outraged by the execution of so many suppliants in their midst, and he could not think of letting them go under safe-conduct and then setting upon them. However, his advisers got their way by arguing that Jews had no rights whatever, and that expediency must be preferred to conventional morality whenever the two were in conflict. So he gave the doomed men a guarantee of safety in ambiguous terms, permitting them to leave only by the road that led to Tiberias. Instantly falling into the trap and suspecting nothing, they loaded themselves with their possessions quite openly and set out along the permitted route. Meanwhile the Romans lined the road all the way to Tiberias so that no one could leave it, and shut them up in the city. Vespasian followed and herded them all into the Stadium. The aged and useless, 1,200 of them, were disposed of by his orders. From the young men he picked out the 6,000 strongest and sent them to Nero at the Isthmus.[1] The rest of the people to the number of 30,400 he auctioned, except those he presented to Agrippa; the men who came from his kingdom Vespasian allowed him to deal with as he pleased, and the king put them too under the hammer. The rest of the mob came from Trachonitis, Gaulonitis, Hippos, and the Gadarene district, and was largely composed of rebels and fugitives whose unsavoury reputation in peacetime made war seem to them attractive. Disaster overtook them on the 8th of Gorpiaios.

After the fall of Jotapata some of the Galilaeans had remained in revolt against Rome; but when Tarichaeae was overwhelmed they surrendered, and the Romans took over all the fortresses and towns except Gischala and the garrison of Mt Tabor. These were supported by Gamala, a town opposite Tarichaeae on the opposite side of the lake. This town was in the territory assigned to Agrippa, as were Sogane and Seleucia. Gamala and Sogane both belonged to Gaulonitis, Sogane being part of Upper Gaulan, as it is called, and Gamala of Lower. Seleucia was near Lake Semechonitis. This lake is three and a half miles wide and seven long. Its marshes stretch as far as Daphne, a pleasant spot in many ways, with springs that feed the Little Jordan under the temple of the golden cow[2] and send it pouring into the Jordan proper. Sogane and Seleucia had been persuaded at the beginning of the revolt to submit to Agrippa; but Gamala had refused to surrender, relying on its inaccessibility even more than Jotapata had done. Sloping down from a towering peak is a spur like a long shaggy neck, behind which rises a symmetrical hump, so that the outline resembles that of a camel; hence the name, the exact form of the word being obscured by the local pronunciation. On the face and both sides it is cut off by impassable ravines. Near the tail it is rather more accessible, where it is detached from the hill; but here too, by digging a trench across, the inhabitants made access very difficult. Built against the almost vertical flank the houses were piled on top of one another, and the town seemed to be hung in air and on the point of tumbling on

1. Nero, who had recently cut the first sod, required navvies to dig the Corinth Canal.
2. At Dan.

top of itself from its very steepness. It faced south and its southern crest, which rose to an immense height, served as citadel, resting on an unwalled precipice that went straight down into the deepest ravine. There was a spring inside the wall at the far side of the town.

Nature having thus made the town well nigh impregnable, Josephus had walled it round and given it the additional protection of trenches and underground passages. Thanks to the natural strength of the position its occupants were more confident than the Jotapatans had been, but they had much fewer fighting-men, being so sure of their defences that they would not admit more. For the town was crowded with refugees because of the protection it offered, as proved by the fact that the forces previously sent by Agrippa to besiege it had made no headway after seven months.

Vespasian set out from Ammathus (i.e. 'warm baths': the town contains a spring of warm water with medicinal qualities) where he had been encamped before Tiberias, and marched to Gamala. Unable to put an unbroken ring of men round the town because of its situation, he posted sentries wherever he could and occupied the hill that overlooked it. When the legions had fortified their camps in the usual way on its slopes, he began to construct platforms at the tail end. In the eastern part of the ridge where rose the highest of the towers the construction was done by the Fifteenth Legion, the Fifth worked opposite the middle of the town, and the filling in of the trenches and ravines was undertaken by the Tenth.

At this juncture King Agrippa approached the walls, and was trying to discuss terms of surrender with the defenders when one of the slingers hit him on the right elbow with a stone. He was immediately surrounded by his own men, but the determination of the Romans to press the siege was redoubled both by indignation on the king's account and by anxiety for their own safety; for men who displayed such savagery towards one of their own race who advised them in their own interest would stick at no brutality in treating foreigners and enemies.

With so many skilled hands the platforms were soon finished and the engines brought up. Chares and Joseph, the most effective leaders in the town, lined up their armed forces, though they had already lost heart because they had little hope of withstanding the siege for long, being short of water and other necessaries. However, their leaders laughed at their fears and led them out on to the wall. For a time they beat back those who were bringing up the engines, but becoming the target for the catapults and stone-throwers they withdrew into the town. Then the Romans brought up the Rams at three points, and battering their way through the wall poured in through the breaches with a great blare of trumpets and din of weapons, and shouting themselves hoarse flung themselves upon the defenders of the town. They for a time stood firm against the first waves of attackers, and offering strenuous resistance prevented the Romans from advancing further. But under heavy pressure from all directions they withdrew to the upper parts of the town, and as the enemy pursued them they swung round and counter-attacked vigorously. Swept down the slope and jammed inextricably in the narrow alleys, the Romans suffered fearful casualties. Unable either to resist those above them or to force their way through the advancing mass of their companions, they climbed on to the roofs of the houses where they rested against the slope. Crowded with men and unequal to the weight these quickly collapsed. As one fell it knocked down many of those underneath, and so on to the bottom. The effect on the Romans was devastating. Completely at a loss, even when they saw the roofs falling in they jumped on to them. Many were buried under the debris, many while trying to escape found one limb or another pinned down, still more were choked by the dust. Seeing in this the hand of God and indifferent to their own losses, the men of Gamala pressed their attack, driving the enemy on to the roofs as they stumbled in the steep, narrow ways, and with a rain of weapons from above dispatching those who fell. The debris furnished them with any number of great stones, and the bodies of the enemy with cold steel: they wrenched the swords from the fallen and used them to finish off those who were slow to die. Many as the houses were actually falling flung themselves to their death. Not even those who fled found it easy to get away; for unacquainted with the roads and choked with the dust they could not even recognize their friends, but in utter confusion attacked each other. At last after long search they found the outlets and escaped from the town.

Vespasian, keeping as close as he could to his struggling soldiers, and deeply moved by the sight of the town falling in ruins about his army, had forgotten his own safety, and without realizing it had gradually reached the highest level of the town, where he found himself in the utmost peril and almost alone. Not even his son Titus was with him at this time, having just been sent to Mucianus in Syria. Flight seemed both dangerous and disgraceful; so remembering his lifetime of struggle and his reputation for prowess he became like one inspired, made his men link their shields to cover their armed bodies, stemmed the wave of attackers that swept down from above, and heedless of the swarms of men and the hail of missiles stood firm, until overawed by his superhuman courage the enemy slackened their attacks. Relieved of their pressure he withdrew step by step, not turning his back till he was outside the walls. Roman losses in this battle were very heavy. One of the fallen was the decurion Aebutius, a man who not only in the action in which he fell but in many earlier battles had shown heroic courage and inflicted very heavy casualties on the Jews. A centurion named Gallus, cut off with ten soldiers in the mêlée, crept into somebody's house. Like the others he was a Syrian, and he overheard the occupants discussing over supper how they would deal with the Romans and look after themselves. In the night he emerged from hiding, cut all their throats, and with his men got back safely to the Roman lines.

Roman morale had suffered severely. Defeat was unfamiliar, disaster on this scale unprecedented, and the soldiers burned with shame to think they had left their commander to his fate. But Vespasian consoled them, suppressing any allusion to himself to avoid the least semblance of reproof. 'What might happen to anyone you must face,' he said, 'like men. Remember it is in the nature of war that bloodless victories do not happen: "fickle-footed Fortune" spares no one. You have killed thousands and thousands of Jews, and her ladyship has only exacted a token payment. If it is vulgar to crow over victory, it is just as cowardly to whine under defeat. You never know how long either will last. A first-class soldier never lets success go to his head; that is why failure never gets him down. As for recent events, they were not due to any slackness of ours or to Jewish prowess: their gain and our loss both came from the difficulty of the ground. With that in mind you might be blamed for your reckless impetuosity: when the enemy retired to the higher ground you should have restrained yourselves and not run your heads into the danger that hung over you. As you were masters of the lower town you should have gradually enticed the enemy down to where you could meet them safely on firm ground. Instead, in your headlong dash for victory you forgot all about safety. Such recklessness in war, such crazy impetuosity is foreign to us Romans, who win all our victories by efficiency and discipline; it is the vice of backward races and the chief cause of Jewish defeats. Well then! It is up to us to rely once more on our own superiority and to see red rather than be down in the mouth about an unlucky reverse. The best encouragement each of you will find is his own right arm; that is how you can avenge the killed and punish the killers. For my own part, I shall try, in this and every battle, to be first to get at the enemy and the last to leave the field.'

With this address Vespasian restored the morale of his army. Meanwhile the people of Gamala were for the moment cheered by their success, so unexpected and so overwhelming; but later, when they realized that they had robbed themselves of any hope of coming to terms and knew in their hearts that they could not escape – already they were short of supplies – they became terribly despondent and their courage failed them. However, they did what they could to make themselves safe: the bolder spirits guarded the gaps in the wall, the rest lined the battlements still standing. But when the Romans raised the platform higher and tried a new assault, most of them began to run out of the town, down almost impassable ravines where no picquets had been posted or through the underground passages. The few who remained from fear of being captured were starving, for every corner had been scraped bare to supply the fighting-men.

While in spite of these privations Gamala still held out, Vespasian diverted some of his strength to deal with the garrison of Mt Tabor, midway between Scythopolis and the Great Plain. This mountain is no less than 20,000 feet high, with the northern face almost unclimbable; the top is a plateau three miles long with a wall right round.[1] This huge rampart Josephus had built in forty days, drawing the material from below, and even his water, as the occupants had nothing but rain. On this plateau vast numbers had gathered; so Vespasian dispatched 600 horsemen under Placidus. He, finding the ascent impossible, called on the rank and file to make peace, offering to intercede for them and obtain terms. They came down, intending to meet guile with guile. Placidus had wooed them with honeyed words in order to capture them in the plain; they came down in apparent compliance, intending to attack him off his guard. However, Placidus won the battle of wits; for when the Jews began the fight he pretended to flee, drew his pursuers far into the plain, turned his horsemen about and routed the enemy, killing vast numbers of them and cutting off the rest so that they could not return. These gave up Tabor for lost

1. *Josephus has multiplied the length by five and the height by ten!*

and fled to Jerusalem; the natives, their safety being guaranteed and their water having failed, handed themselves and the mountain over to Placidus.

At Gamala the more venturesome were slipping away unnoticed, while the combatants sustained the siege and the non-combatants died of starvation. On the 22nd of Hyperberetaios, shortly before stand-to, three soldiers of the Fifteenth Legion crept up to the tower that projected opposite them and noiselessly undermined it. In the darkness the sentries on its battlements failed to observe them either during or after their arrival. Working in silence the soldiers rolled away the five stones forming the base. As they jumped out of the way the tower fell with a resounding crash, bringing the sentries down with it. The other sentry-groups fled in panic; many made a bold effort to break through but were cut down by the Romans, among them Joseph, who was killed by a chance shot as he tried to escape through a gap in the wall. Bewildered by the crash, the whole population lost their heads and ran in all directions as if the entire Roman army had broken in. At that moment Chares, confined to bed and in the doctor's hands, expired, his death caused by terror as much as by his illness. The Romans, however, mindful of their earlier failure, made no attempt to force their way in, till on the 23rd of the month Titus returned and, furious at the blow that had fallen on the Romans in his absence, chose 200 cavalry and some infantry and noiselessly entered the town. Discovering this when he was already inside, the sentry-groups gave the alarm and rushed to their posts. In a moment news of the Roman entry reached the centre of the town. Some snatched their children and dragging their wives with them fled to the citadel, wailing and shouting; others went to meet Titus and were without exception killed. Many were prevented from running up to the heights, and in their helplessness fell into the hands of the Roman guards. There were heart-rending cries as men were slaughtered on every side, and the whole town was deluged with the blood that poured down the slopes.

To deal with those who had retired to the citadel Vespasian came in person at the head of his entire force. The hill-top was rocky and inaccessible on every side, soaring to an immense height, ringed with precipices and thick with people all round. There the Jews inflicted heavy casualties on their attackers, rolling down rocks and hurling missiles of every kind, while they themselves on their lofty perch were almost out of reach. But to ensure their destruction they were struck full in the face by a miraculous tempest, which carried the Roman shafts up to them but checked and turned aside their own. So violent was the blast that they could neither keep their feet on the narrow ledges, having no proper foothold, nor see the approaching enemy. Up came the Romans and hemmed them in: whether they resisted or tried to surrender their fate was the same, for the Romans boiled with rage against them all when they remembered those who perished in the first onslaught. Despairing of escape and hemmed in every way, they flung their wives and children and themselves too into the immensely deep artificial ravine that yawned under the citadel. In fact the fury of the victors seemed less destructive than the suicidal frenzy of the trapped men; 4,000 fell by Roman swords, but those who plunged to destruction proved to be over 5,000. The sole survivors were two women, nieces of Philip son of Jacimus, a man of note who had commanded King Agrippa's army. They survived because when the town fell they eluded the fury of the Romans, who spared then not even babes in arms, but seized all they found and slung them from the citadel. Thus Gamala fell on the 23rd of Hyperberetaios, the revolt having begun on the 24th of Gorpiaios.

CHAPTER 14

Factions in Jerusalem

ONLY Gischala, a little town in Galilee, was left unreduced. The inhabitants were anxious for peace – for the most part they were farmers whose only concern was the prospect of a good harvest; but a powerful gang of bandits had infiltrated into their midst and some of the townsmen had been infected. These were incited and organized for revolt by John son of Levi, an impostor expert in every wile, full of ambitions and with a knack of making them succeed. Anyone could see that he was bent on war as a means of becoming dictator. He was the recognized leader of the insurgent element in Gischala; thanks to them the population, who would gladly have sent envoys offering to surrender, were now preparing a warlike reception for the Romans. To crush this opposition Vespasian dispatched Titus with 1,000 horse, removing the Tenth Legion to Scythopolis. He himself returned to Caesarea with the other two, to rest them after their continuous efforts and in the belief that good living in the city would make them fit and keen in readiness for the coming struggles. It was no light task that he saw awaiting him at Jerusalem, for she was the city of kings and capital of the whole race, and into her was flowing a stream of refugees from the war. Her natural strength and formidable walls caused him no small anxiety; and he realized that the daring spirits within would, even without walls, be hard to subdue. So he trained his soldiers like athletes before a contest.

When Titus rode up to Gischala he saw it would be easy to take the town by assault; but he knew that if it was stormed there would be a wholesale massacre of the population by the soldiery, and he was already sick of bloodshed and grieved that the whole people, without distinction, must share the fate of the guilty. He was therefore anxious to persuade the town to surrender on terms. The wall was crowded with men, mostly members of the corrupt gang; so he asked them what gave them such confidence that when every other town had fallen they alone opposed the Roman arms. They had seen much stronger towns overthrown by a single assault, while all who had accepted Roman terms enjoyed their own possessions in safety. The same terms he now offered them, freely forgiving their truculence. To desire freedom was natural enough: to persist when no possibility remained was inexcusable. If they refused to accept his generous proposals and sincere offers, they would experience the remorselessness of his arms, and learn the terrible lesson that to the Roman engines their wall was just a toy – the wall that gave them such confidence that they were the only Galilaeans to show themselves truculent prisoners.

To these overtures none of the townspeople could make any reply – they could not even go on to the wall; the bandits had already occupied it all, and there were sentries at the gates to see that no one slipped out to accept the offered truce or admitted any of the cavalry into the town. But John replied that he welcomed the proposals himself and would either persuade or constrain any dissidents. However, in accordance with the Jewish Law, Titus must allow them that day, the seventh, on which it was an offence either to take up arms or to make peace. It was known even to the Romans that they did no work of any kind when the seventh day came round; if they were compelled to break that rule, the man who compelled them would be as guilty as themselves. The delay would do Titus no harm; what could be attempted in one night except flight, which would be impossible if he camped round the town? It would be a great gain to them not to infringe any ancestral custom; and gracious in one who granted an unlooked-for peace to respect the laws of those whose lives he spared. With such pleas John beguiled Titus, being less anxious about the seventh day than about his own skin. He was afraid of being left to his fate the moment the town fell, and pinned his hopes of life on darkness and flight. But clearly God was preserving John to bring destruction on Jerusalem, and it was His doing that Titus not only accepted this pretext for delay, but even pitched his camp further from the town, at Cydoessa. This is a strong inland village of the Tyrians, always engaged in bitter strife with the Galilaeans. The size of the population and the strength of the defences enabled it to maintain the struggle against the surrounding nation.

In the night John, seeing no Roman guards round the town, seized his chance, and taking with him not only his armed bodyguard but a large number of non-combatants with their families, fled towards Jerusalem. For two miles or more he managed to carry along a mob of women and children, though spurred on by fear of prison and death; but as he pressed on further they dropped behind, and agonizing were the lamentations of those thus abandoned. The further each found himself from his own kith and kin, the nearer he imagined himself to the enemy. Believing that their captors were hard on their heels, they lost their heads and turned when they heard the footsteps of their fleeing companions, as if their pursuers were upon them. Many lost their way, and even on the highroad many were crushed in the fight to get to the front. Miserable was the plight of women and children; some even ventured to call their husbands or kinsmen back, shrieking and imploring them to wait. But John's commands were obeyed: 'Every man for himself,' he shouted; 'make for the place where you can avenge those left behind, if they fall into Roman hands.' So as every man made what speed his strength allowed, the column of fugitives lengthened out.

When dawn came Titus advanced to the wall to conclude the treaty. The people opened the gates to him, and coming forward with their families hailed him as a benefactor who had delivered the town from oppression. They told him of John's flight and begged him to spare them and to come and punish the remaining rebels. Titus, deciding that the people's requests must take second place, sent a detachment of horse to pursue John, but they failed to overtake him and he reached Jerusalem in safety. Of those who had set out with him, however, some 6,000 were killed, and nearly 3,000 women and children were rounded up and brought back. Titus was vexed at his failure to inflict immediate punishment on John for his deception; but for his baffled rage he had compensation enough in the mass of prisoners and heaps of dead. So he entered the town amid acclamations, and ordering his men to tear down a short section of the wall in token of capture used threats rather than punishment to subdue the disturbers of the peace. For many from personal animosity and private enmity would denounce the innocent, if he tried to pick out those who deserved punishment; it was better to leave the guilty in suspense and fear than to destroy any guiltless person with them; for the guilty man would perhaps change his ways from fear of punishment, appreciating the pardon he had received for the past; but for those needlessly put to death there could be no redress. However, he made the town safe with a garrison, by which he could restrain the disaffected and leave the peaceably inclined more secure.

Thus the whole of Galilee was subdued, after giving the Romans plenty of strenuous exercise in preparation for the assault on Jerusalem.

On John's arrival there the whole population turned out, and round each of his companions in flight a vast crowd collected, crying for news of events outside. Still hot and breathless the fugitives could not hide the stress they were under, but they swaggered in their sorry plight, declaring they had not run from the Romans but had come to give them battle on favourable ground. Obviously it would be senseless and futile to risk their lives in a hopeless struggle for Gischala and other weak little towns, when they ought to save their arms and energies for the united defence of the Capital. Then they mentioned in passing the capture of Gischala, but what they euphemistically described as their withdrawal was generally seen to have been a rout. When, however, the fate of the prisoners became known, utter dismay seized the people, who saw in it an unmistakable omen of their own. John himself, quite unconcerned for those he had left behind, went round urging them one and all to war by false hopes, making out that Roman power was feeble, exaggerating Jewish strength, and ridiculing the ignorance of the inexperienced. Not even if they grew wings could the Romans ever get over the wall of Jerusalem, after being so severely mauled in their attacks on Galilaean villages and wearing out their engines against flimsy walls.

With this nonsense he drew most of the young men into his net and whetted their appetite for war, but of the sensible, older men there was not one but saw what was coming and mourned for the City as if it had perished already. Such was the confused state of the people, but the country population had been torn by dissension before faction reared its head in Jerusalem. For Titus had left Gischala for Caesarea, and Vespasian had marched from Caesarea to Jamnia and Azotus. These towns he reduced and garrisoned, returning with a mass of people who had surrendered on terms. Every town was seething with turmoil and civil war, and as soon as the Romans gave them a breathing-space they turned their hands against each other. Between advocates of war and lovers of peace there was a fierce quarrel. First of all in the home family unity was disrupted by partisan bitterness; then the nearest kinsmen severed all ties of blood, and attaching themselves to men who thought as they did lined up on opposite sides. Faction reigned everywhere, the revolutionaries and jingoes with the boldness of youth silencing the old and sensible. They began by one and all plundering their neighbours, then forming themselves into companies they extended their brigandage all over the country, so that in lawless brutality the Romans were no worse than the victims' own countrymen – in fact those who were stripped bare thought it far preferable to be captured by the Romans.

The garrisons of the towns, partly to avoid trouble and partly to spite the Jews, did little or nothing to protect those attacked. When at last the leaders of the various gangs of bandits had had enough of plundering the countryside, they came together and formed a single pack of rogues. Then they infiltrated into Jerusalem, a city without military command, where by age-old custom any of Jewish race were admitted without scrutiny, and where at this juncture everyone thought that those who were pouring in all came out of kindness as allies. It was this very thing that apart from the faction-fighting ultimately wrecked the City; for a useless and idle mob consumed supplies adequate for the fighting-men, and in addition to war they brought on themselves faction and starvation. Other bandits from the country slipped into the City, and joining forces with the desperadoes within gave themselves to every imaginable crime. They did not limit their insolence to theft and brigandage, but went so far as to commit murder, not by night or secretly or against the common people, but openly by day, beginning with the most eminent. First they seized and imprisoned Antipas, a member of the royal family and one of the most influential men in the City, entrusted with all the public funds. Next came Levias, an eminent man, and Sophas son of Raguel, both of royal blood, then all who were prominent in the country. Terror filled the people, and as if the City had been taken by storm no one thought of anything but his own safety.

The terrorists were not satisfied with imprisoning their captives; they thought it unsafe to keep men of influence in such custody for long, as their households were quite large enough to attempt their rescue, and the whole people might be incensed by their outrageous conduct to rise in revolt. So they decided to murder the prisoners, choosing for their tool the most bloodthirsty assassin among them, one John, whose father was called in the vernacular Dorcas. He with ten others went into the prison sword in hand and ran the prisoners through. This outrageous crime they justified with a monstrous lie; they alleged that the men had approached the Romans about surrendering Jerusalem, and had perished as traitors to their country. In fact, they boasted of their crimes as if they were benefactors and saviours of the City. The result was that the people became so cowed and abject, the terrorists so rabid, that they actually got control of the appointment of chief priests. Setting aside the families which in turn provided these, they appointed obscure persons of no family, to gain partners in crime; those who without deserving it found themselves in the highest office were inevitably the creatures of those who had put them there. Again, they sowed dissension between their rulers by various tricks and scandalous stories, turning the squabbles of those who might have restrained them to their own advantage, till sated with their crimes against men they transferred their insolence to the Deity and entered the Sanctuary with their feet polluted.

The populace were now seething with discontent, urged on by the oldest of the chief priests, Ananus, a man of the soundest judgement who might have saved the City if he had escaped the hands of the plotters. These made the Temple of God their stronghold and refuge from popular upheavals, and the Sanctuary became the centre for their illegal operations. Through their atrocities ran a vein of ironic pretence more exasperating than the actions themselves. For to test the submissiveness of the people and prove their own strength, they attempted to appoint the chief priests by lot, though as we said before the succession was by birth. The excuse given for this arrangement was ancient custom; they said that from time immemorial the chief priesthood had been conferred by lot. In reality this was a reversal of the regular practice and a device for consolidating their power by arbitrary appointments. Assembling one of the chief-priestly clans called Eniachin, they drew lots for a chief priest. The luck of the draw furnished the clearest proof of the depths to which they had sunk. The office fell to one Phanias son of Samuel, of the village of Aphtha, a man not only not descended from chief priests but too boorish to have any clear notion of what the chief-priesthood might be. Anyway they dragged him willy-nilly from his holding and disguised him from head to foot like an actor on the stage, robing him in the sacred vestments and teaching him his cues. To the perpetrators this shocking sacrilege was the occasion for ribald mirth, but the other priests, watching from a distance this mockery of their law, burst into tears, cut to the heart by this travesty of the sacred rites.

Such impudence was more than the people could stand: one and all determined to bring tyranny to an end. Natural leaders like Gorion, son of Joseph, and Gamaliel's son Symeon, by passionate appeals to public meetings and by a door-to-door canvass urged them to act now, punish the destroyers of freedom, and purge the Sanctuary of these blood-guilty men. The most respected of the chief priests, Jeshua

son of Gamalas and Ananus son of Ananus, held meetings at which
they took the people severely to task for their indifference and
incited them against the Zealots; for 'Zealots' they called themselves,
as if they were devoted to good works, not zealous for all that was vile –
vile beyond belief. The populace flocked to a mass meeting where
everyone denounced the invasion of the Sanctuary, the rapine and
bloodshed, but no one was prepared to resist, as it was obvious the
Zealots would be very difficult to tackle. So Ananus stood up in the
middle, and turning again and again to the Temple with his eyes full
of tears began thus:

'How wonderful it would have been if I had died before seeing
the house of God full of countless abominations and its unapproachable, sacred precincts crowded with those whose hands are red with
blood! Yet I who wear the vestments of a chief priest and answer to
the most honoured and august of names, am alive and in love with life,
and cannot face a death that would be the glory of my old age! And
so I'll go alone, and as if no one else existed I'll give my one life for
God. What is the use of living among people blind to calamity and no
longer capable of tackling the troubles on their hands? You are plundered without a protest, beaten without a murmur, witnesses of murder without one audible groan. What unbearable tyranny! But why
blame the tyrants? Don't they owe their existence to you and your
lack of spirit? Wasn't it you who shut your eyes when the gang was
first formed – a mere handful then – encouraged its growth by your
silence, and by standing idly by while they were arming turned those
arms against yourselves? The right thing was to nip their attacks in the
bud when they were pouring abuse on your own flesh and blood; but
you by your utter indifference encouraged these ruffians to plunder.
When houses were ransacked, nobody cared; so they seized their
owners too, and dragged them through the middle of the City without
anyone raising a finger to defend them. Next they flung into jail the
men you had let down – I will not say how many or of what character.
Uncharged, uncondemned, they were imprisoned without a soul
coming to the rescue. The natural consequence was that these same
men were seen murdered. We saw this too – they were like a herd
of dumb animals from which choice victims were in turn dragged
away; yet not a murmur was uttered, not a hand raised!

'Take it calmly then, take it calmly, when you watch your Sanctuary
trampled underfoot. You yourselves built every one of the steps by

which these sacrilegious wretches have climbed so insolently; do not grumble if they have reached the top. Why, by now they would undoubtedly have reached still dizzier heights if there had been anything greater than the Sanctuary to destroy!

'They have seized the strongest place in the City – from now on the Temple must be spoken of as a citadel or fort; tyranny is strongly entrenched and the enemy can be seen over your heads; but what do you mean to do? how can you quieten your fears? will you really wait for the Romans to recover our holy places? have things gone so far in the City, are we so sunk in misery, that we are an object of pity even to our foes? Why don't you rise, you spiritless creatures, and turn to meet the blows, and as you see beasts do kick out at your tormentors? Why don't you remember your own personal miseries, set before your eyes what you have suffered, whet your appetite for their blood? Have you really lost the most honourable and deep-rooted of our instincts, the longing for freedom? Are we in love with slavery and devoted to our masters, as if our father had taught us to be doormats? Why, again and again they fought to the bitter end for independence, defying the might of both Egypt and Persia rather than take orders from anyone! But why talk about our fathers? our present struggle with Rome – never mind whether it is profitable and advantageous or the opposite – what is its object? Isn't it freedom? Then shall we refuse to yield to the masters of the world and put up with tyrants of our own race? Yet submission to a foreign power might be put down to one crushing blow of fortune; but subservience to the scum of our own nation would prove us wilful degenerates.

'Having once mentioned the Romans I will make no secret of what occurred to me as I spoke and turned my thoughts in their direction. Even if we fall into their hands – I do not suggest we shall – we cannot suffer any worse treatment than these men have subjected us to. Could anything be more galling than first to see offerings left in the Temple by our enemies, then spoils seized by men of our own race who have robbed and massacred the nobility of our capital city, murdering men whom even the Romans would have spared in the hour of triumph? The Romans never went beyond the bounds set for unbelievers, never trampled on one of our sacred customs, but reverently gazed from a distance at the walls of the Sanctuary; and men born in this country, brought up in our customs and called Jews, stroll where they like in the Inner Sanctuary, their hands still reeking with the slaughter of their countrymen! In face of that can anyone dread a foreign war, and enemies by comparison far kinder to us than our own people? Why, if we are to call things by their right names, we might well find that the Romans are the champions of our Law, and its enemies are inside the City!

'But that these plotters against our liberty are the scum of the earth, that for what they have done no one could devise the punishment they deserve, I am sure you were all satisfied when you left home, and before I uttered a word you were furious with them because of the things they have made you suffer. Possibly most of you are terrified by their numbers and their temerity, and also by the advantage of their position. But these are the results of your inaction, and now will grow worse still if you procrastinate. Indeed their numbers are increasing daily, since birds of a feather flock together; their temerity is inflamed by the complete lack of opposition; and they will naturally make use of their commanding position and fortify it too, if we give them the chance. But rest assured that if we go over to the offensive they will be defeated by their own guilty conscience, and the advantage of height will be cancelled out by anxiety. Perhaps the Deity they have offended will turn their missiles against themselves, and the ungodly wretches will die by their own weapons. We have only to show ourselves and they are finished! Even if there is some danger involved, it will be a splendid thing to die before the sacred gateways and to sacrifice our lives, if not for our wives and children, yet for God and His Temple. I will champion your cause with head and hand; I will do everything I can think of to secure your safety, and every ounce of my bodily strength is at your disposal.'

With this eloquent appeal Ananus roused the populace against the Zealots, though well aware that they would be most difficult to suppress now, numerous, young, and intrepid as they were, and with such terrible crimes on their consciences; for they would hold out to the last, having no hope of pardon for what they had done. Nevertheless he was ready to endure anything rather than look on when affairs were in such a parlous state. The people for their part clamoured for him to lead them against the enemies he had denounced, every man most anxious to be in the forefront of the fight. But while Ananus was enlisting suitable men and organizing them for battle, the Zealots got wind of what was afoot, as they were kept informed of all that the people were doing. They were furious, and charged out of the

Temple en masse and in large gangs, sparing no one they encountered. The citizens' forces were quickly mustered by Ananus, superior in numbers, but in equipment and training far inferior to the Zealots. However, enthusiasm made up for the deficiencies on both sides. Those from the City fortified themselves with rage more powerful than weapons, those from the Temple with animal courage for which no numbers were a match; the former were convinced that it was impossible to stay in the City unless they rid her of the terrorists, the Zealots that unless they triumphed they would be spared no punishment. So they joined battle, with their passions in command. They started by pelting each other with stones in the streets and in front of the Temple and by hurling spears at long range. When either side retired the victors used their swords. The slaughter on both sides was frightful and the wounded could not be counted. Casualties on the people's side were carried into the houses by their relatives; if a Zealot was hit he went up into the Temple, leaving bloodstains on the sacred floor. It might indeed be said that their blood alone polluted the Sanctuary.

In these encounters the sudden sorties of the bandits were always successful; but the citizens' forces, blazing with fury and constantly growing in numbers, heaped abuse on all who wanted to surrender, while those who turned tail were unable to retire because of the men pushing forward from the rear. Thus they turned their whole strength against their opponents. They, unable to withstand this onslaught any longer, slowly retired into the Temple, Ananus and his men charging in with them. Alarmed by the loss of the first Court, they took refuge in the inner and at once locked the gates. Ananus could not bring himself to attack the sacred gateways, especially as the enemy were hurling missiles from above, and he deemed it unlawful, even if the attack succeeded, to bring in the City crowd unpurified; so he detailed 6,000 armed men to guard the colonnades. These were relieved by others, and every man had to take his turn as sentry; but many members of the upper classes were allowed by their superiors to hire men of humbler means to take their place on guard.

The whole of this citizen army was later destroyed – thanks to John, who, as the reader knows, had ratted from Gischala.

CHAPTER 15

Atrocities in the City. Vespasian's Intervention

JOHN was as crafty as a fox. He was eaten up with the love of despotic power and had long been engaged in treasonable activities. In the present crisis he pretended to be on the citizens' side and went everywhere with Ananus, whether to discuss the situation with the leading men by day or to visit the guardposts by night, afterwards betraying his secrets to the Zealots. Thus every question discussed by the citizens, even before a decision had been reached, was communicated by him to their mortal enemies. In his determination to avoid suspicion he showed the utmost obsequiousness to Ananus and the leaders of the citizens. But his efforts to impress produced the opposite result; for his lick-spittle attitude brought him under greater suspicion, and his habit of pushing his nose in everywhere without an invitation made it look as if he was betraying secrets. For evidently their enemies knew all their intentions, and no one had invited the suspicion of having disclosed them as had John. To get rid of him was another matter; he had strengthened his position by his atrocious conduct, and in any case was not one who could be disregarded; and he had built up a large following among members of the Central Council; so it was decided to make him take an oath of loyalty. John swore readily enough to be loyal to the citizens, to betray neither action nor intention to their enemies, and to put his powers of body and mind at their service for the destruction of their assailants. Ananus and his friends, satisfied with these oaths, now forgot their suspicions and invited him to their discussions: they even commissioned him to arrange a truce with the Zealots; for they were anxious that no act of theirs should desecrate the Temple and that no Jew should fall in its precincts.

John, however, as if he had sworn loyalty *to* the Zealots and not against them, went in, and placing himself in their midst declared that he had often run into danger for their sakes, to keep them informed of all the secret measures concerted against them by Ananus and his friends; now he was face to face with the greatest possible danger, and so were they all, unless providence came to their aid. Ananus was on the move; he had persuaded the people to send a delegation to Vespasian, requesting him to come with all speed and take over the City; and to injure the Zealots he had announced a purification ceremony for the morrow, so that his men could gain admittance either as worshippers or by force and attack them at close quarters. He did not see how they could hold out for long or stand up to such vast numbers. He added that it was by divine providence that he was the one commissioned to arrange a truce; Ananus was making these overtures in the hope of catching them off their guard. They must therefore either humbly beg their besiegers to spare their lives or obtain some help from outside. Anybody who cherished hopes of being pardoned if they suffered defeat must have forgotten their own black record, or imagine that when the offenders expressed regret their victims were obliged to forgive them at once. In actual fact wrongdoers often caused only disgust by eating humble pie, and the wronged were all the more furious when they found they had the whip hand. Lying in wait for the Zealots were the relatives and friends of the murdered, and a mass of people enraged by the suppression of laws and lawcourts. Even if a tiny section of these was sorry for them, the furious majority would obliterate it.

Such was the fanciful story he told to frighten them all. Precisely what 'help from outside' he had in mind he did not venture to explain, but he was hinting at the Idumaeans. To rouse the Zealot leaders to special fury he insinuated that Ananus was a savage brute whose threats were particularly meant for them. The leaders were Eleazar son of Simon, judged the most capable of devising suitable measures and carrying them out, and one Zachariah, son of Amphicalleus, both members of priestly families. When these two beside the general threats heard those directed against them personally, and were told that Ananus and his friends in their determination to make themselves dictators were calling in the Romans – another of John's slanders – they were quite at a loss what to do, being so desperately short of time; for the citizens were prepared to attack them quite soon, and the speed of this design had cut off all hope of reinforcement from outside, as they would be finished entirely before any of their allies was any the wiser. All the same they decided to call in the Idumaeans, and wrote a brief letter saying that Ananus had deceived the people and was betraying the Capital to the Romans; that they themselves had revolted in defence of their freedom and as a result were imprisoned in the Temple; that a few short moments would decide whether they should survive; and that unless the Idumaeans came to their aid with all speed, they would soon be in the hands of Ananus and their mortal enemies, and the City in the hands of the Romans. Further details the messengers were to communicate to the Idumaean chiefs orally. To convey the message they chose two men of great energy, fluent and convincing speakers on public affairs, and – still more important – exceptionally good runners. They knew the Idumaeans would promptly agree, as they were an excitable and undisciplined race, always on the look-out for trouble and with an appetite for revolution, ready at the least flattery from those who sought their aid to take up arms and dash into battle as if to a banquet. The message had to be delivered with all speed – this the messengers (both called Ananias) were only too eager to do, and they very soon reached the Idumaean headquarters.

The rulers, amazed by the letter and the explanations of the bearers, raced about the country like madmen, proclaiming mobilization. The muster was complete before the time appointed, and every man seized his arms to defend the freedom of the Capital. Forming an army 20,000 strong they marched to Jerusalem commanded by four generals, John and James the sons of Sosas, Simon son of Cathla, and Phineas son of Clusoth.

Neither Ananus nor the sentries had noticed the departure of the messengers, but they could not miss the arrival of the Idumaeans. Aware of it in good time Ananus barred the gates against them and posted sentries on the walls. Anxious however not to antagonize them completely he decided to try persuasion before resorting to arms. So taking his stand on the tower facing them Jeshua, the senior chief priest after Ananus, made this appeal.

'Many different disorders have gripped this city: no trick of fortune has astonished me so much as the way scoundrels have received support from unexpected quarters. You, for instance, have come here to help these dregs of humanity against us with more alacrity than could be expected even if the Capital had called on you to resist a foreign attack. If I saw any resemblance between you and those who have fetched you here, your enthusiasm would seem natural enough; no bond is as close as similarity of character. But actually, if they were examined one by one, none of them would be found fit to live a moment longer. The dregs, the scum of the whole country, they have squandered their own property and practised their lunacy upon the towns and villages around, and finally have poured in a stealthy stream into the Holy City, bandits so utterly ungodly that they have desecrated even hallowed ground. They may be seen now shamelessly getting drunk in the Sanctuary and spending what they have stolen from their victims to satisfy their bottomless appetite. But your great army in its shining array is a sight that would be welcomed if the Capital had by common consent invited you to support us against a foreign enemy. What could anybody call this but one of fortune's meanest tricks, when he sees an entire nation take up arms for the sake of the most despicable scoundrels?

'For a long time I have been asking myself what on earth made you move so suddenly. Without good cause you would never have armed yourselves from head to foot to support bandits against your kith and kin. When we heard Rome and treachery mentioned – that is what some of you were shouting a little while ago, and how you had come here to guard the freedom of the Capital – nothing these impudent wretches ever did surprised us as much as this lying invention. Men who are born lovers of liberty, and for liberty above all are ready to fight a foreign enemy, could in no other way be incited against us than by framing a charge that we were betraying their beloved liberty. Think who are the slanderers and who are their victims, and gather the truth not from fairy tales but from known facts. Whatever could induce us to sell ourselves to the Romans now? We need not have revolted at the start; and when we had done so we could quickly have made our submission, before our countryside was ravaged. Now, even if we wanted to, we could not easily obtain an armistice, when the Romans despise us for the loss of Galilee, and it would be a disgrace worse than death to cringe to them when they are on our doorsteps. For myself, I would prefer peace to death, but once war has begun and battle been joined I would rather die bravely than live as a prisoner.

'Which do they say – that we, the citizens' leaders, sent secretly to the Romans, or that the citizens voted us authority to proceed? If they blame us, let them name the friends we sent, the stooges who put the dirty business through! Was anyone spotted on his way there or caught on the way back? Are they in possession of any letters? How did we keep it dark from all these thousands of citizens with whom we rub shoulders all day long, while a handful of men, blockaded and unable even to leave the Temple for the City, were informed of secret goings-on in the country? Has the information reached them only now, when they must pay the penalty for their crimes? and while they had no fear for themselves was none of us suspected of treachery? If on the other hand they lay the blame on the citizens, everything was discussed in public, wasn't it? There was a full attendance at the meeting, so that before your informants arrived rumour would have brought you the news quite openly. Then again, wouldn't they have sent ambassadors if they had voted for an armistice? Who was elected? Let them name him. Gentlemen, this is simply the pretence of men afraid to die and fighting to escape the punishment that is coming to them. Why, if the City *had* been destined to be betrayed, no one but our slanderers would have been vile enough to do it; the list of their villainies is complete already but for this one – treason.

'But now that you are here in arms, your prime duty is to defend the Capital and help us exterminate the usurpers who have suppressed our courts of justice, trampled on our laws, and settled all disputes with their swords. Men of mark, charged with no offence, they have dragged from the middle of the market-place fettered and humiliated, and deaf to protests and entreaties have murdered them. You are free to enter – though not by right of war – and see for yourselves the proofs of what I say: houses emptied by their rapacious hands, wives and children of the murdered men in black, tears and laments in every corner of the City. There is no one who hasn't felt the hand of these grasping scoundrels. Into such a frenzy of madness they have plunged that they have transferred their impudent banditry not only from the country and outlying towns to the very heart of the Jewish world, but even from the City to the Temple! This they have made their headquarters and fortress, the base for their operations against us; and the spot venerated by the whole world and honoured by foreigners from the ends of the earth is trampled on by beasts bred in our midst. Now in their despair they are deliberately setting district against district, town against town, and enlisting the nation to tear out its own vitals. Therefore the right and proper course for you, as I said before, is to help us exterminate the ruffians, and to punish them for cheating you by daring to call you in as allies when they ought to have feared you as avengers.

'But if you can't disregard the appeals of such men, it is still possible to lay aside your arms, come into the City by right of kinship, and holding the balance between both sides serve as arbitrators. Think what they will gain by your judgement on charges unanswerable and very serious. *They* would not hear a word in defence of men charged with no offence at all: still, let them reap the benefit of your coming. But if you will neither share our indignation nor act as judges, there is a third course – to dissociate yourselves from both sides and neither rub salt into our wounds nor give any support to those who wish to destroy the mother-city. However much you suspect that some of us have been in contact with the Romans, you have only to watch the approaches; if any of these slanderous suggestions is found to be true, then you can come and defend the Capital and punish those whose guilt is proved. The enemy couldn't catch you off your guard while you are so near the City. If none of these proposals seems to you acceptable or reasonable, don't be surprised that the gates remain shut as long as you carry arms.'

Jeshua's speech fell on deaf ears. The Idumaean rank and file were furious at not being instantly admitted, while their generals were enraged by the invitation to lay down their arms; they might as well be prisoners as throw them away under compulsion. Simon son of Cathla, one of the generals, managed at last to quieten the uproar of his men, took his stand where the chief priests could hear him, and made his reply.

'It is no longer surprising that the champions of liberty are confined in the Temple, when our people are shut out of the city that belongs to us all – shut out by men who are ready to admit the Romans, perhaps with garlands on the gates, but converse with Idumaeans from the towers, and order them to throw away the arms they have taken up in defence of liberty; who will not trust their kinsmen with the defence of the Capital yet expect those very people to arbitrate in their disagreements, and accuse others of putting men to death without a trial when they themselves are condemning the whole nation to ignominy. The gates of this city have always been wide open to every foreigner for worship, and now you have walled them up against your own country-men! We were racing here to cut your throats, of course, and to attack our own people – we, who were only hastening to keep you free! No doubt those you are blockading have wronged you in the same way, and you have collected an equally convincing assortment of suspicions against them! Then while confining everyone in Jerusalem who cares about the welfare of the state, after shutting your gates without distinction against the peoples who are nearest to you in blood and ordering them about in this insulting way, you complain that you are under the thumb of usurpers and hurl a charge of despotism against the victims of your own usurpation! Who could stomach your hypocrisy when he sees your words contradicted by the facts? – unless perhaps it is you who are being shut out of the Capital by the Idumaeans, the men *you* are excluding from their ancestral rites! One might reasonably blame the men besieged in the Temple because, when they were brave enough to punish the traitors whom you, being equally guilty, call "men of mark, charged with no offence", they didn't start with you and hack off first of all the most vital limbs of this treasonable plot. But if they showed foolish leniency, we Idumaeans will defend the House of God and fight for our common country, firmly resisting both the enemy from without and the traitors within. Here before the walls we shall remain in arms, till the Romans tire of paying attention to you, or you come over to the side of freedom.'

This speech was vociferously applauded by the Idumaean rank and file. Jeshua withdrew in despair, seeing them incapable of moderation and the City assailed from two sides. Nor indeed were the Idumaeans in a happy frame of mind. They were furious and insulted at their exclusion from the City, and the failure of the Zealots, who seemed to be in a strong position, to give them any assistance so bewildered them that many were sorry they had come. But the disgrace of going home with nothing whatever accomplished outweighed their regrets, and they stayed where they were before the wall, encamped in the greatest discomfort. During the night a devastating storm broke; a hurricane raged, rain fell in torrents, lightning flashed continuously, the thunderclaps were terrifying, the earth quaked with deafening roars. Disaster to the human race was plainly foreshadowed by this collapse of the whole framework of things, and no one could doubt that the omens portended a catastrophe without parallel.

The Idumaeans and the people in the City drew the same conclusion. The former felt that God was angry about the expedition and that they would not escape punishment for bearing arms against the Capital; Ananus and his friends were sure that they had gained a victory without a battle and that God was championing their cause. But this guess was wide of the mark – they were predicting for their enemies the fate that awaited their friends. For the Idumaeans pressing close together kept each other warm, and by making a roof overhead with their long shields were little the worse for the downpour; and the Zealots, more anxious about them than about the danger to themselves, met to discuss the possibility of helping them. The hotheads favoured using their weapons to force a way through the lines of guards, and then charging into the middle of the City and defiantly opening the gates to their allies. The guards would fall back confused by their unexpected move, especially as most of them were unarmed and had seen no fighting, while the citizen army could not easily be mustered, as they were confined by the storm to their own houses. If this meant danger, it was their duty to put up with anything rather than stand by while such a huge army perished miserably because of them. The more sensible people on the other hand opposed the use of force, seeing not only that the guards encircling them were at full strength, but that because of the Idumaeans the City wall was carefully guarded. They assumed also that Ananus was everywhere, visiting the guards at all hours. On other nights such was indeed the case, but on this night it was omitted, not through neglect on Ananus' part, but because Fate was determined that he should perish and all his guards with him. It was she who as the night advanced and the storm reached its height put to sleep the sentries guarding the colonnade, and gave the Zealots the idea of borrowing some of the Temple saws and cutting through the bars of the gates. The noise was not heard, thanks to the roar of the wind and the continuous crash of thunder.

They stole out of the Temple and made for the wall; then plying the saws as before opened the gate in front of the Idumaeans. They panicked at first, thinking that Ananus and his men were making an attack, and every man grasped his sword to defend himself; but they soon realized who had come, and passed through the gateway. If they had flung themselves on the City, nothing could have prevented the citizens from perishing to a man, such was their fury; but they were anxious to free the Zealots from their confinement first, as the men who had admitted them implored them not to forget that those they had come to assist were in dire peril, or involve them in greater danger. When they had overwhelmed the guards they could easily attack the City; but if they once roused the City they would never overcome the guards; for as soon as they realized the situation the citizens would form up and block every way to the Temple.

Convinced by this reasoning, the Idumaeans passed through the City and up the slope to the Temple. When they appeared inside, the Zealots, who had been on tenterhooks till they arrived, emerged full of confidence from the inner Temple, and mingling with the Idumaeans attacked the picquets, knifing some of the advanced sentries in their sleep. The shouts of those who were awake roused the whole force. Completely taken aback they snatched their weapons and rallied to the defence. As long as they thought that only the Zealots were attacking them they fought confidently, hoping to win by weight of numbers, but when they saw others streaming in from outside they grasped the fact of the Idumaean irruption. Most of them lost hope, flung away their arms, and gave themselves up to lamentation; but some of the younger men, putting up a wall of shields, fought the Idumaeans tooth and nail and for a long time sheltered the feebler folk. Their cries informed the people in the City of the disastrous situation; but none of these ventured to help them when they learnt that the Idumaeans had broken in; they merely replied with futile shouts and groans, and loud shrieks went up from the women who all had dear ones in danger among the guards. The Zealots echoed the war-cry of the Idumaeans, and the din from every side was made more terrifying by the tempest. No one was spared by the Idumaeans, by nature most barbarous and bloodthirsty, and so knocked about by the storm that they vented their rage on the men who had shut them out, making no distinction between those who cried for mercy and those who fought. Many who reminded them of the ties of blood and begged them to reverence the Temple they shared were run through with swords. There was no room for flight, no hope of safety; they were crushed together and cut down until most of them, driven back, with no way of retreat left, relentlessly assailed by their murderous foes and in a hopeless position, flung themselves headlong into the City, choosing for themselves a fate more pitiable, it seems to me, than the one they were fleeing from. The entire outer Temple was deluged with blood, and 8,500 corpses greeted the rising sun.

This holocaust did not satisfy the Idumaean appetite for blood. Turning to the City they plundered every house and killed anyone they met. Then thinking the common people not worth bothering about they went after the chief priests, most of them rushing off to attack these. The priests were soon caught and killed, and the murderers, standing on their dead bodies, ridiculed Ananus for his devotion to the people and Jeshua for his speech from the wall. So devoid of decency were they that they threw out the dead bodies without burial, though the Jews pay so much regard to obsequies that even those found guilty and crucified are taken down and buried before sunset. I should not be far wrong if I said that the fall of the City began with Ananus'

death, and that the overthrow of the wall and the destruction of the
Jewish state dated from the day when they saw the high priest and
champion of their cause assassinated in the middle of the City. For he
was a man looked up to on every account and entirely honest, and although so distinguished by birth, position, and reputation he loved to
treat even the humblest as equals. Utterly devoted to liberty and with
a passion for democracy, he always made his own interests take second
place to the public advantage and made peace the aim of his life; for
he knew that Rome was invincible. But when he had no option he
made careful preparations for war, in order that if the Jews would
not end hostilities they might carry on the fight efficiently. In
short, had Ananus lived hostilities would indeed have ended; for
he was an eloquent speaker who could mould public opinion and
had already silenced his opponents: if war it was to be, the Jews would
have held up the Roman advance a very long time under such a
general.

His yoke-fellow was Jeshua, not on his level perhaps, but far above
the rest. But I think God had sentenced this polluted city to destruction
and willed that the Sanctuary should be purged by fire, and so cut off
those who clung to them and loved them so dearly. Thus men who a
little while before had been clad in the sacred vestments, and conducting the worship renowned through the world had been revered by
visitors from every land on earth, were thrown out naked, to be
devoured by dogs and wild beasts before all eyes. Virtue herself wept
for these splendid men, I believe, lamenting her total defeat at the
hands of Vice. Yet such was the end of Ananus and Jeshua.

With these two out of the way, the Zealots and a solid mass of
Idumaeans fell upon the population and butchered them like a herd of
unclean animals. Ordinary people were killed where they were caught;
the young nobles were arrested, fettered, and locked up in prison: in
the hope that some would join the rebels, their execution was delayed.
But not a man did so – rather than align themselves with scoundrels
against their own country they all chose death. For this refusal they
paid a terrible price; they were flogged and racked, and only when their
bodies could endure no more torture were they allowed to die by the
sword. Those arrested in the morning were finished off at night, and
the bodies brought up and thrown out to make room for the next
batch. The people were so petrified with fear that no one dared either to
be seen weeping for a dead kinsman or to bury him, but they kept

their tears secret behind locked doors, and made sure that none of their enemies could hear them before they uttered a groan; for the mourner promptly received the same treatment as the mourned. By night they took up a little dust in their hands and sprinkled it on the bodies–or by day, if a man was exceptionally bold. 12,000 of the young nobles died in this way.

Disgusted now with haphazard slaughter, the Zealots set up sham courts and faked trials. They had decided to liquidate one of the most distinguished citizens, Zachariah son of Baruch, as they were annoyed by his burning hatred of wrong and love of freedom, and his wealth made them hope not only to plunder his property but also to get rid of a man capable of destroying them. They therefore issued a categorical order, summoning seventy men in public positions to the Temple, where they turned them into a stage jury with no authority. Then they charged Zachariah with trying to betray their country to Rome and sending an offer of treason to Vespasian. There was no proof of the charges, no evidence at all, but they said that they themselves were quite convinced of his guilt and claimed that this should satisfy anyone. Zachariah realized that his fate was sealed: he had been treacherously summoned to a prison, not a court. But certain death was not going to deprive him of free speech – he stood up, scoffed at the incredibility of the charges, and in a few words disposed of the whole indictment. Then, turning the tables on his accusers, he methodically detailed all their illegalities and mercilessly exposed their mismanagement of affairs. The Zealots howled with rage and could hardly keep their hands off their swords, determined as they were to play out this farce, this sham trial to the end, and eager also to find out whether the jurors would risk their own lives in the cause of justice. But the seventy brought in a unanimous verdict of Not Guilty, choosing to die with the defendant rather than bear the responsibility for his destruction. The Zealots greeted his acquittal with shouts of indignation, and were all enraged with the jury for not realizing that the authority bestowed on them was a mere sham. Two of the most unscrupulous fell upon Zachariah, murdered him in the middle of the Temple, and jested over his dead body: 'Now you have got our verdict too, and your trials are over.' With that they threw him out of the Temple and into the valley beneath. Then they showed their contempt for the jurors by belabouring them with the backs of their swords and driving them from the precincts. For one purpose only they refrained from murdering them – that they might go into every part of the City and let all the citizens know that they were slaves.

The Idumaeans now felt sorry they had come and were disgusted with the goings-on. One of the Zealots came to them privately and held a meeting at which he denounced the excesses they had committed jointly with those who had called them in, and listed the damage done to the Capital. They had taken up arms on the ground that the chief priests were betraying the Capital to the Romans, yet they had found no evidence of treason whatever. But her defenders so-called were all out for war and personal domination. The right time to stop all this had been at the outset; but having once formed a partnership to shed their country's blood, they ought at least to set a limit to their misdeeds and not go on assisting the destroyers of all they held dear. If some of them were vexed at the closing of the gates and the refusal to let them enter at once with their weapons, those responsible had paid for their opposition, hadn't they? Ananus was dead, and in a single night the population had been almost wiped out. This had produced an unmistakable revulsion of feeling in many of their own people, but those who had called them in displayed unparalleled savagery and not a trace of respect for their deliverers. Before the very eyes of their allies they perpetrated the vilest atrocities, and their excesses would be laid at the Idumaeans' door until someone either ended or repudiated what was going on. And so, as the allegation of treason had been exploded and there was no Roman invasion on the horizon, while the City was at the mercy of a caucus that could not be dislodged, their right course was to go back home and have nothing more to do with these contemptible people, and so blot out the memory of all the crimes in which they had been tricked into playing a part.

Accepting his advice the Idumaeans first released from prison about 2,000 citizens who at once left the City and fled to Simon, of whom we shall speak by and by; then turning their backs on Jerusalem they went home. Their departure had a paradoxical effect on both sides: the citizens, unaware of the revulsion of feeling, recovered their spirits for a time as if rid of an enemy, while the Zealots became more arrogant still, not as if they were deserted by allies, but as if relieved of men who frowned upon and interfered with their excesses. No longer was there any hesitation or circumspection about their outrages: they reached all their decisions with the utmost speed and executed them more quickly still. Chief objects of their lust for blood were the brave and the nobly born, the former being victims of their fear, the latter of their envy: they felt their whole safety depended on their leaving no one who counted alive. Along with many others they murdered Gurion, a man with a reputation and of good family, but democratic and passionately devoted to liberty, if ever a Jew was. He owed his ruin mainly to his plain speaking, as well as the advantages he enjoyed. Nor did Niger the Peraean escape their clutches. He had shown amazing courage in the campaigns against the Romans; but now, protesting loudly and displaying his scars, he was dragged through the middle of the City. When pulled outside the gates he despaired of life and pleaded for burial; but they made it brutally clear that the grave he so desired would never be his, and then did the foul deed. As he died, Niger called down on their heads the vengeance of Rome, famine and pestilence, battle and slaughter, and as a final disaster, a death-grapple with their fellow-citizens. All these things heaven visited on the godless wretches; and the retribution was most just, for through their party-strife they were to taste before long the mad fury of their fellow-citizens.

Niger's death lessened their fear of being overthrown, but there was no section of the people for whose destruction they did not invent an excuse. Those with whom any of them had quarrelled had long ago been put away; those who had not collided with them in peacetime were subjected to carefully chosen accusations: if a man never came near them at all he was suspected of arrogance; if he approached them boldly, of contempt; if he was obsequious, of conspiracy. The most serious accusations and the most trifling were alike punished with death, and no one could escape unless he was quite insignificant owing to humble birth or poverty.

In the Roman camp all the generals treated the enemy's internal divisions as a godsend, and in their eagerness to march on the City begged Vespasian, as commander-in-chief, to lose no time. Divine providence, they said, had upheld their cause by setting their enemies at each other's throats; but the pendulum would soon swing back, and at any moment the Jews might be reunited through weariness of mutual injury or some revulsion of feeling. Vespasian replied that they were wide of the mark and were assuming a theatrical pose of warriors in arms – a dangerous pose – oblivious to safety and common-sense. If he did march on the City at once, he would only reunite the enemy and turn their full strength against himself; if he waited, he would find their numbers reduced by their internal divisions. He might safely leave the generalship to God, who was handing over the Jews to the Romans without their lifting a finger, and making them a present of victory with no danger to the army. Very well then; while their opponents, torn by calamitous internal divisions, perished by their own hands, the right thing for them was to watch the dangerous conflict from a safe distance, not to get mixed up with suicidal maniacs locked in a death struggle. 'If anyone thinks', he went on, 'that victory without a fight won't taste so sweet, he had better realize that to win success by biding your time is a sounder policy than courting disaster by plunging into battle. And again, those who shine in physical combat are no more entitled to fame than those who accomplish just as much by self-discipline and brains.' Furthermore, while the enemy were growing weaker his own army would recover from its continuous toil and be stronger than at present.

Finally, this was not the time to set their hearts on a dazzling victory. The Jews were not busy making weapons, building walls or recruiting auxiliaries, in which case postponement would injure those who granted it, but were being bled to death by dissension and civil war, and suffering daily greater miseries than they would themselves inflict on them if they attacked and overwhelmed them. If then safety was to be the criterion, those who were destroying each other should be left to continue the good work; if they asked what kind of success would win the most fame, they would be fools to attack a sick community; for there would be no denying that the victory was due, not to them, but to Jewish divisions.

Vespasian's arguments were accepted by the officers, and any doubt as to the soundness of his judgement was soon dispelled; a steady stream of deserters eluded the Zealots. But flight was difficult as every exit was guarded and anyone caught going out, whatever the reason, was assumed to be on his way to the Romans and dispatched forthwith. However, if he paid enough they let him go, and only if he failed to pay was he a traitor, so that the rich purchased their escape and only the poor were slaughtered. Dead bodies along all the main roads were heaped up high, and many who were anxious to desert decided instead to perish in Jerusalem, for hope of burial made death in their own city seem the lesser evil. But their enemies reached such a pitch of barbarity that they would allow no one, whether killed in the City or on the roads, so much as a hole in the ground. As if they were pledged to destroy the laws of their country and of Nature too, and along with their crimes against mankind to pollute the Deity Himself, they left the dead bodies rotting under the open sky. For those who buried a kinsman, as for deserters, the penalty was death, and anyone who gave burial to another soon needed it himself. In short, no other lofty emotion disappeared so completely amid the horrors of the time as pity; things that deserved compassion were the things that provoked these wretches, who switched their venom from the living to those they had murdered, and from the dead back to the living. Paralysed with fear the survivors envied those already dead – they were at peace – and the tortured occupants of the jails declared that compared with them even the unburied were fortunate. Their persecutors trampled on every ordinance of man, scoffed at the laws of God, and ridiculed the oracles of the prophets as the inventions of tricksters. Yet those prophets clearly discerned the laws of right and wrong, by breaking which the Zealots caused the prophecies against their country to be fulfilled. For there was an age-old saying of inspired men that the City would be taken and the most Holy Temple burnt to the ground by right of war, if ever the citizens strove with each other and Jewish hands were the first to pollute the house of God. The truth of this the Zealots did not question; but they made themselves the means of its fulfilment.

By now John had set his heart on one-man rule and, not content to be on an equality with his fellows, gradually built up a following of the worst types and cut adrift from the rebel organization. He paid no heed whatever to the decisions of the rest and issued his own orders like a lord, obviously aiming at sole sovereignty. Some gave way to him through fear, some were genuine adherents; for he was very clever at winning support by the orator's tricks. Many thought their own skins would be safer if the crimes already committed were laid at one door, not many; and his activity with both hand and brain won him henchmen in plenty. However, a large number of dissidents left him, to some extent prompted by envy and unwillingness to submit to a former equal, but in the main put off by dread of a sovereign ruler; for they could not hope to pull him down easily once he was master, and he would have a handle against them as they had opposed him at the start. Every man chose to face war with all its miseries rather than throw away his liberty and die like a slave. This, then, was the explanation of the rift in the insurgent ranks, and John faced his opponents like a rival monarch. However, they did little more than watch each other's movements, and there was little or no actual fighting: their only rivalry was at the expense of the people – who would bring home the most loot was the point at issue. Now that the storm-tossed city was at the mercy of the three greatest calamities, war, tyranny, and party-strife, by comparison the citizens felt that war was almost endurable. Anyway they fled from their own people and sought sanctuary with foreigners, finding in the Roman camp the safety they had no hope of finding in their own city.

And now a fourth calamity was coming on the doomed nation. Not far from Jerusalem was a well-nigh impregnable fortress built by the kings of long ago for the safe keeping of their treasures and their personal security in the hazards of war. It was called Masada, and was in the hands of the so-called Sicarii. Hitherto they had merely raided the districts nearby to procure supplies: fear prevented any further ravages; but when they heard that the Roman army was making no move, while the Jews in Jerusalem were torn by party-strife and domestic tyranny, they launched out on more ambitious schemes. During the Feast of Unleavened Bread (kept by the Jews in memory of their escape, ever since they were freed from slavery in Egypt and returned to their ancestral home) they eluded those who lay in their path and made a night raid on a little town called Engedi. Those who might have put up a resistance were scattered before they could seize their weapons and form up, and thrown out of the town; those who could not fly, women and children more than 700 in number, were butchered. Then they stripped the houses bare, seized the ripe crops, and brought the loot to Masada. They proceeded to plunder all the villages round the fortress and ravage the whole area, their numbers being daily swelled by a flow of ruffians like themselves from every side.

In all districts of Judaea there was a similar upsurge of terrorism, dormant hitherto; and as in the body if the chief member is inflamed all the others are infected, so when strife and disorder broke out in the Capital the scoundrels in the country could plunder with impunity, and each group after plundering their own village vanished into the wilderness. There they joined forces and organized themselves in companies, smaller than an army but bigger than an armed gang, which swooped on sanctuaries and cities. Those they attacked suffered as severely as if they had lost a war, and were unable to retaliate as the raiders, like all bandits, made off as soon as they had got what they wanted. In fact, every corner of Judaea was going the way of the Metropolis.

All this was reported to Vespasian by deserters; for though the insurgents guarded all the outlets and killed those who went near them, whatever the reason, there were some, nevertheless, who eluded them and fled to the Roman camp, where they begged the commander-in-chief to protect the City and save the remnant of the people – it was because of their loyalty to Rome that so many had lost their lives and danger threatened the survivors. Vespasian, already moved by their misfortunes, set out as if to besiege Jerusalem, but really to end the existing siege. But he was obliged first to reduce the places that were left, so as to leave nothing outside the City to interfere with the siege. He therefore proceeded to Gadara, the strongly fortified capital of Peraea, entering the city on the 4th of Dystros. The authorities, unseen by the insurgents, had sent a deputation to him with an offer of surrender, partly from a longing for peace and partly to safeguard their possessions, many Gadarenes being very rich. Of this deputation their opponents knew nothing; Vespasian was nearly there before they discovered it. They despaired of holding the town themselves as their enemies within outnumbered them and the Romans could be seen not far away. So they decided to flee, but could not bear to do so without spilling blood and wreaking vengeance on those who had brought things to this pass. They seized Dolesus, by birth and reputation the first citizen, but believed to be responsible for the deputation, killed him, and in their uncontrollable rage mutilated his dead body before fleeing from the town. The Roman force now arrived, and the people of Gadara welcomed Vespasian with acclamation and received from him guarantees of protection, as also a garrison of horse and foot to deal with sudden attacks by the fugitives. They had pulled down their walls without orders from the Romans, so as to prove their devotion to peace by their inability to make war even if they wanted to.

To deal with those who had fled from Gadara Vespasian sent Placidus with 500 horse and 3,000 foot, while he himself with the rest of the army went back to Caesarea. When the fugitives suddenly caught sight of the pursuing horsemen, before contact was made they crowded into a village named Bethennabris. Here they found a large number of young men and armed them willy-nilly. Then with utter recklessness they rushed out to attack Placidus. At the first onset his men gave a little ground, scheming to draw the enemy away from the walls; when they had got them where they wanted they encircled them and shot them down. Those who fled the cavalry cut off, those who were pinned down the infantry destroyed without mercy. In their death-struggle the Jews could do no more than display their fearlessness; for as they hurled themselves on the massed Romans behind their impenetrable barrier of steel, they could find no chink for their missiles to enter or means of breaking the enemy ranks, while they themselves were easy targets for Roman missiles and like the wildest of wild beasts charged the opposing steel and perished, some struck with the sword as they faced the enemy, some scattered by the cavalry.

Placidus was determined to block their dashes for the village, so he kept his cavalry moving past them on that side, and then wheeled round and instantly discharged a well-aimed volley, killing those who were near and scaring away the rest, till the bravest of them forced their way through and sought the protection of the walls. The sentries found themselves in a quandary: they could not bear to shut out the men from Gadara and with them their own friends; and if they let them in they would perish with them. This was exactly what happened; for when the Jews forced their way inside the ramparts the Roman cavalry almost managed to burst in with them, and though the gates were shut in the nick of time Placidus launched an attack, and after battling fiercely till evening captured the wall and the entire village. The non-combatants were exterminated, the able-bodied fled, the houses were ransacked by the soldiery, and the village set on fire. Those who escaped raised all the countryfolk, and by exaggerating their own calamities and saying that the entire Roman army was coming against them drove them all out on every side in terror, and with the whole mass fled towards Jericho; this was the only city left strong enough to nourish the hope of survival in view of its large population. Placidus, relying on his cavalry and encouraged by his earlier successes, pursued them to the Jordan, killing all he could catch; and when he had penned the whole mass on the bank of the river, where they were stopped by the current, which was swollen by rain and unfordable, he deployed his forces opposite them. Necessity compelled them to fight, having no way of escape; so they extended their line along the bank as far as they could and faced the missiles and the charges of the horsemen, who wounded many of them and threw them into the swirling waters below. Those who perished by Roman hands numbered 15,000; those who were forced to leap into the Jordan of their own accord could not be counted at all. Some 2,200 were taken prisoner, and there was a rich haul of asses, sheep, camels, and oxen.

The Jews had never suffered a heavier blow than this, and it seemed even heavier than it was; for not only was the whole path of their flight one long trail of slaughter and the Jordan rendered impassable by dead bodies, but the Dead Sea too was filled with corpses which the river carried down into it by the thousand. Placidus, seizing his advantage, launched attacks against the little towns and villages round about, captured Abila, Julias, Besimoth, and all the rest as far as the Dead Sea, and drafted into each the most suitable of the deserters. Then putting the soldiers on board ship he rounded up those who had sought safety on the lake. Thus all Peraea submitted or was crushed as far as Machaerus.

CHAPTER 16

Vespasian Emperor

A T this time news was received of the rising in Gaul, and how
Vindex and the native chiefs had revolted from Nero, as described
in detail by other writers. Vespasian's reaction was to step up his
campaign; he already foresaw the coming civil wars and the danger to
the whole Empire, and felt that if he quickly pacified the eastern areas
he would lighten the anxiety of Italy. While therefore the winter
lasted he secured the conquered towns and villages with garrisons,
posting centurions in the towns and decurions in the villages, and rebuilt many that had been destroyed. In the early days of spring he set
out from Caesarea with most of his army and marched to Antipatris.
There he stayed two days to settle the affairs of the town, and the next
day marched on, destroying and burning all the villages around. After
reducing the toparchy of Thamna and the neighbouring districts he
went on to Lydda and Jamnia. As these two were subdued already he
settled there a sufficient number of those who had submitted, and
advanced to Emmaus. After seizing the approaches to the capital of
this area he fortified a camp, and leaving the Fifth Legion there marched
with the rest of his forces to the toparchy of Bethleptepha. He ravaged
with fire this and the neighbouring district together with the outlying
regions of Idumaea, building guardposts in strategic positions. Then
he captured two villages in the very middle of Idumaea, Betaris, and
Caphartoba, killed over 10,000 inhabitants, took over 1,000 prisoners,
expelled the rest of the population, and placed there a large part of his
own forces. These overran and laid waste all the hill country. Then at
the head of his remaining forces he returned to Emmaus, and from there
through Samaria and past Neapolis,[1] known locally as Mabartha, he
went down to Corea, encamping there on the 2nd of Daisios. The next
day he arrived at Jericho, where Trajan , one of his generals, joined him
with the force from Peraea, the whole area beyond Jordan being subdued already. The bulk of the population, without waiting for their
arrival, had fled from Jericho to the hill country opposite Jerusalem, but

1. *Now Nablus.*

a large section which had stayed behind was put to death. The Romans found the city deserted.

Jericho is situated in a plain above which rises a bare, treeless mountain range of very great length, stretching northwards to the Scythopolis district, and southwards to the region of Sodom and the far end of the Dead Sea. This ridge is uneven all the way along and uninhabited because of its infertility. Beyond Jordan rises a parallel range beginning at Julias in the north and running southwards to Somorrhon, which borders on Petra in Arabia. In this range is the so-called Iron Mountain jutting out into Moab. The country between the two ranges is called the Great Plain, stretching from the village of Ginabrin to the Dead Sea, and measuring 140 miles by 14. It is bisected by the Jordan and has two lakes in it, the Dead Sea and Lake Tiberias, opposite in character: the former is salt and sterile, the latter sweet and prolific. In summertime the plain is burnt up and the absolute drought makes the air unwholesome; for it is entirely waterless except for the Jordan, this being the reason why the palm-groves on the river-banks are more flourishing and bear heavier crops than those at a distance.

However, near Jericho there is an abundant spring, admirably suited for irrigation. It gushes out near the old city, the first in the land of Canaan to be stormed by the Hebrew commander Joshua the son of Nun. This spring, it is said, at first not only blighted fruit-crops but produced miscarriages in women, in fact proved unwholesome and destructive of everything, but was sweetened and changed into a most wholesome and life-giving stream by the prophet Elisha, friend and successor of Elijah. When he had been made welcome by the people of Jericho and most hospitably entertained by them, he repaid them and their country with an undying favour. He went out to the spring and threw into the running water an earthenware jar full of salt, then raised his godly right hand towards heaven and poured atoning libations on the ground, beseeching earth to purify the water and open sweeter veins, and heaven to blend the waters with more life-giving airs and to give the people round about fruits in plenty and children to succeed them, not letting them ever lack water to give these birth, so long as they remained righteous. With these prayers, accompanied by many ritual acts based on deep study, he transformed the spring, so that the water that had hitherto brought childlessness and famine upon them, from then on furnished them with children and all good things. Indeed, for irrigation it is so effective that if it merely comes in contact with the land, it benefits the crops more than waters that soak right in. So while the other streams, even if freely used, do little good, this tiny stream does a great deal. In fact it waters more land than all the rest, covering a plain 8½ miles by 2½ and satisfying the needs of very numerous and very lovely parks. Of the palms which it waters there are many varieties differing in taste and name: the richer ones when trodden underfoot actually yield a large quantity of 'honey', nearly as good as the real thing. Bees too abound in the district, which also produces balsam, the most valuable local crop, the cypress and the ben-nut; so that it would be no exaggeration to call the place divine – a place where the rarest and loveliest things are found in such abundance. For as regards its other crops, it would be hard to find another region in the wide world to compare with it, so large is the yield from the seed sown. This is due, I think, to the warmth of the air and the fertilizing power of the water; the warmth draws out the growing plants and makes them spread, the moisture encourages root-growth in them all and supplies strength for the summer, when the district is so burnt up that no one goes out if he can help it. If the water is drawn before sunrise and then exposed to the air, it becomes extremely cold and quite unlike the atmosphere round it; on the other hand, in winter it warms up and bathers find it most comfortable. The air too is so mild that the inhabitants dress in linen when the rest of Judaea is under snow. Jericho is 18 miles from Jerusalem and 7 from the Jordan.[1] The country between the two cities is a rocky desert; between Jericho and the Jordan and Dead Sea it is more low-lying, but just as barren a desert.

Of Jericho and its great natural advantages enough has been said; but we must also describe the characteristics of the Dead Sea. This, as I said, is bitter and sterile, but because of their relative lightness brings to the surface even the heaviest things thrown into it; in fact it is not easy to go down into the depths even by deliberate effort. Thus when Vespasian came to examine it, he ordered some non-swimmers to be thrown with their hands tied behind them into deep water, and found that they all came to the surface as if blown upwards by a strong wind. In addition to this the changing colour is remarkable: thrice daily it alters its appearance and reflects the sun's rays with varying tints. Moreover in many places it throws up black lumps of asphalt:[2] these as they float are in shape and size like headless bulls. The lakeside

---

1. *Both figures a little too big.*
2. *Hence the Greek name of the Dead Sea – Asphaltitis.*

workers row to the spot, seize the lumps one by one and haul them into their boats. When these are full it is not easy to get the asphalt away, as the boat sticks to the glutinous mass until they loose it with a woman's menstruous blood and urine, to which alone it yields. It is useful not only for caulking ships but also for curing bodily sickness: it is included in many medical prescriptions.

The length of this lake is 67 miles, measured from Zoar in Arabia, the width 17.[1] Next to it lies the land of Sodom,[2] once so rich in crops and in the wealth of its cities, but now dust and ashes. They say that owing to the impiety of its inhabitants it was burnt up by lightning; indeed, there are still marks of the fire from heaven and the outlines of five cities to be seen, and ashes still form part of the growing fruits, which have all the appearance of eatable fruit, but when plucked with the hand dissolve into smoke and ashes. To this extent the stories about the land of Sodom are confirmed by the evidence of our eyes.

In order to make the encirclement of Jerusalem complete, Vespasian constructed camps in Jericho and Adida, garrisoning each with a mixed force of Romans and allies. He also sent Lucius Annius to Gerasa, giving him a squadron of cavalry and an ample number of infantry. Annius took the town by assault, put to death 1,000 of the younger men – all who had failed to escape –, enslaved the women and children, and allowed the soldiers to plunder everything of value, finally setting fire to the houses before he marched against the surrounding villages. The strong fled, the weak perished, and all that was left went up in flames. Now that the war had engulfed the whole region of mountain and plain, it was impossible to leave Jerusalem; those who wanted to desert were watched by the Zealots, and those who did not yet favour the Romans were shut in by the army which surrounded the City on every side.

Vespasian returned to Caesarea, and was getting ready to march his entire force against Jerusalem itself when he received the news that Nero had met a violent end after reigning 13 years[3] and 8 days. I might relate how he abused his position by entrusting the management of affairs to those utter scoundrels, Nymphidius and Tigellinus, two worthless freedmen; how when these plotted against him he was deserted by all his guards, ran away with four faithful freedmen, and

1. *Both figures much too big.*
2. *South of the lake.*
3. *Possibly* eight months *has dropped out of the MSS.*

died in the suburbs by his own hand; or how those who had brought him down soon paid the penalty. I might give an account of the war in Gaul and explain how it ended, how Galba on being invited to mount the throne returned to Rome from Spain, and how he was accused of meanness by the soldiers, assassinated in the middle of the Roman Forum and succeeded by Otho. I might describe Otho's campaign againt Vitellius' generals and his overthrow; the disturbances that followed under Vitellius and the fighting round the Capitol, and the way Antonius Primus and Mucianus destroyed Vitellius and the German Legions and so brought the civil war to an end. But I must excuse myself from describing any of these events in detail, because they are matters of common knowledge and have been dealt with by many Greek and Roman writers; to secure continuity and coherence in the narrative I have summarized the various incidents.

Vespasian's immediate response was to put off his expedition against Jerusalem, waiting anxiously to see who would step into Nero's shoes. Then, when he heard that Galba was on the throne, he refrained from all military activity pending the receipt of a new directive, but sent his son Titus to pay homage and seek the Emperor's instructions for settling the Jewish problem. With the same object Agrippa embarked for Rome along with Titus. But while they sailed along the Greek coast in warships because it was winter, Galba was assassinated, after a reign of seven months and as many days, and his office went to Otho who laid his own claim to the headship of the state. Agrippa decided to complete his journey as if nothing had happened; Titus by a divine impulse sailed back from Greece to Syria and proceeded with all speed to Caesarea to rejoin his father. In their suspense – for the Roman Empire was rocking and everything was in the melting-pot – the two commanders held up operations against the Jews, feeling that while they were so anxious about things at home an invasion of a foreign country would be inopportune.

But there was to be no peace for Jerusalem. There was a young hothead called Simon, son of Gioras, a Gerasene by birth. He was less crafty than John who was master of the City, but superior in physique and daring – the quality which had caused Ananus the high priest to turn him out of his toparchy of Acrabatene, so driving him into the arms of the bandits who had seized Masada. At first they eyed him warily, and only allowed him into the lower part of the fortress with the women he brought with him, occupying the upper part themselves.

Later, as a kindred spirit and to all appearance trustworthy, they took him on their plundering expeditions and raids round about Masada. His eloquence, however, failed to persuade them to attempt anything more ambitious; they were used to the fortress and dared not venture far from their lair. But Simon had made up his mind to usurp supreme power, and when he heard that Ananus was dead he withdrew to the hill country. There he proclaimed liberty for slaves and rewards for the free, so collecting the scum of the whole district. As soon as his force was strong enough he overran the villages in the hill country, until the constant flow of recruits encouraged him to descend to lower levels. Soon he was an object of dread to the towns, and many men of good position were led astray by his strength and continual success, so that his army no longer consisted only of slaves and bandits, but included many respectable citizens who obeyed him like a king. He next overran the toparchy of Acrabatene and the whole area as far as Great Idumaea: near a village called Nain he had built a wall which he used to secure himself from attack; and in the valley of Pharan he found a number of convenient caves and enlarged many others, using them all to safeguard his treasure and to house the loot. There too he stored the corn he had seized and accommodated most of his armed gangs. It was obvious that he was training his army in readiness to attack Jerusalem.

Alarmed at his designs and determined to nip the growing threat in the bud, the Zealots marched out in force under arms. Simon met them and gave battle, inflicting heavy casualties and driving the survivors into the City. He was not yet so sure of himself as to assault the walls: he embarked first on the conquest of Idumaea, setting out for the frontier at the head of 20,000 well-armed men. The Idumaean authorities promptly collected the best fighting-men in the country, about 25,000 of them, and leaving all the rest to guard their homes against raids by the sicarii from Masada, awaited Simon at the frontier. Battle was joined and raged all day long, ending without victory to either side. Simon returned to Nain and the Idumaeans dispersed to their homes. Not long after Simon with a larger force again invaded their territory, and encamped near a village called Tekoa. From there he sent Eleazar, one of his staff, to the garrison of Herodium near by to induce them to surrender the fort. Eleazar was readily admitted by the guards, who did not realize what he had come for; but when he mentioned surrender they drew their swords and chased him until, unable to fly any further, he flung himself from the wall into the ravine below and was instantly killed. But the Idumaeans were now thoroughly alarmed by Simon's strength, and decided not to give battle till they had reconnoitred the enemy forces.

For this duty Jacob, one of their officers, eagerly offered his services with the intention of turning traitor. Setting out from Olurus, the village where the Idumaean army was concentrated at the time, he went straight to Simon and made a compact with him. In return for a solemn undertaking that he should always occupy a position of influence he would first hand over his own home town, and then help Simon subdue the whole of Idumaea. On this understanding he was lavishly entertained by Simon, and buoyed up with dazzling promises returned to his own lines. When by pretending that Simon's army was many times its real size he had undermined the morale of the officers, and gradually of the whole army, he urged them to receive Simon and hand over all authority to him without a struggle. During the negotiations he sent messengers to invite Simon, promising to disperse the Idumaeans, as indeed he did. As the army drew near he was the first to leap on to his horse and flee with his companions in crime. Panic seized the whole defending force, and before battle could be joined they left their posts and every man fled to his own home. Having in this unexpected way swept into Idumaea without bloodshed, Simon by a surprise attack captured the little town of Hebron, where he seized a vast quantity of booty and got possession of ample corn supplies. If the inhabitants are to be believed, Hebron is more ancient than any town in the country – older even than Memphis in Egypt; its age is reckoned as 2300 years. They affirm that it was the home of Abram, the ancestors of the Jews, after his migration from Mesopotamia, and that his descendants went down into Egypt from there. Their tombs are pointed out to this day in the little town, of the finest marble and beautifully fashioned. Three quarters of a mile from the town can be seen an immense terebinth, said to be as old as creation. From there he advanced through the whole country, not only sacking villages and towns but ravaging the countryside: in addition to the heavy infantry he had 40,000 men with him, so that he could not supply his immense host even with the necessities of life. Quite apart from his needs, his brutal nature and vindictiveness against the Idumaean people were major reasons for the devastation of their land. Just as in the wake of locusts we may see a whole forest stripped bare, so in the rear of Simon's army there was nothing left but a desert. Some places they set on fire, some they demolished; everything that grew anywhere in the country they destroyed, either trampling it down or devouring it, and their heavy feet made cultivated land harder than barren soil. In short, not a sign remained to show that what they destroyed had ever existed.

All this roused the Zealots to fresh activity. They dared not face Simon in the open, but they laid ambushes in the passes and captured his wife and many of her servants. Then, as delighted as if they had taken Simon himself prisoner, they went back to the City in the belief that he would at once lay down his arms and plead for the return of his wife. Her capture, however, moved him not to pity but to fury; he came up to the walls of Jerusalem, and like a wounded animal that cannot catch the hunter, he vented his rage upon everyone he met. All who went outside the gates to gather herbs or firewood, old people without arms, he seized and tortured to death. In his boundless indignation he was ready to feed on their dead bodies. Many he sent back after cutting off their hands, in an attempt to terrify his opponents and stir the people to revolt against those responsible. They were ordered to say that Simon swore by God, the Lord of all, that if they did not instantly give him back his wife he would break down their wall and inflict the same punishment on every person in the City, sparing neither young nor old and treating guilty and innocent alike. These threats terrified not only the citizens but the Zealots too, and they sent his wife back to him. Pacified for the time being he took a brief respite from continual bloodshed.

It was not only in Judaea that sedition and civil war were rife, but in Italy too. Galba had been assassinated in the middle of the Roman Forum and his successor Otho was at war with Vitellius, who claimed the throne as the nominee of the legions in Germany. At Bedriacum in Northern Italy battle was joined with Valens and Caecinna, Vitellius' generals. On the first day Otho had the better of it, on the second the army of Vitellius. The carnage was frightful, and when Otho at Brix-ellum learnt of his defeat he committed suicide, after a reign of only three months and two days. His troops went over to Vitellius' generals, and Vitellius himself marched into Rome with his army.

Meanwhile Vespasian left Caesarea, and on the 5th of Daisios launched a campaign against those parts of Judaea that had not yet sub-mitted. Climbing into the hill country he occupied two toparchies, those of Gophna and Acrabetta; then two small towns, Bethel and Ephraim. After garrisoning these he rode as far as Jerusalem, slaughtering many of those he met and taking prisoners by the score. Cerealius, one of his officers, took a small body of horse and foot and ravaged Upper Idumaea, taking Caphethra (which calls itself a town) in his stride and setting it on fire, and after a preliminary assault laying siege to Capharabin too. The wall was very strong indeed, and he was resigning himself to a long wait when without warning the inhabitants opened the gates, came forward with olive-branches in their hands, and gave themselves up. After accepting their surrender Cerealius made for Hebron, another, very ancient, city, situated as we have seen in the hill country not far from Jerusalem. Forcing an entry he slaughtered all he found there, old and young alike, and burnt the city to the ground. Every place had now been reduced but Herodium, Masada, and Machaerus, which were in the hands of the bandits: the target of the Romans was now Jerusalem itself.

When Simon had got back his wife from the Zealots, he returned to what remained of Idumaea, and harrying the nation from every direction forced the majority to flee to Jerusalem. He followed them to the City himself, and again encircling the wall killed any working men he caught going out into the country. The people found Simon outside more terrifying than the Romans, and the Zealots inside more savage than either: of these the Galilaean contingent was pre-eminent in the originality and audacity of their crimes. It was they who had put power in the hands of John, and he from the pinnacle on which they had set him rewarded them by leaving every man free to do as he liked. Their passion for looting was insatiable: they ransacked rich men's houses, murdered men and violated women for sport, and *drank* their spoils washed down with blood: through sheer boredom they shamelessly gave themselves up to effeminate practices, adorning their hair and putting on women's clothes, steeping themselves in scent and painting under their eyes to make themselves attractive. They copied not merely the dress but also the passions of women, and in their utter filthiness invented unlawful pleasures; they wallowed in slime, turning the whole city into a brothel and polluting it with the foulest practices. Yet though they had the faces of women they had the hands of murderers; they approached with mincing steps, then in a flash became fighting-men, and drawing their swords from under their dyed cloaks ran every passer-by through. Those who ran away from John had a more murderous reception from Simon, and anyone who eluded the tyrant within the walls was killed by the tyrant outside the gates. Thus for those who wished to desert to the Romans every way of escape was cut off.

But John's forces were in a mutinous state, and the entire Idumaean contingent detached itself and attacked the usurper from jealousy of his power as well as hatred of his brutality. They joined battle and wiped out many of the Zealots, chasing the rest into the royal palace built by Grapte, a kinswoman of the king of Adiabene, Izas. The Idumaeans poured in with them, then driving them from there into the Temple set about looting John's effects: it was in this palace that he himself was living and storing the spoils of his tyranny. Meanwhile the mass of Zealots scattered all over the City joined forces with the fugitives in the Temple, and John got ready to lead them down against the citizens and the Idumaeans. The latter, being better fighters, feared their onset less than their madness: in the night they might slip out of the Temple, murder their opponents and burn the City to the ground. So they held a joint meeting with the chief priests to discuss the best means of guarding against their onslaught. But God, it seems, turned their thoughts to foolish courses, and to save their lives they chose a remedy worse than death: in order to overthrow John they voted to admit Simon, and olive-branch in hand to bring in a second tyrant to be their master. The resolution was carried out, and they sent the high priest, Matthias, to implore Simon to enter – the man they so greatly feared! The invitation was supported by those citizens who were trying to escape the Zealots and were anxious about their homes and property. He in his lordly way expressed his willingness to be their master, and entered with the air of one who intended to sweep the Zealots out of the City, acclaimed by the citizens as deliverer and protector. But when he and his forces were inside his one purpose was to establish his own supremacy, and he looked upon those who had invited him as enemies no less than those he had been invited to suppress.

Thus in Xanthicos of the third year of the war Simon became master of Jerusalem. John and the Zealots, unable to leave the Temple and with all their possessions in the City lost – for their property had been instantly plundered by Simon's men – saw no hope of safety. Aided by the citizens Simon began an assault on the Temple; the enemy took their stand on the colonnades and battlements and beat off their attacks. Many of Simon's men were killed and many were carried away wounded; for from their commanding position it was easy for the Zealots to aim their shafts with telling effect. Having already the

advantage of position they further constructed four immense towers
to enable them to hurl their missiles from a still greater height – one at
the north-east corner, one above the Gymnasium, the third at another
corner opposite the Lower City, while the last was set up over the roof
of the priests' chambers, where one of the priests invariably stood to
proclaim by trumpet-blast, in the late afternoon the approach of every
seventh day, and on the next evening its close, calling on the people
in the first case to cease work, in the second to resume it. On these
towers they mounted quick-loaders and stone-throwing machines,
along with archers and slingers. Simon's attacks now grew more hesi-
tant, most of the men being dispirited; all the same he hung on, having
the advantage in numbers, though the artillery with its longer range
accounted for many of the men engaged.

While all this was happening Rome herself suffered severe shocks.
Vitellius had arrived from Germany dragging along with his army a
vast mob of hangers-on; and as the accommodation provided for the
soldiers was inadequate, he turned the whole City into a camp and filled
every house with armed men. These were unused to the sight of Roman
wealth and the silver and gold that glittered all around them; they
could hardly restrain their covetous desires, but turned to plunder and
the murder of any who got in their way. Such was the state of affairs
in Italy.

Vespasian, having crushed all opposition in the neighbourhood of
Jerusalem, went back to Caesarea. There he heard of the upheavals in
Rome and the accession of Vitellius. He knew how to obey as well as
how to command, yet the news angered him; he could not accept as
master one who had madly seized on the Empire as if it was derelict;
and in his distress at what had happened he could not endure the torture,
and when his homeland was being ravaged give his attention to wars
elsewhere. But while anger drove him to her defence, the thought of
the distance restrained him; the possibility that fortune might play
many a scurvy trick before he could cross to Italy, especially if he sailed
in the winter season, curbed his indignation which was fast getting out
of control.

But his officers and men in informal groups were already talking
openly of revolution and exploding with rage. 'The soldiers in Rome,
living in luxury and afraid of the very word "war", vote anyone they
fancy on to the throne, and appoint emperors with one eye to the main
chance. We, who have toiled and sweated and grown old in the

service, let others enjoy this privilege, even when we have in our own camp a candidate with much stronger claims. What better way shall we find of repaying his kindness to us, if we throw this chance away? Vespasian's claim to the throne is far stronger than Vitellius's – just as we are far better soldiers than those who appointed him. The wars we have carried through were hardly trifles compared with those in Germany, and as soldiers we can stand comparison with those who brought *that* tyrant with them! But no contest will be necessary – neither Senate nor people will put up with a filthy lout like Vitellius instead of a clean-living man like Vespasian, or turn down a kindly leader in favour of a despotic brute, or choose a childless man as their chief rather than a father; for the best guarantee of peace is the outstanding excellence of princes. If then it takes the experience of years to make good government, we have Vespasian; if the vigour of youth, Titus: the advantages of both ages will be combined. And not only shall we supply strength to those we appoint – we have three legions and contingents from the kings – ; but they will be backed by all the east and as much of Europe as is safely out of Vitellius's reach, and by the allies in Italy, as well as Vespasian's brother and another son. One of these will be joined by many young men of distinction; the other has already been entrusted with control of the City – an immense asset for any candidate for imperial honours. In short, if we lose our chance, the Senate will most likely appoint the very man whose own soldiers, after helping him guard the Empire, have passed him over.'

Such were the remarks passed by the knots of soldiers, who then joined forces and, urging each other on, declared Vespasian emperor and called on him to save the tottering Empire. He indeed had long been anxious about the general weal, but had never sought office for himself; for though aware that in view of his services he had a good claim, he preferred the safety of private life to the dangers of exalted position. But when he turned down their invitation the officers were the more insistent, and the rank and file surrounded him sword in hand, and threatened to kill him if he refused the life that was his due. After earnestly impressing on them his many reasons for declining office, in the end, as he could not convince them, he accepted their nomination.

Mucianus and the other officers now pressed him to assume the sovereignty, while the lower ranks loudly demanded that he should lead them against any that opposed him. But his chief anxiety was to get control of Alexandria, knowing that Egypt was the most important part of the Empire because it supplied corn. Once master of Egypt he felt sure that if hostilities dragged on he could make Vitellius' position impossible, as the people of Rome would not be content to go hungry; secondly he wished to obtain the support of the two legions at Alexandria; and lastly he planned to make the country his shield against the incalculable tricks of fortune. For Egypt is difficult to enter by land, and the coast is almost harbourless; on the west it it is protected by the waterless regions of Libya, on the south by Assuan (separating Egypt from Ethiopia) and the unnavigable cataracts of the Nile, on the east by the Red Sea, which extends as far as Coptus. Its northern bulwarks are the district adjoining Palestine and the Egyptian Sea, where there is no anchorage at all. Thus Egypt is walled in on every side. Its length from Pelusium to Assuan is about 230 miles; the distance by sea from Plinthine to Pelusium is a little over 400.[1] The Nile can be navigated as far as the city of Elephantine, beyond which further progress is barred by the cataracts mentioned above. It is difficult even in peacetime for ships to approach the harbour of Alexandria; the entrance is narrow, and submerged rocks make a straight course impossible. The left side is shut in by artificial moles; on the right the island of Pharos lies off shore, and from this rises an enormous lighthouse whose fires are visible 35 miles away, warning visiting ships to anchor at night well away from the shore because of the difficulty of making the port. The island is surrounded by immense artificial defences; hurling itself against these and breaking round the barriers opposite, the sea makes the channel rough and the narrow entrance treacherous. Inside, however, the harbour is perfectly safe, and is three and a half miles long. To this port is brought everything the country lacks for life and comfort; in return what the land produces in excess of requirements is exported to every part of the world.

Naturally Vespasian was anxious to gain control there and so ensure the stability of the whole Empire. He sent at once to the governor of Egypt and Alexandria, Tiberius Alexander, to inform him of the army's determination, which forced him to shoulder the burden of empire and to seek the co-operation and assistance of the governor. After reading this letter aloud, Alexander enthusiastically called on soldiers and civilians alike to swear allegiance to Vespasian; both were delighted to obey, knowing what an excellent man he was from his conduct of the campaign in Africa. Invited thus to prepare the way for

1. *These figures are wildly out – the first much too small, the second much too big.*

Vespasian's accession, he got everything ready for that general's arrival; and in a flash rumour spread the news of the emperor in the east, and every city celebrated the good news and offered sacrifices on his behalf. The Moesian and Pannonian legions, still furious at the impudence of Vitellius, were even more delighted to swear allegiance to Vespasian. He, setting out from Caesarea, came to Beirut, where many deputations from Syria and many from the other provinces met him, bringing from all the cities crowns and addresses of congratulation. Mucianus, governor of the province, arrived too with news of the universal enthusiasm and the swearing of allegiance in every city.

Everywhere things were going right for Vespasian and with few exceptions were combining to further his ends. He now felt that divine providence was helping him to seize the reins of office and that some just destiny was choosing him as monarch of the world. In one place after another a succession of omens had foretold his reign: he specially remembered the words of Josephus, who while Nero was still alive had dared to address him as Emperor. He was grieved to think that the man was still a prisoner in his hands; so he sent for Mucianus and his other officers and friends, and after first enlarging on Josephus's outstanding energy and the difficulties he had created for the Romans at Jotapata, he went on to describe the predictions which he himself had suspected at the time of being fictions springing from fear, but which had been proved by time and the course of events to be truly inspired. 'It is shocking,' he said, 'that the man who prophesied my rise to power and was the mouthpiece of God should still be treated as a prisoner and endure the lot of a captive'; then summoning Josephus he ordered him to be set free. Seeing a foreigner receive such recompense the officers felt they could confidently expect wonderful things for themselves; but Titus, who was present with his father, exclaimed: 'Father, it is only right that Josephus's disgrace should be removed as well as his fetters. It will be equivalent to a free pardon if instead of unfastening his chains we cut them through.' This is the usual procedure in the case of a man unjustly fettered. Vespasian agreed, and a man came forward and severed the chain with one blow of an axe. Josephus, having thus as a reward for his past prophecies recovered his civil rights, was now believed capable of foretelling what was still to come.

After replying to the deputations Vespasian made a careful choice of governors for the various provinces and then proceeded to Antioch. There he considered what course to take, and decided that his journey to Alexandria was less urgent than a settlement in Rome, since Alexandria was his already but Rome was in a ferment because of Vitellius. So he sent Mucianus to Italy with a formidable body of horse and foot. Mucianus, afraid to sail in the depth of winter, marched his army overland through Cappadocia and Phrygia.

Meanwhile Antonius Primus, at the head of the Third Legion from Moesia, where he was in command, was rapidly advancing to do battle with Vitellius. Vitellius sent Caecina Alienus with a large force to oppose him, having complete confidence in this officer in view of his defeat of Otho. Setting out with all speed from Rome he came face to face with Antonius near Cremona, a Gallic town just over the Italian frontier. But when he saw the size and discipline of the enemy force he had no stomach for a fight, and as retreat seemed dangerous he decided to change sides. Assembling his centurions and tribunes he urged them to go over to Antonius, minimizing the resources of Vitellius and magnifying the strength of Vespasian. The one, he said, was sovereign only in name, the other in fact; it was better for them to recognize the inevitable and adapt themselves to it, and as they were bound to be defeated if they gave battle they must escape the danger by their wits. Vespasian was quite capable, without their assistance, of winning all that was not yet in his grasp: Vitellius, even with it, could not hold what he had.

Speaking to this effect at considerable length Caecina persuaded his whole force to desert to Antonius. But that very night the soldiers changed their minds, realizing with horror that the man who had sent them might prove the winner. So drawing their swords they dashed off to kill Caecina, and would have carried out their intention if the tribunes had not fallen on their knees and begged them not to. They refrained from killing him, but bound the traitor with the intention of sending him to Vitellius. Informed of this, Primus at once summoned his men and led them fully armed against the mutineers. These formed a line and resisted for a while, but soon turned tail and made for Cremona. Primus at the head of his cavalry prevented their entrance, encircled and destroyed the bulk of them before the city, and sweeping in with the survivors gave his troops permission to loot the town. The consequence was that many foreign business men and many of the inhabitants lost their lives, as well as Vitellius' entire army of 30,200 men: of the soldiers from Moesia 4,500 perished. Antonius set free Caecina and sent him to Vespasian to report his triumph. On his arrival Caecina was received with such unexpected honours that his shocking treachery was soon forgotten.

At Rome too Sabinus was more confident now that he knew Antonius was approaching; so collecting the cohorts of armed watchmen he seized the Capitol in the night. At daybreak he was joined by many of the nobles, among them Domitian, his brother's son, the chief pillar of his hopes of victory. Vitellius cared little about Primus, but was furious with those who were supporting Sabinus in his revolt, his congenital brutality making him thirst for noble blood. The part of his army which had returned with him to Rome he flung against the Capitol. The utmost heroism was displayed both by these and by the men who defended the temple; but in the end numbers told and the troops from Germany captured the hill. Domitian and many leading citizens had a remarkable escape, but the rest of the garrison was annihilated. Sabinus was brought before Vitellius and put to death, while the soldiers stripped the temple of its treasures and set it on fire. Next day Antonius marched in with his army; the soldiers of Vitellius met him, joined battle in three areas of the City, and perished to a man. Out of the palace came Vitellius, drunk, and as a last fling gorged to the eyes like the glutton he was. Dragged through the crowd, insulted and tormented in every possible way, he was knifed to death in the heart of his capital, after a reign of 8 months and 5 days: if he had happened to live longer I doubt whether the Empire could have satisfied his lust. Other known casualties totalled more than 50,000 dead. All this took place on the 3rd[1] of Apellaios.

The next day Mucianus entered with his army and stopped further slaughter by Antonius' men, who were still searching the houses and killing many of Vitellius's soldiers and many supposed partisans among the civilians, letting their rage forestall any careful discrimination. He then put forward Domitian, recommending him to the assembled citizens as head of the state till his father arrived. The people, free at last from fear, acclaimed Vespasian as Emperor, and held a combined celebration for his establishment on the throne and Vitellius' overthrow.

After arriving at Alexandria Vespasian received the good news from Rome, and envoys came from all over the world to congratulate their new sovereign, so that the City – bigger than any but Rome – proved too small for the swollen population. Now that the whole Empire was secure and the supremacy of Rome so surprisingly re-established,

1. *The 21st of December by the Roman calendar.*

Vespasian turned his attention to the final stages of the Judaean campaign. He was eager, however, to embark for Rome in person as soon as winter ended, and was putting all his energy into gettings things straight in Alexandria; but he sent Titus with the pick of his army to destroy Jerusalem. Titus marched overland to Nicopolis two and a half miles from Alexandria. There he put his army on board naval vessels and sailed up the Nile past the district of Mendes to the city of Thmuis. Disembarking there he marched to the little town of Tanis, where he camped for the night. His second stopping-place was Heracleopolis, his third Pelusium. Here for two days he rested his army, and the next morning crossed the Pelusian river-mouths, and after marching all day across the desert pitched camp by the temple of Casian Zeus, going on next day to Ostrakine. At this stopping-place there was no water – the inhabitants have to fetch it from elsewhere. After this he broke his journey at Rhinocorura, marching on from there to Raphia, his fourth stopping-place, a town on the Palestinian frontier. His fifth camp he pitched at Gaza, then on to Ascalon, Jamnia, and Joppa, ending up at Caesarea, where he had decided to assemble his other units.

CHAPTER 17

The Siege of Jerusalem – First Stages

TITUS, having in the way we have described crossed the desert from Egypt to Palestine, arrived at Caesarea, where he had decided to concentrate his forces. While he was still at Alexandria helping his father establish the sovereignty newly entrusted to them by God, the faction-fight in Jerusalem had broken out again; a three-cornered fight now, as one party had split in two – in such a miserable situation the best and most providential thing that could happen. The Zealots' attack on the citizens, for the City the beginning of the end, has been described already, with a detailed account of its origin and disastrous progress. We should not be far wrong if we described this as a faction within a faction, like a maddened beast driven by lack of other food to devour its own flesh.

Eleazar (son of Simon), who had at the start separated the Zealots from the citizens and removed them into the Temple precincts, professed indignation at the outrages daily committed by John, whose appetite for blood was still unsatisfied. The truth was that he could not bear to be under the thumb of a usurper who had come on the scene after him: he had set his heart on absolute power and one-man rule. He therefore broke away, taking with him Judas son of Chelcias and Simon son of Ezron, both influential men, together with Hezekiah son of Chobari, quite a well-known person. As each of these was followed by an appreciable number of Zealots, they were able to seize the inner court of the Temple and take up positions over the Holy Gates on the sacred pediment. Provisions were ample, and they had no fears on that score: there was an unlimited supply of sacred commodities for those who had no scruples. But they were alarmed by the smallness of their numbers, and for the most part sat still and made no move. John on the other hand had the advantage in numbers, but this was cancelled out by the awkwardness of his position: with his enemies overhead he could not attack them with any confidence, and if he remained inactive his rage choked him. He suffered more damage than he could do to Eleazar and his men, yet he would not suspend operations: there were constant sorties and showers of missiles, and murder desecrated every corner of the Temple.

Simon son of Gioras, whom the people in their distress had called in, hoping for aid but saddling themselves with one tyrant the more, was master of the Upper City and much of the Lower. He now launched more violent attacks on John's men, since they were being assailed also from above: he himself had to approach them from beneath, as they did those above them. Attacked from both sides, John gave as good as he received, and what he lost by being lower than Eleazar he gained by being higher than Simon. So while easily fighting off with light weapons the attack from below, he used his engines to counter the spears showered on him from the Temple above; for he had plenty of quick-loaders, catapults, and stonethrowers, with which he not only repulsed the attackers but killed many of those who offered sacrifice. For though mad enough to commit any sacrilege, they admitted those who wished to make offerings – natives with suspicion and after cautious search, foreigners with less hesitation. But these, though they gained admission by making the Zealots ashamed of their cruelty, often became victims of the sedition; for the heavy missiles came over with such velocity that they reached the Altar and the Sanctuary, falling on priests and sacrifices; and many who had hastened from the ends of the earth to visit this famous place, which all men held sacred, were themselves struck down before their offerings, and sprinkled with their own blood the altar revered by Greeks and barbarians everywhere. The bodies of natives and aliens, priests and laymen, were piled on each other, and the blood of men and beasts formed lakes in the sacred courts. Unhappy City! what have you suffered from the Romans to compare with this? They entered your gates to purge with fire the filthiness within you: you were no longer the place of God; you could not continue, now that you were the burial-place of your own sons and had turned the Temple into a common grave for those who had slain each other. Even now you might be restored to life, if only you would make atonement to God who destroyed you! But even the deepest emotions must be stifled in obedience to the laws of history: this is not the time for private lamentation but for a record of the facts. So I will explain the subsequent course of the insurrection.

The plotters against the City were now divided into three. Eleazar

and his party, who had the sacred first-fruits in their hands, made
John the target of their drunken rage: John and his men plundered the
citizens and directed his attacks against Simon: Simon in his struggle
against the rival factions was dependent for supplies on the City.
Whenever John was assailed from both sides he made his men face both
ways, raining missiles from the colonnades on those who came up from
the City, and using his artillery to repel those who showered spears on
him from the Temple. Whenever the pressure from above was relaxed
– it was often interrupted by drunkenness and exhaustion – he made
bolder, large-scale sallies against Simon's lines. To whichever part of
the City he turned, he never failed to set fire to the houses that were
stocked with grain and supplies of every kind; when he withdrew
Simon advanced and followed his example. It was as if to oblige the
Romans they were destroying all that the City had laid up against a
siege and hamstringing their own powers. The result at any rate was that
all the buildings round the Temple were burnt to the ground, the City
became a desolate no man's land where they flung themselves at each
other's throats, and almost all the grain – enough to support them
through many years of siege – went up in flames. It was hunger that
defeated them, a thing that could never have happened if they had not
brought it upon themselves.

  The entire City was the battleground for these plotters and their
disreputable followers, and between them the people were being torn
to bits like a great carcase. Old men and women, overwhelmed by
the miseries within, prayed for the Romans to come, and looked forward to the war without, which would free them from the miseries
within. Fear and utter despondency filled the hearts of loyal citizens:
they had no chance to effect a change of policy, no hope of compromise
or flight if they desired it. Guards were everywhere and the bandit
chiefs, quarrelling about everything else, executed as common
enemies all who were for peace with the Romans or were suspected of
intending to desert and agreed on only one thing – to murder those
who deserved to live. The shouting of the combatants went on ceaselessly day and night; more frightful still was the terrified moaning of
the bereaved. One cause of grief after another their disasters furnished,
but their cries were bottled up by overwhelming dread: afraid to
voice their anguish they were racked with stifled groans. The living no
longer counted for anything with their kinsfolk: the dead no one
troubled to bury. The reason in either case was that everyone despaired

of his own life; those who belonged to no party had no interest in any-thing – they would soon be dead anyway. Trampling on the bodies heaped upon each other the partisans were locked in strife, and drawing in draughts of frenzy from the corpses under their feet they became more savage still. They were constantly devising some new means of self-destruction, and relentlessly putting all their resolves into effect they left no method of outrage or barbarity untried. John actually purloined the sacred timber for the construction of engines of war. The chief priests and people had once decided to underprop the Sanctuary and increase its height by 30 feet, and the necessary timber had been brought from Lebanon by King Agrippa at very great labour and expense, baulks astonishingly straight and of immense size. But the war had put a stop to the work and John cut them up and built towers with them, as he found them long enough to reach his enemies on the Temple above. These towers he pushed forward and stationed behind the court over against the western recess, the only possible place, as the other sides were completely cut off by staircases.

With the engines so impiously constructed he hoped to defeat his enemies, but God made his efforts useless by bringing the Romans upon him before he had posted a single man on the towers. For Titus had collected part of his forces, ordering the rest to meet him at Jerusalem, and was marching from Caesarea at the head of the three legions which at his father's bidding had laid waste Judaea, and the Twelfth, which under Cestius had once suffered defeat, but which at all times was renowned for its courage and now, remembering what had happened to it, was advancing the more eagerly to seek revenge. Of these he ordered the Fifth to meet him via Emmaus and the Tenth to go up via Jericho. He himself moved off with the rest, accompanied by much larger contingents from his royal allies and many auxiliaries from Syria. The four legions which Vespasian had depleted by selecting men to go with Mucianus to Italy were brought up to strength with those who had arrived with Titus: he had with him 2,000 picked men from the armies at Alexandria and 3,000 from the garrisons on the Euphrates. With them too came a friend of the most tried loyalty and wisdom, Tiberius Alexander. He had recently been administering Egypt for the Romans, and now was entrusted with the command of the armies as a reward for being the first to welcome the newly emerged imperial house, and with splendid faith to throw in his lot with theirs when the future was uncertain. Years and experience, too, had made him a most competent adviser amid the uncertainties of war.

Titus advanced into enemy country behind an advance guard formed of the royal troops and all the allied contingents. Next came roadmakers and camp-constructors, then the officers' baggage with its armed escort. Behind these came the commander-in-chief with his spearmen and other picked soldiers, followed by the legionary cavalry. These marched in front of the engines, and behind them picked men commanded by tribunes and prefects of cohorts; then the Eagle, surrounded by the standards, with their trumpeters in front, and after them the main column, marching six abreast. The servants belonging to each legion came next, preceded by the baggage; and last of all the mercenaries under the watchful eye of a rearguard. Leading his forces on in good order, as is the Roman way, Titus advanced rapidly through Samaria into Gophna, occupied by his father earlier on and now garrisoned. Having spent one night there he set off at daybreak, and after marching all day pitched camp in the valley which the Jews call the Valley of Thorns near Gabath Saul (Saul's Hill), a village about three and a half miles from Jerusalem. From there with about 600 of his best cavalry he went forward to ascertain the strength of the City and the temper of the Jews – would they at the sight of him be frightened into surrender before a blow was struck? for he had been informed, truthfully enough, that the citizens though under the thumb of insurgents and terrorists were anxious for peace, and submitted only because they were too weak to rebel.

As long as he rode straight along the highway leading to the walls no one showed his face outside the gates; but when he left the road and led his body of horse slantwise towards the tower Psephinus, a horde of Jews suddenly poured out by the Women's Towers through the gate facing Helena's Monuments, burst through his cavalry, and lining up in front of those still galloping along the road prevented him from joining those who had turned aside, so cutting off Titus with a mere handful of men. He could not advance, as all the ground was trenched from the wall for gardening purposes, and divided up by cross-walls and a number of fences; and to withdraw to his own men he realized was impossible with such a mass of enemies in between. Moreover the men on the highway had turned tail, and as most of them had no idea that the prince was in danger, but thought that he had turned about as they had, there was no holding them. Titus, seeing that nothing but his own prowess could save him, wheeled his horse, and shouting to his little group to follow charged into the middle of the foe, determined to hack his way through to his own men. Then, if ever, it became evident that the fortunes of war and the fate of princes are in the hands of God; for when missiles were raining down on Titus, who had neither helmet nor breastplate, having gone forward as I said not to fight but to observe, not one touched his person, but as if badly aimed on purpose every spear whizzed past harmlessly. He with his sword again and again scattered those to right and left of him, and striking down many who opposed him from the front trampled the fallen under his horse's hooves. Caesar's dazzling courage called forth an answering shout and cries of 'Go for him!' But whichever way he rode, his opponents instantly scattered in all directions. Those who shared his peril closed in on him, assailed as they were from flank and rear; for their one chance of survival lay in opening a way through with Titus before they were encircled. Two indeed were further off than the rest; one of these was surrounded and struck down with his horse, the other dismounted but was killed and his horse led away; with the remainder Titus got through safely to his camp. Success in their first attack roused the Jews to unreasoning optimism, and Fortune's fleeting smile filled them with boundless confidence in the future.

During the night Caesar was joined by the legion from Emmaus; at daybreak he set out for Look-Out Hill, the first point from which could be seen the City and the shining mass of the Temple – hence the propriety of the name Look-Out for this slight eminence adjoining the northern region of the City. Three quarters of a mile from the City he ordered a single camp to be constructed for the two legions, with the Fifth 600 yards to the rear, as he thought that men tired out by a night march were entitled to protection, so that they could build their rampart in safety. As soon as they had begun their task the Tenth Legion arrived from Jericho, where a body of infantry was stationed to guard the pass previously occupied by Vespasian. This legion had been ordered to encamp about three quarters of a mile from Jerusalem at the Mount of Olives, which faces the City on the east and is separated from it by a deep ravine known as Kidron.

Within the City the warring factions now for the first time put an end to their incessant, suicidal strife in view of war suddenly descending on them from without in all its fury. The partisans, seeing with consternation the Romans building three separate camps, made an unholy alliance and asked each other what they were waiting for, and what ailed them that they allowed the erection of three fortifications that would suffocate them. The enemy were building a rival city with impunity while they, as if they were watching something wonderful being done in their interest, sat behind their battlements hands on laps and weapons laid by. 'Are we only capable of injuring ourselves?' they shouted: 'are the Romans, as the result of our party quarrels, to capture the City without losing a man?' Urging each other on in this way and combining their forces, they seized their weapons, made a sudden sortie against the Tenth Legion, tore across the ravine with blood-curdling yells, and fell upon the enemy at work on their fortifications. They to speed their labours had dispersed, and had grounded most of their arms, never imagining that the Jews would dare to sally out – if they were disposed to do so, their efforts would be stultified by their dissensions. As a result they were surprised and thrown into disorder. Leaving their tasks some promptly retreated; many ran to their weapons but were struck to the ground before they could turn and face the enemy. The number of Jews was steadily increasing as their early successes encouraged other men, and seemed both to them and to the Romans far greater than it really was, as things were going so well for them. Men highly organized and trained to fight according to the book and in obedience to orders are most quickly demoralized by unorthodox and enterprising tactics. So on this occasion the Romans having left the initiative to the Jews gave way before the onslaught. Whenever some of them were overtaken and faced about, they held up the onrush of the Jews, and catching them off their guard in the excitement of pursuit inflicted casualties on them, but as more and more Jews poured out of the City their confusion grew, till at last they were chased from their camp. It is likely that the situation of the whole legion would have been precarious had not Titus, informed of the position, at once gone to the rescue. Denouncing their cowardice in no uncertain terms he rallied the runaways; then falling on the Jews from the flank at the head of the picked men who were with him he killed many, wounded more, routed them all, and drove them into the ravine. On the downward slope they suffered severely, but when they had crossed they turned about and with the stream between them put up a determined resistance. So it went on till midday; then a few minutes after noon Titus lined up the reinforcements he had brought and the men from the cohorts and sent the rest of the legion to resume their fortification on the ridge.

The Jews took this for a rout, and when the watchman posted on the wall waved his cloak a mass of men, quite fresh, sprang into the open with such ferocity that it was like the charge of a herd of buffaloes. Indeed, not one of their opponents awaited the impact, but as if struck by an artillery barrage they broke ranks, turned, and fled up the hillside leaving Titus with a handful of men halfway up the slope. He was strongly urged by the friends who in loyalty to their commander disregarded their danger and stood firm, to retire before these suicidal Jews and not to risk his life for men whose duty was to stay and defend him, but to bear in mind his unique position and not play the part of a private soldier when he was commander-in-chief of the army and master of the world, or run into such extreme danger when everything depended on him. To such appeals Titus shut his ears. He stood his ground against those who were charging up the slope to get at him, and boldly attacking them as they pressed on cut them up; then falling on the masses behind drove them in a body down the slope. His amazing courage and strength terrified them, but even so they did not retreat into the City, but opening out in both directions to get out of his way went hard on the heels of those fleeing up the slope. So he attacked them from the flank and checked their onrush.

Meanwhile those who were constructing the camp above, seeing the men lower down in flight, were again filled with panic and terror and the whole legion scattered, thinking that the Jewish onrush was irresistible and that Titus himself had been put to flight: the others surely would never have fled while he remained. As if in the grip of panic fear they ran off in all directions, till some caught sight of the general in the thick of the fight, and in great fear for his safety shouted to the whole legion to tell them of his danger. Shame turned them back, and reproaching each other less for their flight than for their abandonment of Caesar they rounded fiercely on the Jews, and after once turning them back pushed them off the hillside into the valley. The retreating Jews disputed every inch, but enjoying the advantage of position the Romans drove them all into the ravine. Titus kept up the pressure on those in front of him, sending the legion back to their camp-building, while he with the same men as before firmly opposed the enemy advance. Thus if truth must be told without adding anything in flattery or subtracting anything through envy, it was Caesar himself who twice saved the whole legion from destruction and enabled them to fortify their camp in safety.

As soon as there was a momentary respite from external war, internal faction again raised its head. When the day of Unleavened Bread arrived (14th Nisan, on which the Jews believe they first escaped from Egypt), Eleazar's men half opened the gates to admit citizens who wished to worship within. But John used the Feast to screen his treacherous intentions, and equipping the most insignificant members of his gang – most of them unpurified – with hidden weapons, managed to get them into the Temple unnoticed with orders to seize it before they were detected. As soon as they were inside they whipped off their disguise, and suddenly showed themselves armed to the teeth. Utter disorder and confusion at once reigned all round the Sanctuary: the people who had had nothing to do with party quarrels supposed that the attack was directed against all without distinction, the Zealots that it was against them alone. They, however, abandoned their watch at the gates, jumped down from the battlements, and before a blow was struck concealed themselves in the Temple vaults; while the people from the City, cowering by the Altar and crowding round the Sanctuary, were trampled on and savagely beaten with swords and cudgels. Through private animosity and hatred many harmless persons were taken for rival partisans and murdered by their enemies: any man who had got across one of the conspirators in the past was now recognized as a Zealot and led away to his doom. When the utmost cruelty had been inflicted on the guiltless a truce was granted to the guilty, who came out of the vaults and were allowed to go. Now that they had seized the Inner Temple and all that was stored in it, the invaders could snap their fingers at Simon. Thus what was recently a three-cornered fight was once more a struggle between two parties.

Titus now decided to leave Look-Out Hill and encamp nearer to the City. To deal with any sorties he posted what he considered an adequate body of horse and foot, instructing the rest of his forces to level the ground as far as the walls. Every fence and hedge which the occupiers had put round their gardens and orchards were thrown down, every fruit-tree in the area felled, the dips and hollows filled in, the rocky projections demolished with iron implements, and the whole space flattened from Look-Out Hill to Herod's Monuments alongside the Serpents' Pool.

At this stage the Jews devised an ingenious ruse to catch the Romans. The more daring of the insurgents streamed out of the Women's Towers, and as if they had been expelled by the peace party and dreaded an attack by the Romans, huddled together in a cowering mass. Others lined the walls and pretended to be ordinary citizens; they clamoured for peace, begged for protection, and invited the Romans in, promising to open the gates. While they shouted thus they pelted their own men with stones, as if attempting to drive them from the gates. They in turn pretended to be trying to force an entry and appealing to the men inside, and repeatedly made a dash for the Roman lines, then turned tail with every sign of panic. The Roman soldiers fell for the trick: they thought they had one group in their power and ready for execution, and hoping that the others would open the gates started out to settle the business. But Titus smelt a rat. Only the previous day he had, through Josephus, invited them to come to terms without receiving a civil answer, so now he ordered the soldiers to stay where they were. However, some of the men posted in front of the works had already seized their weapons and charged for the gates. Those who apparently had been expelled gave ground before them at first, but when they were between the towers of the gate the Jews sallied out, surrounded them and attacked them from the rear; while from the battlements came a hail of stones and missiles of every kind, killing many and wounding far more. For it was not easy to escape from the wall under pressure from the rear, and besides, shame at their blunder and fear of their officers forced them to persist in their mistake. So for a long time they kept up the fight with spears, suffering severely at the hands of the Jews, but certainly giving as good as they received, till at last they broke out of the circle. But as they retired the Jews pursued them as far as Helena's Monuments, pelting them all the way. Then cock-a-hoop over their success they mocked the Romans for being taken in by a trick, and brandishing their shields danced and yelled with delight.

Meanwhile the soldiers were received with threats by their officers and an angry outburst from Caesar. The Jews, he said, whose only leader was desperation, did everything with forethought and common-sense, planning stratagems and ambushes with every care, and their devices were crowned with success because of their obedience and unswerving loyalty to each other; whereas the Romans, who because of their discipline and quickness to obey their leaders could always command success, were now humiliated through behaving in the opposite way, caught out by lack of self-control, and, as a crowning disgrace, through fighting without a leader in the presence of Caesar.

What a blow to the laws of the Service! What a blow to his father when he learnt of this defeat! For he in a lifetime of warfare never suffered such humiliation; and the laws always punished with death those guilty of the smallest breach of discipline, whereas now they had seen a whole army leaving its post. However, those reckless fools should soon learn that with the Romans even victory, if won without orders, counted for nothing. With such vehemence did Titus address his officers that it seemed evident he would deal with all the offenders according to the law. They abandoned all hope, expecting to die immediately as they deserved; but the legions swarmed round Titus and pleaded for their comrades, begging him to overlook the rashness of a few men in view of the good discipline of them all: they would atone for their present blunder by exemplary conduct in the future.

Caesar saw that it was in his own interest to yield to their entreaties; for he thought that while an individual punishment should be actually carried out, collective punishments should not go beyond words. He therefore pardoned the soldiers after warning them most emphatically to be more careful another time. Then he considered privately how to make the Jews pay for their stratagem. Four days were spent in levelling the ground right up to the walls. Then wishing to get his baggage-train and supernumeraries by in safety, Titus deployed his effective forces opposite the wall on the north and west, in a formation seven deep, infantry drawn up in front, cavalry behind, each in three ranks, with a seventh line in between formed of archers. This huge concentration put a stop to Jewish sorties, and the transport of the three legions and the supernumeraries marched by without fear. The general himself pitched his camp about 400 yeards from the wall near the corner opposite the tower called Psephinus, where the encircling wall bent back from the north to the west. The other section of the army threw up a fortification facing the tower known as Hippicus, at the same distance of 400 yards from the City. The Tenth Legion remained where it was on the Mount of Olives.

Jerusalem was defended by three walls except where it was shut in by impassable ravines; so that a single rampart was enough. It was built on two hills facing each other and separated by a central ravine,[1] at which the terraces of houses ended. Of these hills the one occupied by the Upper City was much the higher and straighter along its length; being

1. *The Tyropoeon, or Valley of the Cheesemakers, now filled in.*

so strong it was called the Stronghold by King David, father of Solomon who first built the Temple, though known to us as the Upper Market. The second, called the Citadel and covered with the Lower City, was dome-shaped.[1] Opposite this was a third hill, by nature lower than the Citadel and originally cut off from it by another wide ravine; later, however, when the Hasmonaeans were reigning they filled the ravine in, wishing to join the City to the Temple; they also removed the top of the Citadel to reduce its height so that the Temple could be seen beyond it. The Valley of the Cheese-makers, which as we said separated the hills of the Upper and Lower Cities, goes down to Siloam – such was the name we gave to that sweet and never failing spring. On the outside the City's two hills were surrounded by deep ravines, and the steep cliffs on either side made access everywhere impossible.

Of the three walls the Old, thanks to the ravines, and the hill above them on which it was built, was almost impregnable; and apart from the advantage of the situation it was also strongly constructed, David and Solomon, and later kings too, having tackled the work with enthusiasm. Starting in the north at the Hippicus Tower it stretched to the Gymnasium, then joining the Council-chamber ended at the west colonnade of the Temple. Running in the other, westward, direction from the same starting-point, it went down through the area called Bethso to the Essene Gate, then turned south above the fountain of Siloam, from which it bent again eastwards towards Solomon's Pool and going on as far as a place called Ophel joined the east colonnade of the Temple.

The Second Wall started at the Genrath, a gate in the first wall. It enclosed the northern quarter only and went up as far as Antonia. The Third started at the Hippicus Tower from which it ran as far north as the Psephinus Tower, then going down opposite the Monuments of Helena (daughter of King Izates who became queen of Adiabene), and continuing a long way past the Caves of the Kings bent at a corner tower near the Fuller's Tomb, and joining the Old Wall came to an end at the Kidron Valley.[2] This wall was built by Agrippa to protect the

1. *It is now thought that this hill, not the first, was David's stronghold of Zion.*

2. *Older maps show the Third Wall on the line of the modern wall. Archaeologists however have traced a wall much further north, which is now believed to have been the Third.*

newest parts of the City, hitherto defenceless; for as the population overflowed the City gradually crept beyond its limits, and uniting the area north of the Temple to the hill the people pushed out so far that houses covered a fourth hill, Bezetha. Situated opposite Antonia this was cut off from it by a deep trench, dug purposely so that the foundations of Antonia should not be in contact with the hill and be approachable and too low: the relative height of the towers was greatly increased by the depth of the ditch. The new housing estate was known locally as Bezetha, which might be translated New City. When he saw the occupants of the estate in need of protection, the father of the present king, like him called Agrippa, began the wall mentioned above, but fearing that when Claudius Caesar saw how massive the ramparts were he would suspect him of planning revolt and insurrection, he stopped when he had only laid the foundations. If the wall had been finished as it was begun, the City could never have been taken, for it was built of bonded stones 30 feet long and 15 broad, so that it would have been very difficult to undermine with iron tools or shake with engines. The wall itself was 15 feet thick, and its height would no doubt have been greater if the enthusiasm of its designer had not been damped. Later, though its erection by the Jews was hasty, it rose to 30 feet and was surrounded by battlements 3 feet and ramparts 4½ feet high; so the total height reached 37½ feet.

From the wall rose towers 30 feet wide and 30 high, square and solid like the wall itself, the stones as beautiful and perfectly fitted as in a temple. Above the compact mass that towered up 30 feet there were magnificent halls, and over these upper rooms and tanks to hold rainwater. Each tower had a wide spiral staircase. The third Wall had 90 such towers 100 yards apart; the Middle Wall was divided up by 14 towers, the Old by 60. The whole circuit of the City was 3¾ miles.[1] The whole of the Third Wall was wonderful, but not so wonderful as the Psephinus Tower, which rose at the north west corner near the spot where Titus later pitched his camp. 105 feet high, when the sun was up it afforded a prospect of Arabia and the farthest extent of Hebrew possessions as far as the sea. It was octagonal.

Opposite this tower was Hippicus and near to it two others, all

---

1. *If the third wall was on the line favoured by modern scholars the circuit of the City was, as stated by Josephus, 3¾ miles. His earlier figures are obviously wildly out, for 90 towers 30 feet wide and 100 yards apart would make the third wall alone 9900 yards (over 5½ miles) long!*

three built by King Herod in the Old Wall, and superior in size, beauty, and strength to any in the whole world. For apart from his love of grandeur and his ambitions for the City, the king made the splendour of these works a means of expressing his own emotions, naming the towers after the three persons he cared for most, his brother, friend, and wife, to whose memory he dedicated them. His wife, as related already, he had himself killed through passionate love; the other two had fallen in battle, covered with glory. Hippicus, named after the friend, was of square section, 37½ feet each way, and 45 feet high, with no empty space anywhere in it. On top of this solid structure of fitted stones was a reservoir to hold rain-water 30 feet deep, and over this a two-storey building 37½ feet high divided into various chambers. Above this again rose a ring of turrets 3 feet high with ramparts 4½ feet high, making the total height 120 feet.

The second tower, named Phasael after Herod's brother, was of equal length and width, 60 feet each way, the height of the solid part being also 60 feet. Round the top ran a colonnade 15 feet high, protected by breastworks and bulwarks. Rising from the middle of the colonnade was another tower, divided into splendid apartments which even included a bathroom, that the tower might lack nothing to make it seem a palace. The top was equipped with ramparts and turrets. The total height was about 135 feet, the general appearance like that of the tower at Pharos that shows the light of its fires to sailors approaching Alexandria; but the measurement round was much greater. During the siege it served as headquarters for the autocrat Simon.

The third tower, Mariamme – for this was the queen's name – was solid for the first thirty feet, and was also 30 feet long and of equal width. The building on top was more splendid and elaborate than the others, as the king felt it incumbent on him to make the one named after a woman more ornate than those named after men, while theirs were sturdier than hers. The total height in this case was 82½ feet.

The great size of these three towers seemed much greater still because of their site. For the Old Wall in which they were placed was built on a high hill, and above the hill a sort of crest rose 45 feet higher. Erected on this the towers gained enormously in height. Another remarkable feature was the size of the stones: they did not consist of ordinary small stones or lumps that men might carry, but of white marble, cut into blocks, each 30 feet long, 15 wide, and 7½ deep, so perfectly united that each tower looked like a single rock, sent up by mother earth and later cut and polished by artists' hands into shape and angles; so invisible from any viewpoint was the fitting of the joints.

A little way south of these towers and sheltered by them was the king's palace, which no tongue could describe. Its magnificence and equipment were unsurpassable, surrounded as it was on every side by a wall 45 feet high, with ornamental towers evenly spaced along it, and containing huge banqueting halls and guestrooms with 100 beds. Words cannot express the varied beauty of the stones, for kinds rare everywhere else were here brought together in quantity. There were ceilings remarkable for the length of the beams and the splendour of the ornamentation, and rooms without number, no two designed alike, and all luxuriously furnished, most of their contents being of gold or silver. On every side were numbers of intersecting colonnades, each differing in the design of its pillars. The open spaces between them were all green lawns, with coppices of different trees traversed by long walks, which were edged with deep canals and cisterns everywhere plentifully adorned with bronze statues through which the water poured out. Flanking the streams were numerous cotes for tame pigeons. But indeed no words are adequate to portray the Palace, and the memory of it is agonizing, since it brings to mind the destruction wrought by the bandits' fires. For the Palace was not fired by the Romans but, as we said earlier, by the plotters within the City, who when the revolt began lit a fire at Antonia which spread to the Palace and reached the upper storeys of the three towers.

The Temple, as stated earlier, was built on a strong hill.[1] At first the level ground at the top was hardly spacious enough for Sanctuary and Altar, as it was surrounded by steep cliffs.[2] King Solomon, who originally founded the Sanctuary, walled up the eastern side and erected a single colonnade on the platform thus created: on the remaining sides the Sanctuary was bare. In successive generations the people kept extending the platform, and the flat hilltop grew wider. Then they cut through the south wall and took in all the ground later included within the periphery of the whole Temple. Having walled in

1. *As Josephus was familiar with the Temple, his account is naturally more reliable than our other written authority, Middoth, written about 80 years after the destruction; but in important particulars it cannot be reconciled with the conclusions of archaeologists.*

2. *Throughout this translation 'Sanctuary' represents Greek* naos *and denotes the central shrine, while 'Temple' represents* hieron *and includes the courts, colonnades, etc. surrounding the shrine.*

the hill from its base on three sides and completed a task to stagger the imagination – a task on which they spent long ages and all their sacred treasures, replenished as they were by tribute sent from every corner of the world as a gift to God – they built round the Sanctuary both the upper enclosures and the lower Temple courts. These where the ground was lowest had to be built up 450 feet, in some places even more. The whole depth of the foundations did not meet the eye, as the ravines were largely filled in from a wish to level the streets of the town. Stones 60 feet long were used in the building; for the unlimited funds and popular enthusiasm resulted in undertakings beyond belief, and a task with no end in sight was through patience and the passage of time completed.

Of such foundations the works above were entirely worthy. The colonnades were all double, the supporting pillars were 37½ feet high, cut from single blocks of the whitest marble, and the ceiling was panelled with cedar. The natural magnificence of it all, the perfect polish, the accurate jointing, afforded a remarkable spectacle, without any superficial ornament either painted or carved. The colonnades were 45 feet wide and the complete circuit of them measures ¾ mile, Antonia being enclosed within them. The whole area open to the sky was paved with stones of every kind and colour. Anyone passing through this towards the second court found it enclosed within a stone balustrade 4½ feet high, a perfect specimen of craftsmanship. In this at equal intervals stood slabs announcing the law of purification, some in Greek, some in Roman characters. No foreigner was to enter the Sacred Precincts – this was the name given to the second court. Fourteen steps led up to it from the first: the elevated area was rectangular and had a protecting wall of its own. The height of this on the outside was 60 feet, but it was concealed by the steps: on the inside it was only 37½ feet. For the interior was perched up at the top of the steps and so could not all be seen, concealed as it was by being higher up the hill. Beyond the fourteen steps there was a space of fourteen feet to the wall, quite flat. From there other flights of five steps led up to the gates. On the north and south the gates numbered eight, four in each case; on the east there were bound to be two, for on this side a special place was walled off for the women to worship in, necessitating a second gate, which opened facing the first. On the other sides there was one north and one south gate through which the Court of the Women could be entered; for through the others women were not admitted, nor might they go by their own gate past the dividing wall. This court was open for worship alike to native women and to Jewesses from abroad. The western part had no gate at all, there being no openings in the wall on that side. The colonnades between the gates faced inwards from the wall in front of the treasury, and rested on pillars of exceptional height and beauty; they were single, but apart from size were in every way equal to those round the lower court.

Of the gates nine were completely covered with gold and silver, as were the posts and lintels, but the one outside the Sanctuary was of Corinthian bronze, and far more valuable than those overlaid with silver or even with gold. Every gateway had double doors, each half being 45 feet high and 22½ wide. On the inner side however the gateways widened out, and on either hand there was a gate-room 45 feet square, shaped like a tower and over 60 feet high. Each room was supported by two pillars 18 feet round. The other gates were all of the same size, but the one beyond the Corinthian Gate, opening out from the Court of the Women on the east and facing the gate of the Sanctuary was much bigger; for its height was 75 feet, that of the doors 50, and the decoration was more magnificent, the gold and silver plates being extremely thick. This plating was the gift of Alexander, father of Tiberius.[1] Fifteen steps went up from the women's enclosure to the Greater Gate, shallower steps than the five at the other gates.

The Sanctuary itself, the Holy Temple, situated in the middle, was reached by a flight of twelve steps. Seen from the front it was of the same height and width, each 150 feet, but behind it was 60 feet narrower, for the entrance was flanked by shoulders, as it were, projecting 30 feet on either side. The first gate was 105 feet high and 37½ wide; it had no doors, symbolizing thus the vast, inexclusible expanse of heaven. The face was covered with gold all over, and through the arch the first chamber could all be seen from without, huge as it was, and the inner gate and its surrounding wall, all glistening with gold, struck the beholder's eye. The Sanctuary was divided into two chambers, but only the first was visible all the way up, as it rose 135 feet from the ground, its length being 75 and its width 30. The gate of this was, as I said, covered with gold all over, as was the entire wall surrounding it. Above it were the golden grape-vines, from which hung bunches as big as a man. The Sanctuary was two storeys high and so appeared lower inside than outside. There were golden doors 82½

1. *Not the emperor but an officer on Vespasian's staff.*

feet high and 24 wide. In front of these was a curtain of the same length, Babylonian tapestry embroidered with blue, scarlet, linen thread, and purple, a marvellous example of the craftsman's art. The mixture of materials had a clear mystic meaning, typifying all creation: it seemed that scarlet symbolized fire, linen the earth, blue the air, and purple the sea. In two cases the resemblance was one of colour; in the linen and purple it was a question of origin, as the first comes from the earth, the second from the sea.[1] Worked in the tapestry was the whole vista of the heavens except for the signs of the Zodiac.

Passing through the gate one entered the ground-floor chamber of the Sanctuary, 90 feet high, 90 long, and 30 wide. But the length was again divided. In the first part, partitioned off at 60 feet, were three most wonderful, world-famous works of art, a lampstand,[2] a table, and an altar of incense. The seven lamps branching off from the lampstand symbolized the planets; the twelve loaves[3] on the table the Zodiac circle and the year. The altar of incense, by the thirteen spices from sea and land, inhabited and uninhabited, with which it was kept supplied, signified that all things are from God and for God.

The inmost chamber measures 30 feet and was similarly separated by a curtain from the outer part. Nothing at all was kept in it; it was unapproachable, inviolable, and invisible to all, and was called the Holy of Holies.

Along the sides of the lower part of the Sanctuary were a number of intercommunicating chambers on three floors, approached by passages on both sides of the entrance. The upper part had no such chambers, as it was narrower; it rose 60 feet higher and was less ornate than the lower part. Thus with the 90 feet of the bottom storey we get 150 as the total height.

Viewed from without the Sanctuary had everything that could amaze either mind or eyes. Overlaid all round with stout plates of gold, in the first rays of the sun it reflected so fierce a blaze of fire that those who endeavoured to look at it were forced to turn away as if they had looked straight at the sun. To strangers as they approached it seemed in the distance like a mountain covered with snow; for any part not covered with gold was dazzling white. From the very top rose sharp gold spikes to prevent birds from perching on the roof and soiling it. Of the

---

1. *Purple dye was made from shellfish.*
2. *Not a candlestick, as generally represented.*
3. *The shewbread.*

stones in the building some were 67½ feet long, 9 wide, and 7½ deep.[1] In front of the Sanctuary stood the Altar, 22½ feet high and as much as 75 feet long and 75 wide, with the four corners jutting out like horns, and with a gentle slope leading up to it from the south. It was built without the use of iron, and no iron ever came in contact with it. Round the Sanctuary and the Altar ran a graceful parapet of beautiful stone about 18 inches high, separating the laity from the priests inside.

Sufferers from venereal disease or leprosy were debarred from entering the City at all; from the Temple women were excluded during their monthly periods, and even when ceremonially clean they could not go beyond the barrier already described. As for men, those not thoroughly sanctified were not admitted to the inner court, nor were priests during their time of ceremonial cleansing.

Of those who were priests by descent any disqualified by physical defect from officiating were allowed inside the parapet like those fully qualified and received the portions to which their birth entitled them, but wore ordinary clothes: vestments were worn by the officiating priests alone. Priests without blemish went up to the Altar and Sanctuary robed in fine linen, rigorously abstaining from strong wine through respect for their ministry, lest they should transgress in any way while officiating. The high priest went up with them, not always but on sabbaths and new moons, and whenever a traditional feast or annual assembly of the nation occurred. He officiated in breeches that covered his thighs to the crutch, with a linen shirt and over that an ankle-length blue robe, circular and tasselled; to the tassels were attached alternately golden bells and pomegranates, thunder being signified by the bells, lightning by the pomegranates. The sash that bound the robe to the breast was adorned by five bands in different colours – gold, purple, scarlet, linen, and blue, with which as we said the Sanctuary curtains also were embroidered. The same combination appeared in the high priest's ephod, gold being most prominent. It was shaped like a fitted breastplate, and secured by two round gold brooches, which were set with very large and very lovely sardonyxes engraved with the names of the tribes that make up the nation. To the other side were attached twelve more stones in four groups of three – sardius, topaz, and emerald; carbuncle, jasper, and sapphire; agate,

---

1. *It would be interesting to know how such stones could be carried up the hill and placed in position. Later, in* Antiquities, *our author gave quite different measurements, almost doubling the volume of each stone, which now becomes 7100 cubic feet.*

amethyst, and jacinth; onyx, beryl, and chrysolite. On each of these again was engraved the name of one tribe. On his head the high priest wore a linen mitre wreathed with blue and encircled by a crown of gold, which bore in relief the sacred letters – four vowels.[1] He did not normally wear these vestments: he put on less ornate garments except when he entered the inmost shrine, which he did once a year – alone – on the day observed by all as a fast to God.[2] The City, and the Sanctuary with its customs and laws, we shall describe in greater detail in a later work; for we have only touched the fringe of the subject.

Antonia, situated at the junction of two colonnades of the first Temple court, the western and northern, was built on a rock 75 feet high and precipitous on every side. It was the work of King Herod and revealed in the highest degree the grandeur of his conceptions. In the first place, from the very bottom the rock was faced with polished stone slabs, both for ornament and to ensure that anyone who tried to climb up or down would slip off; next, before the actual tower was a 4½ foot wall, and inside this the whole elevation of Antonia rose 60 feet into the air. The interior was like a palace in spaciousness and completeness; for it was divided into rooms of every kind to serve every need, colonnades, bathrooms, and wide courtyards where troops could encamp, so that in having all conveniences it was virtually a town, in its splendour a palace. In general design it was a tower with four other towers attached, one at each corner; of these three were 75 feet high, and the one at the south-east corner 105 feet, so that from it the whole Temple could be viewed. Where it joined the Temple colonnades stairs led down to both,[3] and by these the guards descended; for a Roman infantry unit was always stationed there, and at the festivals they extended along the colonnades fully armed and watched for any sign of popular discontent. The City was dominated by the Temple, the Temple by Antonia, so that Antonia housed the guards of all three. The Upper City had a stronghold of its own – Herod's Palace. Bezetha Hill was cut off, as I mentioned, from Antonia. This hill, on which part of the New City was built, was the highest of them all, and on the north it alone obscured the view of the Temple. I intend in a later work to describe the City and its walls in much greater detail, so for the present this must suffice.

1. *Vowels? The mitre was surely inscribed with the Hebrew forms of the consonants YHVH, standing for Yahveh. Josephus has perhaps transliterated it into the Greek form IAUE.*   2. *The Day of Atonement.*   3. *See Acts xxi 40.*

CHAPTER 18

Two Walls Captured

INSIDE the City the partisan fighters under Simon's command, not counting the Idumaeans, numbered 10,000, under 50 officers, with Simon as commander-in-chief. His Idumaean allies were 5,000 strong, with ten officers, of whom Jacob son of Sosas and Simon son of Cathla were the accepted leaders. John, after his seizure of the Temple, had 6,000 fully armed men under 20 officers. Later he was joined by the Zealots, who had laid aside their quarrel. These numbered 2,400, led by their old commander Eleazar and Simon son of Arinus. While these factions, as we said, were fighting each other, the citizens were assailed from two directions at once, and those who would not be accessories to crime were plundered by both parties. Simon held the Upper City and the Great Wall as far as the Kidron, with as much of the Old Wall as bent eastward from Siloam and went down to the palace of Monobazus, king of Adiabene east of Euphrates. He also held the Fountain and part of the 'Citadel', or Lower City, as far as the castle of Helena, Monobazus' mother. John held the Temple and much of the surrounding area, with Ophel and the Kidron Valley. Everything that lay between them they burnt down to leave room for their fratricidal conflict. For even when the Romans were encamped close to the walls the internal strife continued to rage. At the time of the first sortie they had momentarily recovered their wits; but their frenzy had quickly returned, co-operation was at an end, and the internal struggle was resumed as if their one desire was to play into the hands of the besiegers. They suffered nothing worse at Roman hands than they had endured at each other's, and when they had finished there was nothing new left for the City to undergo – she went through greater agony before she fell, and her destroyers accomplished something greater. I mean that her internal divisions destroyed the City, and the Romans destroyed the internal divisions, which were far more firmly established than her walls; and the misery of it all could reasonably be put down to her own people, the justice of it to the Romans. But everyone must interpret the facts in his own way.

Such being the state of affairs within the City, Titus with some picked horsemen rode round outside, looking for the best point for an assault on the walls. Seeing no hope anywhere else, as where the valleys ran there was no access and elsewhere the first wall seemed too solid for his engines, he decided to deliver his assault near the tomb of John the high priest; for there the first rampart was lower and the second was not joined to it, little trouble having been taken with the fortifications where the New City was thinly populated, while it was easy to approach the third through which he planned to invade the Upper City, force his way through Antonia, and capture the Temple. While he was riding round an arrow struck one of his staff, Nicanor, in the left shoulder, as a result of his approaching too near with Josephus in an endeavour to put peace proposals before the sentries on the walls, who knew him well. This brought home to Caesar their determination, for they would not leave unmolested even those who came near to save them: it spurred him on to begin the siege, and he at once gave his infantry leave to devastate the suburbs, and ordered timber to be collected and platforms constructed. Dividing his army into three sections till this work was done, he stationed the spearmen and archers between the platforms and in front of these the quick-loaders, catapults, and stone-throwers, to prevent any enemy sorties directed against the works and any attempted interference from the wall. The felling of the trees at once stripped the suburbs bare, but the collection of the timber for the platforms and the concentration of the whole army on the work were accompanied by feverish activity on the Jewish side. Consequently the citizens who had been at the mercy of bandits and cut-throats now recovered their spirits, confident that they would have a breathing-space while the enemy without kept their persecutors busy, and that they would be revenged on them if the Romans were victorious.

John, however, though his men were eager to attack the Romans, was immobilized by fear of Simon. Simon on the other hand was active enough, being nearer to the besiegers. He mounted his artillery along the wall, the weapons taken from Cestius earlier on and those captured when they overwhelmed the defenders of Antonia. These, however, most of the men were unable to use owing to in-experience, but following instruction from deserters a few managed to use their engines after a fashion, besides showering stones and arrows on the builders from the wall and dashing out in company strength to engage them hand to hand. The workmen were shielded from the missiles by wicker screens laid across palisades, while the artillery halted the sorties. The engines of all the legions were master-pieces of construction, but none were equal to those of the Tenth; their quick-loaders were more powerful and their stone-throwers bigger, so that they could repulse not only the sorties but also the fighters on the wall. The stone missiles weighed half a hundredweight and travelled 400 yards or more; no one who got in their way, whether in the front line or far behind, remained standing. At first the Jews kept watch for the stone – it was white, so that not only was it heard whizzing through the air: its shining surface could easily be seen. Look-outs posted on the towers gave them warning every time a stone was shot from the engine and came hurtling towards them, by shouting 'Baby on the way!' Those in its path at once scattered and fell prone, a precaution which resulted in the stone's passing harmlessly through till it came to a stop. The Roman counter was to blacken the stone. As it could not then be seen so easily, they hit their target, destroying many with a single shot. But in spite of their casualties the Jews did not allow the Romans to raise their platforms in safety; every device of inventive-ness and daring was called into play as they fought night and day to keep them out.

When the works were finished the engineers measured the distance to the wall by throwing lead and line from the platforms: no other way was possible under the barrage from above. When they found that the Batterers could reach it, they brought them up. Titus next posted his artillery nearer to prevent the Jews from keeping the Rams away, and ordered the battering to begin. From three sides a frightful din suddenly resounded round the City, a shout went up from those within and the partisans were as terrified as the rest. Both parties seeing the common danger realized at last that they must make a com-mon defence. The rivals shouted across to each other that they were giving the enemy every possible assistance, when the right thing, even if God did not give them permanent concord, was for the moment at any rate to set aside their mutual animosities and unite against the Romans. Simon then announced that everyone was free to proceed from the Temple to the wall, and John gave his permission though suspicious of Simon. Hatred and private differences utterly forgotten they became one body, and manning the wall they flung firebrands by the hundred against the engines, and showered weapons continuously on the men shoving the Batterers. The bolder spirits sprang forward in tight groups, tore to pieces the screens over the engines, and falling on the crews overpowered them, not so much by skill as by reckless courage. To the help of those in difficulty Titus himself never failed to come: he placed the cavalry and bowmen on either side of the engines, beat off the fire-throwers, repulsed those who were hurling missiles from the towers, and got the Batterers into action. Yet the wall did not give way under the blows, except that the Fifteenth Legion's Ram knocked away the corner of a tower. The wall itself was undamaged: it was not in the same immediate danger as the tower, which projected a long way and could not easily involve the collapse of any part of the actual rampart.

Suspending their sorties for a while the Jews kept watch on the Romans, who had scattered to their tasks and about the camps under the impression that the defenders had withdrawn through exhaustion and terror. Suddenly they poured out en masse by a hidden gate near the tower Hippicus, armed with brands to set fire to the works and bent on reaching the Roman fortifications. At their shouts the front-line troops manned their posts and the supports came running up. But the reckless courage of the Jews was too quick for the solid defence of the Romans: they routed their foremost opponents and swept on to attack the reserves. A furious battle was joined round the engines, one side straining every nerve to set them on fire, the other to prevent it: a babel of sounds arose from both and many of those in the fore-front were killed. The Jews were gaining the advantage through sheer desperation, the works were catching fire and were in danger of being completely destroyed, engines and all, had not the picked troops from Alexandria with few exceptions stood fast, surpassing their own reputation for gallantry; for in this battle they put more famous legions in the shade. At last Caesar brought up the flower of his cavalry and charged the enemy. Twelve of the leading Jews he killed with his right hand. Their fate broke the resistance of the rest: Titus followed, drove them in a body into the City, and saved the works from the flames. It happened that in this battle one of the Jews was taken alive. Titus ordered him to be crucified before the walls, hoping that the sight would terrify the rest into surrender. After the withdrawal John, the Idumaean leader, was talking to a soldier of his acquaintance before the wall when he was struck in the breast by an Arab arrow and died instantly – a terrible shock to the Idumaeans and grief to the insurgents; for his prowess and ability were both outstanding.

The next night the Romans were thrown into confusion by a surprising occurrence. Titus had ordered the construction of three towers 75 feet high, to be set up on three platforms so that from them he might bombard the defenders on the wall. But in the middle of the night one of these fell down spontaneously with a tremendous crash, causing panic in the army. Convinced that an attack was imminent all rushed for their weapons, and wild confusion seized the legions. As no one could say what had occurred, they scattered in all directions with cries of anguish, and when no enemy appeared they grew scared of each other, and everyone anxiously asked his neighbour for the password as if the Jews had broken into their camps. They were like men in the grip of panic fear, till learning what had occurred Titus ordered it to be explained to them all, and at long last they recovered from their confusion.

The Jews stood up obstinately to every other form of attack but were in great difficulty from the towers. From them they were pelted by the lighter engines and by the spearmen, archers, and stone-throwers. On their lofty perch these men were beyond the reach of Jewish weapons, and there was no way to capture the towers, which were difficult to overturn because of their weight and could not be set alight because of the iron that encased them. So they withdrew out of range, abandoning the attempt to hold off the assaults of the Romans, which by their incessant blows were little by little effecting their purpose. Already the wall was giving way before Victor; for so the Jews nicknamed the biggest Roman Batterer, as being victorious over everything; and they had long been worn out by fighting and sentry-go and night-duty far from the City. Besides, through laziness and their habit of deciding wrongly, they thought it a waste of effort to defend this wall as there remained two more behind it. Most of them slacked off and retired; and when the Romans climbed through the breach made by Victor they all left their posts and ran helter-skelter to the second wall. Those who had broken through then opened the gates and let in the whole army. Having thus mastered the first wall on the fifteenth day of the siege – the 7th of Artemisios – the Romans demolished a large part of it, together with the northern suburbs of the City, so recently destroyed by Cestius.

Titus now accommodated his troops within the first wall in the traditional Camp of the Assyrians, occupying all the intervening ground as far as the Kidron, but out of bowshot from the second wall, and at once began probing attacks. Dividing their forces the Jews kept up an obstinate defence from the wall, John's men fighting from Antonia and the northern colonnade of the Temple and before the tomb of King Alexander, Simon's brigade occupying the approach near the tomb of John the high priest and defending the ground as far as the gate by which water was brought in to the Hippicus Tower. Over and over again they sprang out from the gates and fought at close quarters; and though chased back to the wall and worsted in these hand-to-hand struggles, being far less skilled than the Romans, they scored in the wall-fighting. The Romans were upheld by the combination of strength with experience, the Jews by reckless courage nourished by fear, and by their characteristic obstinacy amid disasters; and they still had hopes of survival, as the Romans had of a quick victory. Neither side showed any sign of flagging: assaults, wall-fighting, sorties at company strength went on continuously all day long: no method of attack was left untried. Dusk hardly availed to break off the battles begun at dawn, and there was no sleep for either side – indeed the night was less endurable than the day, the Jews expecting every moment the capture of the wall, the Romans an assault on their camps. Both passed the night in arms; yet the first glimmer of dawn found them ready for battle.

Among the Jews the great ambition was to show outstanding courage and earn the gratitude of their officers. Simon was held in special respect and awe, and so devoted to him was every man under his command that none would have hesitated a moment to kill himself at Simon's bidding. With the Romans the great inducements to valour were the habit of victory and unfamiliarity with defeat, their constant campaigning and uninterrupted training, and the greatness of the Empire – above all the fact that always, in every place, by every man stood Titus. To show weakness when Caesar was there, fighting at their side, was unthinkable, while the man who fought valiantly did so before the eyes of the one who would reward him; indeed, he was paid already if Caesar had recognized his courage. As a result many showed courage beyond their strength through sheer enthusiasm. Here is an instance. On one of those days the Jews were drawn up before the wall in force, and the opposing lines were still exchanging spears at long range. Suddenly Longinus, a cavalryman, leapt out of the Roman ranks and charged the very middle of the Jewish phalanx. Scattering them by his onslaught he killed two of the most stalwart, striking one in the face as he came to meet him, withdrawing the spear and transfixing the other through the side as he turned away. Then back from the middle of the enemy he ran to his own lines unscathed. When he had given this demonstration of prowess there were many who imitated his valour. The Jews on their side, heedless of the damage they suffered, were concerned only with what they could inflict, and death had no terrors for them if only it fell on one of the enemy too. But Titus was as anxious for the safety of his men as for victory itself. He declared that incautious enthusiasm was utter madness, and heroism was heroic only when it went with prudent regard for the hero's own safety. His men were forbidden to risk their own lives in order to display their fearlessness.

He now brought up the Batterer against the middle tower of the north wall. There a cunning Jew named Castor lay in ambush with ten others like himself, the rest having withdrawn to escape the arrows. These for a time kept quiet, crouching behind the parapet, but when the tower began to disintegrate they stood up and Castor, holding out his hands as if in supplication, called on Caesar and in heart-rending tones besought him to pity them. Guileless himself, Titus believed him, and hoping that the Jews had at last come to their senses stopped the Ram, allowed no arrows to be aimed at the suppliants, and invited Castor to state his wishes. When he replied that he would like to come down under a guarantee of impunity, Titus expressed delight at his good sense; he was still more delighted if everyone felt the same, and gladly gave the City his word. Of the ten men five pretended to join in Castor's supplication, but the rest loudly protested that they would never be slaves of the Romans while they could die as free men. During the long wrangle that followed the assault was held up, and Castor sent to Simon bidding him take his time in deciding the necessary steps, as he could delude the Roman command indefinitely. At the same time as he sent this message he made it appear that he was urging the objectors to accept the guarantee. They made a show of indignation, brandishing their naked swords above the parapet, then struck their own breastplates and fell down as if run through. Titus and his staff were dumbfounded at the extraordinary courage of the men, and being unable to see from below just what had happened admired their fortitude and pitied their misfortune.

At this point someone shot an arrow and hit Castor at the side of his nose. He at once drew it out and showed it to Titus, complaining of unfair treatment. Reprimanding the archer Caesar deputed Josephus, who was standing by, to convey the guarantee to Castor and shake hands on it. But Josephus refused to go himself, since the petitioners meant no good, and restrained those of his friends who were anxious to take his place. However Aeneas, one of the deserters, said he would go, and when Castor called for someone to receive the money that he had with him, Aeneas spread out his garments to catch it and ran towards him more eagerly. Castor promptly picked up a huge stone and flung it at him. Aeneas dodged out of the way, but it injured another soldier who had come forward. When Caesar saw how he had been tricked he realized that it was fatal to show pity in war: sterner measures gave the trickster less opportunity. Furious that he had been fooled, he stepped up the assaults of the Batterer. As the tower was on the point of collapse Castor and his men set fire to it, and leaping through the blaze into the vault beneath again gave the Romans the impression of fortitude by apparently flinging himself into the fire.

Caesar captured the wall at this point four days after capturing the first, and as the Jews had retired from it he entered with 1,000 heavy infantry and his special bodyguard, in that part of the New City where the wool-shops, forges, and cloth-market were, and the streets ran slantwise to the wall. If he had without hesitation demolished a longer stretch of the wall, or after entering had by right of conquest sacked what he had taken, his victory would not, I think, have been cancelled out by a reverse. As it was, hoping to shame the Jews by waiving his right to do them hurt, he refrained from widening the breach to ensure an easy retreat: he never imagined they would repay his kindness with treachery. So after his entry he forbade his men to kill any prisoners or set the houses on fire; the partisans he informed that if they wished to fight without harming the citizens they were free to march out; to the citizens he promised the return of their property. For his chief concern was to preserve the City for himself and the Temple for the City.

The people had been ready from the first to accept his demands, but the war-party took humanity for weakness and imagined that it was through inability to take the rest of the City that Titus made these offers. Threatening the townsfolk with death if there was any suggestion of surrender, and murdering all who mentioned the word 'peace', they attacked the Romans inside the wall, some pouncing on them in the narrow streets, some from the houses, while others made a dash outside the wall from the upper gates. In hopeless confusion the guards on the wall jumped down from the towers and withdrew to their camps. A clamour arose from those within, completely encircled by the enemy, and from those without, in fear for those left behind. The Jews, every minute more numerous, and at a great advantage through familiarity with the streets, wounded many and by relentless pressure forced them towards the exit. They, having no other choice, continued to resist; for it was impossible to escape in a body through the narrow gap in the wall. It is probable that all who had entered the City would have been cut to pieces had not Titus come to the rescue. Placing his bowmen at the ends of the streets and taking his own stand where the enemy were thickest, he stopped their advance with his arrows, aided by Domitius Sabinus, who in this battle again showed his worth. Firm as a rock, Caesar kept up a constant stream of arrows and pinned down the Jews till all his men had got clear.

Thus the Romans after capturing the second wall were driven out again. The war-party in Jerusalem were elated, carried away by their success, and convinced that if the Romans ever did venture to set foot in the City again they were doomed to defeat. For God was blinding their eyes because of their transgressions, and they saw neither the strength of the remaining Roman forces – so much more numerous than those they had ejected – nor the famine that was creeping towards them. It was still possible to feed on the public miseries and drink the City's life-blood, though want had long been assailing honest men and for lack of necessities many were at death's door. But the destruction of the people the partisans welcomed: it left more for them. The only people who, in their opinion, deserved to survive were those who had no use for peace and only lived to defeat the Romans: the masses who opposed them were a mere drag, and they were glad to see them go. Such was their attitude to those within the walls: the Romans, when they again tried to break in, they held up by filling the breach and walling it up with their bodies. For three days they stood their ground, resisting with the utmost determination; but on the fourth Titus delivered a violent onslaught which overcame their defence and forced them to retire as before. Once more in possession of the wall, he at once threw down the northern stretch from end to end, and placing garrisons in the towers on the portion towards the south began to plan the assault on the third wall.

He now resolved to suspend the siege for a time and so afford the partisans an interval for deliberation, in the hope that they would be inclined to surrender in view of the demolition of the second wall or through fear of starvation; for plunder would not keep them going for long. This interval he turned to his own advantage as follows. When the soldiers' pay-day arrived, he ordered the officers to parade their troops in full view of the enemy and there count out the money to each man. In accordance with custom the soldiers removed from their armour the protective coverings and advanced in full panoply, the horsemen leading their chargers decked in all their trappings. Every yard of ground before the City shone with silver and gold, a spectacle that filled the Romans with delight, their enemies with terror. Spectators crowded the whole length of the Old Wall and the north side of the Temple, and behind the wall eyes could be seen peering from every window – nowhere in the City was there an inch of ground not hidden by the crowds. Utter consternation seized even the boldest when they saw the entire army assembled, the splendour of their armour and the perfect discipline of the men. I have little doubt that at this sight the partisans would have abandoned their stand, had not the limitless mischief they had done to the citizens destroyed all hope of pardon by the Romans. Death by torture awaited them if they turned back now: death in battle was greatly to be preferred. Fate, too, ordained that with the guilty should perish the innocent, and with the warring factions the entire City.

In four days the Romans completed the payment of all the legions. On the fifth, as no request for peace came from the Jews, Titus divided his legions into two groups and began building platforms in front of Antonia and the Tomb of John, planning to invade the Upper City at the Tomb and the Temple via Antonia: if the Temple was not taken, not even possession of the town would be secure. At each of these points work on two platforms was begun, every legion being responsible for one. The men working alongside the Tomb were hindered by the Idumaeans and Simon's infantry, who made surprise sorties; those before Antonia by John's men and the Zealot groups. These attackers had the advantage not only with hand-thrown missiles which they threw from a greater height, but also because they had now learnt to use their engines; for daily practice had steadily increased their skill. They had 300 quick-loaders and 40 stone-throwers, enabling them to make work on the Roman platforms difficult. Titus knew that the survival or destruction of the City mattered very much to himself; so while he prosecuted the siege he did not fail to urge the Jews to reverse their policy, combining military activity with good advice. Knowing too that very often the sword is less effective than the tongue, he called on them repeatedly to save themselves by handing over the City, virtually his already, and sent Josephus to talk to them in their own language, thinking they would perhaps yield to the persuasions of a fellow-countryman.

Josephus circled the wall, striving to keep out of range but within hearing, and appealing to them again and again to spare themselves and their people, their country and their temple, and not to show themselves more indifferent than were foreigners. The Romans, who had no share in them, respected their enemies' holy places and till now had kept their hands off them, while those who had been brought up in them, and if they survived would alone possess them, were doing their best to destroy them. Did they not see their strongest walls lying flat, and only the weakest one still standing? Did they not know that the might of Rome was invincible, and submission to her an everyday experience? If it indeed was right to fight for freedom, they should have done so at the start; once they had been crushed, and had submitted for many years, to try then to shake off the yoke was to show, not a love of freedom, but a morbid desire for death. It might well be reasonable to disdain meaner masters, but not the lords of the whole world. What corner of the earth had escaped the Romans, unless heat or cold made it of no value to them? From every side fortune had passed to them, and God, who handed dominion over from nation to nation round the world, abode now in Italy. It was an immutable and unchallenged law among beasts and men alike, that all must submit to the stronger, and that power belonged to those supreme in arms. That was why their ancestors, in soul and body and in resources far superior to themselves, had submitted to Rome – which they could not have borne to do if they had not known that God was on the Roman side.

As for themselves, what gave them confidence to hold out, when most of the City was already captured and those inside, even if the walls were still standing, were worse off than if the City had fallen? The Romans were well aware of the famine within, which was now destroying the civilian population and would soon destroy the fighting-men as well. Even if the Romans suspended operations and made no armed assault on the City, yet a war there was no resisting was raging in their midst and growing every hour – unless they could take arms and fight against famine itself, and alone among men master even hunger! They had better change their ways, he went on, before it was too late, and veer to a safer course while they could: the Romans would bear them no grudge for their past folly unless they brazened it out to the end: they were by nature merciful in victory, and they never allowed bitter feelings to stand in the way of their interests, which would not be served by having the City uninhabited or the country desolate. And so Caesar was ready even now to offer them guarantees; but he would not spare a single man if he took the City by storm, least of all if even at their last gasp they turned down his offers. That the third wall would be quickly captured was evident from the capture of the other two: even if that barrier defied attack, hunger would fight for the Romans and against them.

These appeals of Josephus were received by the defenders generally with howls of derision or execration, sometimes with showers of stones. As frank advice was lost on them, he turned to the story of the nation's past.

'You wretched people!' he cried, 'you forget your real allies. Are you fighting the Romans with weapons and your own right hand? Who else have we defeated in that way? and when did God our Creator fail to avenge our wrongs? Turn round and look at the place you are setting out from to the fight, and think how powerful an Ally you have grossly insulted! Have you forgotten the miraculous achievements of your fathers, and the terrible wars this place has won for you in days gone by? For my part, I shudder to recall the works of God in your unworthy hearing – listen all the same, and realize that you are fighting not only the Romans but God as well.

'Pharaoh Necho, king of Egypt at the time, descended on this land with an immense army and seized Sarah the Princess, mother of our nation. And what did her husband, our forefather Abraham, do? Did he avenge the insult by force of arms? Yet he had 318 officers under him, with unlimited manpower at their disposal! Did he not regard them as valueless without the help of God, and stretch out clean hands towards the place you now have desecrated, enlisting the Almighty as his Helper? Wasn't the queen sent back to her husband the very next evening, unsullied, while the Egyptian, reverencing the place stained by you with your countrymen's blood and shaken by terrible dreams in the night, fled, showering silver and gold on God's beloved Hebrews?[1]

'Need I speak of our fathers' sojourn in Egypt? They were crushed and subject to foreign rulers for 400 years; but though they might have resisted with weapons and their own right hand, they committed their cause to God. Who has not heard of Egypt, overrun with every wild beast and wasted by every disease, the barren land, the shrunken Nile, the ten plagues in swift succession, and the consequent departure of our fathers, sent on their way with no bloodshed and no danger, led forth by God to establish His temple-worship? Again, when the Syrians carried off our sacred Ark, did not Philistia and Dagon the idol, did not the whole nation of plunderers rue the day? Their hidden parts suppurating, their bowels prolapsed, they brought it back with the hands that stole it, propitiating the Sanctuary with the sound of cymbals and timbrels and with peace-offerings of every kind. It was God whose generalship won this victory for our fathers, because they placed no trust in their right arm or their weapons but committed to Him the decision of the issue.

'When the king of Assyria, Sennacherib, brought all Asia with him and encamped round this City, did he fall by human hands? Wasn't it when those hands were unarmed and raised in supplication that an angel of God in one night destroyed that innumerable army, so that when he arose in the early morning the Assyrian found 185,000 dead corpses, and fled with the survivors from unarmed Hebrews who attempted no pursuit? You know too of the bondage in Babylon, where the people lived in exile for seventy years, and never tried to shake off the yoke till Cyrus granted them liberty as an offering to God. They were sent on their way by him to re-establish the temple-worship of their Ally.

'In short, on no occasion did our fathers succeed by force of arms, or fail without them after committing their cause to God. If they remained still they were victorious as it seemed good to their Judge: if they gave battle they were beaten every time. For instance, when the king of Babylon was besieging this city, and our king Zedekiah disregarding Jeremiah's prophecies gave battle, he was taken prisoner himself and saw the town and the Temple razed to the ground. Yet how moderate that king was compared to your leaders, and his subjects compared to you! Jeremiah shouted from the housetops that they were

1. *Where* did *Josephus find this fantastic story? Not in Holy Writ!*

hated by God for their iniquities against Him, and would be taken into captivity unless they surrendered the City; yet neither king nor people put him to death. But you! I will say nothing of happenings in the City – I have no words to describe the atrocities you have perpetrated; but when I appeal to you to save yourselves you greet me with howls of execration and showers of stones, enraged at being reminded of your sins and unable to endure any mention of the outrages you openly commit day after day!

'Again, when Antiochus Epiphanes was blockading the City and had committed gross sacrilege, and our ancestors advanced in arms against him, what happened? They were cut to pieces in the battle, the town was plundered by the enemy, and the Sanctuary was desolated for three years and a half. Need I go on with the story? But who enlisted the Romans against our country? Wasn't the impiety of the inhabitants responsible? And what began our servitude? Wasn't it civil strife among our ancestors, when the insane rivalry of Aristobulus and Hyrcanus brought Pompey against the City and God put beneath the Roman heel those who did not deserve to be free? After three months' siege they surrendered, though they had not sinned against the Sanctuary and the Law as you have done – and were far better equipped for war. And we know the end of Antigonus, the son of Aristobulus, don't we? In his reign God by a further capture of the City smote the people for their iniquities: Herod, Antipater's heir, brought Sossius, and Sossius a Roman army, which blockaded and besieged them for six months, till as the punishment of their sins they saw the City captured and plundered by their enemies.

'Thus it was never intended that our nation should bear arms, and war has invariably ended in defeat. It is the duty, I believe, of those who dwell on holy ground to commit all things to the judgement of God, and to scorn the aid of human hands whenever they can reach the ear of the heavenly Judge. But which of the things blessed by the lawgiver have *you* done? Which of the things cursed by him have you left undone? How far those who were defeated in earlier days fell short of your impiety! You have not eschewed the secret sins – theft, treachery, adultery; in plundering and murder you vie with each other; you open up new avenues of vice. The Temple has become a sink for the nation's dregs, and native hands have polluted the hallowed spot that even Romans venerated from a distance, setting aside many of their own customs from regard for your Law.

'After all this do you expect Him you have dishonoured to be your ally? You are indeed righteous suppliants and it is with clean hands that you beseech your Helper! With such hands no doubt our king made supplications for aid against the Assyrian, when in one night that mighty army was struck down by God! Are the Romans behaving so like the Assyrian that you can expect a like vengeance on them? Isn't the truth that whereas he received money from our king on the understanding that he would not sack the City, and then descended on us, in defiance of his oaths, to burn the Sanctuary, the Romans are only demanding the customary tribute which our fathers paid to theirs? When they obtain this they will neither sack the City nor lay a finger on your holy places: they will give you everything else, the freedom of your children, the security of your property, and the preservation of your holy Law. It is madness to expect God to treat the just as He treated the unjust!

'Again, He knows how to take immediate vengeance when there is need; thus on the very night the Assyrians pitched their camp by the City He crushed them. So if He had judged our generation worthy of liberty or the Romans of chastisement, He would immediately have fallen upon them as He fell upon the Assyrians. When? When Pompey meddled with our affairs, when later Sossius came against us, when Vespasian was laying Galilee waste, last of all when Titus was but now drawing near the City. And yet Magnus and Sossius not only suffered no setback but took the City by assault, Vespasian made his war against us the stepping-stone to the throne, while for Titus the very springs flow more abundantly, springs that had dried up for you! Before his advent you know that Siloam was failing, as were all the springs outside the town, so that water had to be bought by the pailful; but now they are in such full flood for your enemies that not only for them and their beasts but even for gardens there is more than enough. The same portent you saw happen once before at the capture of the City, when the Babylonian already referred to marched against it, took the City and Temple and burnt them both, though that generation was surely guilty of no such impiety as yours. So I am sure the Almighty has quitted your holy places and stands now on the side of your enemies. Why, when a good man will quit a licentious house and abominate its occupants, do you think God can endure the wickedness of His household – God, who sees each hidden thing and hears what is wrapped in silence? But what do you wrap in silence or keep hidden?

What have you not paraded before your enemies? You boast of your unspeakable crimes and daily vie with one another who can be the worst, as proud of your vices as if they were virtues!

'In spite of all, a way of salvation still remains if you will follow it, and the Almighty is ready to pardon those who confess and repent. You obdurate fools! throw away your weapons, take pity on your birthplace at this moment plunging to ruin, turn round and gaze at the beauty of what you are betraying – what a city! what a temple! what gifts from all the Gentile world! Against these will any man direct the flames? Does any man wish these things to pass away? What better deserves to be kept safe than these, you inhuman, stony-hearted monsters! If the sight of these things leaves you unmoved, at least pity your families, and let each man set before his eyes his wife and children and parents, so soon to perish by famine or the sword. I know that danger threatens my own mother and wife, a family of great promise, and a house famous from of old; and perhaps you think it is for their sake I advise you. Kill them! take my flesh and blood as the price of your own salvation! I too am ready to die, if thereby you can learn wisdom.'

CHAPTER 19

The Horrors of the Siege

TEARS ran down Josephus' face as he concluded his vehement appeal. The partisans would not give way as they thought a change of front would be disastrous, but among the common people there was a movement in favour of desertion. Some sold all their property at a dead loss, others parted with the more valuable of their treasures. Then to frustrate the bandits they swallowed their gold pieces, and deserting to the Romans had only to empty their bowels to have ample provision for their needs. For most of them were allowed by Titus to go through into the countryside in any direction they chose. This made them still more ready to desert, as they would thus escape from the horrors within the City without being enslaved by the Romans. The partisans of John and Simon made greater efforts to keep these men in than to keep the Romans out, and anyone who afforded even a shadow of suspicion was promptly put to death.

For the wealthy it was just as dangerous to stay in the City as to leave it; for on the pretext that he was a deserter many a man was killed for the sake of his money. As the famine grew worse, the frenzy of the partisans increased with it, and every day these two terrors strengthened their grip. For as nowhere was there corn to be seen, men broke into the houses and ransacked them. If they found some they maltreated the occupants for saying there was none; if they did not, they suspected them of having hidden it more carefully and tortured them. Proof that they had or had not food was provided by the appearance of the unhappy wretches. If they still had flesh on their bones they were deemed to have plenty of stores; if they were already reduced to skeletons they were passed over, for it seemed pointless to dispatch those who were certain to die of starvation before long. Many secretly exchanged their possessions for one measure of corn – wheat if they happened to be rich, barley if they were poor. Then they shut themselves up in the darkest corners of their houses, where some through extreme hunger ate their grain as it was, others made bread, necessity and fear being the only guides. Nowhere was a table laid – they snatched the food from the fire while still uncooked and ate like wolves.

The sight of such misery would have brought tears to the eyes, for while the strong had more than enough the weak were in desperate straits. All human feelings, alas, yield to hunger, of which decency is always the first victim; for when hunger reigns restraint is abandoned. Thus it was that wives robbed their husbands, children their fathers, and – most horrible of all – mothers their babes, snatching the food out of their very mouths; and when their dearest ones were dying in their arms, they did not hesitate to deprive them of the morsels that might have kept them alive. This way of satisfying their hunger did not go unnoticed: everywhere the partisans were ready to swoop even on such pickings. Wherever they saw a locked door they concluded that those within were having a meal, and instantly bursting the door open they rushed in, and hardly stopped short at squeezing their throats to force out the morsels of food! They beat old men who held on to their crusts, and tore the hair of women who hid what was in their hands. They showed no pity for grey hairs or helpless babyhood, but picked up the children as they clung to their precious scraps and dashed them on the floor. If anyone anticipated their entry by gulping down what they hoped to seize, they felt themselves defrauded and retaliated with worse savagery still.

Terrible were the methods of torture they devised in their quest for food. They stuffed bitter vetch up the genital passages of their victims, and drove sharp stakes into their seats. Torments horrible even to hear about they inflicted on people to make them admit possession of one loaf or reveal the hiding-place of a single handful of barley. It was not that the tormentors were hungry – their actions would have been less barbarous had they sprung from necessity – but rather they were keeping their passions exercised and laying in stores for use in the coming days. Again, when men had crawled out in the night as far as the Roman guardposts to collect wild plants and herbs, just when they thought they had got safely away from the enemy lines these marauders met them and snatched their treasures from them. Piteous entreaties and appeals to the awful Name of God could not secure the return of even a fraction of what they had collected at such risk: they were lucky to be only robbed and not killed as well.

While the humbler folk suffered thus at the hands of mere henchmen, men of position or wealth were dragged before the party chiefs. Some of them were falsely accused of plotting and destroyed, others were charged with betraying the City to the Romans; but the favourite

device was to pay an informer to allege that they were planning to
desert. When a man had been stripped by Simon he was sent to John:
when someone had been plundered by John, Simon took him over.
They drank each other's health in the blood of their countrymen and
divided the carcases of the wretches between them. In their desire for
domination the two were at daggers drawn, in their crimes they were
blood-brothers; for the one who did not give his partner a share in the
fruits of other people's misery was deemed an utter scoundrel, while
the one who received no share, as if robbed of a prize, was furious at
being excluded from the savagery. To give a detailed account of their
outrageous conduct is impossible, but we may sum it up by saying
that no other city has ever endured such horrors, and no generation
in history has fathered such wickedness. In the end they brought the
whole Hebrew race into contempt in order to make their own impiety
seem less outrageous in foreign eyes, and confessed the painful truth
that they were slaves, the dregs of humanity, bastards, and outcasts of
their nation. The overthrow of the City was their work, though they
forced the unwilling Romans to be credited with a melancholy victory, and almost hurried the flames to the Temple as if they were too
slow! It is certain that when from the Upper City they watched the
Temple burning they did not turn a hair, though many of the Romans
were moved to tears. But of this I shall speak later at the proper time,
giving a full account of the circumstances.

On the Roman side the platforms were nearing completion, though
the defenders' missiles caused many casualties among the soldiers.
Titus himself detailed a section of the cavalry to ambush those who
sallied out along the valleys in search of food. Some of these were
fighting-men no longer satisfied with what they could steal, but the
majority were penniless workers, afraid to desert lest their families
should be penalized; for they knew the partisans would catch them if
they tried to get their wives and children through the lines, and they
could not bear to leave them behind for the bandits to murder in their
stead. But hunger gave them courage for these sallies, the only thing
left being to slip out and fall into enemy hands. When caught they
were forced to offer resistance, and when the fighting ended it seemed
too late to sue for mercy. Scourged and subjected before death to every
torture, they were finally crucified in view of the wall. Titus indeed
realized the horror of what was happening, for every day 500 – sometimes even more – fell into his hands. However it was not safe to let

V, 460   THE HORRORS OF THE SIEGE   315

men captured by force go free, and to guard such a host of prisoners would tie up a great proportion of his troops. But his chief reason for not stopping the slaughter was the hope that the sight of it would perhaps induce the Jews to surrender in order to avoid the same fate. The soldiers themselves through rage and bitterness nailed up their victims in various attitudes as a grim joke, till owing to the vast numbers there was no room for the crosses, and no crosses for the bodies.

So far were the partisans from changing their policy in view of this calamity that they went to the opposite extreme in tricking the rest of the people. They dragged the families of the deserters on to the wall with those members of the public who were ready to accept Roman assurances, and showed them what happened to men who deserted to the enemy, declaring that the victims were suppliants, not prisoners. This caused many who were eager to desert to remain in the City, until the truth came out; but some crossed over without further delay, knowing the fate that awaited them but regarding death at enemy hands as a deliverance, compared with starvation. Many of these prisoners Titus ordered to have their hands cut off, that they might not be thought to have deserted and might be believed because of their horrible treatment. Then he sent them to Simon and John, urging these two to put an immediate end to their resistance and not compel him to destroy the City, but reap the benefit of a change of heart, belated as it was, and save their own lives, their wonderful birthplace, and the Temple that was theirs alone. At the same time he went from platform to platform urging on the workers, to show that he would shortly follow up words with deed. In answer the men on the wall hurled insults at Caesar himself and at his father, and shouted that they cared nothing for death, but preferred it to slavery, as men should. They would do all possible damage to the Romans while they had breath in them. What did their birthplace matter to those who, as he himself said, were doomed to die? As for the Temple, God had a better one in the world itself; but this one too would be saved by Him who dwelt in it, and having Him on their side they would laugh at every threat not backed by deeds; for the issue lay with God. Such were the retorts which they yelled, along with mere abuse.

At this time Antiochus Epiphanes arrived with a large force of heavy infantry and a bodyguard of so-called Macedonians, all just out of their teens, tall, and trained and equipped in the Macedonian manner – hence the title, though few of them bore much resemblance to that martial race! As it happened, the most prosperous of Rome's vassals was the king of Commagene – until his luck changed. In his old age he declared that no man before his death should be called happy. But Antiochus, who had arrived while his father still flourished, expressed amazement that the Romans should hesitate to approach the wall. He himself was a born fighter, naturally venturesome, and so phenomenally strong that his audacity rarely failed to achieve its end. Titus smiled and said that they were partners in the struggle; so without more ado Antiochus led his Macedonians in a sudden onslaught on the wall. He himself, thanks to his strength and skill, was untouched by the Jewish missiles as he shot his arrows at them. But his youngsters were severely battered, except a very few; for to fulfil their promise they fought tooth and nail, and when they at last retired many had become casualties. No doubt they said to themselves that even real Macedonians could only conquer if they had Alexander's luck!

The Romans had begun work on the 12th of Artemisios, but they only completed the platforms on the 29th, after seventeen days of continuous toil; for all four were of vast size. One, facing Antonia, was raised by the Fifth Legion opposite the middle of the Quince Pool; another, built by the Twelfth, was thirty feet away. A long way from these, to the north of the City, was the work of the Tenth, near the Almond Pool; forty-five feet from this the Fifteenth built theirs by the High Priest's Monument. But from within the City John tunnelled through the ground near Antonia, supporting the galleries with wooden props, and by the time the engines were brought up he had reached the platforms and left the works without solid support. Next he carried in faggots daubed with pitch and bitumen and set them alight, so that as soon as the props were burnt away the entire tunnel collapsed, and with a thunderous crash the platforms fell into the cavity. At once there arose a dense cloud of smoke and dust as the flames were choked by the debris; then when the mass of timber was burnt away a brilliant flame broke through. This sudden blow filled the Romans with consternation, the ingenuity of the Jews plunged them into despondency; as they had felt sure that victory was imminent the shock froze their hope of success even in the future. To fight the flames seemed useless, for even if they did put them out their platforms were already swallowed up.

Two days later Simon's forces assaulted the other two platforms; for the Romans had brought up their Batterers on this side and were already rocking the wall. Tephthaeus, who came from Garis in Galilee, and Megassarus, a servant of Queen Mariamme, accompanied by a man from Adiabene (the son of Nabataeus) nicknamed because of a disability Ceagiras ('Cripple'), picked up firebrands and rushed at the engines. In the whole course of the war the City produced no one more heroic than these three, or more terrifying. They dashed out as if towards friends, not massed enemies; they neither hesitated nor shrank back, but charged through the centre of the foe and set the engines on fire. Pelted with missiles and thrust at with swords on every side, they refused to withdraw from their perilous situation till the weapons were ablaze. When the flames were already shooting up the Romans came running from the camps to the rescue. But the Jews advanced from the wall to stop them, grappling with those who attempted to quench the flames and utterly disregarding their personal danger. The Romans tugged at the Batterers while the wicker covers blazed; the Jews, surrounded with the flames, pulled the other way, and seizing the red-hot iron would not leave go of the Rams. From the engines the fire spread to the platforms outstripping the defenders. Meantime, the Romans were enveloped in flames, and despairing of saving their handiwork began to withdraw to their camps. The Jews pressed them hard, their numbers constantly swelled by reinforcements from the City, and emboldened by their success attacked with the utmost violence till they actually reached the Roman fortifications and engaged the defenders.

There is an armed picquet, periodically relieved, which occupies a position in front of every Roman camp and is subject to the very drastic regulation that a man who retires, no matter what the circumstances, must be executed. These men, preferring death with honour to death as a penalty, stood their ground, and their desperate plight shamed many of the runaways into making a stand. Quick-loaders were set up on the wall to drive off the mass of men that poured out of the City without the slightest thought for their own safety. These grappled with all who stood in their path, falling recklessly upon the Roman spears and flinging their very bodies against the foe. It was less by actions than by supreme confidence that they gained the advantage, and it was Jewish audacity rather than their own casualties that made the Romans give ground.

At this crisis Titus arrived from Antonia, to which he had withdrawn to choose a site for more platforms. He expressed the utmost contempt for the soldiers, who after capturing the enemy's walls were in danger of losing their own, and were enduring a siege themselves through letting the Jews out of prison to attack them! Then he put himself at the head of a body of picked men and tried to turn the flank of the enemy, who although assailed from the front wheeled round to meet this new threat and resisted stubbornly. In the confusion that followed, blinded by the dust and deafened by the uproar, neither side could distinguish friend from foe. The Jews stood firm, not so much through prowess now as through despair of victory; the Romans were braced by respect for the honour of their arms, especially as Caesar was in the forefront of danger. The struggle would probably have ended, such was the fury of the Romans, with the capture of the whole mass of Jews, had they not forestalled the crisis of the battle by retreating to the City. With their platforms destroyed the Romans were downhearted, having lost the fruits of their prolonged labours in a single hour; many indeed felt that with conventional weapons they would never take the City.

Titus held a council of war. The more sanguine spirits were for bringing the whole army into action in a full-scale assault. Hitherto only a fraction of their forces had been engaged with the enemy; if they advanced en masse the Jews would yield to the first onslaught, overwhelmed by the rain of missiles. The more cautious urged either that the platforms should be reconstructed, or that abandoning these they should merely blockade the City and prevent the inhabitants from making sallies or bringing in food, leaving them to starve and refraining from combat. For there was no battling with despair, when men desired only to die by the sword and so escape a more horrible fate. Titus himself thought it unwise to let so large a force remain idle, while there was no point in fighting those who were certain to destroy each other. To throw up platforms was a hopeless task with timber so scarce, to prevent sallies still more hopeless. For to form a ring of men round so big a City and over such difficult terrain was impracticable, and highly dangerous in view of sudden attacks. The known paths might be blocked, but the Jews would contrive secret ways out, driven by necessity and knowing the ground. Again, if provisions were smuggled in the siege would be prolonged still further, and he was afraid the lustre of his triumph would be dimmed by its slowness in coming. Given time anything could be accomplished, but reputations were won by speed. If he was to combine speed with safety he must build a wall round the entire City. That was the only way to block all egress and force the Jews to abandon their last hope of survival and surrender the City. If they did not, hunger would make them easy victims. For he would not wait for things to happen, but would resume construction of the platforms when resistance had been weakened. If anyone thought the task too great to carry out, he must remember that little tasks were beneath the dignity of Rome, and that without hard work nothing great could be achieved, unless by a miracle.

Having thus convinced the generals Titus ordered them to divide up the work between their units. An inspired enthusiasm seized the soldiers, and when the circuit had been marked out there was competition not only between legions but even between cohorts. The private was eager to please his decurion, the decurion his centurion, the centurion his tribune; the tribunes were ambitious for the praise of the generals; and of the rivalry between the generals Caesar himself was judge. He personally went round several times every day to inspect the work. Starting at the Assyrians' Camp, where his own quarters were, he took the wall to the New City below, and from there through the Kidron to the Mount of Olives. Then he bent the line towards the south enclosing the Mount (as far as the rock called the Dovecot) and the next eminence, which overhangs the valley near Siloam. From there he went in a westerly direction down into Fountain Valley, then up by the tomb of Ananus the high priest, embracing the hill where Pompey's camp had been. Then turning north he passed the village called The House of Peas, and rounding Herod's Tomb went east till he finished up at his own camp, the starting-place. The wall measured 4½ miles, and outside were built on thirteen forts with a combined circumference of over a mile. Yet the whole task was completed in three days, though it might well have taken months – the speed passed belief. Having surrounded the City with this wall and garrisoned the forts, Titus himself took the first night watch and went the rounds; the second he entrusted to Alexander; the third was assigned to the legion commanders. The guards drew lots for periods of sleep, and all night long they patrolled the intervals between the forts.

The Jews, unable to leave the City, were deprived of all hope of survival. The famine became more intense and devoured whole houses and families. The roofs were covered with women and babes too weak to stand, the streets full of old men already dead. Young men and boys, swollen with hunger, haunted the squares like ghosts and fell wherever faintness overcame them. To bury their kinsfolk was beyond the strength of the sick, and those who were fit shirked the task because of the number of the dead and uncertainty about their own fate; for many while burying others fell dead themselves, and many set out for their graves before their hour struck. In their misery no weeping or lamentation was heard; hunger stifled emotion; with dry eyes and grinning mouths those who were slow to die watched those whose end came sooner. Deep silence enfolded the City, and a darkness burdened with death. Worse still were the bandits, who broke like tomb-robbers into the houses of the dead and stripped the bodies, snatching off their wrappings, then came out laughing. They tried the points of their swords on the corpses, and even transfixed some of those who lay helpless but still alive, to test the steel. But if any begged for a sword-thrust to end their sufferings, they contemptuously left them to die of hunger. Everyone as he breathed his last fixed his eyes on the Temple, turning his back on the partisans he was leaving alive. The latter at first ordered the dead to be buried at public expense as they could not bear the stench; later, when this proved impossible, they threw them from the walls into the valleys. When in the course of his rounds Titus saw these choked with dead, and a putrid stream trickling from under the decomposing bodies, he groaned, and uplifting his hands called God to witness that this was not his doing.

While such were the conditions in the City the Romans were exuberant, for none of the partisans sallied out now that they too were despondent and hungry. There was an abundance of corn and other necessaries from Syria and the neighbouring provinces, and the soldiers delighted to stand near the wall and display their ample supplies of food, by their own abundance inflaming the hunger of the enemy. But when suffering made the partisans no more ready to submit, Titus took pity on the remnant of the people, and in his anxiety to rescue the survivors again began constructing platforms, though it was difficult to get timber. Round the City it had all been cut down for the previous works, and the soldiers had to collect new supplies from more than ten miles away. Concentrating on Antonia, from four directions they raised platforms much bigger than the earlier ones. Caesar made the round of the legions, speeding the work and showing the bandits they were in his hands. But they alone seemed to have lost all sense of remorse, and making a division between soul and body acted as if neither belonged to them. For their souls were as insensitive to suffering as their bodies to pain – they tore the carcase of the nation with their fangs, and filled the prisons with the defenceless.

Simon actually put Matthias, who had made him master of the City, to death by torture. The son of Boethus and the scion of the chief priests, he enjoyed the absolute trust and respect of the people. When the masses were being roughly handled by the Zealots whom John had already joined, he persuaded the people to accept Simon's aid, having made no pact with him but expecting no mischief from him. When however Simon arrived and got the City into his power, he treated Matthias as an enemy like the rest, and the furtherer of his cause as a mere simpleton. Matthias was brought before him and accused of favouring the Romans, and without being allowed to defend himself, was condemned to die with three of his sons. The fourth had already made his escape to Titus. When Matthias begged to be killed before his children, pleading for this as a favour because he had opened the gates to Simon, the monster ordered him to be killed last. So his sons were murdered before his eyes and then his dead body was thrown on to theirs, in full view of the Romans. Such were the instructions that Simon had given to Ananus, son of Bagadates, the most brutal of his henchmen; and he mockingly enquired whether Matthias hoped for assistance from his new friends. Burial of the bodies was forbidden. After their deaths an eminent priest named Ananias, son of Masbalus, and the clerk of the Sanhedrin, Aristaeus, whose home was Emmaus, together with fifteen distinguished citizens, were put to death. Josephus' father was kept under lock and key, and an edict forbade anyone in the City to associate with him through fear of betrayal. Any who condoled with him were executed without trial.

Seeing all this Judas, son of Judas, a subordinate whom Simon had entrusted with command of a tower, partly through disgust at these brutal murders but chiefly with an eye to his own safety, collected the ten most reliable of his men. 'How long,' he asked, 'shall we endure these horrors? What hope of survival have we if we remain loyal to a scoundrel? We are starving already and the Romans have almost got in. Simon is betraying his best friends and is likely soon to jump on us; but the word of the Romans can be trusted. So come on! Let us surrender the wall and save ourselves and the City! Simon had lost hope already! it won't hurt him if he gets his deserts a bit sooner.' This argument convinced the ten, and at stand-to he sent off the rest in different directions to avoid discovery. Three hours later he shouted from his tower to the Romans, but some of them were scornful, others mistrustful, the majority uninterested: in any case the City would soon fall into their lap. Titus advanced with his heavy infantry towards the wall, But Simon stole a march on him, occupied the tower first, arrested the men, executed them before the eyes of the Romans, and threw their mutilated bodies over the wall.

At this time, as he went round making yet another appeal, Josephus was struck on the head by a stone and fell to the ground unconscious. Seeing him fall the Jews ran out, and would have dragged him into the City had not Caesar promptly sent men to protect him. While they fought Josephus was picked up, knowing little of what was going on. The partisans thought they had disposed of the man they hated most, and whooped for joy. When the report spread through the City the survivors of the populace were overcome with despair, believing that they had really lost the man with whose help they hoped to desert. When Josephus' mother was told in prison that her son was dead, she said to the guards that she had foreseen this ever since Jotapata; while he was alive she might as well have had no son. Privately she lamented to her maids that this was the only result of bringing children into the world – she would not even bury the son whom she had expected to bury her. But the false report neither grieved her nor cheered the bandits for long. Josephus soon recovered from the blow, and went forward to shout that it would not be long before they paid the penalty for wounding him, and to implore the people to trust him. His reappearance brought new hope to the common folk, to the partisans consternation.

Some of the deserters, seeing no other way, promptly jumped from the wall. Others advanced as if to battle armed with stones, then fled to the Romans. Their fate was worse than if they had stayed in the City, and the hunger they had left behind was, as they discovered, less lethal than the plenty the Romans provided. They arrived blown up by starvation as if by dropsy, then stuffed their empty bellies non-stop till they burst – except for those who were wise enough to restrain their appetites and take the unaccustomed food a little at a time. Those who escaped this danger fell victims to another disaster. In the Syrian camp one deserter was caught picking gold coins out of his excreta. As I mentioned, they swallowed coins before leaving, because they were all searched by the partisans, and there was a great deal of gold in the City. In fact it fetched less than half the old price. But when the trick was discovered through one man, the rumour ran round the camps that the deserters were arriving stuffed with gold. The Arab unit and the Syrians cut open the refugees and ransacked their bellies. To me this seems the most terrible calamity that happened to the Jews: in a single night nearly two thousand were ripped up.

When Titus learnt of this atrocity he was on the point of surrounding the perpetrators with his cavalry and shooting them down. But far too many were involved; in fact those to be punished far outnumbered their victims. Instead he summoned both the auxiliary and the legionary commanders, some of whose men were accused of participating, and spoke angrily to both groups. Was it possible that some of his own soldiers did such things on the off chance of gain, and had no respect for their own weapons that were made of silver and gold? The Arabs and Syrians, serving in a war that was not the concern of their own nation, began by indulging their passions in an undisciplined fashion, and ended by letting Romans take the blame for their bloodthirsty butchery and their hatred for the Jews; for some of his own soldiers shared their evil reputation. The foreigners therefore he threatened to punish with death if any man was caught after this committing such a crime. The legionary commanders he instructed to ferret out suspected offenders and bring them before him.

But avarice, it seems, scorns every penalty and an extraordinary love of gain is innate in man, nor is any emotion as strong as covetousness. At other times these passions are kept within bounds and overawed by fear. But it was God who condemned the whole nation and turned every means of escape to their destruction. So what Caesar forebade with threats was still done to the deserters in secret, and the refugees, before the rest noticed them, were met and murdered by the foreign soldiers, who looked round in case any Roman saw them, then ripped them up and pulled the filthy money out of their bowels. In few however was any found, the majority being victims of an empty hope. Fear of this fate caused many of the deserters to return.

John, when there was nothing left that he could extort from the people, turned to sacrilege and melted down many of the offerings in the Temple and many of the vessels required for services, basins, dishes, and tables, not even keeping his hands off the flagons presented by Augustus and his consort. For the Roman emperors honoured and adorned this shrine at all times. But now this Jew stole even the gifts of foreigners, telling his companions that they need not hesitate to use

God's property for God's benefit, and that those who fought for the Sanctuary were entitled to live on it. Accordingly he emptied out the sacred corn and oil which the priests kept in the Inner Temple to pour on burnt offerings, and shared them out to the crowd, who without a qualm swallowed a pailful or smeared it on themselves. I cannot refrain from saying what my feelings dictate. I think that if the Romans had delayed their attack on these sacrilegious ruffians, either the ground would have opened and swallowed up the City, or a flood would have overwhelmed it, or lightning would have destroyed it like Sodom. For it produced a generation far more godless than those who perished thus, a generation whose mad folly involved the nation in ruin.

But why should I describe these calamities one by one? While they were happening Mannaeus, the son of Lazarus, fled to Titus and told him that through a single gate which had been entrusted to him 115,880 corpses had been carried out between the day the Romans pitched their camp near the City – 14th of Xanthicos – and 1st of Panemos. All these were the bodies of paupers. Though he was not himself in charge he had to pay the expenses out of public funds, so was obliged to keep count. The rest were buried by their own kin, who merely brought them out and threw them clear of the City. After Mannaeus many distinguished citizens deserted, and these reported that in all 600,000 pauper bodies had been thrown out at the gates: of the others the number was unknown. When it was no longer possible to carry out the penniless, they said, the corpses had been heaped up in the biggest houses and the doors locked. The price of corn was fantastically high, and now that the City was walled round and they could not even gather herbs, some were in such dire straits that they raked the sewers and old dunghills and swallowed the refuse they found there, so that what once they could not bear to look at now became their food.

When the Romans heard of all this misery they felt pity: the partisans, who saw it with their own eyes, showed no regrets but allowed these things to come upon them too; for they were blinded by the doom that was closing in on the City and on themselves.

CHAPTER 20

Antonia Captured and Destroyed

As the days wore on the plight of Jerusalem grew steadily worse, the partisans being goaded to greater fury by successive calamities, while the famine that devoured the people now preyed on themselves. The innumerable corpses piled up all over the City not merely were a revolting sight and emitted a pestilential stench: they obstructed the fighting-men as they made their sorties; for like men marching across a battlefield littered with thousands of dead they were forced to trample on the bodies. But as they trod them underfoot they gave no shudder, felt no pity, and saw no ill omen to themselves in this insult to the departed. Their hands drenched with their country's blood they rushed out to battle with foreigners, reproaching the Almighty, it seems to me, for His slowness in punishing them; for it was not hope of victory but despair of deliverance now that emboldened them for the fight. The Romans, though it was a terrible struggle to collect the timber, raised their platforms in twenty-one days, having as described before stripped the whole area in a circle round the town to a distance of ten miles. The countryside like the City was a pitiful sight; for where once there had been a lovely vista of woods and parks there was now nothing but desert and the stumps of trees. No one – not even a foreigner – who had seen the old Judaea and the glorious suburbs of the City, and now set eyes on her present desolation, could have helped sighing and groaning at so terrible a change; for every trace of beauty had been blotted out by the war, and nobody who had known it in the past and came upon it suddenly would have recognized the place: when he was already there he would still have been looking for the City.

To Romans and Jews alike the completion of the platforms brought a new terror. The Jews felt sure that unless they burnt these too the City would fall, the Romans that it would never be taken if they went the way of the others. For no more timber was available, and the soldiers' physical strength had been sapped by toil, their morale by constant reverses. Indeed, the disastrous conditions in the City proved more discouraging to the Romans than to the inhabitants: they found the fighting-men not in the least subdued by their severe reverses, while their own hopes were continually frustrated, their platforms rendered useless by stratagems, their engines by the strength of the wall, their skill in close combat by the daring of their adversaries. Worst blow of all, they discovered that the Jews had an inner courage that rose superior to faction, famine, war, and disasters beyond number. They began to think the onslaughts of these men irresistible, and their equanimity amidst disasters unshakable – what would they not endure if fortune favoured them, seeing that calamity only whetted their appetite for battle? Small wonder, then, that the Romans made the guard-posts of the platforms stronger still.

John's forces in Antonia were building up their strength for eventualities, in case the wall was thrown down. At the same time they forestalled the onslaught of the Rams by an assault on the Roman works. The attempt was a failure: they advanced torch in hand, but before nearing the platforms lost hope completely and turned back. In the first place there seemed to be no agreed plan – they dashed out a few at a time, at intervals, with hesitation and fear – in short, unlike Jews; there was little sign of the national characteristics, boldness, dash, the massed charge, the refusal to acknowledge defeat. But while the customary vigour was lacking in their advance, they found the Romans formed up in unusual strength; with their mail-clad bodies they surrounded the platforms with so complete a bulwark as to leave no chink anywhere for the passage of a firebrand, and every man braced himself to die rather than budge from his post. For apart from the destruction of all their hopes if these works too went up in flames, the soldiers could not bear the thought that trickery should triumph every time over prowess, desperation over skill at arms, numbers over experience, and Jews over Romans. Furthermore the artillery co-operated by dropping missiles on the leading Jewish files: the fallen held up those immediately behind, and the risk of going to the fore quenched their ardour. Of those who pushed beyond the beaten zone, some before coming to close quarters took fright at the disciplined and serried ranks of the enemy, others took to flight only when pricked by their lances. At last flinging the word 'coward' at each other, they withdrew with nothing to show. It was on the 1st of Panemos that the attempt was made.

After the Jewish withdrawal the Romans brought up the Batterers, pelted with lumps of rock from Antonia, with firebrands, arrows, and every weapon with which necessity furnished the Jews; for though they felt sure of their wall and despised the engines, they nevertheless tried to prevent them from being brought up. The Romans, assuming that the anxiety of the Jews to avert an assault on Antonia was due to the weakness of the wall, and hoping that the foundations were unsound, made strenuous counter-efforts. The wall stood up to the blows, but the Romans under a deluge of missiles paid no heed to any danger from above and kept the Batterers constantly at work. As however they were awkwardly placed and crushed by the lumps of rock, other men working under a roof of shields strove with hands and crowbars to undermine the foundations, and by strenuous efforts levered out four stones. Darkness ended the activities of both sides, but in the night, at the point where, by the measures he had devised against the earlier platforms, John had undermined the wall, the tunnel fell in and the wall, already shaken by the Rams, suddenly collapsed.

This occurrence had an astonishing effect on both sides. The Jews, who might have been expected to lose heart because the collapse was unlooked for and they were unprepared for it, took it quite calmly as Antonia remained; but the Romans' unlooked for delight at the downfall was quickly extinguished by the sight of another wall which John's men had built just behind. Certainly this one appeared easier to assail than the other: to climb up over the ruins seemed a simple matter, and it was assumed that the wall was much weaker than that of Antonia, and that as it had been erected in an emergency it would quickly disintegrate. However, no one dared to climb up: for those who led the way it meant certain death.

Believing that zest for battle is roused most effectively by words of encouragement, and that incentives and promises often make men oblivious of danger, sometimes contemptuous of death itself, Titus got together the élite of his army and put them to the test.

'My fellow-soldiers,' he began, 'to urge men on to actions involving no risk is a deliberate insult to them and an unmistakable proof of the speaker's cowardice. Incentives, surely, are needed only for dangerous enterprises: the other sort men will undertake without any inducement. So I tell you here and now that the ascent to this wall is a formidable task: the point I would emphasize is that the first duty of those who pride themselves on their courage is to battle with difficulties, that it is a splendid thing to die with honour, and that the heroism of those who lead the way will be amply rewarded. In the first place, what might well be a deterrent to some should be an incentive to you – the endurance of these Jews and their fortitude in distress. It would be scandalous for men who are Romans and my soldiers, in peacetime trained for war, in war accustomed to triumph, to be outshone by Jews in strength or determination, and that on the brink of victory and with God to assist us! For our setbacks are the result of Jewish desperation; their difficulties are increased both by your prowess and by God's assistance. Faction, hunger, siege, walls that fall when no engine is at work – what else can be the cause but God's anger with them and aid to ourselves? So to be outdone by our inferiors and to betray God our Ally as well would be unworthy of us. It would be utterly disgraceful that Jews, whose reputation suffers little from defeat as they have learnt to endure slavery, should in order to escape from it despise death and repeatedly sally out against our full strength, not in the hope of victory but merely to prove their courage, while you, the lords of almost every land and sea, who could not hold up your heads if victory escaped you, never once hazarded a direct encounter with the enemy, but waited for starvation or bad luck to bring them to their knees, while you sat idle with such weapons in your hands, and that when at a trifling hazard you could win a resounding victory! Once on top of Antonia and the City is at our mercy; for even if there is some further fighting against the men inside – I do not anticipate any – we shall be sitting on top, squeezing the breath out of them; and that means victory, speedy and complete.

'I have no intention at this moment of singing the praises of death in battle and the immortality given to those who are killed when fighting-mad; as for those who are not made that way, curse them, I hope they will die in a bed of disease, condemned body and soul to the grave. For every good soldier knows that souls set free from the flesh on the battlefield by the sword are given a welcome by the purest element, ether, and set among the stars, and that as friendly spirits and genial heroes they appear to their own descendants; while souls that waste away in sick bodies, even if completely free from spots and stains, vanish into darkness underground and sink deep into oblivion, life, body, and memory too annihilated at one stroke. But if it is fated that all men must die and a kindlier minister of death than any sickness is the sword, how contemptible it would be not to give to the service of our country what we must yield up to fate!

'I have spoken so far as if those who make the attempt cannot possibly come through alive; but it *is* possible for those who play the man to come safely through the very greatest dangers. First, the ruined wall will be easy to climb; then all the new structure will be easy to throw down. More and more of you must call up your courage for the task and give each other encouragement and support; your determination will soon take the heart out of the Jews. It is quite possible that you will win a bloodless victory once you take the first step. As you climb they will presumably try to stop you; but if you once force your way through undetected, there will be no further resistance, even if only a few of you get there. As for the man who takes the lead, I should be ashamed if when honours are awarded I did not make him an object o envy. Finally the survivor shall be promoted over his present equals, and the fallen shall receive the coveted meed of valour.'

Listening to this speech the bulk of the army were appalled by the greatness of the danger; but in one of the cohorts was a man called Sabinus, a Syrian by race, who in prowess and courage proved himself outstanding. And yet anyone who had seen him before would have concluded from his physical appearance that he was not even an average soldier. His skin was black, his flesh lean and shrunken; but in his frail body, far too slender for its own prowess, dwelt a heroic soul. Springing to his feet he cried: 'I gladly offer you my services, Caesar. I am the first to scale the wall. I trust my strength and determination will have the benefit of your usual luck; but if I am thwarted in my efforts, rest assured I am quite prepared for failure and for your sake have chosen death with my eyes open.'

So saying, with his left hand he held his shield in front of and over his head, and drawing his sword with his right stepped out towards the wall, just about midday. He was followed by eleven of the others, the only ones to emulate his courage; but he went on far ahead of them all, driven by some supernatural impulse. The guards on the battlements flung spears at them, discharged volleys of arrows from all directions and rolled down great lumps of rock, which swept away some of the eleven; but Sabinus, charging into the missiles and buried under the arrows, did not falter for a moment till he had got to the top and routed the enemy. For the Jews, astounded by his dynamic energy and remorseless determination, and thinking too that others had climbed up, turned tail. And here one might well complain of Fortune, so jealous of heroic deeds and ever ready to prevent brilliant successes. For this brave man, just as he achieved his purpose, tripped up, and stumbling over a big stone fell flat on top of it with a great crash. The Jews swung round, and seeing him alone and on the ground pelted him from all directions. He got up on one knee, and covering himself with his shield for a time fought back, wounding many who came near him; but soon, riddled with wounds, he lost the use of his right hand and at length, before he breathed his last, he was buried under the arrows. So brave a man deserved a better fate, yet his fall was a fitting end to such an enterprise. Of the others, three who had already reached the top were battered to death with stones, the other eight were dragged down wounded and carried back to camp. This incident took place on the 3rd of Panemos.

Two days later twenty of the men guarding the advanced posts on the platforms got together, and calling on the standard-bearer of the Fifth Legion, two soldiers from the cavalry squadrons and one trumpeter, at 2 a.m. moved forward in silence through the ruins of Antonia. Disposing of the first sentries in their sleep, they got possession of the wall and ordered the trumpeter to sound. The other guards instantly leapt to their feet and ran away without staying to see how many had climbed up; for the trumpet-call and the resulting panic deluded them into thinking that the enemy had climbed up en masse. When Caesar heard the signal he armed his forces with all speed, and with his generals and picked troops led the way to the top. The Jews had taken refuge in the Temple, and the Romans poured in through the tunnel John had dug to the Roman platforms. The partisans of both groups, John's and Simon's, drawn up separately, blocked their way, displaying strength and determination to the very limit; they realized that a Roman entry into the Sanctuary would be the beginning of the end, while the Romans saw in it the dawn of victory. Round the entrances they grappled in a life and death struggle, the Romans driving on relentlessly to get possession of the Temple, the Jews pushing them back towards Antonia. Arrows and spears were of no use to either side; they drew their swords and closed; in the milling mass it was impossible to distinguish one side from the other, as the men were locked together inextricably in the confined space, and amidst the uproar their shouts conveyed no meaning to the ear. The carnage on both sides was terrible, and the mail-clad bodies of the fallen were trampled and crushed by the combatants. Whichever way the tide of battle swung, always there followed the cheers of the victors, the groans of the routed. There was room for neither flight nor pursuit: in the confused struggle the turns of the scale, the movements this way and that, were infinitesimal. Those in front must either kill or be killed – there could be no retreat; for on either side those behind pressed their own men forward and left no space between the opposing lines. But the time came when Jewish fury got the better of Roman skill and the line began to give from end to end. After all, they had fought without a break from two in the morning till one in the afternoon, the Jews in full strength and with the danger of utter defeat as a spur to their valour, the Romans with only a tiny part of their army, since the legions those actually fighting counted on had not yet followed them up the slope. So it was sufficient for the present to be in possession of Antonia.

Standing by Titus' side in Antonia was a centurion from Bithynia called Julian, a man of note and far more remarkable for skill in arms, physical strength, and fearless spirit than anyone I met with from beginning to end of the war. When he saw the Romans already giving way and putting up a poor defence, he sprang forward and drove back the already victorious Jews, unaided, as far as the corner of the Inner Temple. The whole mass fled, convinced that such strength and audacity could not be those of a mere man. This way and that he charged through their midst as they scattered, killing all he could reach : never had Caesar beheld so amazing a sight, or the other side one so terrifying. But he too was pursued by Fate, from whom there is no escape for mortal man. He was wearing the ordinary military boots studded with masses of sharp nails, and as he ran across the stone pavement he slipped and fell flat on his back, his armour clanging so loudly that the runaways turned to look. A shout went up from the Romans in Antonia, alarmed for their champion's safety, while the Jews crowded round him and aimed blows from all directions with their lances and broadswords. Many heavy blows he stopped with his shield; time after time he tried to stand up but was knocked down by the mass of assailants. Even then as he lay he stabbed many with his sword; for he could not be finished off easily, as he was protected in every vital part by helmet and breastplate and kept his head down. But at last, when all his limbs were slashed and no one dared come to his aid, he ceased to struggle.

Caesar was greatly distressed at the death of so gallant a soldier, killed before so many eyes. He himself was prevented by his situation from going to the rescue, though anxious to do so. Those who might have gone were too terrified. So Julian, after a long fight for life in which he allowed few of his assailants to go unscathed, at long last received the *coup de grâce*, leaving behind him, not only with Caesar but even with his foes, a glorious reputation. The Jews snatched the body and again drove the Romans back, shutting them up in Antonia. Those on their side who distinguished themselves in this battle were Alexas and Gyphthaeus among John's followers, among Simon's Malachias, Judas son of Merto, and Jacob son of Sosas, commanding the Idumaeans, and of the Zealots two brothers, sons of Jairus, by name Simon and Judas.

Titus ordered the soldiers with him to lay Antonia flat and make the ascent easy for the whole army. Then he put up Josephus to speak; for he was informed that on that day, the 17th of Panemos, through lack of men the Continual Sacrifice had been discontinued, and that the people were consequently in the depths of despair. Josephus was to make John the same offer as before: if he was possessed by some morbid craving for a fight, he was free to come out with as many men as he liked and join battle without at the same time bringing destruction on the City and Sanctuary; but he must stop polluting the Holy Place and offending against God. Moreover he was permitted to choose any Jews he liked to offer the discontinued sacrifices.

Josephus took his stand where he could be heard not only by John but by the masses and delivered Caesar's message in Aramaic, appealing to them eloquently to spare their birthplace, to beat out the flames already enveloping the Sanctuary and to restore to God the due oblations. Listening to him the people remained silent and dejected; but the chief gangster poured abuse and curses on the head of Josephus, finally adding that he would never be afraid of capture, as the City was God's. Josephus loudly retorted:

'Of course, you have kept it perfectly pure for God, and the Holy Place remains unpolluted! You have never dishonoured your hoped-for Ally! He still receives the customary sacrifices! If anyone robbed you of your daily food, you godless creature, you would regard him as your enemy; and do you think you can count on God, whom you have denied His everlasting worship, to be your Ally in the war? And do you blame your own sins on the Romans, who have throughout respected our Law and are now pressing you to restore to God the sacrifices you have interrupted? Who would not groan with anguish at the astounding change that has come over the City, when foreigners and enemies atone for your ungodliness and you, a Jew, cradled in the Law, do more hurt than they? But consider, John! To turn your back on evil ways is no disgrace, even at the last moment. If you wish to save your birthplace, you have a splendid example before you in Jeconiah, king of the Jews. He, when the king of Babylon made war on him through his own fault, of his own accord left the City before its capture, and with his family submitted to voluntary imprisonment rather than surrender these holy places to the enemy and see the House of God go up in flames. For that he is celebrated by all Jews in the sacred record, and memory, flowing through the ages eternally new, passes him on to future generations immortal. A splendid example, John, even if it were dangerous! But I can guarantee your pardon from the Romans. Remember this is the advice of a fellow-country-man and the promise of a Jew; it is sensible to consider who is counsell-ing you and where he comes from. I trust that never while I live shall I become such an abject slave as to deny my birth or forget my heritage!

'Once more you rage against me with loud-mouthed abuse. I deserve even worse for flying in the face of fate to advise you, and fighting to save men damned by God. Who doesn't know the writings of the old prophets and the oracle pronounced against this unhappy city and now about to be fulfilled? They foretold the day of her fall – the day when some man began the slaughter of his fellow-country-men. And aren't the City and Temple full of your dead bodies? It is God then, God Himself who is bringing with the Romans fire to purge the Temple and is blotting out the City, brimful of corruption, as if it had never been.'

As Josephus spoke thus, with groanings and tears, sobs choked his voice. Even the Romans were moved by his distress and applauded his determination; but John's party were the more incensed with the Romans, and mad to get Josephus into their clutches. However, many citizens of good family were shaken by his speech. Some of them were too frightened of the partisan guards to move, though they had given up themselves and the City for lost; but a few watched their oppor-tunity to escape and sought asylum with the Romans. These included the chief priests Joseph and Jeshua and several sons of chief priests, three sons of Ishmael who had been beheaded in Cyrene, four of Matthias and one of another Matthias; this man had run away after the death of his father, who had been murdered by Simon son of Gioras with three sons, as explained above. Many other citizens of good family went over with the chief priests. Caesar received them with all possible kindness, and knowing that foreign customs would make life distasteful for them he sent them to Gophna, where he advised them to remain for the time being: he would restore every man's possessions as soon as he had got the war off his hands. So they retired to the little town allotted to them in perfect safety and supremely content.

When they did not reappear, the partisans again spread the tale that the Romans had butchered the deserters, obviously in the hope that the rest would be too frightened to run away. As before, the trick worked for a time; terror effectively put a stop to desertions. But when the men were brought back from Gophna by Titus and ordered to go round the wall with Josephus under the eyes of the people, there was a wholesale flight to the Romans. All the fugitives joined together, and standing in front of the Roman lines wept and wailed as they besought the partisans, if they could bring themselves to do it, to fling their gates wide open to the Romans; if not, at least to withdraw from the Temple and save their treasured Sanctuary: the Romans would never bring themselves, unless absolutely driven to it, to burn down the sacred buildings. This appeal provoked a violent reaction; a volley of abuse was hurled at the deserters, and above the sacred gates quick-loaders, catapults, and stone-throwers were set in line, so that the Temple courts, littered with bodies, were like a vast graveyard, the Sanctuary itself like a fortress. Into the sacred, untrodden precincts they poured armed to the teeth, their hands still dripping with the blood of their own countrymen. So monstrous was their conduct that the indignation the Jews might well have felt if the Romans had committed such outrages against them, was felt by the Romans now against the Jews who profaned their own holy ground. In fact, among the soldiers there was not a man who was not filled with reverent awe when his eyes rested on the Sanctuary, or who did not pray that the terrorists would see the light before all was lost. Greatly distressed, Titus again reproached John and his supporters.

'You disgusting people! Didn't you put up that balustrade to guard your Holy House? Didn't you at intervals along it place slabs inscribed in Greek characters and our own, forbidding anyone to go beyond the parapet? And didn't we give you leave to execute anyone who did go beyond it, even if he was a Roman? Why then, you guilty men, are you now trampling dead bodies inside it? Why are you polluting your Sanctuary with the blood of foreigner and native? I call the gods of my fathers and any god that ever watched over this place – I do not believe there is one now – I call my own army, the Jews in my camp, and you yourselves to witness that *I* am not compelling you to desecrate your Temple. If you change the battle-ground, no Roman shall go near your holy places or insult them: I will protect the Sanctuary for you, whether you wish it or not.'

As Josephus made known this promise on Caesar's behalf, the terrorists and their chief, assuming that not good-will but cowardice lay behind his exhortations, received them with scorn. When Titus saw that these men had no mercy on themselves and no concern for the Sanctuary, he resumed hostilities, though much against his will. It was not possible to bring up his whole army against them as there was not room enough; so he picked out from every century the thirty best soldiers and put a tribune in charge of every thousand, the entire force being under the command of Cerealius, with orders to attack the guardposts an hour before sunrise. He was himself in arms and ready to go down with them, but his friends held him back because the danger was so great, and because the officers insisted that he would do more good by sitting quiet in Antonia in general control of the operations of his men than by going down into the forefront of the battle; if Caesar was watching every man would fight to the death. Yielding to their arguments Caesar explained to the men that he was staying behind for one purpose only – to be judge of their exploits, so that no brave man should go unrewarded, no coward unpunished, through not being seen, and to be an eyewitness of every deed, able as he was both to punish and to reward. So he sent them to their task at the time mentioned above, and going himself to an excellent forward observation-post he remained in Antonia, anxiously awaiting the outcome.

However, the task-force did not find the guards asleep, as they hoped; they leapt to their feet with loud yells and a hand-to-hand struggle instantly began. When the shout of the sentries was heard within, the rest of the guard poured out in a body. Under the onslaught of the leading ranks the Romans stood firm; those who followed collided with their own troops and many treated friends as foes. They could not distinguish voices because of the confused hubbub, nor faces because it was night. They were blinded also, some by fury, some by fear; consequently they struck out indiscriminately at all in their path. The Romans locked their shields together and charged in their units, so suffering less from this bewilderment; and every man remembered the password. The Jews were continually scattering, their attacks and retreats were haphazard, and they repeatedly took each other for enemies; in the darkness any man who moved to the rear was invariably received by his friends as an advancing Roman. In fact more were wounded by their comrades than by the enemy, till day broke and it was possible to see what was happening in the battle. The two sides now separated into opposing formations and began to hurl missiles in an orderly engagement. Neither side gave an inch or showed any sign of weariness. The Romans, as Caesar was watching, individually and by companies vied with each other, every man convinced that his promotion would date from that day if he distinguished himself in the fight: the Jews had as judge of their prowess their fear for themselves and for the Temple, and the taskmaster who stood over them rousing them to action, some with encouragement, some with threats or the lash. In the main the battle was stationary, the ebb and flow very slight and very rapid: flight and pursuit were alike impossible. All the time the shouts from Antonia changed with the fortunes of their own men: at every advance they were loudly cheered, at every retreat they were urged to stand fast. It was like a battle in an amphitheatre: Titus and his staff could see every detail of the fighting. At last, after battling from before dawn to nearly midday, they broke off the fight, without either side having really budged the other from the spot where the first blow was struck, and without any decision being reached. On the Roman side many had fought magnificently; on the Jewish, of Simon's followers Judas son of Merto and Simon son of Josiah, of the Idumaeans Jacob and Simon, sons of Sosas and Cathla respectively, of John's men Gyphthaeus and Alexas, and of the Zealots Simon son of Jairus.

Meanwhile the rest of the Roman army had in one week laid Antonia flat and engineered a wide road to the Temple. Advancing near to the first rampart the legions now set to work on four platforms, one opposite the north-west corner of the Inner Temple, one near the northern arcade between the two gates, and of the other two one opposite the western colonnade of the Outer Temple, the other farther out opposite the northern. The progress of the work, however, cost them much toil and sweat, as they had to fetch the timber eleven or twelve miles. Sometimes they suffered losses through Jewish stratagems, as their crushing superiority made them over-confident just when despair of survival made the Jews more daring than ever. For instance some of the mounted men, every time they went out to collect firewood or fodder, used while they were foraging to let their horses graze free and unbridled; these the Jews by a sudden sortie in strength seized and carried off. This happened so often that Caesar, correctly diagnosing the cause of these losses as less the valour of the Jews than the negligence of his own soldiers, decided to take measures to ensure better care of the horses in future. He commanded one of the men who had lost their mounts to be led off for execution, so terrifying the rest that he made sure their horses should be safe. They never again left them behind to graze, but took them on all their forays as if horse and rider were one. So the war against the Temple continued and the platforms neared completition.

The very day after the ascent of the legions many of the partisans, as the supply of loot was running out and hunger was pressing, made a united attack on the Roman posts on the Mount of Olives an hour before sunset, hoping they would catch them off their guard and already busy with their personal needs, and so force their way through without difficulty. But the Romans saw them coming, and instantly closing in from the neighbouring guard-posts prevented them from climbing over the camp wall or cutting through it by force. Followed a fierce struggle, with many instances of heroic courage on both sides, the Romans showing a combination of strength and tactical skill, the Jews unlimited vigour and uncontrollable fury. Shame was in command of one side, necessity of the other: to let the Jews slip out of the net that enveloped them seemed to the Romans an appalling disgrace: their opponents had one solitary hope of survival – to break through the wall by sheer force. A mounted man from one cohort, by name Pedanius, seeing the Jews at last routed and pushed down into the valley, drove his horse alongside at a furious pace and snatched up one of the enemy as he fled, a young man of sturdy build and in full armour too, seizing him by the ankle – so far did he lean over from the saddle, so magnificently did he display strength of hand and body combined with magnificent horsemanship. Then as if he had got hold of a treasure he rode off with his prisoner to Caesar. Titus congratulated the captor on his amazing strength, and ordered the captive to be executed for his part in the attempt on the wall, then turned his personal attention to the battle for the Temple and the speedier construction of the platforms.

The Jews were suffering so severely in every engagement, as the war slowly but surely approached its culmination and crept nearer to the Sanctuary, that they severed as from a diseased body the affected limbs to prevent the spread of the infection. The part of the north-west colonnade that was joined to Antonia they set on fire, afterwards breaking off some 30 feet, with their own hands beginning the burning down of their holy places. Two days later, on the 24th of the last-named month, the adjoining colonnade was fired by the Romans. When the flames had advanced over 20 feet the Jews as before cut away the roof, and showing no regard whatever for this masterpiece of architecture severed the link it provided with Antonia. With this in mind, though they had a chance to stop the lighting of the fire, they did not even lift a finger as the flames approached, and regarded the progress of the fire in the light of their own advantage. Around the Temple there was no break in the fighting, battle raging continuously between small raiding parties of both sides.

During this period one of the Jews called Jonathan, a man of small stature and nothing much to look at, whose birth and attainments were negligible, stepped forward opposite the tomb of John the High Priest, heaped contempt and abuse on the heads of the Romans, and challenged the bravest of them to single combat. Of the Romans lined up at that point the majority treated him with contempt, some in all probability were frightened, a few were struck by the very reasonable thought that a man who was looking for death was not one to be engaged at close quarters: those who despaired of their lives might well have uncontrollable passions and the willing help of the Almighty; and to risk everything in a duel with one whose defeat would be nothing to boast of, his victory disgraceful as well as dangerous, was an act not of courage but of recklessness. For a long time no one came forward and the Jew hurled a volley of gibes at their cowardice, for he had a great admiration for himself and contempt for the Romans. But at last one Pudens, a member of a cavalry squadron, sickened by his arrogant vapourings and no doubt foolishly overconfident because of his small stature, ran out, joined battle, and was getting the better of it when fortune left him in the lurch: he fell, and Jonathan ran up and dispatched him. Then standing on the body he brandished his dripping sword and with his left hand waved his shield, shouting vociferously at the troops, crowing over the fallen man, and mocking the Romans as they watched. At length, while he still jumped about and played the fool, Priscus, a centurion, shot an arrow which pierced him through; at this shouts went up from Jews and Romans – very different in character. Jonathan, spinning round in his agony, fell down on the body of his foe, clear proof that in war undeserved success instantly brings on itself the vengeance of heaven.

The partisans in the Temple never slackened their overt endeavours to cause daily losses to the soldiers working on the platforms, and on the 27th of the same month they devised the following ruse. In the western colonnade they filled the space between the joists and the ceiling below them with dry wood, bitumen, and pitch, then withdrew as if tired out. Thereupon many thoughtless soldiers, carried away by reckless eagerness, charged after those retreating, and erecting ladders ran up to the colonnade. The more sensible men, suspicious of the unexplained Jewish withdrawal, made no move. However, the colonnade was crowded with the men who had climbed on to it, and at that moment the Jews fired it from end to end. As the flames shot up suddenly all round, the Romans who were out of danger were seized with utter consternation, the trapped men with complete helplessness. Encircled by the blaze some flung themselves down into the City behind them, some into the thick of the foe; many in the hope of escaping with their lives jumped down among their own men and broke their legs; most for all their haste were too slow for the fire; a few cheated the flames with their own daggers. Even those destined for a different end were promptly trapped by the wide extension of the conflagration. Caesar, though angry with the victims for having climbed on to the colonnade without orders, was at the same time moved with human compassion; and though no one could hope to rescue them, it was some comfort to the dying men to see the one for whom they were giving their lives so distressed; for as he called out to them, and dashed forward and urged those around him to do everything possible to help them, he could be seen by all. Taking with him those shouts, that sympathy, like a glorious winding-sheet, every man died happy. Some indeed retired to the wide colonnade wall and got clear of the fire, but they were trapped by the Jews and, after long holding out in spite of their many wounds, finally perished to a man.

Last to fall was a young man named Longus, who added glory to the whole tragic tale, and when every one of all the men who died deserved to be mentioned outshone them all. Full of admiration for his prowess and in any case unable to get at him, the Jews invited him to come down to them under a pledge of safety; his brother Cornelius, on the other hand, adjured him not to tarnish his own renown and disgrace the Roman army. Convinced that he was right, Longus held up his sword in the sight of the opposing lines and plunged it in his heart. Among those trapped by the flames one Artorius saved his life by a trick. He called to him a fellow-soldier, Lucius, who shared his tent, and yelled: 'I will leave you everything I have if you will come close and catch me.' Lucius eagerly ran to his aid; then Artorius jumped on top of him and survived, but his weight dashed his rescuer to the stone pavement, killing him instantly.

For a time this terrible blow filled the Romans with despondency; but it helped them in the long run by making them more wary and putting them on their guard against Jewish traps, in which they suffered chiefly through ignorance of the ground and through the character of their opponents. The colonnade was burnt down as far as the tower which John in his struggle with Simon had built over the gates opening on to the Gymnasium; the rest, now that the men who had climbed on to it had been wiped out, the Jews cut away. The next day the Romans took a turn, setting light to the entire northern colonnade as far as its junction with the eastern where the angle between the two overhung the Kidron Valley, to which there was a terrifying drop. Here for the present we leave the struggle for the Temple.

In the City famine raged, its victims dropping dead in countless numbers, and the horrors were unspeakable. In every home, if the shadow of something to eat was anywhere detected, war broke out and the best of friends came to grips with each other, snatching away the wretchedest means of support. Not even the dying were believed to be in want; at their last gasp they were searched by the bandits in case some of them had food inside their clothes and were feigning death. Open-mouthed with hunger like mad dogs, the desperadoes stumbled and staggered along, hammering at the doors like drunken men, and in their helpless state breaking into the same houses two or three times in a single hour. Necessity made them put their teeth in everything; things not even the filthiest of dumb animals would look at they picked up and brought themselves to swallow. In the end they actually devoured belts and shoes, and stripped off the leather from their shields and chewed it. Some tried to live on scraps of old hay; for there were people who collected the stalks and sold a tiny bunch for four Attic drachmas!

But why should I speak of the inanimate things that hunger made them shameless enough to eat? I am going now to relate a deed for which there is no parallel in the annals of Greece or any other country, a deed horrible to speak of and incredible to hear. For myself, I am so anxious that future ages should not suspect me of grotesque inventions that I would gladly have passed over this calamity in silence, had there not been countless witnesses of my own generation to bear me out; and besides, my country would have little reason to thank me if I drew a veil over the miseries that were so real to her.

There was a woman, Mary the daughter of Eleazar, who lived east of Jordan in the village of Bethezub ('House of Hyssop'). She was of good family and very rich, and had fled with the rest of the population to Jerusalem, where she shared in the horrors of the siege. Most of the property she had packed up and moved from Peraea into the City had been plundered by the party chiefs; the remnants of her treasures and any food she had managed to obtain were being carried off in daily raids by their henchmen. The wretched woman was filled with uncontrollable fury, and let loose a stream of abuse and curses that enraged the looters against her. When neither resentment nor pity caused anyone to kill her and she grew tired of finding food for others – and whichever way she turned it was almost impossible to find – and while hunger was eating her heart out and rage was consuming her still faster, she yielded to the suggestions of fury and necessity, and in defiance of all natural feeling laid hands on her own child, a babe at the breast. 'Poor little mite!' she cried. 'In war, famine, and civil strife why should I keep you alive? With the Romans there is only slavery, even if we are alive when they come; but famine is forestalling slavery, and the partisans are crueller than either. Come, you must be food for me, to the partisans an avenging spirit, and to the world a tale, the only thing left to fill up the measure of Jewish misery.' As she spoke she killed her son, then roasted him and ate one half, concealing and saving up the rest.

At once the partisans appeared, and sniffing the unholy smell threatened that if she did not produce what she had prepared they would kill her on the spot. She replied that she had kept a fine helping for them, and uncovered what was left of her child. They, overcome with instant horror and amazement, could not take their eyes off the sight. But she went on: 'This child is my own, and the deed is mine too. Help yourselves: I have had my share. Don't be softer than a woman or more tender-hearted than a mother. But if you are squeamish and don't approve of my sacrifice – well, I have eaten half, so you may as well leave me the rest.' That was the last straw, and they went away quivering. They had never before shrunk from anything, and did not much like giving up even this food to the mother. From that moment the entire city could think of nothing else but this abomination; everyone saw the tragedy before his own eyes and shuddered as if the crime was his. The one desire of the starving was for death: how they envied those who had gone before seeing or hearing of these appalling horrors!

It was not long before the dreadful news reached the Romans. Some of them refused to believe, some were distressed, on most the effect was to add enormously to their detestation of the Jewish race. Caesar disclaimed all responsibility in the sight of God for this latest tragedy. He had offered the Jews peace and self-government with an amnesty for all offenders; but they had rejected concord in favour of strife, peace in favour of war, plenty and abundance in favour of hunger, and with their own hands had tried to burn down the Temple which the Romans were safeguarding on their behalf; so this food was just what they deserved. Nevertheless he would bury this abomination of infanticide and cannibalism under the ruins of their country, and would not leave in the wide world under the sun a city in which mothers fed themselves thus. It was even more revolting for mothers to eat such food than for fathers, who even after such appalling tragedies remained in arms. While he made this clear, he was thinking too of the desperation of these men: they would never see reason after enduring all the agonies they might so easily have avoided by a change of heart.

CHAPTER 21

The Temple Burnt and the City Taken

By now two of the legions had completed their platforms, and on the 8th of Loös Titus ordered the Rams to be brought up opposite the western arcade of the Outer Temple. For six days before they arrived the most powerful Batterer of all had pounded the wall incessantly without result: this like the others made no impression on stones so huge and so perfectly bonded. At the northern gate a second team attempted to undermine the foundations, and by tremendous efforts they did lever out the stones in front; but the inner stones supported the weight and the gate stood firm, till despairing of all attempts with engines and crowbars they set up ladders against the colonnades. The Jews were in no hurry to stop them, but when they climbed up they were violently assailed; some were pushed backwards and sent headlong, others clashed with the defenders and were killed; many as they stepped off the ladders were unable to get behind their shields before they were run through with swords, while a few ladders crowded with heavy infantry were pushed sideways at the top and overturned; the Jews too suffered severe losses. Those who had brought up the standards fought hard for them, knowing that it would be a terrible disgrace if they were captured; but in the end the Jews even captured the standards, destroying every man who climbed up. The rest, demoralized by the fate of the fallen, withdrew. On the Roman side not a man died till he had accomplished something; of the partisans all who had distinguished themselves in earlier battles shone once more in this, as did Eleazar, nephew of the party chief Simon. Titus, seeing that his attempts to spare a foreign temple meant injury and death to his soldiers, ordered the gates to be set on fire.

At this time two men deserted to him, Ananus from Emmaus, the most bloodthirsty of Simon's henchmen, and Archelaus son of Magadatus, expecting a free pardon as they were quitting the Jews when they were getting the better of it. Denouncing this as another of their dirty tricks and aware of their habitual cruelty to their own people, Titus was strongly inclined to kill them both, pointing out that they had been forced to it by necessity and had not come by free choice, and that men did not deserve to live if they first set their own city on fire and then jumped clear. However, anger could not stand against his own pledged word and he let the men go, though he did not grant them the same privileges as the others.

By now the soldiers were piling fire against the gates. The silver melted and ran, quickly exposing the woodwork to the flames, which were carried from there in a solid wall and fastened on to the colonnades. When the Jews saw the ring of fire they lost all power of body and mind; such was their consternation that not a finger was raised to keep out or quench the flames; they stood looking on in utter helplessness. Yet their dismay at the present destruction made them no wiser for the future, but as if the Sanctuary itself was already in flames they whipped up their rage against the Romans. All that day and the following night the flames were in possession: the colonnades could not be fired all at once but only bit by bit.

The next day Titus ordered a section of his army to put out the fire, and to make a road close to the gates for the easier ascent of the legions. Then he summoned a council of war, attended by the six senior generals – Tiberius Alexander the chief of staff; Sextus Cerealius, Larcius Lepidus, and Titus Phrygius, commanding the Fifth, Tenth, and Fifteenth Legions respectively; Aeternius Fronto, tribune in charge of the two legions from Alexandria; and Marcus Antonius Julianus, procurator of Judaea. After these the other procurators and tribunes were brought in, and Titus invited opinions on the question of the Sanctuary. Some insisted that they should enforce the law of war: there would be continual revolts while the Temple remained as a rallying-point for Jews all over the world. Others argued that if the Jews evacuated it and no armed man was allowed on it, it should be spared, but if they climbed on it for military purposes it should be burnt down. It would in that case be a fortress, not a sanctuary, and from then on the impiety would be blameable not on the Romans but on those who forced their hands. Titus replied that even if the Jews did climb on it for military purposes he would not make war on inanimate objects instead of men, or whatever happened burn down such a work of art: it was the Romans who would lose thereby, just as their empire would gain an ornament if it was preserved. Fronto, Alexander, and Cerealius now confidently came over to this opinion. Titus thereupon adjourned the meeting, and instructing the officers to give the remainder of the army time for rest, so that he should find them full of new vigour when fighting was resumed, he ordered the picked men of all the cohorts to make a road through the ruins and put out the fire.

All that day exhaustion and consternation subdued the enterprise of the Jews; but on the next, having recovered both strength and confidence, they made a sortie through the East Gate against the garrison of the Outer Temple at about 8 a.m. Their onslaught met with stubborn resistance from the Romans, who sheltered behind a wall of steel and closed their ranks, though it was obvious that they could not hold together long as the raiding party surpassed them in numbers and determination. Anticipating the collapse of the line Caesar, who was watching from Antonia, came to the rescue with his picked horsemen. The Jews broke before their onset, and when the front-rank men fell the rest withdrew. But whenever the Romans gave ground they whipped round and pressed them hard: when the Romans turned about they retreated again, till at about 11 o'clock they were overpowered and shut up in the Inner Temple.

Titus retired to Antonia, intending at stand-to next day to launch a full-scale attack and surround the Sanctuary completely. It had however been condemned to the flames by God long ago: by the turning of time's wheel the fated day had now come, the 10th of Loös, the day which centuries before had seen it burnt by the king of Babylon. But it was the Jews themselves who caused and started this conflagration. When Titus had retired the partisans remained quiet for a time, then again attacked the Romans, the garrison of the Sanctuary clashing with those who were putting out the fire in the Inner Temple, and who routed the Jews and chased them as far as the Sanctuary. Then one of the soldiers, without waiting for orders and without a qualm for the terrible consequences of his action but urged on by some unseen force, snatched up a blazing piece of wood and climbing on another soldier's back hurled the brand through a golden aperture giving access on the north side to the chambers built round the Sanctuary. As the flames shot into the air the Jews sent up a cry that matched the calamity and dashed to the rescue, with no thought now of saving their lives or husbanding their strength; for that which hitherto they had guarded so devotedly was disappearing before their eyes.

A runner brought the news to Titus as he was resting in his tent after the battle. He leapt up as he was and ran to the Sanctuary to extinguish the blaze. His whole staff panted after him, followed by the excited legions with all the shouting and confusion inseparable from the disorganized rush of an immense army. Caesar shouted and waved to the combatants to put out the fire; but his shouts were unheard as their ears were deafened with a greater din, and his hand-signals went unheeded amidst the distractions of battle and bloodshed. As the legions charged in, neither persuasion nor threat could check their impetuosity: passion alone was in command. Crowded together round the entrances many were trampled by their friends, many fell among the still hot and smoking ruins of the colonnades and died as miserably as the defeated. As they neared the Sanctuary they pretended not even to hear Caesar's commands and urged the men in front to throw in more firebrands. The partisans were no longer in a position to help; everywhere was slaughter and flight. Most of the victims were peaceful citizens, weak, and unarmed, butchered wherever they were caught. Round the Altar the heap of corpses grew higher and higher, while down the Sanctuary steps poured a river of blood and the bodies of those killed at the top slithered to the bottom. The soldiers were like men possessed and there was no holding them, nor was there any arguing with the fire. Caesar therefore led his staff inside the building and viewed the Holy Place of the Sanctuary with its furnishings, which went far beyond the accounts circulating in foreign countries, and fully justified their splendid reputation in our own. The flames were not yet effecting an entry from any direction but were feeding on the chambers built round the Sanctuary; so realizing that there was still time to save the glorious edifice, Titus dashed out and by personal efforts strove to persuade his men to put out the fire, instructing Liberalius, a centurion of his bodyguard of spearmen, to lay his staff across the shoulders of any who disobeyed. But their respect for Caesar and their fear of the centurion's staff were powerless against their fury, their detestation of the Jews, and an uncontrollable lust for battle. Most of them again were spurred on by the expectation of loot, being convinced that the interior was bursting with money and seeing that everything outside was of gold. But they were forestalled by one of those who had gone in. He, when Caesar dashed out to restrain his men, pushed a firebrand into the hinges of the gate. Then from within a flame suddenly shot up, Caesar and his staff withdrew, and those outside were free to start what fires they liked. Thus the Sanctuary in defiance of Caesar's wishes was set on fire.

Grief might well be bitter for the destruction of the most wonderful edifice ever seen or heard of, both for its size and construction and for the lavish perfection of detail and the glory of its holy places; yet we find very real comfort in the thought that Fate is inexorable, not only towards living beings but also towards buildings and sites. We may wonder too at the exactness of the cycle of Fate: she kept, as I said, to the very month and day which centuries before had seen the Sanctuary burnt by the Babylonians. From its first foundation by King Solomon to its present destruction, which occurred in the second year of Vespasian's reign, was a period of 1,130 years, 7 months, 15 days; from its rebuilding in the second year of King Cyrus, for which Haggai was responsible, to its capture under Vespasian was 639 years, 45 days.[1]

While the Sanctuary was burning, looting went on right and left and all who were caught were put to the sword. There was no pity for age, no regard for rank; little children and old men, laymen and priests alike were butchered; every class was held in the iron embrace of war, whether they defended themselves or cried for mercy. Through the roar of the flames as they swept relentlessly on could be heard the groans of the falling: such were the height of the hill and the vastness of the blazing edifice that the entire city seemed to be on fire, while as for the noise, nothing could be imagined more shattering or more horrifying. There was the war-cry of the Roman Legions as they converged; the yells of the partisans encircled with fire and sword; the panic flight into the arms of the enemy of the people cut off above, their shrieks as the end approached. The cries from the hill were answered from the crowded streets; and now many who were wasted with hunger and beyond speech, when they saw the Sanctuary in flames, found strength to moan and wail. Back from Peraea and the mountains round about came the echo in a thunderous bass.

Yet more terrible than the din were the sights that met the eye. The Temple Hill, enveloped in flames from top to bottom, appeared to be boiling up from its very roots; yet the sea of flame was nothing to the ocean of blood, or the companies of killers to the armies of killed: nowhere could the ground be seen between the corpses, and the soldiers climbed over heaps of bodies as they chased the fugitives. The partisan horde pushed the Romans back, and by a violent struggle burst through into the Outer Temple and from there into the City, the few surviving members of the public taking refuge on the outer

1. *For all their apparent accuracy, these figures are considerably out: the second should be 589 years, the first approximately 1041.*

colonnade. Some of the priests at first tore up from the Sanctuary the spikes with their lead sockets and threw them at the Romans. Then as they were no better off and the flames were leaping towards them, they retired to the wall, which was twelve feet wide, and stayed there. However, two men of note, in a position either to save their lives by going over to the Romans or to face with the others whatever came their way, threw themselves into the fire and were burnt to ashes with the Sanctuary – Meirus son of Belgas and Joseph son of Dalaeus.

The Romans, judging it useless to spare the outbuildings now that the Sanctuary was in flames, set fire to them all – what remained of the colonnades and all the gates except two, one on the east end, the other on the south, both of which they later demolished. They also burnt the treasuries which housed huge sums of money, huge quantities of clothing, and other precious things; here, in fact, all the wealth of the Jews was piled up, for the rich had dismantled their houses and brought the contents here for safe keeping. Next they came to the last surviving colonnade of the Outer Temple. On this women and children and a mixed crowd of citizens had found a refuge – 6,000 in all. Before Caesar could reach a decision about them or instruct his officers, the soldiers, carried away by their fury, fired the colonnade from below; as a result some flung themselves out of the flames to their death, others perished in the blaze: of that vast number there escaped not one. Their destruction was due to a false prophet who that very day had declared to the people in the City that God commanded them to go up into the Temple to receive the signs of their deliverance. A number of hireling prophets had been put up in recent days by the party chiefs to deceive the people by exhorting them to await help from God, and so reduce the number of deserters and buoy up with hope those who were above fear and anxiety. Man is readily persuaded in adversity: when the deceiver actually promises deliverance from the miseries that envelop him, then the sufferer becomes the willing slave of hope. So it was that the unhappy people were beguiled at that stage by cheats and false messengers of God, while the unmistakable portents that foreshadowed the coming desolation they treated with indifference and incredulity, disregarding God's warnings as if they were moonstruck, blind and senseless. First a star stood over the City, very like a broadsword, and a comet that remained a whole year. Then before the revolt and the movement to war, while the people were assembling for the Feast of Unleavened Bread, on the 8th of Xanthicos at three in the morning so bright a light shone round the Altar and the Sanctuary that it might have been midday. This lasted half an hour. The inexperienced took it for a good omen, but the sacred scribes at once gave an interpretation which the event proved right. During the same feast a cow brought by someone to be sacrificed gave birth to a lamb in the middle of the Temple courts, while at midnight it was observed that the East Gate of the Inner Sanctuary had opened of its own accord – a gate made of bronze and so solid that every evening twenty strong men were required to shut it, fastened with iron-bound bars and secured by bolts which were lowered a long way into a threshold fashioned from a single slab of stone. The temple-guards ran with the news to the Captain, who came up and by a great effort managed to shut it. This like the other seemed to the laity to be the best of omens: had not God opened to them the gate of happiness? But the learned perceived that the security of the Sanctuary was dissolving of its own accord, and that the opening of the gate was a gift to the enemy; and they admitted in their hearts that the sign was a portent of desolation.

A few days after the Feast, on the 21st of Artemisios, a supernatural apparition was seen, too amazing to be believed. What I have to relate would, I suppose, have been dismissed as an invention had it not been vouched for by eyewitnesses and followed by disasters that bore out the signs. Before sunset there were seen in the sky over the whole country, chariots and regiments in arms speeding through the clouds and encircling the towns. Again, at the Feast of Pentecost, when the priests had gone into the Inner Temple at night to perform the usual ceremonies, they declared that they were aware, first of a violent movement and a loud crash, then of a concerted cry: 'Let us go hence.'

An incident more alarming still had occurred four years before the war at a time of exceptional peace and prosperity for the City. One Jeshua son of Ananias, a very ordinary yokel, came to the feast at which every Jew is expected to set up a tabernacle for God. As he stood in the Temple he suddenly began to shout: 'A voice from the east, a voice from the west, a voice from the four winds, a voice against Jerusalem and the Sanctuary, a voice against bridegrooms and brides, a voice against the whole people.' Day and night he uttered this cry as he went through all the streets. Some of the more prominent citizens, very annoyed at these ominous words, laid hold of the fellow and beat him savagely. Without saying a word in his own defence or for the private information of his persecutors, he persisted in shouting the same warning as before. The Jewish authorities, rightly concluding that some supernatural force was responsible for the man's behaviour, took him before the Roman procurator. There, though scourged till his flesh hung in ribbons, he neither begged for mercy nor shed a tear, but lowering his voice to the most mournful of tones answered every blow with 'Woe to Jerusalem!' When Albinus – for that was the procurator's name – demanded to know who he was, where he came from and why he uttered such cries, he made no reply whatever to the questions but endlessly repeated his lament over the City, till Albinus decided he was a madman and released him. All the time till the war broke out he never approached another citizen or was seen in conversation, but daily as if he had learnt a prayer by heart he recited his lament: 'Woe to Jerusalem!' Those who daily cursed him he never cursed; those who gave him food he never thanked: his only response to anyone was that dismal foreboding. His voice was heard most of all at the feasts. For seven years and five months he went on ceaselessly, his voice as strong as ever and his vigour unabated, till during the siege after seeing the fulfilment of his foreboding he was silenced. He was going round on the wall uttering his piercing cry: 'Woe again to the City, the people, and the Sanctuary!' and as he added a last word: 'Woe to me also!' a stone shot from an engine struck him, killing him instantly. Thus he uttered those same forebodings to the very end.

Anyone who ponders these things will find that God cares for mankind and in all possible ways foreshows to His people the means of salvation, and that it is through folly and evils of their own choosing that they come to destruction. Thus the Jews after pulling down Antonia made the Temple square, in spite of the warning in their prophetic books that when the Temple became a square the City and Sanctuary would fall. But their chief inducement to go to war was an equivocal oracle also found in their sacred writings, announcing that at that time a man from their country would become monarch of the whole world. This they took to mean the triumph of their own race, and many of their scholars were wildly out in their interpretation. In fact the oracle pointed to the accession of Vespasian; for it was in Judaea he was proclaimed emperor. But it is not possible for men to escape from fate even if they see it coming. The Jews interpreted some of the prophecies to suit themselves and laughed the others off, till by the fall of their city and their own destruction their folly stood revealed.

As the partisans had fled into the City, and flames were consuming the Sanctuary itself and all its surroundings, the Romans brought their standards into the Temple area, and erecting them opposite the East Gate sacrificed to them there, and with thunderous acclamations hailed Titus as *Imperator*. So laden with plunder was every single soldier that all over Syria the value of gold was reduced by half. With the priests holding out on the Sanctuary wall was a lad parched with thirst. He begged the Roman guards to give him safe conduct, openly admitting his thirst. They felt sorry that a mere child should be suffering so, and granted the safe conduct. He came down, drank what he needed, filled the vessel he had brought with water, and dashed off full speed to his friends aloft. He was far too quick for the guards, who swore at him for breaking his word; but he retorted that he had done no such thing, for the agreement had not been that he should stay with them, but only that he should come down and get some water. That was exactly what he had done, so how had he broken his word? Such sharp practice in one so young astounded the victims of his trickery. However, after four days the starving priests came down and were taken by the guards to Titus, whom they begged to spare their lives. He replied that the time for pardon was past, that the one thing that would have justified their being spared had gone, and that the duty of priests was to perish with their sanctuary. Then he pronounced sentence of death.

The partisans and their chiefs, beaten in the war all ways and shut in by a wall that left them no possibility of escape, invited Titus to a parley. Such was his natural kindness that he was eager to save the town, and urged by his friends, who concluded that the terrorists had at last come to their senses, he took his stand to the west of the Outer Temple; for here above the Gymnasium there were gates, and a bridge linked the Temple with the Upper City; this now separated the party chiefs from Caesar. On either side stood a dense crowd – Jews round Simon and John on tiptoe with hope of pardon, Romans eager to see how Titus would receive their appeal. Titus called on his men to control their fury and their weapons, and placing his interpreter by his side exercised the victor's privilege and spoke first.

'Are you satisfied now, gentlemen, with the sufferings of your country? you who, in utter disregard of our strength and your weakness, have through your reckless impetuosity and madness destroyed your people, your city, and your temple, and richly deserve the destruction that is coming to yourselves; you who from the moment Pompey's forces crushed you have never stopped rebelling, and now have made open war on Rome. Did you rely on numbers? Why, a tiny fraction of the Roman army sufficed to deal with you! Well then; on the trustworthiness of your allies? And which of the nations outside our empire was going to prefer Jews to Romans? Or on your wonderful physique? Yet you know that the Germans are our slaves. On the strength of your walls? What wall could be a better obstacle than the open sea that is the bulwark of Britain? But Britain was brought to her knees by the arms of Rome! On your invincible determination and the wiles of your generals? Yet you know that even Carthage was overwhelmed!

'There is only one answer. You were incited against the Romans by Roman kindness. First we gave you the land to occupy and set over you kings of your own race; then we upheld the laws of your fathers, and allowed you complete control of your internal and external affairs; above all, we permitted you to raise taxes for God and to collect offerings, and we neither discouraged nor interfered with those who brought them – so that you could grow richer to our detriment and prepare at our expense to make war on us! Then, enjoying such advantages, you flung your abundance at the heads of those who furnished it, and like beasts you bit the hand that fed you!

'No doubt you despised Nero for his idleness, and like lesions or sprains you remained quiescent but malignant for a time, and when a more serious illness broke out you came out into the open and let your limitless ambitions grow into insolent presumption. My father came into the country, not to punish you for what you did in Cestius' time, but to caution you. If he had come to put an end to the nation, the right thing would have been to go straight to the root of your strength and sack this city at once. In actual fact he ravaged Galilee and the outlying districts, giving you time to come to your senses. But you took generosity for weakness, and our gentleness only served to increase your audacity. When Nero died you sank to the lowest level of depravity. You took advantage of our difficulties at home, and when my father and I had gone away to Egypt you jumped at the chance to prepare for war, and shamelessly created difficulties now that we were emperors, though when we were generals you had found us so considerate. When the whole Empire had come to us for protection, when all its inhabitants were enjoying the blessings of peace and countries outside were sending embassies to congratulate us, once again the Jews rose against us. You sent embassies beyond the Euphrates to stir up a revolt; you rebuilt your city walls; there were faction-fights, rival party chiefs, civil war – just what we should expect from men so depraved!

'I came to the city bearing sombre injunctions which it had pained my father to give. When I heard that the citizens were peace-minded I was delighted. You others I begged to desist before hostilities began; long after you had begun them I spared you, giving safe conduct to deserters and keeping faith with them when they came to me for protection. For many prisoners I showed pity: the warmongers I punished with torture and death. Most unwillingly I brought engines to bear on your walls: my soldiers, ever thirsting for your blood, I held in leash: after every victory, as if it was a defeat, I appealed to you for an armistice. When I got near to the Temple I again deliberately forwent my rights as victor and appealed to you to spare your own holy places and preserve the Sanctuary for your own use, offering you free-dom to come out and a guarantee of safety or, if you wished, a chance to fight on other ground. Every proposal you treated with scorn, and your Sanctuary you set on fire with your own hands!

'After all that, you disgusting people, do you now invite me to a conference? What have you to save that can be compared with what has gone? What security do you think you deserve after the loss of your sanctuary? Why, even now you stand in arms, and not even at your last gasp so much as pretend to be asking for mercy. You poor fools, what are you pinning your faith on? Aren't your people dead, your sanctuary gone, your city in my power, your very lives in my hands? Do you think you will win renown for your courage by putting off death till the last moment? I shall not compete with you in craziness. If you throw down your arms and surrender your persons I will grant you your lives; like an easy-going head of a house, I will punish what cannot be cured and spare the rest for my own use.'

To this they replied that they could accept no terms from him as they had sworn never to do this; but they asked leave to go out through the encircling wall with their wives and children, in which case they would go away into the desert and leave the City to him. Titus, furious that men no better than prisoners should put forward demands as if they had defeated him, ordered it to be announced that it was no longer any use their deserting or hoping for terms, as he would spare no one: they must fight to the last ditch and save themselves in any way they could; from now on he would insist on all his rights as victor. Then he gave his men leave to burn and sack the City. They did nothing that day, but on the next they fired the Muniment Office, the Citadel, the Council Chamber, and the area known as Ophel. The fire spread as far as Helena's Palace in the centre of the Citadel, consuming the narrow streets and the houses full of the bodies of those who had died of starvation.

On the same day King Azates' sons and brothers, joined by many prominent citizens, besought Caesar to grant them protection. He, though furious with all the survivors, lived up to his character and received the applicants. For the time being he kept them all in custody; the king's sons and kinsmen he put in chains and later conveyed to Rome to serve as hostages.

The partisans made a rush towards the Royal Palace, which was so solidly built that many had stored their property there. They drove away the Romans, slaughtered the people who had crowded into the building, 8,400 in number, and looted the riches. They also took two of the Romans alive, a cavalryman and an infantryman. The infantryman they butchered then and there and dragged round the City, as if by proxy they were revenging themselves on all the Romans. As the cavalryman said he had something to suggest that might save their lives, he was taken into Simon's presence; but when he got there he had nothing to say, so was handed over to Ardalas, one of the officers, to be executed. Ardalas tied his hands behind him and blindfolded him, then marched him forward in full view of the Romans with the intention of cutting off his head; but by a sudden movement the man dashed away to the Roman lines just as the Jew drew his sword. As he had made his escape from the enemy Titus could not very well put him to death, but deciding that he was unfit to be a soldier of Rome as he had let himself be taken alive, he stripped him of his arms and expelled him from the legion, to a man with any self-respect a punishment worse than death.

Next day the Romans drove the terrorists from the Lower City and burnt the whole place as far as Siloam. They were glad enough to see the town destroyed but got precious little loot, as the whole area had been cleaned out by the partisans before they withdrew to the Upper City. These men felt no remorse for the mischief they had done – they boasted as if they were proud of it: when they saw the City burning they laughed heartily and said they were happily awaiting the end; for as the people were slaughtered, the Sanctuary burnt to the ground, and the town blazing they were leaving nothing to the enemy. Yet to the very last Josephus never wearied of appealing to them to spare what was left of the City, though however much he might say against their savagery and impiety, however much advice he might give them for their own good, he got nothing but ridicule in return. As they could not very well surrender because of their oath and were unable now to fight the Romans on equal terms, they were like caged animals, so used to killing that they thirsted for blood. They scattered through the outskirts of the City and lay in wait among the ruins for would-be deserters. Many in fact were caught, and as hunger had left them too weak even to run away, all were butchered and their bodies thrown to the dogs. But any kind of death was more bearable than starvation, so that although they had no hope now of mercy from the Romans they still fled to them, falling into the murderous hands of the partisans with their eyes open. Not one spot in the whole City was empty: every single one had its corpse, the victim of hunger or faction.

The last hope that bolstered up the party chiefs and their terrorist gangs lay in the underground sewers. If they took refuge in them they did not expect to be tracked down, and after the final capture of the City and the subsequent departure of the Romans their intention was to come out and make good their escape. But this was only an idle dream: they were not fated to escape from either God or the Romans. At the time, however, they had such faith in their bolt-holes that they lit more fires than did the Romans. Those who fled from the burning buildings into the sewers they killed without hesitation and plundered; if they found anyone with food they snatched it away and swallowed it, dripping with the wretched man's blood. By now they were actually fighting each other for the loot; and I have little doubt that if capture had not forestalled it their utter bestiality would have made them get their teeth into the very corpses.

Owing to the steep approach on every side it was not feasible to master the Upper City without platforms, so on the 20th of Loös Caesar divided up the work among the troops. It was difficult to transport the timber since, as mentioned before, all the neighbourhood for eleven or twelve miles had been stripped bare for the earlier platforms. The four legions raised their works on the west side of the City opposite the Royal Palace, while the whole body of allies and the rest of the army worked near the Gymnasium, the bridge and Simon's tower, built during the struggle with John as a stronghold for himself.

At this time the Idumaean chiefs at a secret meeting discussed the question of piecemeal surrender, and sent five men to Titus to implore his protection. He, hoping that the party chiefs too would give in if they lost the support of the Idumaeans who had made so large a contribution to the war, hesitated at first, but finally granted them their lives and sent the men back. But as they got ready to go Simon saw what was afoot, immediately put to death the five who had gone to Titus, seized the chiefs of whom the most prominent was Jacob son of Sosas, and threw them into prison. On the Idumaean rank and file, at a loss without their leaders, he kept a careful eye, posting more efficient sentry-groups along the wall. However, the sentries were unable to cope with the deserters: many as were the killed, far more got away. The Romans received them all, Titus through kindness of heart disregarding his earlier proclamation, and the men holding their hands because they were sick of killing and hopeful of gain. For only the townsmen were kept back – all the rest were sold along with the women and children, the retail price being very low, as supply was far in excess of demand. In spite of his earlier announcement that no one must desert alone, but must bring his family with him, he nevertheless received such people; but he appointed officers to separate from them anyone deserving punishment. The number sold was enormous: the number of townsmen spared was over 40,000; these were free to go wherever they thought fit.

During this same period a priest named Jeshua, son of Thebuthi, obtained from Caesar a sworn guarantee of safety on condition that he should hand over some of the sacred treasures. He came out and handed over from the Sanctuary wall two lampstands closely resembling those kept in the Sanctuary, as well as tables, basins, and cups, all of solid gold and very heavy. He also handed over the curtains, the vestments of the chief priests with the precious stones, and many other articles required for the Temple services. In addition the Temple treasurer Phineas, when taken prisoner, produced the tunics and girdles of the priests, a large supply of purple and scarlet kept in store for repairing the great curtain, together with cinnamon in bulk, cassia, and quantities of other spices, which were blended and daily burnt as incense to God. He handed over many of the other treasures too with Temple ornaments in abundance, thus earning though a prisoner the pardon granted to deserters.

In 18 days the platforms were ready for use, and on the 7th of Gorpiaios the Romans brought up their engines. Some of the partisans, already despairing of the City, withdrew from the wall to the Citadel, others plunged into the sewers; but many ranged themselves along the ramparts and tried to repulse the Batterer crews. These too the Romans overwhelmed by numbers and by force, and above all by confidence in face of despondency and half-heartedness. When a section of the wall was broken through and some of the towers gave way before the assault of the Rams, there was an immediate flight from the battlements, and even the party chiefs were filled with terror unjustified by the situation: before the enemy got through they were stunned and ready to fly, and men once arrogant and bragging about their ungodly deeds could now be seen abject and trembling, insomuch that even in these vile scoundrels it was pitiful to note the change. Their one desire was to dash for the wall that shut them in, repulse the guards and hack their way through to safety; but when their old faithful supporters were nowhere to be seen – they had been forced to scatter in all directions – and when runners announced that the whole west wall was down, or that the Romans had broken in and were just round the corner seeking them, while others blinded by terror declared that from the towers they could actually see the enemy, they fell on their faces bewailing their own insane folly, and as if hamstrung were incapable of flight.

What happened would serve as an object-lesson, showing both the power of God over the wicked and the luck of the Romans. For the party chiefs divested themselves of their safety, and of their own accord came down from the towers on which they could never have been subdued by force but only by starvation; and the Romans, who had toiled so hard to break through the weaker walls, captured by sheer luck those the engines could not touch; for no mechanical device could have made any impression on the three towers described elsewhere. Abandoning these, or rather driven down from them by God, they took refuge for a moment in the ravine below Siloam; later, when they had recovered somewhat from their terror, they made a dash for the nearest section of the Roman wall. But their strength was broken now by terror and disaster, and their courage could not rise to the occasion; so they were repulsed by the guards, scattered this way and that, and plunged into the sewers.

Masters now of the walls, the Romans set up their standards on the towers and with clapping and singing celebrated their victory, having found the end of the war much easier than the beginning. They had surmounted the last wall without losing a man – it seemed too good to be true – and when they found no one to oppose them they could make nothing of it. They poured into the streets sword in hand, cut down without mercy all who came within reach, and burnt the houses of any who took refuge indoors, occupants and all. Many they raided, and as they entered in search of plunder they found whole families dead and the rooms full of the victims of starvation: horrified by the sight, they emerged empty-handed. Pity for those who had died in this way was matched by no such feeling for the living: they ran every man through whom they met and blocked the narrow streets with corpses, deluging the whole City with gore so that many of the fires were quenched by the blood of the slain. At dusk the slaughter ceased, but in the night the fire gained the mastery, and on the 8th of Gorpiaios the sun rose over Jerusalem in flames – a city that during the siege had suffered such disasters that if from her foundation she had enjoyed as many blessings she would have been the envy of the world; a city that deserved these terrible misfortunes on no other account than that she produced a generation such as brought about her ruin.

When Titus entered he was astounded by the strength of the city, and especially by the towers which the party chiefs in their mad folly had abandoned. Observing how solid they were all the way up, how huge each block of stone and how accurately fitted, how great their breadth and how immense their height, he exclaimed aloud: 'God has been on our side; it is God who brought the Jews down from these strongholds; for what could human hands or instruments do against such towers?' At that time he made many such remarks to his friends, and he set free all persons imprisoned by the party chiefs and found in the forts. Later, when he destroyed the rest of the City and pulled down the walls, he left the towers as a monument to his own luck, which had proved his ally and enabled him to overcome impregnable defences.

As the soldiers were now growing weary of bloodshed and survivors were still appearing in large numbers, Caesar gave orders that only men who offered armed resistance were to be killed, and everyone else taken alive. But as well as those covered by the orders the aged and infirm were slaughtered: men in their prime who might be useful were herded into the Temple and shut up in the Court of the Women. To guard them Caesar appointed one of his freedmen, and his friend Fronto to decide each man's fate according to his deserts. Those who had taken part in sedition and terrorism informed against each other, and Fronto executed the lot. Of the youngsters he picked out the tallest and handsomest to be kept for the triumphal procession; of the rest, those over seventeen were put in irons and sent to hard labour in Egypt, while great numbers were presented by Titus to the provinces to perish in the theatres by the sword or by wild beasts; those under seventeen were sold. During the days in which Fronto was sorting them out starvation killed 11,000 of the prisoners, some because the guards hated them too bitterly to allow them any food, others because they would not accept it when offered; in any case to fill so many mouths there was not even enough corn.

All the prisoners taken from beginning to end of the war totalled 97,000; those who perished in the long siege 1,100,000. Of these the majority were Jews by race but not Jerusalem citizens: they had come together from the whole country for the Feast of Unleavened Bread and had suddenly been caught up in the war, so that first the over-crowding meant death by pestilence, and later hunger took a heavier toll. That so many could crowd into the City was shown by the census held in Cestius' time. He, wishing to bring home the strength of the city to Nero, who despised the nation, instructed the chief priests to hold a census of the population if it was possible to do so. They chose the time of the Passover Feast, at which sacrifice is offered from three to five in the afternoon, and as it is not permissible to feast alone a sort of fraternal group is formed round each victim, consisting of at least ten adult males, while many groups have twenty members. The count showed that there were 255,600 victims; the men, reckoning ten diners to each victim, totalled 2,700,000, all ceremonially clean; for persons suffering from leprosy, venereal disease, monthly periods, or any form of defilement were debarred from participation, as were the foreigners who came from abroad in large numbers to be present at the ceremonies.

But now fate had decreed that one prison should confine the whole nation and that a city solid with men should be held fast in war's embrace. No destruction ever wrought by God or man approached the wholesale carnage of this war. Every man who showed himself was either killed or captured by the Romans, and then those in the sewers were ferreted out, the ground was torn up, and all who were trapped were killed. There too were found the bodies of more than 2,000, some killed by their own hand, some by one another's, but most by starvation. So foul a stench of human flesh greeted those who charged in that many turned back at once. Others were so avaricious that they pushed on, climbing over the piles of corpses; for many valuables were found in the passages and all scruples were silenced by the prospect of gain. Many prisoners of the party chiefs were brought up; for not even at their last gasp had they abandoned their brutality. But God rewarded them both as they deserved: John, starving to death with his brothers in the sewers, after so many scornful refusals at last appealed to the Romans for mercy, while Simon after battling long against the inevitable, as will be described later, gave himself up. John was sentenced to life-imprisonment, but Simon was kept for the triumphal procession and ultimate execution. The Romans now fired the out-lying districts of the town and demolished the walls.

So fell Jerusalem in the second year of Vespasian's reign, on the 8th of Gorpiaios, captured five times before and now for the second time laid utterly waste. Shishak king of Egypt, followed by Antiochus, then Pompey, and after that Sossius and Herod together, captured the City but spared it. Earlier on[1] the king of Babylon had stormed it and laid it waste 1,468 years, 6 months from its foundation. It was originally founded by a Canaanite chieftain called in the vernacular 'King of Righteousness', for such he was. On that account he was the first priest of God and the first to build the Temple and in its honour to give the name of Jerusalem to the City, previously called Salem. The Canaanite inhabitants were driven out by the Jewish king David, who settled his own people there; and 477 years, 6 months after his time it was utterly destroyed by the Babylonians. From King David, the first Jew to reign in it, to the destruction by Titus was 1,179 years.[2] But neither its long history, nor its vast wealth, nor its people dispersed through the whole world, nor the unparalleled renown of its worship sufficed to avert its ruin. So ended the siege of Jerusalem.

---

1. *Not earlier than Shishak.*
2. *The three figures given here are again far too big.*

CHAPTER 22

Jerusalem Destroyed: Roman Celebrations

THERE was no one left for the soldiers to kill or plunder, not a soul on which to vent their fury; for mercy would never have made them keep their hands off anyone if action was possible. So Caesar now ordered them to raze the whole City and Sanctuary to the ground, leaving the towers that overtopped the others, Phasael, Hippicus, and Mariamme, and the stretch of wall enclosing the City on the west – the wall to serve as protection for the garrison that was to be left, the towers to show later generations what a proud and mighty city had been humbled by the gallant sons of Rome. All the rest of the fortifications encircling the City were so completely levelled with the ground that no one visiting the spot would believe it had once been inhabited. This then was the end to which the mad folly of revolutionaries brought Jerusalem, a magnificent city renowned to the ends of the earth.

To guard the site Caesar decided to leave the Tenth Legion with a few troops of horse and companies of foot; and having now settled all problems arising from the war he desired to congratulate the whole army on its achievements and to bestow suitable rewards on those whose services were outstanding. A wide dais was erected for him in the middle of his old camp-site, and on it he took his stand flanked by his staff, where the whole army could hear him. He thanked them heartily for their unfailing loyalty to him, and praised their obedience throughout the war, shown along with personal heroism in many dangerous situations. By their own efforts they had increased the power of their country and had made it plain to all men that neither the number of their enemies, the strength of their defences, the size of their cities, nor the reckless daring and brutal savagery of their warriors could ever hold out against Roman valour, even if some of them found in fortune a constant ally. It had been a magnificent feat to bring to an end a war that had raged so long: they could not have wished for anything better when they embarked on it. But it was a much more splendid and brilliant achievement to have elected and sent home as rulers and governors of the Roman Empire men whom all were delighted to welcome, and whose decisions they loyally obeyed, full of gratitude to those who had chosen them. He was full of admiration and affection, he went on, for them all, knowing that every man's ability had been fully equalled by his enthusiasm; some however, blest with superior strength, had fought with greater distinction, not only shedding glory on their own lives by their gallant deeds, but making his campaign a more brilliant success by their exploits: on these he would at once bestow their honours and distinctions, and no one who had been prepared to put more into it than the next man should get less than his due. He would, indeed, give this matter his closest attention, as he was more interested in rewarding the courage and initiative of his fellow-soldiers than in punishing slackers.

Accordingly he at once ordered officers detailed for the task to read out the name of every man who in the course of the war had performed any outstanding exploit. Calling them by name he praised them as they came forward, as delighted as a man could be over his own exploits. He put golden crowns on their heads, gave them gold torques, miniature gold spears and standards made of silver, and promoted every man to higher rank. In addition he assigned to them out of the spoils silver, gold, and garments, with any amount of other booty. When he had rewarded them all according to his own opinion of their deserts, he offered prayers on behalf of the whole army, and stepped down amidst thunderous applause, then turned his attention to sacrifices in honour of his victory. A great number of bullocks were herded round the altars: all these he sacrificed and divided among the troops for a victory feast. He himself spent three days celebrating with his senior officers, and then dispatched the bulk of his army to the destinations selected for the various units: the Tenth Legion he detailed to guard Jerusalem instead of sending it to the Euphrates where it had been before. Remembering that while Cestius was in command the Twelfth Legion had given way before the Jews, he banished it from Syria altogether – it had earlier been stationed at Raphanaeae – and sent it away to Melitine, beside the Euphrates between Armenia and Cappadocia. Two legions he decided should stay with him till his arrival in Egypt, the Fifth and the Fifteenth. Then he went down with his army to Caesarea on the coast, where he deposited the bulk of the spoil and arranged for the custody of the prisoners, the voyage to Italy being impossible now that the summer was over.

At the time when Titus Caesar was busy directing the siege of

Jerusalem, Vespasian had embarked on a merchantman and crossed from Alexandria to Rhodes. From there he sailed in a fleet of triremes, calling at every city on the way and welcomed everywhere with enthusiasm. From Ionia he went on to Greece, and from there via Corcyra to the Promontory of Iapyx, whence he continued his journey overland.

From Caesarea on the coast Titus marched to Caesarea Philippi, where he stayed a long time exhibiting shows of every kind. Many of the prisoners perished here, some thrown to wild beasts, others forced to meet each other in full-scale battles. Here also Titus was informed of the capture of Simon son of Gioras, which had happened as follows. During the siege of Jerusalem Simon had been in the Upper City; but when the Roman army was inside the walls sacking the entire city he took his most trustworthy friends, and with them some tunnellers equipped with the tools of their trade and supplies of food sufficient for several weeks, and thus accompanied went down into one of the concealed sewers. They advanced through the old tunnel as far as it went, and when they reached solid earth they tried to hack through it, hoping to push ahead till they could emerge at a safe spot and get clear away. But the hope was baffled when the task was attempted; for progress was slow though the miners toiled hard, and in spite of careful rationing the food was on the point of giving out. So Simon, thinking to frighten the Romans by a trick, dressed himself up in several short white tunics with a crimson cape fastened over them, and at the very spot where the Temple had once stood he appeared out of the ground. At first those who saw him were too taken aback to move, but after a while they came nearer and asked who he was. This Simon refused to tell them: they must summon the general. They ran to fetch him, and Terentius Rufus, left in command of the garrison, came at once. Learning the whole truth from Simon he kept him fettered and sent an account of his capture to Caesar.

Thus as the just punishment of his brutality to his fellow-citizens, whom he had subjected to such savage tyranny, Simon was put by God beneath the heel of his most bitter enemies. He had not been brought into their power by force but had voluntarily thrown himself in the way of vengeance – the very thing for which he had put so many to a horrible death on the false charge of going over to the Romans. For wickedness cannot evade the divine wrath, and Justice is not weak: in time she overtakes those who offend against her, and brings heavier vengeance on the wicked when they think they are out of her reach because punishment has not been immediate. This was brought home to Simon himself when he fell into the hands of the furious Romans. His emergence from the ground meant that in the next few days a great many more partisans were discovered in the sewers. When Caesar returned to Caesarea by the sea, Simon was brought before him in fetters, and was ordered to be reserved for the triumphal procession through Rome which he was planning.

While he remained there he celebrated his brother's birthday[1] in the grand style, reserving much of his vengeance on the Jews for this notable occasion. The number of those who perished in combats with wild beasts or in fighting each other or by being burnt alive exceeded 2,500. Yet all this seemed to the Romans, though their victims were dying a thousand different deaths, to be too light a penalty. Caesar next went on to Beirut, a town in Phoenicia and a Roman colony. Here he made a longer stay, celebrating his father's birthday[2] with a still more lavish display, both in the magnificence of the shows and in the originality of the other costly entertainments. Vast numbers of prisoners perished in the same way as before.

It happened about this time that the surviving Jews in Antioch were the targets of accusations that might well mean their destruction; for the local population had been roused against them both by slanders of which they were at present the victims and by events that had occurred shortly before. Of these I must first give a short account, in order to make my exposition of what occurred later easier to follow.

Men of Jewish blood in great numbers are diffused among the native populations all over the world, especially in Syria, where the two nations are neighbours. The biggest Jewish colony was at Antioch owing to the size of the city, and still more because the kings who followed Antiochus had made it safe for them to settle there. Antiochus Epiphanes indeed had sacked Jerusalem and looted the Sanctuary; but his successors restored all the offerings made of bronze to the Antioch Jews as a gift for their synagogue, and further gave them the same civil privileges as the Greeks. As the later kings treated them in the same way they grew in numbers, and with their elaborate and costly offerings beautified the Temple. All the time they were attracting to their worship a great number of Greeks, making them virtually members of their own community. But at the time of the declaration

1. *24th October.*   2. *17th November.*

of war, when Vespasian had just landed in Syria and when the universal hatred of the Jews was at its peak, a certain Antiochus, a Jew himself and greatly respected because of his father, the magistrate responsible for the Antioch Jews, took advantage of a public gathering to go into the theatre and denounce his own father and the others, accusing them of a conspiracy to burn down the whole city in a single night. He also handed over some Jews from abroad as accomplices in the plot. When the people heard this they could not control their anger, and demanded that those handed over should be at once consigned to the flames, and then and there they were all burnt to death in the theatre. The crowd then hurled themselves at the main body of Jews, thinking that on their swift punishment the safety of their own home-town depended. Antiochus whetted their anger still more: he thought he could provide proof of his conversion and his hatred of Jewish customs by sacrificing according to Greek rites, and suggested that the others should be forced to do the same, as refusal to do so would show who were in the plot. When the Antiochenes applied the test a few gave way and those who refused were put to death. Antiochus now borrowed soldiers from the Roman general and began to tyrannize over his fellow-citizens, not allowing them to rest on the seventh day, but forcing them to do everything just as on the other days. Such strong compulsion did he bring to bear that not only at Antioch was the seventh day rest abolished, but starting from there the new rule was enforced in the other cities too for a short time.

Such miseries having befallen the Antioch Jews at that time, they were now struck by a second disaster, to the story of which the last paragraph will serve as prologue. It happened that a fire destroyed the Square Market, the City Hall, the Record Office, and the Law Courts, and it proved difficult to check the flames as they violently swept on through the whole city. With responsibility for this Antiochus saddled the Jews. Even if they had not already viewed them with bitter hostility, in the uproar that followed the incident the Antiochenes would have been deceived by this slander: after what had happened earlier they were much more ready to swallow everything this man said, and to convince themselves they had as good as seen with their own eyes the fires being lit by the Jews. So as if they had gone mad they all rushed in an absolute frenzy upon the victims of the slander. It was with the greatest difficulty that their impetuosity was checked by Gnaeus Collega, the governor's deputy, who insisted that they should allow Caesar to be informed of what had occurred; for though the governor of Syria, Caesennius Paetus, had already been sent out by Vespasian, it happened that he was not yet on the spot. By painstaking enquiry Collega found out the truth. Of the Jews on whom Antiochus had laid the blame not one had had any share in the business, which was entirely the work of some unscrupulous wretches who, unable to settle their debts, decided that if they burnt the Market and the public records they could not be called on for repayment. So with these accusations hanging over them the Jews were still anxious about the future, tossed as they were on a sea of painful fears.

When Titus Caesar received news of the delight with which his father's arrival had been greeted in all the cities of Italy, and of the matchless enthusiasm and splendour of his welcome in Rome, his pleasure and satisfaction knew no bounds; all anxiety on his father's behalf had been most happily dispelled. For long before Vespasian appeared the whole population of Italy were paying him homage in their hearts as if he was already there; eager anticipation made them mistake the prospect of his coming for his actual arrival, and their devotion to him was entirely spontaneous. The Senate had not forgotten the disastrous consequences of the rapid succession of emperors: it was a godsend to have once again an emperor possessing the dignity of mature years and a magnificent record in war, whose supremacy, they were well aware, would only be for the safety of his subjects. The people, worn out by the miseries of civil war, were still more eager for his coming: now at last they would be freed for ever from their wretchedness, and would again enjoy security and prosperity too, without a doubt. Above all the soldiery pinned their faith on him: they knew better than anyone the magnitude of the wars he had won, and having seen for themselves the incompetence and cowardice of the other emperors, they were eager to close that long and painful chapter, and prayed that the one man who could give them safety and honour should be at their head. Amidst all this devotion on every side citizens of distinguished status could no longer bear to wait, and hastened a very long way from Rome to be the first to welcome him. Nor indeed could any of the humbler folk endure the delay in meeting him: they all felt it was simpler and easier to go than to stay behind; so they all streamed out in such masses that the City itself enjoyed the unwonted pleasure of finding itself sparsely inhabited; for those who went outnumbered those who stayed behind. But when his imminent rarival was announced, and those who had been to the fore exclaimed over the friendly welcome he had given to every group, all the rest of the population with their wives and children now lined the roadside to cheer; each group as he passed were so delighted to see him, and so impressed by the gentleness of his bearing, that they uttered cries of every kind, greeting him as 'benefactor', 'saviour', and 'the only worthy emperor of Rome'. The whole City was as full of garlands and incense as a temple. Making his way with difficulty through the crowd that thronged him to the palace, he offered personal sacrifices to the household gods in thanksgiving for his arrival. The crowd then turned to celebration, and feasting by tribes, families, and neighbourhoods they offered prayers and libations to God, asking that Vespasian himself might remain for very many years at the helm of the Roman state, and that for his sons and all the generations of their descendants the throne might be preserved unchallenged.

After this enthusiastic reception of Vespasian the city of Rome made a rapid advance to great prosperity; but earlier on, while he was at Alexandria and Titus was busy with the siege of Jerusalem, a large section of the Germans had been roused to revolt, and in sympathy with them their Gallic neighbours had made concerted measures by which they had high hopes of even throwing off the Roman yoke. The motives that induced the Germans to engage in this revolt and take the field were these; first, their national character, incapable of logical thought and ready with little grounds for hope to rush into danger; secondly, hatred of their masters, for they know that only the Romans have ever forced their race into subjection. But nothing did so much to give them confidence as the opportunity then presented. They saw the Roman Empire paralysed at the centre by the continual changes at the head of affairs, and were informed that every corner of Rome's wide-flung dominions was in a state of excitement and agitation; so they felt that this was a splendid opportunity presented to them by the calamitous dissensions of the enemy. Their plan was abetted and their fantastic hopes encouraged by Classicus and Civilis, two of their chiefs, who had evidently set their hearts on this rebellion a long time back, and were encouraged by this opportunity to declare their intention: they were to find the masses only too ready to take the plunge.

A large section of the Germans had already agreed on revolt and the rest had raised no objection when Vespasian, as if by divine providence, sent dispatches to Petilius Cerealis, hitherto commander in Germany, conferring on him the rank of consul and ordering him to proceed to Britain as the new governor. He accordingly set out for his new command; but receiving news of the German revolt he fell on them when they had assembled their forces and in a pitched battle inflicted immense casualties, compelling them to abandon their mad scheme and learn sense. Even if Cerealis had not come on the scene so expeditiously, they were fated to meet their deserts before long. For the moment news of their revolt burst on Rome and reached the ears of Caesar Domitian, he, though only in his teens, did not hesitate as anyone else would have done at his age, but shouldered this immense burden of responsibility. He had inherited his father's fighting spirit and had progressed beyond his years in the school of war: now he instantly hurled himself at the barbarian hordes. At the rumour of his approach their courage failed: they submitted to him without a blow, reaping from their terror the great reward of being brought once more under the same yoke without suffering disaster. As soon as he had put all the affairs of Gaul on such a sound basis that no further disturbance was ever likely to occur there, Domitian returned to Rome covered with glory and admired by all for exploits amazing in one so young, and worthy of his father.[1]

The German revolt which I have described coincided with a bold Scythian attack on the Romans. A very large Scythian tribe called the Sarmatians crossed unnoticed to the right bank of the Danube, and launched a very violent attack so completely unexpected that resistance was swept aside. Many of the Roman guards were killed, and when the consular legate Fonteius Agrippa advanced to meet them and put up a strenuous fight he too fell. The whole of the province was overrun and stripped bare. When news of these events and of the devastation of Moesia reached Vespasian, he sent out Rubrius Gallus to punish the Sarmatians. Rubrius slaughtered vast numbers of them in a series of battles, the panic-stricken survivors scurrying back to their own country. Having brought the war to this conclusion the general provided for security in the future by stationing garrisons in greater number and strength about the area, so that the natives were denied the least chance of getting across again. Thus the Moesian war was very quickly settled.

Titus Caesar spent some time in Beirut, as we mentioned before.

1. *And apparently existing only in Josephus' imagination.*

From there he passed through a number of Syrian towns, exhibiting in them all lavish spectacles in which Jewish prisoners were forced to make a show of their own destruction. As he travelled he saw a river whose character merits description. Flowing between Arcea in Agrippa's kingdom and Raphanaea, it has a remarkable peculiarity. When it flows it fills its channel and the current is strong; then it fails completely at its source and for six days the bed is bone-dry; after that, just as if nothing had happened, the water gushes out on the seventh day exactly as before. From this timetable it has never been known to deviate; so it is called the Sabbatical River after the seventh day which the Jews keep holy.

When the citizens of Antioch learnt that Titus was near, they were too delighted to stay within their walls and ran out to meet him, proceeding nearly four miles, not only men but crowds of women with their children pouring out of the city. When they saw him coming, they lined both sides of the road, extending their right arms in salute; then calling down every kind of blessing on his head escorted him to Antioch; but all their acclamations were mingled with a constant appeal for the expulsion of the Jews. Titus took no notice of this appeal but listened impassively to what was said, so that having no clue to his thoughts and intentions the Jews were kept in prolonged and painful suspense. For Titus did not stay in Antioch but marched on immediately to Zeugma on the Euphrates. There he was met by envoys from the Parthian king, Vologeses, who bestowed on him a golden crown in honour of his victory over the Jews. Accepting this he feasted the king's emissaries, then returned to Antioch. After repeated invitations from senate and people to visit the theatre, where the whole population had crowded in to greet him, he graciously gave his consent. But when they again pressed him with extreme earnestness and continuous appeals to drive the Jews out of the city, his reply was brief and to the point: 'Their own country, to which as they are Jews we should have to banish them, has been destroyed, and they would not be admitted anywhere else now.' As that appeal had failed the Antiochenes tried another: they asked him to remove the bronze tablets engraved with the Jews' privileges. Titus would not grant that either; but leaving the position of the Antioch Jews exactly as it was he left for Egypt.

On the way he called at Jerusalem. There he contrasted the grievous desolation that met his eyes with the splendour of the city that was, and calling to mind the mighty structures in ruins now but once so beautiful, he was pained by the city's destruction. Unlike anyone else, he did not boast that though it was so great and so strong he had taken it by storm, but cursed and cursed again those who had instigated the revolt and caused this retribution to fall on the city: so clear did he make it that he would never have wished the terrible punishment that had been inflicted to serve as proof of his prowess. Of the city's great wealth quantities were still being found among the ruins. Much of this was dug up by the Romans, but still more came into their hands as a result of information from the prisoners – gold and silver and the most valuable articles of other kinds, which in view of the incalculable chances of war the owners had stowed underground.

Resuming his interrupted journey to Egypt, Titus crossed the desert by the shortest route and arrived at Alexandria. His intention being to sail for Italy, he sent each of the two legions that had accompanied him back to its old station, the Fifth to Moesia, and the Fifteenth to Pannonia. Of the prisoners he ordered the leaders, Simon and John, with 700 of the rank and file picked out for their exceptional stature and physique, to be conveyed to Italy without a moment's delay, intending to display them in his triumphal procession. The voyage went according to plan, and Rome gave him as warm a welcome as it had given his father; but it was a more glorious occasion for Titus because his father himself came out to welcome him. The throng of citizens could not contain their joy when they saw all three together. A few days later they decided to celebrate a single triumph in common in honour of their exploits, though the Senate had decreed a separate triumph for each. Notice was given in advance of the day appointed for the victory procession, and not one person stayed at home out of the immense population of the City: everyone came out and, although there was only standing-room, found a place somewhere, so that there was barely enough room left for the procession itself to pass.

While it was still night all the soldiers had marched out under their commanders by centuries and cohorts, and had formed up not round the gates of the Upper Palace but near the Temple of Isis; for there the victorious generals had slept that night. As soon as day began to break Vespasian and Titus came out wreathed with bay and wearing the traditional crimson robes, and proceeded to the Octavian Walks; for there the Senate and senior magistrates and knights were awaiting their arrival. A dais had been set up in front of the colonnades, and on it placed ready for them were ivory chairs. On these they proceeded to sit; whereupon the soldiery shouted acclamations, one and all bearing full testimony to their prowess. The central figures were unarmed, in silken robes and wreathed with bay. Having received their acclamations Vespasian, though they had more to say, gave the signal for silence. A complete hush fell on all and the emperor, rising from his seat and wrapping most of his head in his cloak, offered the customary prayers, Titus then doing the same. After the prayers Vespasian made a short speech to the whole gathering, dismissed the soldiers to the breakfast which it was customary for victorious generals to provide, and himself retired to the gate which took its name from the triumphal processions that always pass through it. There they first tasted food, then put on the triumphal robes and sacrificed to the gods that stand on either side of the gate, and finally resumed their triumphal advance, driving through the theatres to give the crowds a better view.

It is impossible to give a satisfactory account of the innumerable spectacles, so magnificent in every way one could think of, whether as works of art or varities of wealth or rarities of nature; almost all the treasures that have ever come one at a time into the hands of fortune's favourites – the priceless marvels of many different peoples – were brought together on that day, showing forth the greatness of the Roman Empire. Masses of silver and gold and ivory in every shape known to the craftsman's art could be seen, not as if carried in procession but like a flowing river. There were hangings borne along, some in the rarest shades of crimson, others embroidered with life-like portraits by Babylonian artists; transparent stones, some set in golden crowns, some in other mounts, were carried past in such numbers that we could see how foolish we had been to suppose any of them rare. In the procession too were images of the Roman gods wonderful in size and of true artistic merit, every one of them made from costly materials; and animals of many kinds were led past, all decked with the proper trappings. Every item in the procession was escorted by a large group of men arrayed in garments of true scarlet dye interwoven with gold; those chosen to take part in the procession itself had about them the choicest and most astonishing wealth of ornament. Furthermore, not even the host of captives went unadorned: under their elaborate and beautiful garments any disfigurement due to physical sufferings was hidden from view.

But what caused the greatest wonder was the structure of the travelling stages; indeed their immense size caused alarm through mistrust of their stability, as many of them were three or even four storeys high, while their lavish equipment was viewed with delighted surprise. Many were hung with curtains interwoven with gold, and all were framed in wrought ivory and gold. Numbers of tableaux showed the successive stages of the war most vividly portrayed. Here was to be seen a smiling countryside laid waste, there whole formations of the enemy put to the sword; men in flight and men led off to captivity; walls of enormous size thrown down by engines, great strongholds stormed, cities whose battlements were lined with defenders utterly overwhelmed, an army streaming inside the ramparts, the whole place reeking of slaughter, those unable to resist raising their hands in supplication, temples set on fire and houses torn down over the heads of their occupants, and after utter desolation and misery rivers flowing, not over tilled fields, supplying drink to men and animals but through a countryside still blazing on every hand. Such were the agonies to which the Jews condemned themselves when they embarked on this war; and the art and marvellous craftsmanship of these constructions now revealed the incidents to those who had not seen them happen as clearly as if they had been there. Placed on each stage was the commander of a captured town just as he had been when captured. A number of ships followed.

Most of the spoils that were carried were heaped up indiscriminately, but more prominent than all the rest were those captured in the Temple at Jerusalem – a golden table weighing several hundredweight, and a lampstand similarly made of gold but differently constructed from those we normally use. The central shaft was fixed to a base, and from it extended slender branches placed like the prongs of a trident, and with the end of each one forged into a lamp: these numbered seven, signifying the honour paid to that number by the Jews. After these was carried the Jewish Law, the last of the spoils. Next came a large group carrying images of Victory, all fashioned of ivory and gold. Behind them drove Vespasian first with Titus behind him: Domitian rode alongside, magnificently adorned himself, and with his horse a splendid sight.

The procession finished at the Temple of Jupiter Capitolinus, where they came to a halt: it was an ancient custom to wait there till news came that the commander-in-chief of the enemy was dead. This was Simon son of Gioras, who had been marching in the procession among the prisoners, and now with a noose thrown round him was being dragged to the usual spot in the Forum while his escort knocked him about. That is the spot laid down by the law of Rome for the execution of those condemned to death for their misdeeds. When the news of his end arrived it was received with universal acclamation, and the sacrifices were begun. When the customary prayers had been offered and the omens proved favourable, the princes went back to the Palace. Some they entertained at the imperial table; for all the rest sumptuous banquets had been prepared at home. All day long the City of Rome celebrated the triumphant issue of the campaign against her enemies, the end of civil strife, and the beginning of hope for a joyous future.

When the triumphal ceremonies were over, as the Roman Empire was now most firmly established, Vespasian made up his mind to build a temple of Peace. This was completed with remarkable speed and surpassed all human imagination. Not only did he have unlimited wealth at his disposal; he also adorned it with paintings and statues by the greatest of the old masters. In fact, in that temple were collected and deposited all those works that men had hitherto travelled over the whole world to see, longing to set eyes on them even when scattered in different lands. There too he laid up the golden vessels from the Temple of the Jews, for he prided himself on them; but their Law and the crimson curtains of the Inner Sanctuary he ordered to be deposited in the Palace for safe keeping.

CHAPTER 23

Cleaning-up Operations

To Judaea a new legate had been sent, Lucilius Bassus, who took over the command from Cerealius Vetilianus. He first secured the submission of the fortress at Herodium together with its defenders; then concentrating all available troops, hitherto very widely dispersed and including the Tenth Legion, he determined to march against Machaerus. It was absolutely necessary to destroy this fortress, for fear that its strength might tempt large numbers to revolt, since the character of the terrain might well fill its defenders with confident hopes of survival and its assailants with despondency and fear. The defended area is itself a rocky hill rising to an immense height, and for that very reason it is almost impregnable; and nature has found means to make it unapproachable too. For it is trenched on every side with ravines too deep for their bottoms to be seen, difficult to cross and quite impossible to fill in. The one which shuts it in on the west stretches seven miles, ending at the Dead Sea; somewhere in this region the soaring peak of Machaerus itself towers aloft. The ravines to the north and south are considerably smaller, but just as serious an obstacle to an attacker; that to the east is found to be at least 150 feet deep, and it extends as far as a mountain situated opposite Machaerus.

Realizing that the site had many natural advantages, the Jewish king Alexander had been the first to build a fortress there, only to be demolished by Gabinius in his war against Aristobulus. When Herod came to the throne he decided that no place would better repay attention and the strongest fortification, especially in view of the proximity of Arabia; for its situation was most opportune, commanding as it did a view of Arab territory. So he surrounded a large area with walls and towers and founded a city there, from which an ascent led up to the ridge itself. Not content with that he built a wall round the very summit and erected towers at the corners, each 90 feet high. In the middle of this enclosure he built a palace, breath-taking in the size and beauty of the various rooms; and at carefully chosen spots he constructed a number of tanks to receive rain-water and maintain a constant supply. He might well have been competing with nature in the hope that the impregnability the place had received from her might be outdone by his own artificial defences. He further provided an ample store of weapons and engines, and managed to think of everything that could enable the occupants to snap their fingers at the longest siege.

There grew in the palace a plant of rue of an astonishing size – it was every bit as tall and stout as a fig-tree. It was popularly believed to have been there since Herod's time, and it might well have lived much longer if it had escaped the axes of the Jewish settlers. In the ravine that protects the town on the north is a place called Baaras, where grows a root of the same name. This is flame-coloured, and at dusk it sends out brilliant flashes so that those who come near in the hope of plucking it cannot take hold of it, as it slips away and will not stay still until it is drenched with a woman's urine or menstrual blood. Even then to touch it means certain death, unless one happens to have brought an exactly similar root dangling from the wrist. It can also be secured another way without risk, thus – they dig right round it, so as to leave the smallest possible piece of root in the ground; then they tie a dog to it, and when he springs forward to follow the man who tied him it is easily pulled up, but the dog dies instantly, a substitute for the person who was going to remove the plant; for no danger remains for those who subsequently handle it. Despite the greatness of the danger it has one virtue that makes it sought after; for the so-called devils – in reality the spirits of evil-doers that enter the living and kill them if they are not rescued – are quickly cast out by this plant if it so much as touches the possessed. Here too flow springs of hot water, differing widely in flavour, as some are bitter, others very sweet indeed. There are also many fountains of cold water, and these do not all issue from wells on low ground in a row: the truth is more surprising, for there is a cave to be seen near by, not hollowed out to any great depth, and sheltered by a rock that juts out. Above this protrude, as it were, two breasts a little way apart, sending out water, in one case icy, in the other boiling hot. When mixed these furnish a most pleasant bath, beneficial in many sicknesses and giving special relief to tired muscles. The region also contains sulphur and alum mines.

After viewing the position from various angles Bassus decided to approach by filling in the ravine to the east. He promptly set to work, endeavouring to raise the platform with the utmost speed and thereby making the siege easy. The Jews trapped inside separated themselves make the siege easy. The Jews trapped inside separated themselves from the Gentiles: these they considered a useless mob and forced to

stay in the town below to face the first onslaught, while they themselves seized and held the fortress above, both because of the strength
of its defences and to ensure their own safety: they felt certain they
could win pardon by surrendering the place to the Romans. First,
however, they wanted to test their prospects of escaping a siege; so
they made vigorous sorties every day and grappled with all they encountered, at heavy cost to both sides. On every occasion it was the
circumstances of the moment that decided the issue in favour of one
side or the other – of the Jews if they caught the Romans off their guard,
of the men on the platforms if they had seen the attack coming and
were lined up to meet it. However, it was not this skirmishing that was
to terminate the siege: a fortuitous and astonishing occurrence forced
the Jews to surrender the fortress.

Among the besieged was a young man, bold in enterprise and
energetic in action, named Eleazar. He had been prominent in the
sorties, inciting the majority of the defenders to issue forth and interrupt the building of the platforms, and in the encounters doing a great
deal of damage to the Romans; for those who dared to sally out with
him he smoothed the way to the attack, and made retreat safe by being
the last to withdraw. One day, when the battle had been broken off
and both sides had retired, he, confidently supposing that none of the
enemy would start further fighting now, stayed outside the gates
talking to the defenders on the wall and with no thought for anyone
else. A soldier from the Roman camp, an Egyptian named Rufus,
saw his chance and performed a breath-taking feat: he made a sudden
rush, picked the man up armour and all, and before the spectators on
the wall could recover from their astonishment carried him off to the
Roman camp. The commander ordered him to be stripped, taken
where he would be most clearly seen by the watchers in the town, and
flogged with whips. The Jews were terribly distressed by the young
man's agony, and the whole town burst into tears, showing most
unusual concern for one unfortunate individual. Seeing this, Bassus
proceeded to play a trick on the enemy, wishing to aggravate their
grief, and so induce them in return for the man's life to surrender the
fortress; nor was his hope disappointed. He ordered a cross to be set up
as if he would crucify Eleazar forthwith. When the defenders saw this
they were filled with still greater distress, and their shrieks were deafening as they cried out that they could not endure the horror of it. Then
Eleazar implored them not to stand by while he suffered the most

pitiable of deaths, but to save their own lives by submitting to the might and fortune of Rome, by which all others had now been crushed. Such an appeal was irresistible, and many inside the town pleaded on his behalf, for he came of an eminent and very numerous family; so, contrary to their nature, they yielded to pity and hastily dispatched a delegation to discuss the surrender of the fortress, on the understanding that they should be free to go away, taking Eleazar with them. To this the Romans and their commander agreed.

When the people in the town below learnt of the separate agreement reached by the Jews, they decided that their own best plan was to steal away in the night. But as soon as they opened the gates those who had come to terms with Bassus informed him of what was happening, perhaps grudging the others their lives, perhaps through fear that they themselves might be held responsible for their escape. The boldest of those who left the town succeeded in breaking through and getting clear, but of those left behind the men were massacred, 1,700 of them, the women and children enslaved. Feeling that he must honour the agreement made with those who had surrendered the fortress, Bassus let them go and sent back Eleazar.

Having settled these problems, he made a rapid march to the Forest of Jardes; for news had reached him that many who had earlier escaped from the sieges of Jerusalem and Machaerus had collected there. Arriving at the spot and finding the information correct, he first encircled the whole area with his cavalry, so that any Jews who tried to break through would find their flight cut off; then he ordered the infantry to cut down the trees amongst which they were hiding. These measures compelled the Jews to attempt some heroic feat, in the hope that by a supreme effort they might get clear. So rushing out en masse with loud hurrahs they fell on the encircling enemy. They met with stubborn resistance, and as one side fought with the fury of despair, the other with the utmost pertinacity, the battle was very prolonged; but it ended very differently for the combatants, Roman casualties being no more than twelve killed and a handful wounded, whereas of the Jews not one survived the encounter; three thousand in all, they perished to a man. Among them was their general, Judas son of Jairus, who as stated already commanded a unit at the siege of Jerusalem, and by making his way through some of the sewers slipped unnoticed through the Roman lines.

About the same time Caesar sent a message to Bassus and Liberius

Maximus the procurator, instructing them to sell all Jewish territory. He founded no city there but treated the country as his own property, merely allowing 800 men discharged from the forces to settle in Emmaus $3\frac{1}{2}$ miles from Jerusalem. He imposed a tax on the Jews wherever they lived, ordering them to pay each year into the Capitol 2 drachmas a head, the sum they had previously paid into the Temple at Jerusalem. Here for the moment we will leave the affairs of the Jews.

In the fourth year of Vespasian's reign the king of Commagene, Antiochus, found himself and all his family in a most disastrous situation. It happened thus. Caesennius Paetus, governor of Syria at the time – either in good faith or to spite Antiochus, it is not certain which – sent a dispatch to Caesar alleging that Antiochus and his son Epiphanes intended to revolt from Rome and had reached an understanding with the king of Parthia: preventive action was therefore called for, to forestall a sudden move that would throw the whole Empire into a state of war. Caesar could hardly overlook an urgent report of such a character; the proximity of the two monarchs made the matter particularly pressing. Samosata, the biggest city of Commagene, lies on the Euphrates, making it very easy for the Parthians, if they had a mind to it, to get across, and guaranteeing them a friendly reception. So Paetus, being trusted and empowered to use his own judgement, wasted no time: suddenly, before Antiochus and his staff had any suspicion, he invaded Commagene at the head of the Sixth Legion, supported by some cohorts and a few troops of horse, and further assisted by the kings of Chalcidice and Emesa, Aristobulus and Soaemus. Their invasion was unopposed, as none of the inhabitants was prepared to lift a hand against them. Antiochus, suddenly faced with the news, did not for a moment contemplate war with Rome, but decided to leave his kingdom just as it was and slip away with his wife and children, thinking thereby to convince the Romans of his innocence. So he travelled fourteen miles from the city and encamped in the plain.

Paetus sent a force to occupy Samosata, thus securing the city while he with the rest of his troops set off in pursuit of Antiochus. Not even his desperate situation could tempt the king to take any warlike measures against the Romans: bewailing his lot he awaited what was coming to him. His sons on the other hand, young, experienced in war and phenomenally strong, could not bring themselves to submit to such a calamity without a struggle, and so Epiphanes and Callinicus resorted to arms. The battle was violent and lasted the whole day, the two leaders displaying noteworthy courage: their forces were intact when dusk broke off the struggle. But not even when the battle ended thus did Antiochus see fit to stay: he took his wife and daughters and fled with them into Cilicia, doing irreparable damage to the morale of his own men; for as he had evidently written off his own kingdom they mutinied and went over to the Romans, and there was no mistaking the universal despair. So before they were completely bereft of allies Epiphanes and his brother were obliged to run from the enemy, no more than ten horsemen crossing the Euphrates with them: from there they rode without interference to the Parthian court, where Vologeses, so far from despising them as runaways, received them, as if they still enjoyed their old prosperity, with all honour. When Antiochus arrived at Tarsus in Cilicia, Paetus sent a centurion to dispatch him in fetters to Rome. But Vespasian refused to let the king be brought to him in this condition, thinking it better to honour their old friendship than to make the war a pretext for relentless animosity. He gave instructions that while he was still on the way he should be freed from his fetters, and instead of continuing his journey to Rome should remain for the present in Sparta. He further assigned him a large revenue, enabling him to live not only in luxury but in royal state. When news of this reached Epiphanes and his brother, who had hitherto been extremely anxious about Antiochus, it was a very great load off their minds. They had hoped that Caesar would be reconciled to them as Vologeses had intervened on their behalf; for though they were living in comfort they were most unwilling to live outside the Roman Empire. Caesar graciously promised them safe conduct, and they travelled to Rome where their father at once joined them from Sparta. They were treated with all honour and settled in the City.

In an earlier chapter we referred[1] to the Alani, a Scythian tribe living near the Don and the Sea of Azov. At this stage in the story, as they planned a raid into Media and beyond in search of loot, they negotiated with the king of Hyrcania, as master of the pass which King Alexander had closed with gates of iron. He granted them admission, and they poured through en masse; then falling on the unsuspecting Medes, they plundered a populous countryside full of livestock of every kind, meeting with no opposition at all. Pacorus, king of the district, had fled in terror to his hide-outs leaving every-

---

1. *Nowhere in the book as we have it.*

thing behind except his wife and concubines, who had been taken prisoners and whom he recovered only by the payment of 100 talents. So they continued their raids with the utmost ease and without opposition, advancing as far as Armenia and leaving a trail of destruction behind them. Armenia was ruled by Tiridates, who met them and gave battle, but came within an inch of being taken alive during the fighting; he was lassoed from a distance and would have been dragged off if he had not whipped out his sword and slashed the rope just in time. This battle made the invaders still more savage: they turned the countryside into a desert, and carrying off a large part of the population and quantities of booty from both kingdoms returned to their own country.

In Judaea Bassus had died and the new governor was Flavius Silva, who, seeing the rest of the country reduced to impotence and only one fortress still holding out, marched against it with all available forces. The fortress was Masada, occupied by the Sicarii under the command of an influential man called Eleazar, a descendant of the Judas who had persuaded many Jews, as recorded earlier, not to register when Quirinius was sent as censor into Judaea. At this time the Sicarii combined against those prepared to submit to Rome, and in every way treated them as enemies, looting their property, rounding up their cattle, and setting their dwellings on fire: they were no better than foreigners, they declared, throwing away in this cowardly fashion the freedom won by the Jews at such cost, and avowedly choosing slavery under the Romans. In reality this was a mere excuse, intended to cloak their barbarity and avarice: the proof lay in their own actions; for their victims had joined with them in the rebellion and fought by their side against Rome; yet it was from them that still more brutal treatment was received, and when they were again proved guilty of hollow pretence they did still more mischief to those who in justifying themselves condemned the wickedness of their tormentors.

Somehow those days had become so productive of every kind of wickedness among the Jews as to leave no deed of shame uncommitted; and even if someone had used all his powers of invention he could not have thought of any vice that remained untried: so corrupt was the public and private life of the whole nation, so determined were they to outdo each other in impiety towards God and injustice to their neighbours, the classes ill-using the masses, and the masses striving to overthrow the classes. One group was bent on domination, the other on violence and on robbing the rich. First to begin this lawlessness and this barbarity to kinsmen were the Sicarii, who left no word unspoken, no deed untried, to insult and destroy the objects of their foul plots. Yet even they appeared gentle by the side of John. He not only put to death all advocates of just and profitable courses, treating such as his most bitter foes among the citizens: by his public actions he subjected his country to countless woes, as a man was sure to do if he had already dared to be impious even towards God. On his table he had unlawful dishes served, and the purifications observed by our fathers he set aside; so it was no longer surprising if gentleness and kindness towards men were not shown by one too mad to show piety towards God.

Think too of Simon, son of Gioras. What crime did he not commit? What outrage was not done to free citizens by the men who gave him unlimited power? What friendship or kinship was there that did not increase the wantonness of their daily murders? The ill-treatment of aliens they looked on as the work of a common criminal, but thought it a proof of brilliance to savage their own kith and kin. But even their madness was nothing to the frenzy of the Idumaeans. These disgusting people butchered the chief priests so that no trace of divine worship should be left, and then destroyed everything that remained of civil organization, permeating the whole system with utter lawlessness. In this no one could equal the Zealots, a party which justified its title by its deeds; they followed every bad example, and there was no crime in the records that they did not zealously reproduce. And yet they gave themselves this title in view of their zeal for what was good, either mocking their victims, brutes that they were, or regarding the greatest evils as good! Thus it was that each of them found a fitting end, God sentencing them all to the penalty they deserved. Every torment mankind can endure fell upon them to the very end of their lives, when they came face to face with death in all its most agonizing forms. Yet it would be true to say that they suffered less misery than they had caused: to suffer what they deserved was impossible. But this is not the time to lament for the victims of their savagery, richly as they deserve it; so I will take up the story where I broke it off.[1]

Against Eleazar and the Sicarii who with him held Masada came the Roman general at the head of his forces. He at once subdued the whole

1. *The reader cannot fail to observe the lack of precise charges in this irrelevant, vindictive, and self-righteous digression.*

area, and stationing garrisons at strategic points threw a wall right round the fortress so that none of the besieged should find it easy to escape, and posted sentries. He established his own headquarters at a place that seemed most opportune for directing the siege, where the rocks on which the fortress stood were linked to the mountain near by, though it was an awkward position for bringing up necessary supplies. For not only was food brought from a distance at the cost of painful toil for the Jews detailed for the task; even drinking-water had to be fetched to the camp as the neighbourhood possessed no spring. These preliminary dispositions completed, Silva began the siege-operations, which called for great skill and immense exertions in view of the strength of the fortress, which I will now describe.

A rock with a very large perimeter and lofty all the way along is on every side broken off by deep ravines. Their bottom is out of sight, and from it rise sheer cliffs on which no animal can get a foothold except in two places where the rock can with great difficulty be climbed. One of these paths comes from the Dead Sea to the east, the other from the west – an easier route. They call the first one the Snake, with reference to its narrowness and constant windings: it is broken as it rounds the projecting cliffs and often turns back on itself, then lengthening out again a little at a time manages to make some trifling advance. Walking along it is like balancing on a tight-rope. The least slip means death; for on either side yawns an abyss so terrifying that it could make the boldest tremble. After an agonizing march of 3½ miles the summit is reached, which does not narrow to a sharp point but is a sort of elevated plateau. On this the high priest Jonathan first built a fortress and named it Masada: later King Herod devoted great care to the improvement of the place. The entire summit, measuring ¾ mile round, he enclosed within a limestone wall 18 feet high and 12 wide, in which he erected 37 towers 75 feet high: from these one could pass through a ring of chambers right round the inside of the wall. For the plateau was of rich soil more workable than any plain, and the king reserved it for cultivation, so that if ever there was a shortage of food from without this should not injure those who had entrusted their safety to these ramparts. He built a palace, too, on the western slope, below the fortifications on the crest and inclining in a northerly direction. The palace wall was of great height and strongly built, with 90 foot towers at the four corners. The design of the apartments within the colonnades, and bathrooms, was varied and magnificent, the supporting pillars cut from a single block in every case, the partition walls and floors of the room tiled with stones of many hues. At every spot where people lived, whether on the plateau, round the palace, or before the wall, he had cut out in the rock numbers of great tanks to hold water, ensuring a supply as great as where spring water can be used. A sunken road led from the palace to the hill-top, invisible from outside. Nor was it easy for an enemy to use even the visible roads: the eastern one, as already explained, was by nature unusable; the western was guarded by a large fort at its narrowest point, at least 500 yards from the crest. To pass this was impossible, to capture it by no means easy, while it had been made difficult even for innocent travellers to get away. So strong had the fortress's defences against enemy attack been made both by nature and by human effort.

The provisions stored inside were even more astonishing in their abundance and diversity, and in their perfect preservation. The stores included a great quantity of corn – more than enough to last for many years – and quantities of wine and oil, with pulse of all varieties and dates in great heaps. All these Eleazar found when by a trick he and his Sicarii made themselves masters of the fortress: they were perfectly fresh and just as good as on the day they were laid in. Yet from that day to the capture by the Romans was about 100 years! In fact, the Romans found what was left of the various foods in excellent condition. We should not be far wrong if we put down their preservation to the atmosphere, which at the height of the plateau is free from any earthy, filthy taint. There was found too a quantity of weapons of every kind, stored there by the king, and enough for 10,000 men, as well as unwrought iron and bronze and a store of lead. For these preparations, indeed, there were very strong reasons: it is believed that Herod equipped this fortress as a refuge for himself, suspecting a double danger – the danger from the Jewish masses, who might push him off his throne and restore to power the royal house that had preceded him, and the greater and more terrible danger from the Egyptian queen, Cleopatra. For she did not conceal her intentions but constantly appealed to Antony, begging him to destroy Herod and requesting the transfer to herself of the kingdom of Judaea. The surprising thing is not that there should have been any question of his gratifying her, but that he did not yield to her demands, hopelessly enslaved as he was by his passion for her. Such were the fears that made Herod fortify Masada, little dreaming that he was to leave it to the Romans as their very last task in the war against the Jews.

As he had now finished the projected exterior wall encircling the whole position, to make absolutely sure that no one slipped out, the Roman commander actively prosecuted the siege, though he had found only one place where it was possible to construct platforms. Behind the tower that guarded the road leading from the west to the palace and the ridge was a rocky projection, quite wide enough and running out a long way, but 450 feet below the level of Masada: it was called the White Cliff. So climbing up and taking possession of this Silva ordered the troops to heap earth on it. They worked with a will and with ample man-power, and soon a solid platform had been raised to a height of 300 feet. As however this did not seem either strong or big enough to carry the engines, they built on top of it a pier composed of great stones fitted together, 75 feet wide and the same height. The engines were similar in construction to those devised by Vespasian first and later by Titus for their siege-operations. Further, a tower was erected 90 feet high and covered all over with iron plates: on this the Romans mounted a number of quick-loaders and stone-throwers which pelted the defenders, driving them from the battlements and forcing them to keep under cover. Silva had had a great Ram constructed: now by his orders it was swung continuously against the wall till at long last a breach was made and a small section collapsed.

Inside however the Sicarii had lost no time in building a second wall, which even the engines were likely to find a tougher proposition: it was pliant and capable of absorbing the impetus of the blows owing to its peculiar construction. Huge baulks were laid lengthwise and fastened together at the ends: these were in two parallel rows separated by the width of a wall and with the space between filled with earth. So that as the height increased the soil should not fall out, they laid beams across the long baulks to secure them. To the enemy the rampart looked like a normal construction, but the blows of the engines falling on yielding earth were absorbed: the concussion shook it together and made it more solid. Seeing this Silva decided that fire was the best weapon against such a wall and instructed his men to direct a volley of burning torches at it. Being made mostly of wood it soon caught fire: owing to its loose construction the whole thickness was soon ablaze and a mass of flame shot up. Just as the fire broke out a gust of wind from the north alarmed the Romans: it blew back the flame from above and drove it in their faces, and as their engines seemed on the point of being consumed in the blaze they were plunged into despair. Then all of a sudden as if by divine providence the wind swung to the south, and blowing strongly in the reverse direction carried and flung the flames against the wall, turning it into one solid blazing mass. God was indeed on the side of the Romans, who returned to camp full of delight, intending to assail the enemy early next day, and all night long kept watch with unusual vigilance to ensure that none of them slipped out unobserved. But Eleazar had no intention of slipping out himself, or of allowing anyone else to do so. He saw his wall going up in flames; he could think of no other means of escape or heroic endeavour; he had a clear picture of what the Romans would do to men, women, and children if they won the day; and death seemed to him the right choice for them all. Making up his mind that in the circumstances this was the wisest course, he collected the toughest of his comrades and urged it upon them in a speech of which this was the substance:

'My loyal followers, long ago we resolved to serve neither the Romans nor anyone else but only God, who alone is the true and righteous Lord of men: now the time has come that bids us prove our determination by our deeds. At such a time we must not disgrace ourselves: hitherto we have never submitted to slavery, even when it brought no danger with it: we must not choose slavery now, and with it penalties that will mean the end of everything if we fall alive into the hands of the Romans. For we were the first of all to revolt, and shall be the last to break off the struggle. And I think it is God who has given us this privilege, that we can die nobly and as free men, unlike others who were unexpectedly defeated. In our case it is evident that daybreak will end our resistance, but we are free to choose an honourable death with our loved ones. This our enemies cannot prevent, however earnestly they may pray to take us alive; nor can we defeat them in battle.

'From the very first, when we were bent on claiming our freedom but suffered such constant misery at each other's hands and worse at the enemy's, we ought perhaps to have read the mind of God and realized that His once beloved Jewish race had been sentenced to extinction. For if He had remained gracious or only slightly indignant with us, He would not have shut His eyes to the destruction of so many thousands or allowed His most holy City to be burnt to the ground by our enemies. We hoped, or so it would seem, that of all the Jewish race we alone would come through safe, still in possession of our freedom, as if we had committed no sin against God and taken part in no crime – we who had taught the others! Now see how He shows the folly of our hopes, plunging us into miseries more terrible than any we had dreamt of. Not even the impregnability of our fortress has sufficed to save us, but though we have food in abundance, ample supplies of arms, and more than enough of every other requisite, God Himself without a doubt has taken away all hope of survival. The fire that was being carried into the enemy lines did not turn back of its own accord towards the wall we had built: these things are God's vengeance for the many wrongs that in our madness we dared to do to our own countrymen.

'For those wrongs let us pay the penalty not to our bitterest enemies, the Romans, but to God – by our own hands. It will be easier to bear. Let our wives die unabused, our children without knowledge of slavery: after that, let us do each other an ungrudging kindness, preserving our freedom as a glorious winding-sheet. But first let our possessions and the whole fortress go up in flames: it will be a bitter blow to the Romans, that I know, to find our persons beyond their reach and nothing left for them to loot. One thing only let us spare – our store of food: it will bear witness when we are dead to the fact that we perished, not through want but because, as we resolved at the beginning, we chose death rather than slavery.'

Such was Eleazar's appeal. It did not meet with the same response from all his hearers: some were eager to do as he said, and filled with something like rapture at the thought that death was so noble; others less heroic were moved by pity for their wives and families, and certainly too by the prospect of their own end; and as they exchanged glances the tears in their eyes betrayed the repugnance they felt. When he saw them playing the coward and their spirits quailing before the bold sweep of his plan, Eleazar was afraid that even those who had not flinched when they heard his proposal might be unmanned by other men's tears and laments. So instead of abandoning his appeal he roused himself, and bursting with ardour began a more dazzling display of oratory on the immortality of the soul. Looking hard at his wet-eyed listeners and complaining bitterly he began:

'I made a sad mistake in thinking I had the support of loyal followers in the struggle for freedom, men resolved to live honourably or die. You are not a bit different from all and sundry in courage and bold-ness, you who fear death even when it means the end of utter misery, a course in which you ought not to hesitate or wait for someone to advise you. Ever since primitive man began to think, the words of our ancestors and of the gods, supported by the actions and spirit of our forefathers, have constantly impressed on us that *life* is the calamity for man, not death. Death gives freedom to our souls and lets them depart to their own pure home where they will know nothing of any calamity; but while they are confined within a mortal body and share its miseries, in strict truth they are dead. For association of the divine with the mortal is most improper. Certainly the soul can do a great deal even when imprisoned in the body: it makes the body its own organ of sense, moving it invisibly and impelling it in its actions further than mortal nature can reach. But when, freed from the weight that drags it down to earth and is hung about it, the soul returns to its own place, then in truth it partakes of a blessed power and an utterly unfettered strength, remaining as invisible to human eyes as God Himself. Not even while it is in the body can it be viewed; it enters undetected and departs unseen, having itself one imperishable nature, but causing a change in the body; for whatever the soul touches lives and blossoms, whatever it deserts withers and dies: such a superabundance it has of immortality.

'Sleep will provide you with the clearest proof of what I say. In sleep souls left to themselves and free from bodily distractions enjoy the most blissful repose, and consorting with God whose kin they are they go wherever they will and foretell many of the things to come. Why, pray, should we fear death if we love to repose in sleep? And isn't it absurd to run after the freedom of this life and grudge ourselves the freedom of eternity?

'It might be expected that we, so carefully taught at home, would be an example to others of readiness to die. But if we do need the testimony of foreigners, let us look to those Indians who profess to practise philosophy. They are men of true courage who, regarding this life as a kind of service we must render to nature, undergo it with reluctance and hasten to release their souls from their bodies; and though no misfortune presses or drives them away, desire for immortal life impels them to inform their friends that they are going to depart. No one tries to stop them, but everyone congratulates them and gives them messages for his dear ones: so confidently and so truly do they believe that the souls share a common life. Then after receiving these commissions they consign their bodies to the flames, that the soul may be as pure as possible when it is separated from the body, and hymns are sung to them as they die. In fact they are sent off more happily by their dearest ones to death than other men are sent by their fellow-citizens on a long journey: the bereaved may weep for themselves, but the departed they deem happy, ranked now among the immortals. Well then! Are we not ashamed to show a poorer spirit than Indians, and by our want of courage to bring the Law of our fathers, the envy of all the world, into utter contempt?

'Even if from the very first we had been taught the contrary belief, that life is indeed the greatest good of mankind and death a disaster, the situation is such, that we should still be called upon to bear it with a stout heart, for God's will and sheer necessity doom us to death. Long ago, it seems, God issued this warning to the whole Jewish race together, that life would be taken from us if we misused it. Do not fasten the blame on yourselves or give the Romans the credit for the fact that we are all ruined by the war against them: it is not through their power that these things have happened – a mightier hand has intervened to give them the outward shape of victory. What Roman weapons slew the Jews who lived in Caesarea? Why, they had no thought of rebelling against Rome, but were in the middle of their seventh-day ceremonies when the Caesarean mob rushed at them, and though they offered no resistance butchered them with their wives and children, paying no heed to the Romans who were treating none as enemies except ourselves, who had in fact rebelled. No doubt I shall be told that the Caesareans had a permanent quarrel with the Jews in their midst and simply seized their chance to vent their old hatred. Then what are we to say of the Jews in Scythopolis? They had the effrontery to make war on us to please the Greeks, and would not join with us, their own kith and kin, to drive out the Romans. Much good they got from their faithful support of the Greeks! They were brutally massacred by them, they and their entire households – such was the reward their alliance brought them! What they saved the Greeks from suffering at our hands they themselves endured as if it was they who had wished to inflict it! It would take too long to speak now about every individual case: you know that of all the towns in Syria there isn't one that hasn't exterminated its Jewish inhabitants, though they were more hostile to us than the Romans. As a single instance, the Damascenes, though they couldn't even fake a plausible excuse, made their own city reek with the most loathsome slaughter, butchering

18,000 Jews and their wives and families as well. As for those tortured to death in Egypt, it was stated that the number was something over 60,000.

'They, perhaps, died in this way because in a foreign land they could find no answer to their enemies; but all those who in their own took up arms against Rome had everything, hadn't they, that could give them hope of certain victory? Weapons, walls, impregnable fortresses, and a spirit that in the cause of liberty no danger could shake, encouraged all to rebel. But these things were effective for a very short time: they raised our hopes only to prove the beginning of worse misfortunes. All were captured; all came into the enemy's hands as if provided specially to make their victory more splendid, not to save the lives of those who fashioned them! Those who died in battle we may well congratulate: they died defending their freedom, not betraying it. But the masses who are now under the thumb of Rome who would not pity? Who would not hasten to die rather than share their fate? Some of them have been broken on the rack or tortured to death at the stake or by the lash; some have been half-eaten by savage beasts and then kept alive to be their food a second time, after providing amusement and sport for their enemies. Of them all we have most cause to pity those who are still alive; for they pray and pray for the death that never comes.

'Where is the mighty city, the mother-city of the whole Jewish race, secure within so many encircling walls, sheltering behind so many forts and lofty towers, bursting with warlike stores, and defended by thousands and thousands of determined men? Where now is the city that was believed to have God for her Founder? She has been torn up by the roots, and the only memorial of her that is left is the camp of her destroyers that still occupies her ruins! Old men with streaming eyes sit by the ashes of the Shrine, with a few women kept by the enemy as victims of their lust.

'Which of us, realizing these facts, could bear to see the light of day, even if he could live free from danger? Who is such an enemy to his country, who so unmanly and so wedded to life as not to be sorry he is alive today? If only we had all died before seeing the Sacred City utterly destroyed by enemy hands, the Holy Sanctuary so impiously uprooted! But since an honourable ambition deluded us into thinking that perhaps we should succeed in avenging her of her enemies, and now all hope has fled, abandoning us to our fate, let us at once choose death with honour and do the kindest thing we can for ourselves, our wives and children, while it is still possible to show ourselves any kindness. After all we were born to die, we and those we brought into the world: this even the luckiest must face. But outrage, slavery, and the sight of our wives led away to shame with our children – these are not evils to which man is subject by the laws of nature: men undergo them through their own cowardice if they have a chance to forestall them by death and will not take it. We were very proud of our courage, so we revolted from Rome: now in the final stages they have offered to spare our lives and we have turned the offer down. Is anyone too blind to see how furious they will be if they take us alive? Pity the young whose bodies are strong enough to survive prolonged torture; pity the not-so-young whose old frames would break under such ill-usage. A man will see his wife violently carried off; he will hear the voice of his child crying "Daddy!" when his own hands are fettered. Come! while our hands are free and can hold a sword, let them do a noble service! Let us die unenslaved by our enemies, and leave this world as free men in company with our wives and children. That is what the Law ordains, that is what our wives and children demand of us, the necessity God has laid on us, the opposite of what the Romans wish – they are anxious none of us should die before the town is captured. So let us deny the enemy their hoped-for pleasure at our expense, and without more ado leave them to be dumbfounded by our death and awed by our courage.'

Eleazar had many more arguments to urge, but all his listeners cut him short and full of uncontrollable enthusiasm made haste to do the deed. As if possessed they rushed off, everyone anxious to be quicker than the next man, and regarding it as proof positive of manliness and wisdom not to be found among the last: so irresistible a desire had seized them to slaughter their wives, their little ones, and themselves. It might have been thought that as they approached their task their determination would have weakened; but they clung resolutely to the purpose they had formed while listening to the appeal, and while they all retained feelings of personal affection, reason, which had urged what was best for their dear ones, won the day. For at the very moment when with streaming eyes they embraced and caressed their wives, and taking their children in their arms pressed upon them the last, lingering kisses, hands other than their own seemed to assist them and they carried out their purpose, the thought of the agonies they would suffer at the hands of the enemy consoling them for the necessity of killing them. In the end not a man failed to carry out his terrible resolve, but one and all disposed of their entire families, victims of cruel necessity who with their own hands murdered their wives and children and felt it to be the lightest of evils!

Unable to endure any longer the horror of what they had done, and thinking they would be wronging the dead if they outlived them a moment longer, they quickly made one heap of all they possessed and set it on fire; and when ten of them had been chosen by lot to be the executioners of the rest, every man lay down beside his wife and children where they lay, flung his arms round them, and exposed his throat to those who must perform the painful office. These unflinchingly slaughtered them all, then agreed on the same rule for each other, so that the one who drew the lot should kill the nine and last of all himself: such perfect confidence they all had in each other that neither in doing nor in suffering would one differ from another.[1] So finally the nine presented their throats, and the one man left till last first surveyed the serried ranks of the dead, in case amidst all the slaughter someone was still left in need of his hand; then finding that all had been dispatched set the palace blazing fiercely, and summoning all his strength drove his sword right through his body and fell dead by the side of his family. Thus these men died supposing that they had left no living soul to fall into the hands of the Romans; but an old woman escaped, along with another who was related to Eleazar, in intelligence and education superior to most women, and five little children. They had hidden in the conduits that brought drinking-water underground while the rest were intent upon the suicide-pact. These numbered 960, women and children included. The tragedy was enacted on 15th of Xanthicos.

Expecting further resistance, the Romans armed themselves at dawn and with gangways bridged the gap between platform and ramparts, then made their assault. Seeing no enemy, but dreadful solitude on every side, fire within, and silence, they were at a loss to guess what had happened. At last, as if giving the signal for a volley, they shouted, in the hope that some of those inside would show themselves. The noise came to the ears of the women, who emerged from the conduits and gave the Romans a detailed account of what had happened, the second of them providing a lucid report of Eleazar's speech and the action that had followed. They found it difficult to believe her and were

1. *What a contrast with the author's own perfidy at Jotapatal*

sceptical of such astounding resolution; but they attempted to extinguish the blaze and quickly cut a way through to the inside of the palace. When they came upon the rows of dead bodies, they did not exult over them as enemies but admired the nobility of their resolve, and the way in which so many had shown in carrying it out without a tremor an utter contempt of death.

Masada having fallen thus, the general left a garrison in the fortress and returned with the rest of his army to Caesarea. For nowhere was there an enemy left: the whole country had been subdued in the long war which had made itself felt by many even of the remotest inhabitants and had endangered their peace.

The next incident occurred in Egypt, and cost the lives of many Jews. Some members of the party of the Sicarii had managed to escape to Alexandria, where not satisfied with being still alive they started a subversive movement, urging many of their hosts to claim their freedom and to regard the Romans as no whit their superiors, honouring God as their only master. When certain Jews in prominent positions objected, they were murdered: the rest were constantly urged to revolt. Seeing the mad folly of the agitators, the leaders of the senate decided that it was no longer safe to overlook what was going on, and summoning all the Jews to a mass meeting exposed the mad folly of the Sicarii, showing them to be the cause of all the trouble. Now, they went on, not even after their escape had they any certain hope of safety, since once recognized by the Romans they would instantly be killed; so they were trying to bring the disaster due to themselves on those who had had no part in their crimes. So they urged the gathering to take care that these men did not bring them to ruin: they could justify themselves to the Romans by handing them over. Recognizing that the danger was very real the audience accepted their advice, and making a furious rush at the Sicarii rounded them up. 600 were caught then and there: a number escaped into Egypt and Egyptian Thebes, but were soon apprehended and brought back. There was universal astonishment at the fortitude and desperation – or was it strength of mind? – that they displayed. Subjected to every form of torture and bodily suffering that could be thought of, for the one purpose of making them acknowledge Caesar as lord, not a man gave in or came near to saying it, but rising above the strongest compulsion they all maintained their resolve, and it seemed as if their bodies felt no pain and their souls were almost exultant as they met the tortures and the flames. But nothing amazed the spectators as much as the behaviour of young children; for not one of them could be constrained to call Caesar lord. So far did the strength of a brave spirit prevail over the weakness of their little bodies.

Lupus, who was in charge of Alexandria at the time, promptly reported this disturbance to Caesar. He, viewing with suspicion the continual turbulence of the Jews, and fearing that they might again assemble their forces and win new adherents, instructed Lupus to pull down the Jewish sanctuary in the district of Onias.

Onias is in Egypt, a settlement that was founded and received this name in the following circumstances. Onias, son of Simon, and one of the chief priests in Jerusalem, fled from Antiochus the Syrian king during his war with the Jews and came to Alexandria, where he was given a friendly reception by Ptolemy, who detested Antiochus. Onias declared that he would win him the support of the whole Jewish race if he would agree to his suggestions. When the king undertook to do all he could, Onias asked leave to build a Sanctuary somewhere in Egypt where he could worship God as his fathers had done. This would make the Jews still more hostile to Antiochus, who had plundered their temple at Jerusalem, and more friendly disposed to himself, and freedom of worship would bring many of them to his side.

Pleased with this suggestion, Ptolemy gave him a piece of ground 21 miles from Memphis: the district is called the Nome of Heliopolis. There Onias constructed a fortress and built his Sanctuary – not like that in Jerusalem but resembling a tower – of large blocks of stone and to a height of 90 feet. But in designing the altar he copied the one at home, and he enriched the Temple with the same kind of offerings, except for the shape of the lampstand. He did not make a stand at all, but simply had a lamp hammered out of gold: it gave a bright light and was hung by a gold chain. The whole temple precincts were encircled with a wall of baked brick, in which the gateways were of stone. The king further allotted him a large district to bring him in revenue, so that the priests should enjoy abundance and God should have ample provision for His worship. Unfortunately the motive of Onias in doing all this was not to his credit: he was anxious to outdo the Jews in Jerusalem, as he bore them a grudge for his exile, and thought that by raising this temple he could induce the masses to leave them for it. There had been too, an ancient prophecy made about 600 years before:[1]

1. *550 would be a nearer figure. The prophecy will be found in* Is. xix. 19.

Isaiah was the name of the man who foretold that this Sanctuary would be raised in Egypt by a Jew. So it was that the Temple came to be built.

On receipt of this dispatch Lupus proceeded to the temple, brought out some of the offerings and shut up the building. Soon afterwards Lupus died and Paulinus, the new governor, stripped the temple bare, threatening the priests with dire consequences if they did not produce every single offering. He then forbade would-be worshippers to come near the precincts, and locking the gates put the place entirely out of bounds, leaving not a vestige of divine worship there. The time from the building of the sanctuary to its closure was 343 years.[1]

The towns in the neighbourhood of Cyrene were also infected by the mad folly of the Sicarii. Into Cyrene slipped an unprincipled scoundrel called Jonathan, by trade a weaver, who persuaded a number of men of the poorer classes to listen to him, and led them out into the desert promising to show them signs and portents. Few of the citizens were aware of his fraudulent activities, but the leading Jews in Cyrene reported his exodus with all his paraphernalia to the governor of Libyan Pentapolis, Catullus, who promptly dispatched contingents of horse and foot. They easily crushed the unarmed mob, destroying the majority in the engagement: the few who were taken alive were brought before Catullus. The ringleader, Jonathan, escaped for the moment, but a long and very careful search of the whole country led to his ultimate capture. Brought before the governor, he contrived to save his own skin but gave Catullus a pretext for shocking injustice. Against the wealthiest of the Jews he brought the monstrous charge that they had given him his instructions, and Catullus, welcoming these charges with delight, grossly exaggerated the significance of what had happened, dramatizing it with a vengeance in order that he too might be credited with a victory over the Jews. But what was crueller still – besides being absurdly credulous he even gave the Sicarii lessons in the art of lying. Thus he ordered Jonathan to name one of the Jews, Alexander, of whom he had fallen foul some time before, the resulting quarrel being public knowledge, involving also his wife Berenice in the allegations. Having got rid of these, he next murdered all the wealthier Jews to the number of 3,000: in doing this he felt quite safe, as he confiscated their possessions for the benefit of Caesar's revenues.

1. 100 years too many; perhaps a deliberate invention, since 343 is the cube of 7. (So Dr Eisler.)

For fear that some of the Jews elsewhere might show up his iniquitous conduct, he increased the scope of his calumnies, inviting Jonathan and some of his fellow-prisoners to prefer a charge of subversive activities against the most respectable Jews in both Alexandria and Rome. One of the objects of this trumped-up charge was Josephus, the writer of this history. However, Catullus did not profit as he had expected from his fabrication. He arrived in Rome bringing Jonathan and his associates in fetters, and satisfied that the lies told in his presence and at his prompting would be accepted without question. But Vespasian smelt a rat and enquired into the facts, and finding no justification for the accusation brought against the men acquitted them of the charges at the instance of Titus, and gave Jonathan the punishment he deserved: he was first tortured, then burnt alive. Catullus for the time being profited by the lenience of the two emperors and received no more than a reprimand; but soon afterwards he succumbed to a complicated sickness beyond remedy and died miserably, not only chastened in body but suffering from a much more terrible disease of the mind. He was tormented by terrors, constantly calling out that he saw the ghosts of those he had murdered standing before him; and losing control of himself he would spring from his bed as if he himself was being tortured and burnt. His malady grew rapidly worse and worse, and his bowels were eaten through and fell out. Such was his end – proof, if ever there was one, of the providence of God, who executes judgement on the wicked.

*

And here we bring our story to an end – the story which we promised to set down with the utmost accuracy for the benefit of those who wished to learn how the Romans fought this war against the Jews. Its literary merits must be left to the judgement of the readers: as to its truth, I should not hesitate to declare without fear of contradiction that from the first word to the last I have aimed at nothing else.

The Slavonic Additions

THE Slavonic Version of the Jewish War, surviving in Russian and Rumanian copies, which at some points differ slightly from one another, was made accessible to Western readers by the late Dr Berendts. Though in the view of Dr Eisler it reveals some traces of a Semitic original, the MS from which the version was made was undoubtedly written in Greek. Perhaps this was the first Greek version of the Aramaic to which the Preface refers, published in Titus' reign and followed in Domitian's by a considerably revised second edition, forming our present text. The Slavonic lacks a great many passages of that text, has others in a different and apparently more primitive form, and contains additional matter entirely missing from the Greek. Most of these passages are of little intrinsic interest and may well have been omitted from the later edition in the course of a literary tidying-up: for none of them could an interpolator have had any motive. Others, which bitterly attacked the venality and treachery of the Romans, may well have given offence and have been omitted later in response to protests. The crudeness of the original account of Josephus' contemptible conduct after the fall of Jotapata may likewise have been felt to need toning down. Instead of 'Josephus – shall we put it down to divine providence, or just to luck? – was left with one other man', it runs 'After saying this he counted the numbers cunningly and so deceived them all.'

Some few passages, however, are of the greatest interest, containing as they do records of John the Baptist, Jesus Christ, and the early Christians. These records, like the famous allusions in *Antiquities*, are condemned as spurious by critics who, victims of their own wishful thinking and bent on destruction, are prepared without a trace of MS authority to bracket or reverse the meaning of any passage that conflicts with their pet theories. Such a proceeding is in the last degree unscientific. It is to be observed also that the forging of these passages for propaganda purposes could not have rendered the least service to a Christian apologist; they could never influence anyone not already convinced by the Gospels; they are in many important points irreconcileable with Christian tradition; and they clearly reveal their author not as a believer but as a doubting, if curious, onlooker.

If then these passages are genuine, how did they come to be omitted from our Greek text? The answer is surely simple. If that text represents the final form of the book, an edition published when Domitian, the hater and persecutor of Christianity, was at the height of his power, would it not have been the last degree of folly – most improbable in one as careful of his own skin as Josephus – to include references to Christ as a benefactor and miracle-worker, something more than a man, unjustly condemned by Roman authority and perhaps raised from the dead, whose followers too had worked wonders and 'signs' beyond the power of medicine? And if it was not safe to speak thus of Christ, could it be safe to speak of the man who had foretold his kingship? It should be remembered that in Josephus, as in the New Testament, the words 'king' and 'Roman emperor' are interchangeable.

The substance of these controversial passages is given in the paraphrases that follow.

I. JOHN THE FORERUNNER[1]

At that time a man was going about Judaea remarkably dressed: he wore animal hair on those parts of his body not covered by his own. His face was like a savage's. He called on the Jews to claim their freedom, crying: 'God sent me to show you the way of the Law, so that you can shake off any human yoke: no man shall rule you, but only the Most High who sent me.' His message was eagerly welcomed, and he was followed by all Judaea and the district round Jerusalem. All he did was to baptize them in the Jordan and dismiss them with an earnest exhortation to abandon their evil ways: if they did so they would be given a king who would liberate them and master the unruly, while himself acknowledging no master. This promise was derided by some but believed by others.

The man was brought before Archelaus[2] and an assemblage of lawyers, who asked who he was and where he had been. He replied: 'I am a man called by the Spirit of God, and I live on stems, roots, and fruit.' When he was threatened with torture if he did not stop behaving and talking like this, he retorted: 'It would be more to the point if you stopped acting so disgracefully and submitted to the God you profess to worship.'

Simon, a scribe of Essene origin, sprang up and exclaimed angrily: 'We study Holy Writ every day; you have just come out of the forest like a wild animal; and do you dare put us right and mislead the people with your damnable nonsense?' Simon then rushed at him to tear him to pieces. But the man replied with a warning: 'I will not reveal to you the secret that is in your midst, as you have refused to listen and so have brought immeasurable disaster upon your own heads.' Then off he went to the other side of Jordan, where he resumed his work unmolested.

1. Following 'their money' on page 124.
2. At the time of Archelaus' expulsion John cannot have been more than thirteen!

2. JOHN, PHILIP, AND ANTIPAS[1]

During his reign Philip dreamt that an eagle pecked out both his eyes. He summoned his advisers, and when they had given a variety of interpretations in came unannounced the man mentioned above, who used to go round in animal hair and cleanse people in the River Jordan. He began: 'Listen to God's message – the dream you had. The eagle, with its ferocious rapacity, represents your own cupidity – the sin that will cost you your two eyes; that is to say, your throne and your wife.' Before sunset Philip was dead and his throne passed to Agrippa.[2] His wife Herodias then married his brother Herod.[3] This shocked and disgusted all who respected the Law, but they dared not take Herod to task. The man we referred to as a savage, and he alone, faced Herod and fiercely assailed him. 'You have married your brother's wife in defiance of the Law, and just as he died a cruel death, so will divine vengeance bring your life to an end. The judgement of God is inexorable, and you are doomed to die miserably in exile.[4] For *you* are not "raising up seed unto your brother": you are indulging your own lust and committing adultery, considering that he has left four children.'[5] This attack infuriated Herod, who ordered the man to be flogged and kicked out. But he constantly waylaid the tetrarch and reiterated his accusations, till Herod lost control altogether and ordered him to be killed.

He was a strange creature, not like a man at all. He lived like a disembodied spirit. He never touched bread; even at the Passover Feast he would not eat the unleavened bread or pronounce the words 'In thankfulness to God, who delivered the nation from slavery, shall you eat this; it was given for the flight, because the journey was made in haste.' Wine and other strong drink he would not allow to be brought anywhere near him, and animal food he absolutely refused – fruit was all that he needed. The whole object of his life was to show evil in its true colours.

3. THE MINISTRY AND CRUCIFIXION OF JESUS[6]

It was at that time that a man appeared – if 'man' is the right word[7] – who had all the attributes of a man but seemed to be something greater. His

1. *Following 'in Peraea' on page 130.*
2. *Philip died in 33 or 34 A.D., several years after John, and three years before Agrippa's accession.*
3. *Antipas. According to* Antiquities *her first husband was not this Philip but a half-brother of Antipas, who was still alive when Antipas married her.*
4. *He died at Lyons in 39 A.D.*
5. *According to* Antiquities, *only Salome.*
6. *Following 'Jerusalem forthwith' on page 131.*
7. *There is in* Antiquities *a similar sentence, where Jesus is named.*

actions, certainly, were superhuman, for he worked such wonderful and amazing miracles that I for one cannot regard him as a man; yet in view of his likeness to ourselves I cannot regard him as an angel either. Everything that some hidden power enabled him to do he did by an authoritative word. Some people said that their first Lawgiver had risen from the dead and had effected many marvellous cures; other thought he was a messenger from heaven. However, in many ways he broke the Law – for instance, he did not observe the Sabbath in the traditional manner. At the same time his conduct was above reproach. He did not need to use his hands: a word sufficed to fulfil his every purpose.

Many of the common people flocked after him and followed his teaching. There was a wave of excited expectation that he would enable the Jewish tribes to throw off the Roman yoke. As a rule he was to be found opposite the City on the Mount of Olives, where also he healed the sick. He gathered round him 150 assistants and masses of followers. When they saw his ability to do whatever he wished by a word, they told him that they wanted him to enter the City, destroy the Roman troops, and make himself king; but he took no notice.

When the suggestion came to the ears of the Jewish authorities, they met under the chairmanship of the high priest and exclaimed: 'We are utterly incapable of resisting the Romans; but as the blow is about to fall we'd better go and tell Pilate what we've heard, and steer clear of trouble, in case he gets to know from someone else and confiscates our property, puts us to death, and turns our children adrift.' So they went and told Pilate, who sent troops and butchered many of the common people. He then had the Miracle-worker brought before him, held an inquiry, and expressed the opinion that he was a benefactor, not a criminal or agitator or a would-be king. Then he let him go, as he had cured Pilate's wife when she was at the point of death.

Returning to his usual haunts he resumed his normal work. When the crowds grew bigger than ever, he earned by his actions an incomparable reputation. The exponents of the Law were mad with jealousy, and gave Pilate 30 talents to have him executed. Accepting the bribe, he gave them permission to carry out their wishes themselves. So they seized him and crucified him in defiance of all Jewish tradition.

4. THE EARLY CHRISTIANS[1]

In the time of Cuspius Fadus and Tiberius Alexander many of the Miracle-worker's followers came forward and declared to the adherents of their master that, although he had died, he was now alive and would free them from their slavery. Many of the common people listened to

1. *Replacing last half of paragraph ending 'Greater Armenia' on page 135.*

their preaching and accepted their call – not because they were men of mark, for they were working men, some only shoemakers, others cobblers, others labourers. But they worked marvellous 'signs'; in fact nothing was beyond their power.

Seeing the unsettlement of the people, these excellent procurators decided after consulting the scribes to arrest the men and put them to death, for fear that the movement, though of no consequence at the moment, might end in a major upheaval. But in face of the 'signs' they hesitated and dared not take any action, convinced that no medical treatment could account for such marvellous cures, and surmising that if these were not the work of God Himself they would soon be shown up. So they gave the men complete freedom of action. Later, however, they were persuaded by the scribes to send them to Rome or Antioch to be tried, banishing others to distant countries.

5. A TEMPLE INSCRIPTION ABOUT JESUS[1]

Above these announcements was hung a fourth in the same characters (Greek, Latin, and Jewish) declaring that Jesus, the king who never reigned, was crucified by the Jews because he foretold the end of the City and the utter destruction of the Temple.

6. THE RENDING OF THE VEIL AND THE RESURRECTION[2]

In the days of our pious fathers this curtain was intact, but in our own generation it was a sorry sight, for it had been suddenly rent from top to bottom at the time when by bribery they had secured the execution of the benefactor of men – the one who by his actions proved that he was no mere man. Many other awe-inspiring 'signs' happened at the same moment. It is also stated that after his execution and entombment he disappeared entirely. Some people actually assert that he had risen; others retort that his friends stole him away. I for one cannot decide where the truth lies. A dead man cannot rise by his own power; but he might rise if aided by the prayer of another righteous man. Again, if an angel or other heavenly being, or God Himself, takes human form to fulfil his purpose, and after living among men dies and is buried, he can rise again at will. Moreover it is stated that he could not have been stolen away, as guards were posted round his tomb, 30 Romans and 1,000 Jews.[3]

1. Following 'wall of its own' on page 291.
2. Following 'signs of the Zodiac' on page 293.
3. The exaggerated numbers are in the best Josephan style.

7. THE ORACLE OF THE WORLD-RULER[1]

Some took this as a reference to Herod, others to the crucified Miracle-worker Jesus, and others to Vespasian.

1. *Replacing the passage beginning 'This they took to mean' on page 350.*

Correlation of this Version with Whiston's

THIS VERSION	WHISTON'S
Ch. 1	Bk 1 Ch. 1–9
2	10–14
3	15–21
4	22–27
5	28–33
6	Bk 2 Ch. 1–7
7	8–13
8	14–17
9	17–19
10	20–22
11	Bk 3 Ch. 1–7
12	7–8
13	9–10 and Bk 4 Ch. 1
14	Bk 4 Ch. 2–3
15	3–7
16	8–11
17	Bk 5 Ch. 1–5
18	6–9
19	10–13
20	Bk 6 Ch. 1–3
21	4–10
22	Bk 7 Ch. 1–5
23	6–11

List of Dates

B.C.	170	Jerusalem captured by Antiochus Epiphanes
	167–161	Judas Maccabaeus
	161–143	Jonathan
	142–135	Simon
	135–105	John Hyrcanus
	105–104	Aristobulus, the first king
	104–78	Alexander Jannaeus
	78–69	Alexandra
	69–62	Aristobulus II
	63	Jerusalem captured by Pompey
	57–55	Gabinius governor
	53	Temple plundered by Crassus
	53–51	Cassius
	48	Death of Pompey
	44	Death of Julius Caesar
	42	Death of Cassius
	40	Jerusalem pillaged by Parthians
		Herod king of the Jews
	37	Jerusalem captured by Herod
	31	Antony defeated at Actium
	29	Murder of Mariamme
	20	Work on Temple begun
	6	Execution of Alexander and Aristobulus
	4	Execution of Antipater
		Death of Herod (March)
		Accession of Archelaus
A.D.	6	Deposition of Archelaus
	6–9	Coponius procurator
	14	Accession of Tiberius
	26–36	Pilate procurator
	37	Accession of Gaius (Caligula)
	41	Accession of Claudius
	41–4	Agrippa I king of Judaea
	52–60	Felix procurator
	53	Agrippa II king of Trachonitis etc.
	54	Accession of Nero
	60–2	Festus procurator
	62–4	Albinus procurator
	64–6	Florus procurator

66	Outbreak of the Jewish War
	Jerusalem pillaged by Florus
	Masada taken by insurgents
	Roman surrender in Jerusalem
	Defeat of Cestius (November)
	Josephus governor of Galilee
67	Arrival of Vespasian
	Siege of Jotapata (May to July)
	Capture of Tarichaeae (September)
	Capture of Gamala (October)
	All Galilee subdued
	Jerusalem in hands of terrorists
68	Gadara occupied by Romans (March)
	Peraea subdued
	Judaea and Idumaea subdued
	Vespasian at Jericho (June)
	Gerasa captured
	Death of Nero (June)
69	Death of Galba (January)
	Simon in Idumaea
	Death of Otho (April)
	Simon in Jerusalem
	Vespasian hailed as emperor
	Death of Vitellius (December)
70	Three factions in Jerusalem
	Siege begun (March)
	Two walls captured (May)
	Circumvallation (May–June)
	Antonia captured (July)
	Temple fired (August)
	City destroyed (September)
71	'Triumph' of Vespasian and Titus
72	Capture of Machaerus
73	Capture of Masada
	Temple of Onias closed
75	Temple of Peace dedicated

The Calendar

The calendar employed by Josephus in this book is the Macedonian, which was in regular use in Asia Minor and the Near East. The names of the months, and their approximate Julian equivalents, are as follows:

Dios	November
Apellaios	December
Andynaios	January
Peritios	February
Dystros	March
Xanthicos	April
Artemisios	May
Daisios	June
Panemos	July
Loös	August
Gorpiaios	September
Hyperberetaios	October

If Niese is correct, the Macedonian months lagged about eighteen days behind the Julian. Thus the 7th of Artemisios is about the 25th of May, and the 29th of the same month is about the 16th of June.

Money

In his vaguer references to money Josephus sometimes mentions 'gold coins'; but whenever he states a precise sum he invariably gives it either in drachmas or in talents, occasionally adding the words 'of silver', or specifying Attic drachmas. The drachma, of which the Roman *denarius* was the rough equivalent, was the 'penny' of the gospels where – for instance in the Parable of the Labourers in the Vineyard – it represents a labourer's wage for a day's work. As a rule it is only small sums that are measured in drachmas, though in one passage we find 'five hundred thousand silver drachmas' as the sum bestowed by Augustus on Herod's unmarried daughters. Large sums are normally measured in talents, and range from the 8 talents given by John the tax-collector to Florus as a bribe to the 3,000 or more plundered by Hyrcanus from the tomb of David.

The precise value of these two monetary units is difficult to determine – it varied in different places and at different times. According to Liddell and Scott the Attic drachma was a silver coin worth 9¾d., and the talent was equivalent to 60,000 drachmas, i.e. £243 15s. 0d. But students must remember that in the many decades that have elapsed since those eminent scholars produced their great work the price of silver and gold has shot up, and pounds, shillings and pence have lost about five-sixths of their value. If therefore we have purchasing power in mind we had best think of the drachma as about 5 shillings, and the talent as about £1,400; but by the time that this book is in the reader's hands even these figures may be too low.

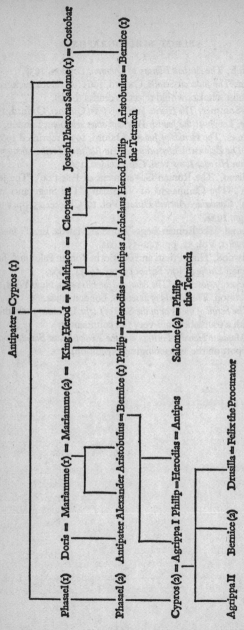

Chief members of the Herodian family

Antipater = Cypros (1)

Phasael (1)   Doris = Marianne (1) = King Herod = Malthace = Cleopatra   Joseph Pheoras Salome (1) = Costobar

Phasael (2)   Antipater Alexander Aristobulus = Bernice (1) Philip = Herodias = Antipas Archelaus Herod Philip   Aristobulus = Bernice (1)
                                                                                                          the Tetrarch

Cypros (2) = Agrippa I Philip = Herodias = Antipas   Salome (2) = Philip
                                                                                  the Tetrarch

Agrippa II   Bernice (2)   Drusilla = Felix the Procurator

Only a few members of this vast family with its numerous internal and at times incestuous alliances are shown above. King Herod is known to have had ten wives and fifteen children.

Bernice (2) had two husbands and was mistress to Vespasian, Titus, and probably her own brother, Agrippa II, the last monarch of Herod's line, retired like Josephus to Rome, where in A.D. 100 both died.

SELECT BIBLIOGRAPHY

F. H. Cross, Jr, *The Ancient Library of Qumran*, London, 1958.

G. R. Driver, *The Judaean Scrolls*, Oxford, 1965 (useful for background, though most scholars would reject its central thesis).

A. Dupont-Sommer, *The Essene Writings from Qumran*, Oxford, 1961.

M. I. Finley, *Josephus: the Jewish War and other selections*, London, 1966.

A. H. M. Jones, *The Herods of Judaea*, Oxford, 1938, reprinted 1967.

M. Hengel, *Die Zeloten: Untersuchungen zur Jüdischen Freiheitsbewegung in der Zeit von Herodes I. bis 70 n. Chr.*, Leiden, 1961.

A. Momigliano, 'The Roman Government of Palestine', 'The Jewish Rebellion', 'The Campaigns of Vespasian', 'The Siege and Fall of Jerusalem', *Cambridge Ancient History* Vol. 10, Chapter 25, pp. 850–65, Cambridge, 1934.

I. A. Richmond, 'The Roman Siege-Works at Masada, Israel', *Journal of Roman Studies*, Vol. 52, pp. 142–55, 1962.

E. M. Smallwood, 'High Priests and Politics in Roman Palestine', *Journal of Theological Studies*, New Series 13, pp. 14–34, 1962.

H. St J. Thackeray, *Josephus: The Man and the Historian*, New York, 1929.

G. A. Williamson, *The World of Josephus*, London, 1964.

Y. Yadin, *The Scroll of the War of the Sons of Light*, London, 1962 (the text edited with a translation and very full commentary).

Y. Yadin, *Masada: Herod's Fortress and the Zealots' Last Stand*, London, 1966 (a report on the archaeological expedition).

Index

Abila, 138, 258

Abraham (Abram), 265, 307

Absalom, lieutenant of Menahem, 159

Acchabaron, 171

Acedasa, 29

Achaia, 93, 170, 180, 185

Achiab, cousin of Herod, 111, 118–19, 121

Acme, maidservant of Julia, 108, 110

Acrabata, 184

Acrabatene, 137, 179, 184, 263–4

Acrabetta, 171, 266

Actian War, 70

Actium, 70, 73

Adiabene, 166, 268, 287, 296, 317

Adida, 262

Adoreus, 43

Adriatic Sea, 45

Aebutius, a decurion, 191, 226

Aemilius Jucundus, 168

Aeneas, a deserter, 303

Aeternius Fronto, a tribune, 344, 359

Africa, 188, 271

Agesilaus, conqueror of Asia, 149

Agrippa, Fonteius, a consular legate, 368

Agrippa, Vipsanius, favourite of Caesar, 75; friend of Herod, 75, 77

Agrippa I, 8, 96; accuses Herod, 131; visits Claudius, 134; given dominion by Claudius, 135; wealth of, 135; builds wall round Jerusalem, 135, 287–8; death of, 135

Agrippa II, 8, 170, 173–4, 183–4, 229, 279, 288, 369, 398; Agrippias named after, 37; succeeds Herod King of Chalcis, 135; visits Rome, 138; Kingdom extended by Nero, 138; travels to Alexandria 144, 147; meets Neapolitanus, 147; and the Jews, 147–8; speech at the Gymnasium, 148–54; and Florus, 148, 154, 156; tries to delay the War, 154; sends help to Jerusalem, 156; palace destroyed, 157; and Noarus,

162; aids Cestius, 164, 166; and revolt of Tiberias, 177; and Vespasian, 182, 185, 215–16, 223–4; adorns Paneum, 220; and Titus, 263

Agrippeum, 77

Agrippias (formerly Anthedon), 34, 37

Agrippina, wife of Agrippa, 138

Alani Tribe, 379

Albinus, procurator, 141, 350

Alexander the Great, 150, 162, 316, 379

Alexander, a bandit, 137

Alexander, father of Tiberius, 292

Alexander, son of Alexander, 96

Alexander, officer of Titus, 319

Alexander, King, 301

Alexander Tiberius, 135–6, 144, 163, 271–2, 279–80, 344, 399

Alexander Jannaeus, 33–7, 374

Alexander, the false, 123–4

Alexander, husband of Berenice, 394

Alexander, son of Aristobulus, 53, 80; escapes from Pompey, 42; and Gabinius, 42–4; flees to Alexandreum, 42–3; leads further revolt, 44–5

Alexander, son of Herod, 80, 96–7, 100–103, 106, 135; hatred of father, 81–2; charged with attempting to poison father, 82–3; and Antipater, 84–5, 88, 91–3; rumours concerning, 84–93; helped by Archelaus, 88–90; and Eurycles, 91–3; and Tiro, 94–5; tried at Beirut, 93–4; and Trypho, 95; death, 95

Alexandra, wife of Alexander Jannaeus, 35, 37

Alexandreum, 39, 42–3, 63, 92, 95

Alexandria, 58, 102, 144, 147, 152, 162–4, 180, 185, 221, 270–71, 273–6, 279, 289, 299, 344, 363, 367, 370, 392–3, 395

Alexas, friend of Antony, 74

Alexas, friend of Herod, 98, 110–11

Alexas, follower of John, 332, 336

Almond Pool, 316

Alps, 151

Amathus, 33–4, 43

Ammathus, 224

Ananias, chief priest, 137, 155–8

Ananias, a messenger, 242

Ananias, priest (son of Masbalus), 321

Ananias, son of Zadok, 159, 176

Ananus, father of Jonathan, 137

Ananus, son of Ananias, 137

Ananus, son of Jonathan, 167

Ananus, son of Bagadates, 321

Ananus of Emmaus, officer of Simon, 343

Ananus, High Priest, 251, 264, 319; repairs City Walls, 170, 178; tries to avert war, 179; urges discontent, 235–8; raises forces, 239; and John, 240; sends delegation to Vespasian, 240–41; and Idumaeans, 241–2; 246–8; death, 248–9; ousts Simon, 263

Andromeda, 213

Annaeus of Tarichaeae, 173

Annius, Lucius, 262

Anthedon, 34, 43, 74, 77, 160

Antigonus, son of Aristobulus, 45, 57, 70, 309; captured by Pompey, 42; escapes from Rome, 44; interview with Caesar, 47; returns from exile, 52; banished again, 53; attacks Hyrcanus, 54–5, 57; made King, 56; disliked by Antony, 58; besieges Masada, 60; and Silo, 60–62; attacked by Herod, 63–5; and Machaerus, 64; and Joseph, 64–5; sends Pappus to oppose Herod, 66–7; surrenders to Sossius, 68; death, 69

Antigonus, son of Hyrcanus, 31–3

Antiochus, king of Syria, 393

Antiochus the Aspendian, 31

Antiochus Dionysius, 35

Antiochus Eupator, 28–31

Antiochus the Jew, 365–6

Antiochus of Commagene, 316; surrenders Samosata, 64; aids

Cestius, 164; aids Titus and Vespasian, 185; attacked by Caesennius Paetus, 378–9

Antiochus Epiphanes (1), 23, 309, 360; and Ptolemy VI, 27; invades Judaea, 27–8, 364; death, 28

Antiochus Epiphanes (2), attacks Jerusalem, 315–16; attacked by Caesennius Paetus, 378–9

Antioch, 45, 53, 65, 78, 90, 115, 117, 121, 132–3, 138, 142, 162, 164, 182, 272, 364–5, 369, 400

Antipas, son of Herod, 8, 97, 111, 398; named Herod's successor, 108, 115; claims Kingdom, 115, 122; tetrarch, 122, 130; and the two Agrippas, 125–40

Antipas, kinsman of Agrippa, 156, 170, 234

Antipater the Samaritan, chief executive of Antipater, 101

Antipater, son of Salome, 98, 115–16

Antipater, father of Herod, 23, 42, 50, 57–8, 309; allied with Hyrcanus, 38, 44; opposes Aristobulus, 37–8, 45; allied with Caesar, 45–6; appointed Commissioner for all Judaea, 47; undisputed head of state, 48; death, 51

Antipater, son of Herod, 53, 80, 95, 109; preferred by father, 82–5, 92; slanders his brothers, 82–5, 88, 96; and Eurycles, 91–2; undisputed heir, 96; fears for his succession, 97; and Pheroras, 98–102; conspiracy of, 98–105; trial of, 105–8; execution of, 110–11

Antipatris, 35, 77, 165, 169, 259

Antiphilus, 101–2, 108

Antonia, daughter of Claudius, 138

Antonia, a fort, 32, 37, 75, 146, 154, 157, 287–8, 290–91, 295, 297, 301, 305, 316, 320, 325–8, 330–32, 335–6, 338, 345, 350

Antonius Primus, 263, 273–4

Antonius of Ascalon, 181–2

Antonius, a centurion, 206–7

Antony, Mark, 37, 54, 58, 60–63, 81;

attacks Alexander, 42–3; returns
body of Aristobulus, 45; declares
war on Cassius and Brutus, 51–2;
receives Jewish deputations, 53;
and Cleopatra, 53, 69–70, 73–4;
and Herod, 53, 58–9, 64–5, 67, 70,
73, 75; dislike of Antigonus, 58;
attacks Samosata, 64; makes Sossius
governor of Syria, 65
Anvath Borceos, 184
Apamea, 50, 69, 162
Aphek, 165
Aphtha, 235
Apollonia, 43
Arabia and Arabs, 21, 56, 77, 150, 184,
260, 262, 288, 299, 374; Obodas,
34, 87; and Antiochus Dionysius,
35; and Aretas, 38; invaded by
Scaurus, 42; and Antipater, 45; and
Herod, 57–8, 71–3; and Joseph, 60;
and Cleopatra, 69–70; and Corinthus, 99; and Varus, 120–21; and
bowmen, 185, 193, 197, 201; and
Vespasian, 193, 197; butchery of
Jews, 323
Arabia Felix, 152
Arbela, 62
Arcea, 369
Archelaus, ethnarch, 97, 125, 130; and
Antipater, 102, 108; named as
Herod's heir, 111; arranges Herod's
funeral, 112–13; rise and fall of,
113–24; appeases subjects, 113; and
revolutionaries, 113–14; and Sabinus, 114–15; visits Rome, 115;
dispute over Herod's will, 115–
17; dispute with Jews, 121;
appointed ethnarch, 122; banished
by Caesar, 124; and Glaphyra, 124;
and John the Baptist, 397
Archelaus, king of Cappadocia, 8, 12,
94, 97, 124; father-in-law of Alexander, 82–3; entertains Herod, 83;
assists son-in-law against Herod,
88–90; rewarded by Herod, 90;
and Eurycles, 91–3
Archelaus, son of Magdatus, 343
Ardalas, Roman officer, 354

Aretas (1), king of Coele-Syria, 35,
38, 42
Aretas (2), King, 99, 120
Arethusa, 42
Argos, 77
Aristaeus, clerk of the Sanhedrin, 321
Aristobulus I, 31–3
Aristobulus II, 45, 47, 52–3, 374; and
mother Alexandra, 36–7; pro-
claims himself king, 37; and
Hyrcanus, 37–8, 309; and Anti-
pater, 37–8; attacked by Aretas, 38;
and Scaurus, 38–9; and Pompey,
39–42, 309; escapes from Rome,
43; defeated by Romans, 43–4
Aristobulus, son of Aristobulus, 96
Aristobulus, son of Herod, 96–7, 131,
135, 138; and Alexander, 80–88,
91–5, 100, 102–3, 123; and Anti-
pater, 84; and Salome, 86; rumours
concerning, 88; and Eurycles, 91–3;
and Tiro, 94–5
Aristobulus, King of Chalcidice, 378
Arius, 120
Armenia, 37–8, 135, 138, 362, 380
Arpha, 184
Artabazes, son of Tigranes, 69
Artaxerxes, 121n.
Artorius, 340
Arus, 120
Asamon, 165
Ascalon, 45, 78, 123, 160–61, 181–2,
185n., 275
Asia, 149–50
Asochis, 33
Assuan, 271
Assyria and Assyrians, 21–2, 300, 308,
310, 319
Athenio, Cleopatra's general, 70–71
Athens and Athenians, 63, 78, 149
Athrongaeus, a shepherd, 119
Atlantic ocean, 152
Atratinus, 58
Augustus Harbour, Caesarea, 104
Auranitis, 74, 122, 135, 156
Azates, King, 354
Azotus, 42–3, 123, 233
Azov, Sea of, 150, 379

Baaras, 375

Babylon and Babylonians, 21, 31, 121, 293, 308, 310, 333, 345, 347, 360, 371

Baca, 183

Bacchides, 27

Balanea, 78

Baris, 32, 37

Bar-Kochbar, 9

Barzapharnes, seizes Syria, 54; and Phasael, 55; overruns Palestine, 80; captures Hyrcanus, 80

Basle, 15

Bassus, Caecilianus, 50

Bassus, Lucilius, succeeds Cerealius Vetilianus in Judaea, 374; attacks Machaerus, 374–7; death, 380

Batanaea, 74, 122, 138, 156, 162, 184

Bathyllus, freedman of Antipater, 102

Bedriacum, 266

Beirut, 16, 78, 93, 120, 164, 272, 364, 368

Beleus, river, 132

Belzedek, 182

Bemeselis, 35

Bercinianus, son of Bernice, 135

Berendts, Dr, 396

Berenice, wife of Alexander, 394

Bernice, mother of Agrippa, 96

Bernice, daughter of Agrippa, 8, 135; and Florus, 144–5, 147; writes to Cestius, 147; and Agrippa, 148, 154, 157, 173

Bersabe, 171, 183

Besimoth, 258

Betaris, 259

Betharamatha, 119

Bethezub, 341

Beth-horon, 136, 165–6, 168–9

Bethleptepha, 259

Bethsaron, 28

Bethso, 287

Bethzachariah, 28

Bezetha, 146, 166, 288, 295

Bithynia, 53, 150, 331

Black Sea, 150

Borcius, 166

Bosporus, 150

Britain and Britons, 150–51, 180, 352, 368

Brittanicus, son of Agrippa, 138

Brixellum, 266

Brundisium, 58

Brutus, 50–51

Byblus, 78

Cadiz, 150

Caecin(n)a Alienus, 266, 273–4

Caesar, Augustus, 23, 37, 51, 125, 130, 323; and Herod, 58–9, 61, 73–7, 82–5, 87, 92, 94, 107–8, 111, 135; and Antony, 73–4; and Alexander, 82–3, 90; and Eurycles, 93; and Antipater, 96, 99, 103, 105–6, 110; and Syllaeus, 99; and Acme, 110; and Archelaus, 113, 115–17; adjudicates on Herod's succession, 115–17, 121–3; and Alexander the false, 124

Caesar, Julius, 16, 48, 58n., 129n., 163; releases Aristobulus, 45; courted by Antipater, 45–6; and Hyrcanus, 46; and Antigonus, 47; murdered, 50

Caesar, Sextus, 48–50

Caesarea, 33, 42, 77, 94–5, 104, 114–15, 130, 135–7, 140, 142–3, 145, 147, 154, 159–60, 164–5, 185, 213, 215, 220, 230, 233, 256, 259, 262–3, 266, 269, 272, 275–6, 279, 362–4, 388, 392

Caesarea Philippi, 130, 215, 220n., 363

Caesennius Gallus, 165, 182

Caesennius Paetus, 366, 378–9

Caligula, 9

Callinicus, 378

Callirrhoe, 110

Calvarius, Sextus, a tribune, 206

Cana, 35, 66

Canaan, 260, 360

Canatha, 70

Cantabria, 151

Capernaum, 221

Capharabin, 267

Caphartoba, 259

Caphethra, 267
Capito, 143
Cappadocia, 82, 89, 93, 96, 124, 150, 273, 362
Cappareccho, 171
Carthage and Carthaginians, 152, 352
Casian Zeus, 275
Cassius, 44–5, 50–53, 58
Castor, a Jew, 302–3
Catiline, 13
Catullus, 394–5
Cavalry Town, 183
Caves of the Kings, 287
Ceagiras, 317
Celadus, 123–4
Celenderis, 104
Celer, a tribune, 138
Celts, 21
Cendebaeus, 29
Cerealis, 14n., 368
Cerealius, 205, 267, 335, 344, 374
Cestius, 10, 23, 170, 180, 190, 213, 279, 297, 300, 352, 359, 362; and Florus, 142, 147; and Agrippa, 162; attacks Zebulon, 164; attacks Joppa and Narbatene, 164–5; attacks Antipatris and Lydda, 165; appeals to Jews, 166; and Ananus, 167; makes for Beth-Loron, 168–9; flees from Jews, 169
Chaallis, 182
Chalcidice, 378
Chalcis, 45, 135, 138
Chares, 224, 228
Cilicia and Cilicians, 34, 42, 78, 83, 103, 150, 379
Civilis, 367
Classicus, 367
Claudius, 138, 288; succeeds Gaius, 133–4; and Agrippa, 134–5; and Vespasian, 180
Cleopatra, mother of Ptolemy, 33, 37
Cleopatra of Jerusalem, wife of Herod, 97
Cleopatra, 383; and Antony, 53, 69–70, 73–4; and Herod, 58, 69, 73; intrigues, 69–70; and Lysanias, 81; and Malichus, 81

Clitus, 178
Coele-Syria, 35, 41, 49, 70
Colchians, 150
Collega, Gnaeus, 365–6
Commagene, 164n., 316, 378
Coponius, 125
Coptus, 271
Corban aqueduct, 131
Corcyra, 363
Coreae, 39, 259
Corinth, 223n.
Corinthian Gate, 292
Corinthus, 99
Cornelius, brother of Longus, 339
Cornelius Faustus, son of Sulla, 41
Cos, 78
Costobar, 87, 156, 170
Crassus, 44
Cremona, 273
Crete, 123
Cumanus, procurator, 136–8
Cuspius Fadus, procurator, 135, 399
Cuthaea, 30
Cydoessa, 231
Cypris, wife of Antipater, 45
Cypros, wife of Agrippa, 135
Cypros fort, 75, 77, 162
Cyprus, 123
Cyrene and Cyrenians, 152, 333, 394
Cyrus, King, 308, 347

Dabarittha, 173
Dacians, 151
Dagon, 30, 308
Dalmatia, 150–51
Damascus and Damascenes, 35, 37–8, 49, 52, 69, 74, 78, 170, 388
Dan, 223n.
Danube, river, 150–51, 188, 368
Daphne, 53, 65, 223
Dardanelles, 149n., 180
Darius, cavalry commander, 156
Darius Hystaspes, 85
David, King, 30, 287, 360
Dead Sea, 12, 17, 110, 221, 258, 260–62, 374, 382
Decapolis, 184n., 215
Dellius, 60

Delta, 163
Demetrius, 34–6
Demosthenes, 13
Diogenes, 36
Diophantus, Herod's secretary, 92
Diospolis, 39, 70
Dolesus, 256
Domitian, 14n., 372; joins Sabinus at Rome, 274; and Mucianus, 274; crushes German revolt, 368; hater of Christianity, 396–7
Domitias Sabinus, a tribune, 206, 304
Don, river, 379
Dora, 29, 42, 76
Doreon, 31
Doris, 53, 80, 82, 85, 97, 100; divorced by Herod, 80; returns to Herod, 82; hatred of Alexander, 85; banished again by Herod, 101
Dovecot, 319
Drusilla, daughter of Agrippa, 135
Drusium, 76

Ecdippon, 55
Egypt and Egyptians, 24, 42, 47, 74, 76, 213, 237, 255, 276, 284, 352, 359, 362, 389; and Ptolemy, 33; and Gabinius, 44; and Mithridates, 45–6; and Antony, 65, 81; and Antipater, 101–2; false prophet of, 139; and Alexander, 144; mentioned in Agrippa's speech, 150, 152; conquered by Romans with Jewish help, 162–3; and descendants of Abraham, 265; and Mucianus, 270–71; and Tiberius Alexander, 271, 279; cited in speech by Josephus, 307–8; Shishak king of, 360; and Titus, 369–70; Rufus, 376; Cleopatra, queen of, 383; incidents at Orias, 392–4
Egyptian Sea, 271
Eisler, Dr, 12, 394n., 396
Eleazar, son of Ananias, 155–6, 158–9
Eleazar, son of Dinaeus, 137–8
Eleazar, brother of Judas, 28
Eleazar, father of Mary, 341
Eleazar, son of Neus, 170

Eleazar, son of Samias, 198
Eleazar, son of Simon, 170, 241, 276–7, 284
Eleazar, nephew of Simon, 343
Eleazar of Masada, 159, 391; commander of Sicarii, 380–81; trickery of, 383; speech by, 385–90
Eleazar of Machaerus, 376–7
Eleazar, member of Simon's staff, 264–5
Elephantine, 271
Eleusa, 83
Eleutherus, river, 69
Elijah, prophet, 260
Elis, 78
Elisha, prophet, 260–61
Elpis, wife of Herod, 97
Elthemus, 72
Emesa, 378
Emmaus, 50, 64, 119–20, 171, 184, 259, 279, 281, 321, 343, 378
Eniachin, 235
Engedi, 184, 255
Ephraim, 266
Essenes, 7, 11, 124–9, 171
Ethiopia, 152, 271
Euphrates, river, 42, 44–5, 64, 69, 80, 150, 152, 188, 279, 296, 353, 362, 369. 378–9.
Euripides, 13
Europe, 149
Eurycles, 90–93
Evarestus of Cos, 93
Ezra, 121n.

Fabatus, Caesar's treasurer, 99
Fabius, centurion, 41–52
Felix, procurator, 138–40
Festus, procurator, 141
Florus, Gessius, 160, 170; and Agrippa II, 141–54; and bandits, 141; character of, 141–2; and Cestus, 142, 147; bribed by Jews, 142–3; outrages Jews in Jerusalem, 143–6; avarice of, 143; and Bernice, 145; attacks Jewish insurgents, 146; and Agrippa, 147, 154; denunciation of urged by Jews, 148; receives

delegation of Simon, 156; bribes Tyrannius Priscus, 167.
Forest of Jardes, 377
Fountain Valley, 319
Fuller's Tomb, 287
Furius, centurion, 41

Gaba, 160, 183
Gabara, 177n., 190
Gabath Saul, 280
Gabinius, 39; succeeds Scaurus in Syria, 42; marches against Alexander, 42–3; reinstates Hyrcanus, 43; and Aristobulus, 43–4, 374; and Antony, 53
Gadara, 33, 41, 43, 74, 122, 160, 162, 177n., 183, 256–7
Gadarenes, 223, 256
Gaius, son of Agrippa, 115, 120
Gaius Caesar, 131–4
Galba, 263, 266
Galilee and Galileans, 10–11, 17, 24, 32, 43, 48–50, 52, 55, 60, 62–3, 65, 74, 117, 119–20, 122, 130, 132, 136–8, 164–5, 170–73, 176, 178, 182–5, 189–90, 196, 198–9, 203–4, 223, 230–33, 243, 267, 310, 317, 352
Gallus, centurion, 226
Gallicanus, 207
Gallus, Rubrius, 368
Gamala, 15n., 30, 36, 43, 171, 177, 184, 223–5, 227–9
Garis, 317
Garstang, Sir John, 8n.
Gaul and Gauls, 21, 74, 81, 112, 124, 150–51, 259, 263, 368
Gaulan, 223
Gaulane, 34, 36
Gaulonitis, 130, 138, 160, 171, 183, 223
Gaza, 34, 42, 74, 122, 160, 275
Gazara, 29
Gema, 136
Geneva, 15
Gennesareth, Lake, 17, 171, 217, 220–21
Genrath, 287
Gerasa, 36, 160, 162, 184, 262

Gerizim, 30
Germanicus, 131
Germany and Germans, 150–51, 180, 263, 266, 269–70, 274, 352, 367–8
Gibeon, 165, 168
Gilead, 34
Ginabrin, 260
Ginaea, 184
Gischala, 171–2, 176–7, 223, 230, 233, 239
Gittha, 65
Glaphyra, wife of Alexander, 85–6, 96, 124
Gophna, 28, 171, 184, 266, 280, 334
Gophra, 50
Gorion, son of Nicomedes, 159
Gorion, son of Joseph, 235
Grapte, kinswoman of Izas, 268
Gratus, commander of Royal Infantry, 118–20
Great Plain, 173, 183–4, 227, 260
Greece, 78, 90, 93, 129, 149, 263, 340, 363
Gurion, 252
Gyphthaeus, follower of John, 332, 336

Hadrian, 9
Haggai, 347
Hannibal, 152
Hasmonaeons, 23, 287
Hebron, 265, 267
Helena's Monuments and Palace, 280, 285, 287, 354
Helena, mother of Morobazus, 296
Heliopolis, 27; Nome of, 393
Helix, 52
Heniochi, 150
Hera, 77
Heracleopolis, 275
Herod, King, 7–8, 12, 45, 113–24, 131, 135, 138, 157, 183, 309, 319, 360, 398; building operations of, 13, 31, 42, 56, 75–8, 140, 289, 374–5, 382–3; death of, 13, 23, 111–12; predecessors of, 27–46; renames Anthedon, 34; rise to power of, 47–59; character of, 48; and

Hezekiah, 48, 119; and Sextus Caesar, 48–9; and Hyrcanus, 48–9, 52–3; and Cassius, 50–52; and Malichus, 50–52, 57, 60; and Murcus, 51; and Helix, 52; and Marion of Tyre, 52; and Antigonus, 52–4, 60–69; and Pacorus, 54–5; flight to Masada, 56; and Cleopatra, 58, 70; and Antony, 58–9, 64–5, 67, 69–70, 73, 75; made king, 58–9, 67; master of Palestine, 60–79; and Silo, 60–61, 63; attacks Joppa, 60–61; frees Masada, 61; occupies Idumaea, 62; occupies Sepphoris, 62; invited to join in Parthian War, 63; and Machaeras, 64; and Pappus, 67; and Sossius, 67–9; captures Hyrcania, 70; and Athenio, 70; speech to his army, 71–2; war with Arabs, 70–73; visits Caesar, 73–4; and Alexas, 74; kingdom extended by Caesar, 74; physical abilities of, 78–9; murder of Mariamme and her children, 80–95; divorces first wife, 80; banishes Antipater, 80; executes Hyrcanus, 80; murders Jonathan, 80–81; jealousy of Mariamme, 80–81; recalls Antipater, 82; accuses Alexander of poison attempt, 82–3; and Archelaus, 83, 89–90; proclaims his sons Kings, 83–4; and Antipater, Aristobulus and Alexander, 85–95; and Salome, 86–8, 93, 95, 98, 110; and Pheroras, 86–90, 95, 98–102, 107; and Eurycles, 90–92; and Tiro, 94–5; murder of Antipater and death, 96–112; marriage plans of, 96–7; banishes Doris, 101; and Samaritan Antipater, 101; and Antiphilus, 101–2; and Bathyllus, 102; and Varus, 104–8; popular rising against, 109; appoints Archelaus his heir, 111; funeral of, 112

Herod, son of Cleopatra, 97
Herod, son of Herod, 97, 99, 101, 398
Herod, king of Chalcis, 96, 135

Herod's Monuments, 284
Herodias, daughter of Aristobulus, 96, 131–2, 398
Herodium, 56, 77, 112, 184, 264, 267, 374
Herodotus, 13
Hezekiah, brother of Ananias, 157–8
Hezekiah, son of Chobari, 276
Hezekiah, bandit, 48, 119
High Priest's Monument, 316
Hippicus, 158, 286–9, 299, 301, 361
Hippos, 122, 160, 162, 183, 223
Hippus, 42, 74
House of Peas, 319
Huleh, Lake, 221n.
Hyrcania, 70, 111, 379
Hyrcanium, 42–3
Hyrcanus, son of Bernice, 135
Hyrcanus, John, 29–31
Hyrcanus, High Priest, 56, 91, 309; appointed High Priest, 36; and Aristobulus, 37–41; heir to the throne, 37; and Antipater, 38, 42, 44, 51; and Aretas, 38; and Scaurus, 38, 42; and Pompey, 39–41; and Alexander, 42; and Gabinius, 43–4; High-Priesthood confirmed by Caesar, 46–7; and Antigonus, 47–8, 56–7; and Herod, 49, 52–3; and Malichus, 51–2; and Phasael, 52–3, 55, 57; and Helix, 52; and Lysanias, 54; and Barzaphrnes, 55, 80; tortured by Antigonus, 57; cowardice of, 57; captured by Parthians, 57

Iapyx Promontory, 363
Idumaea and Idumaeans, 31, 38, 56, 62, 65, 117–18, 122, 170–71, 179, 182, 184, 241–2, 245–9, 251, 259, 264–5, 267–8, 296, 299, 305, 332, 336, 356, 381
Illyrians, 150–51
India, 152
Indian Ocean, 152
Innano, 122
Ionia, 78, 363
Iranaeus, orator, 115

Iron Mountain, 260
Isaiah, prophet, 394
Ishmael, 333
Ixion, 129
Izas, king of Adiabene, 268
Izates, King, 287

Jacob, son of Sosas, 296, 332, 336, 356
Jacob, traitor, 265
Jairus, father of Eleazar (of Masada), 159
Jairus, father of Simon and Judas, 332, 336, 377
Jamblichus, 45
James, son of Sosas, 242
Jamnia, 29, 42–3, 123, 130, 147, 184, 233, 259, 275
Jamnith, 171
Japha, 171, 203
Jardan, 184
Jeconiah, king, 333
Jeremiah, prophet, 308
Jericho, 7, 30, 37, 39, 43, 61–2, 64–6, 69, 75, 77, 80, 110–11, 113, 117, 119, 162, 171, 184, 257, 259–62, 279, 281
Jerusalem (or 'the City'), 8–9, 14, 15n., 17, 21–4, 27–31, 34–5, 38–9, 42–4, 48–53, 55–7, 60–61, 66–7, 69, 75n., 77, 80, 83, 100, 108, 115, 117, 120–22, 130–32, 135–9, 141–5, 147, 151, 157, 165–6, 170, 176–8, 180, 184, 191, 214–15, 228, 230–34, 242, 245, 251, 253, 255–6, 259, 261–4, 266–9, 275–325, 341, 343–73, 377–8, 393, 397
Jeshua, son of Ananias, 349–50
Jeshua, son of Gamalus, a chief priest; and Ananus 235–6; incites people against Zealots, 236; speech by, 242–5; unable to restrain Idumaeans, 246; murdered, 248–9
Jeshua of Tiberius (son of Shaphat), 170, 174, 216–17, 219–20
Jeshua, son of Thebuthi, 356
Jeshua, priest, 333
Jesus Christ, 396–401
Joesdrus, son of Nomicus, 176

John, son of Ananias, 171
John, the Baptist, 396–8
John, son of Dorcas, 234
John, the Essene, 171, 181
John, of Gischala, 239, 263, 279, 301, 305, 321, 336, 381; and Josephus, 11, 13, 172–7; fortifies Gischala, 171, 173; character of, 172; a bandit, 172–3; plunders Galilee, 173; acquires oil monopoly, 173; and Titus, 230–33; and Ananus, 240; seeks one-man rule, 254; looting by, 267; mutiny against, 268; and Eleazar, 276–8; attacked by Simon, 277–8; seizes the Temple, 284, 296; and Simon, 296–8, 312, 314–15, 330, 340, 351, 356, 370; at Antonia, 316, 326–7; sacrilege by, 323–4; speech by Josephus, 332–3; reproached by Titus, 334–5; sentenced to life imprisonment, 360
John, Idumaean leader, 299
John, brother of Judas, 29
John, son of Sosas, 242
John, the tax-gatherer, 142–3
John, High Priest, 297, 301, 305, 338
Jonathan, brother of John, 29
Jonathan, brother of Mariamme, 80–81
Jonathan, father of Simon and Jude, 177
Jonathan, soldier, 338
Jonathan, priest, 137, 139, 382
Jonathan of Egypt, 394–5
Joppa, 29, 35, 42, 60–61, 74, 76, 122, 164, 171, 184, 213–14, 275
Jordan, river and country, 17, 33, 50, 62, 72, 75, 110, 117, 119, 130, 171, 183–4, 220–21, 223, 257–8, 260–61, 341, 397–8
Joseph of Gamala, 224, 228
Joseph, son of Dalaeus, 348
Joseph, son of Gorion, 170
Joseph, nephew of Herod, 97, 120
Joseph, brother of Herod, 45, 56, 60, 62, 64–5, 67
Joseph, husband of Salome, 81
Joseph, son of Simon, 171
Joseph, priest, 333

Josephus, 7–17, 21–5, 29n., 31n., 56n., 72n., 91n., 124n., 125n., 139n., 142n., 169n., 217, 224, 227, 288n., 290n., 295n., 297, 321, 368n., 395–6; birth and early years, 9–10; visits Rome, 10; governor of Galilee, 10–11, 170–79; prisoner of Vespasian, 10, 196–212; becomes Roman citizen, 10; literary works, 10–17; character of, 11–12; truthfulness of, 13–15, 22–3; fortifies Galilee, 171; and John of Gischala, 172–8; and Clitus, 178; and Placidus, 185; flees from Vespasian, 190; at Tiberias, 190–91; and Vespasian, 190–203, 207–8, 212, 272; at Jotapata, 191–203, 206–7; speeches by, 196–7, 209–10, 307–11, 333–4; and Nicanor, 207–8, 211; tries to avert mass suicide, 210; attacked for his life, 210–11; pressure for his execution, 213; rumoured killed, 214–15; and Titus, 285, 332, 334; and Castor, 303; and siege of Jerusalem, 297, 303, 306–12, 321–2, 332–5, 355
Joshua, son of Nun, 260
Jotapata, 11, 15n., 171, 189, 191–3, 200, 203–4, 207, 212, 214–15, 223–4, 272, 322, 391n., 396
Jotape, daughter of Aristobulus, 135
Juba, king of Libya, 124
Jucundus, 92, 143
Judaea, 17, 24, 27–30, 35–6, 38–9, 42, 44, 47, 51–4, 60, 63–4, 69–71, 82, 88, 90, 94, 103, 110, 114, 117, 119, 122, 124, 130, 132–3, 138, 140, 181, 184, 191, 213, 255, 261, 266, 275, 279, 325, 344, 350, 374, 380, 383, 397
Judas, son of Chelcias, 276
Judas, the Essene, 32
Judas of Galilee, 125, 157, 380
Judas, son of Hezekiah, 119
Judas, son of Jairus, 332, 377
Judas, son of Jonathan, 159
Judas, son of Judas, 321–2
Judas, son of Matthias, 28–9

Judas, son of Merto, 332, 336
Judas, son of Sepphoraeus, 109
Jude, son of Jonathan, 177
Julian, of Bithynia, 331–2
Julianus, Marcus Antonius, 344
Julia (Livia), 98, 108, 115n., 130
Julias, 130, 138, 184, 221, 258
Jupiter Capitolinus, Temple, 372

Kedasa, 160
Kidron Valley, 281, 287, 296, 300, 319, 340
King's Towers, 158

Laodicea, 51, 78
Lebanon, 45, 65, 279
Lepidus, Larcius, 344
Levi, guard of Josephus, 178
Levias, 234
Liberalius, a centurion, 346
Liberius Maximus, procurator, 377–8
Libya, 124, 150, 163, 271, 394
Lollius, 38
Longinus, tribune, 168
Longinus, cavalryman, 301–2
Longus, 339–40
Look-out Hill, 166, 168, 281, 284
Lusitania, 151
Lucius, 340
Lucullus, 37
Lupus, ruler of Alexandria, 393–4
Lycia, 78, 150
Lydda, 62, 137–8, 165, 171, 184, 259
Lyons, 398n.
Lysanias, King, 54, 74, 81, 135, 138

Mabartha, 259
Macedon and Macedonians, 150, 152, 162, 315–16
Machaeras, Roman commander, 64–6
Machaerus, 14, 17, 42–3, 162, 183, 258, 267, 374, 377
Magadatus, father of Archelaus, 343
Magnus see Pompey
Malachias, follower of Simon, 332
Malchus, king, 185
Malichus, 42, 50–52, 57–58, 60, 69, 81
Malthace, wife of Herod, 97, 117

Manasseh, 171
Mannaeus, son of Lazarus, 324
Mariamme, wife of Herod, 53, 56, 67, 80–82, 86, 91, 95, 97–102, 289, 317
Mariamme, daughter of Aristobulus, 96
Mariamme, wife of Archelaus, 124
Mariamme, daughter of Agrippa, 135
Mariamme, wife of Herod, King of Chalcis, 135
Mariamme Tower, 289, 361
Marion of Tyre, 52
Marisa, 31, 42–3, 56
Marmaridae, 152
Mary, daughter of Eleazar, 341–2
Masada, 7, 14, 15n., 17, 52, 56, 60–62, 155, 157, 159, 179, 255, 263–5, 380–84, 392
Matthias, son of Asamonaeus, 27–8
Matthias, son of Margalus, 109
Matthias, High Priest, 268, 321, 333
Matthias, father of Josephus, 21, 171, 321
Matthias, 333
Medabe, 30
Medes, 22
Media, 379
Megassarus, servant of Mariamme, 317
Meirus, son of Belgas, 348
Meleager, 13
Melians, 123–4
Melitine, 362
Melos, 123
Memphis, 46, 265, 393
Menahem, son of Judas, 157–9
Mendes, 275
Mennaeus, 35, 45, 54
Mero, 171
Meroth, 183
Mesopotamia, 265
Messala, 53, 58
Messalina, wife of Agrippa, 138
Metellus, 38
Metilius, 159
Middoth, 290
Mithridates, 39, 44–6
Moab, 34, 184, 260

Modein, 27
Moesia and Moesians, 272–3, 368, 370
Monobazus, king of Adiabene, 166, 296
Moors, 152
Mount Athos, 149n.
Mount Carmel, 31, 54, 132, 183
Mount Gerizim, 204
Mount Lebanon, 184
Mount of Olives, 139, 281, 286, 319, 337, 399
Mount Scopus, 166n.
Mount Tabor, 44, 171, 223, 227
Mucianus, 225, 263, 270, 272–4, 279
Murcus, 50–51
Mysian Pergamum, 78

Nabataeans, 44
Nabataeus of Adiabene, 317
Nablus, 259n.
Nain, 264
Narbata, 143
Narbatene, 164
Nasamonians, 152
Neapolis, 259
Neapolitanus, tribune, 147
Necho, king, 307
Neiras, 199
Nero, 140, 148, 163, 169, 207, 352, 359; and the burning of Rome, 9–10; and Vespasian, 23, 180, 212, 223, 263; death of, 24, 262; savagery and madness of, 138; gives control of Caesarea to the Greeks, 142; entrusts Egypt to Alexander, 144; receives Saul, 170; and Josephus, 212, 272; and Vindex, 259; and Nymphiduis and Tigellinus, 262–3
Neus, High Priest, 170
Nicanor, tribune, 207–8, 211, 297
Nicolas (Nicolaus) of Damascus, Herod's gentleman, 12, 99, 106–7, 114–17, 122
Nicopolis (in Greece), 78
Nicopolis (in Egypt), 275
Niger the Peraean, 166, 171, 181–2, 252

Nile, river, 221, 271, 275, 308
Noarus, 162
Numidians, 152
Numidius, Quadratus, legate of Syria, 137
Nymphidius, 262

Obadas, King, 34, 87
Octavia, daughter of Claudius, 138
Octavian, 58n.
Octavian Walks, 370
Olurus, 265
Olympias, daughter of Herod, 97
Olympus, 93
Onias, priest (son of Simon), 27, 46, 393
Onias (settlement in Egypt), 393
Onias, Temple of, 17, 393–4
Ophales, 159
Ophel, 287, 296, 354
Ophellius, 55
Ormiza, 70
Orsanes, 44
Ostrakine, 275
Otho, 263, 266, 273

Pacorus, cup-bearer, 54–6
Pacorus, 54–5, 64
Pacorus, king, 379–80
Palatine, 121
Palestine, 7, 13, 15, 17, 27, 30, 44, 47, 80, 271, 275–6
Pallas, brother of Felix, 138
Pallas, wife of Herod, 97
Pamphylia, 58, 150
Paneas, river, 130
Paneum, 75, 220
Pannonia, 272, 370
Pannychis, 90
Pappus, associate of Antigonus, 66–7
Papyron, 38
Parthia and Parthians, 29–30, 44–5, 54–60, 63–4, 69, 80, 87, 117, 152, 369, 378–9
Paulinus, tribune, 207
Paulinus, governor of Alexandria, 394
Pedanius, legate of Saturninus, 94
Pedanius, a trooper, 337

Peitholaus, chief of staff in Jerusalem, 42–5
Pella, 9, 36, 39, 42, 160, 184
Pelusium, 45–6, 58, 69, 74, 271, 275
Pentapolis, 394
Peraea and Peraeans, 17, 100, 117, 119, 122, 130, 138, 166, 171, 181, 183, 184n., 252, 256, 258–9, 341, 347
Persia, 237
Petina, wife of Claudius, 138
Petra, 38, 56, 99, 101, 260
Petronius, 132–3
Phoebus, 166
Phaedra, wife of Herod, 97
Phallion, brother of Antipater, 38
Phanias, son of Samuel, 235
Pharan, 264
Pharisees, 11, 36–7, 98, 125, 129–30, 155
Pharos, 271, 289
Phasael, son of Antipater, 45; appointed governor of Jerusalem, 48; and Malichus, 50–51; and Helix, 52; and Antony, 53; and Antigonus, 54–5, 57; and Barzapharnes, 55; death of, 57–8; tower named after, 77, 117, 289, 361
Phasael, son of Herod, 97
Phasaelis, 77–8, 123, 130
Pheroras, son of Antipater, 45, 94, 123; fortifies Alexandreum, 63; and Antigonus, 65; and Pappus, 67; and Antipater, 85, 96–9, 101–2, 107; and Alexander and Aristobulus, 85–6, 88; love of slave-girl, 87; accused of conspiracy, 87–8; and Salome, 88, 95; incurs Herod's anger, 89; and Archelaus, 89–90; pressured by Herod to divorce wife, 99; death of, 100, 103; accusations against, 100–101
Philadelphia, 30, 38, 72, 160, 184
Philip of Macedon, 150
Philip of Ruma, 199
Philip, son of Jacimus, 156, 170, 229
Philip, son of Herod, 97, 130–31, 138, 220, 398; and Antipater, 102, 108;

made heir to Trachonites, 111; governor of the palace, 114; and Archelaus, 121; made tetrarch, 122
Philippi, 53
Philippion, son of Ptolemy, 45
Philistia, 308
Phineas, son of Clusoth, 242
Phineas, treasurer, 356
Phoenicia, 67, 76, 152, 183, 213, 364
Phrygius Titus, 344
Phrygia, 273
Pilate, Pontius, 8, 130–31, 399
Pillars of Hercules, 151–2
Piraeus, 76
Pisidians, 34
Piso, 40
Placidus, tribune, sent to Sepphoris by Vespasian, 184; attacks Jotapata, 189, 191, 206; attacks Mount Tabor, 227–8; attacks Bethennabris, 256–8; captures Abila, Julias and Besimoth, 258
Plataea, 149
Platana, 94
Plinthine, 271
Pompey (Pompeius Magnus), 23, 38, 44, 47, 67, 149, 153, 309–10, 319, 352, 360; and Aristobulus, 39–42; and Hyrcanus, 41; over-runs Jerusalem, 39–41; rebuilds Gadara, 41; flees with the Senate, 45; death of, 45; and Bassus, 50
Pomponius, Secundus, 133
Poplas, 114
Priscus, centurion, 338
Priscus, Roman commander, 167–8
Psephinus, 280, 286, 288
Ptolemais, 17, 29, 37, 54, 60, 74, 78, 120, 132–3, 160–61, 164, 182–5, 188–9, 213
Ptolemy, friend of Herod, 58, 63, 85, 111, 114, 119–20
Ptolemy, son of Mennaeus, 35–7, 44–5, 52–4
Ptolemy VI, 27, 393
Ptolemy, son-in-law of Simon, 29–30
Ptolemy Lathyrus, 33
Ptolemy, brother of Nicolaus, 115

Ptolemy, minister of Agrippa, 173
Pudens, cavalry officer, 338
Puteoli, 123
Pyrenees, 151

Quince Pool, 316
Quintilius Varus, 23
Quintus Didius, 73
Quirinius, 157, 380
Qumran, 7

Radice, Betty, 17
Raphanaea(e), 362, 369
Raphia, 34, 43, 275
Red Sea, 271
Rhine, river, 151, 188
Rhinocorura, 58, 275
Rhodes, 58, 73, 78, 363
Rieu, Dr E. V., 17
Rome, 10, 12–13, 15, 21, 24, 27–9, 42–5, 47, 50, 58, 67, 77–8, 80, 82–3, 86, 88, 90, 93, 96, 99–105, 110, 115, 121, 123, 125, 131–2, 134, 138, 147, 149–56, 158–9, 170–71, 177–8, 180, 188, 223, 237, 243, 249–50, 252, 256, 263, 266, 269, 271, 273–5, 306, 316, 319, 352, 354, 361, 364, 366–8, 370, 373, 378–80, 388–90, 395, 400
Roth, Dr Cecil, 11
Roxane, daughter of Herod, 97
Rufus of Sebaste, 118, 120
Rufus, Terentius, 363
Rufus the Egyptian, 376
Ruma, 199

Saba, 198
Sabbatical River, 369
Sabinus the Syrian, 329–30
Sabinus, Flavius, 274
Sabinus, procurator, 114–20
Sadducees, 11, 125, 130
Salamis, 149
Sallust, 13
Salome, daughter of Antipater, 45, 82, 94–5, 130, 398n.; slander of husband Joseph, 81; and Antipater, 85–6, 98–9, 108; and Alexander and Aristobulus, 85–6, 88, 93; slandered

by Pheroras, 87; and Syllaeus, 87, 93, 98; and Julia, 98; and Alexas, 98, 110–11; disobeys Herod, 111; and Archelaus, 114, 123; and Antipas, 115; mistress of Jamnia, 122–3

Salome, daughter of Herod, 97

Samaria and Samaritans, 9, 17, 31, 42–3, 49, 51, 61–3, 66–7, 74–5, 120, 122, 124, 136–8, 183–4, 204–5, 259, 280

Samias, father of Eleazar, 198

Samos, 78

Samosata, 64–5, 378

Sanhedrin, 146–7, 321

Sapphas, father of Jeshua, 170, 174

Sapphinius, friend of Herod, 58

Sappho, 120

Sarah, Princess, 307

Saramalla, the Syrian, 55

Sarmatians, 368

Saturninus, Sextus, Consul, 133

Saturninus, governor of Syria, 94, 96, 99

Saul, 156, 161, 170

Scaurus, 38–9, 42

Scipio, Africanus, 152

Scipio, Metellus, 45, 47

Scythians, 368, 379

Scythopolis, 17, 31, 39, 42–3, 160–61, 183, 213, 215, 227, 230, 260, 388

Sebaste, 16, 31, 37, 75, 95, 118–20, 122, 142–3, 160

Sebastos, 37

Sebonitis, 160

Selame, 171

Seleucus, 35

Seleucia, 36, 171, 223

Semechonitis, Lake, 221, 223

Sennabris, 215

Sennacherib, king of Assyria, 308, 310

Seph, 171

Sepphoraeus, 109

Sepphoris, 43, 62, 119–20, 165, 171, 177–8, 182–5, 190

Serpents' Pool, 284

Servilius, 43

Shishak, king of Egypt, 360

Sicarii, 157, 255, 380–81, 383–4, 392, 394

Sichem, 34

Sidon, 54, 69, 78, 94, 123, 162, 164

Sigoph, 171

Silas, the Babylonian, 166, 175, 181

Silbonitis, 184

Silo, 60–63

Silo, Antonius, 218

Siloam, 147, 287, 296, 310, 319, 354, 357

Silva, Flavius, 380, 382, 384

Simon, the Essene, 124, 397

Simon, a slave, 119

Simon, son of Ananias, 156

Simon, son of Arinus, 296

Simon, son of Boethus, 321

Simon, son of Cathla, 242, 245, 296, 336

Simon, son of Ezron, 276

Simon, son of Jairus, 332, 336

Simon, son of Jonathan, 177

Simon, brother of Jonathan, 29–30

Simon, son of Josiah, 336

Simon, son of Saul, 161

Simon, son of Gioras, 251, 289, 381; attacks Romans at Beth-horon, 166; and Ananus, 179, 263; at Masada, 179, 263; qualities of, 263, gains confidence of Jews, 264; seeks supreme power, 264; overruns Acrabatene, 264; and Idumaeans, 264–5, 267–8; and Jacob, 265; captures Hebron, 265; wife captured, 266–7; attacks Jerusalem, 266–7; and Zealots, 264, 266–9, 296; and Matthias, 268; master of Jerusalem, 268, 277; and John, 267–9, 277–8, 284, 296–8, 312, 314–15, 330, 340, 351, 356, 360, 370; Idumaean allies of, 296; during siege of Jerusalem, 296–305, 312–16, 321–2, 330, 332–3, 336, 340, 343, 351, 354, 356, 360, 363–4; and Castor, 302; and Matthias, 321, 333; and Judas, 321; captured, 363–4, 370; death of, 372

Sisenna, 43
Sisyphus, 129
Snake Path, 382
Soaemus, King, 162, 164, 185, 378
Soaemus of Petra, 99
Sodom, 260, 262, 324
Sogane (Soganaea), 171, 223
Solomon, King, 287, 290, 347
Solomon's Pool, 287
Somorrhon, 260
Sophas, son of Raguel, 234
Sophocles, 13
Sosas, 242, 296, 332, 336, 356
Sossius, 23, 65, 67–9, 309–10, 360
Spain, 131, 151, 263
Sparta and Spartans, 78, 91, 149, 152, 379
Stephen, 136
Strato's Tower, 32–3, 42, 74, 76, 122
Suetonius, 129
Syllaeus, 87, 93, 98–100, 103, 107
Symeon, son of Gamaliel, 235
Syria and Syrians, 17, 28–9, 38–9, 42, 44–6, 48, 50–52, 54, 60, 65, 67, 69, 74, 94, 96, 99, 104, 114, 117, 122, 132, 137, 140, 142, 160, 162, 164, 173, 176, 180, 182–5, 197, 213, 225, 263, 272, 279, 308, 320, 322–3, 351, 362, 364–6, 369, 378, 388, 393
Syrtes, 152

Tanis, 275
Tantalus, 129
Tarentum, 103
Tarichaeae, 44, 138, 171, 173–5, 177–8, 215–17, 222–3
Tarsus, 379
Tekoa, 264
Temenus, 85
Temple Hill, 347
Tephthaeus of Galilee, 317
Thackeray, St John, 13, 15
Thamna, 171, 184, 259
Thebes, 392
Thella, 183
Theodorus, son of Zero, 33–4, 36
Thermopylae, 149
Theudion, uncle of Antipater, 101

Thmuis, 275
Thracians, 112, 150
Thresa, 56, 61
Thucydides, 13
Tiberias, 12, 132, 138, 171, 174–5, 177–8, 183, (lake) 184, 190–91, 215–17, 222–4, (lake) 260
Tiberius, Emperor, 130–31
Tigellinus, 262
Tigranes, son of Alexander, 96
Tigranes, king of Armenia, 37–8, 69
Tigris, river, 152, 166n.
Tiridates of Armenia, 380
Tiro, 94–5
Titus, 11–12, 14, 22, 24–5, 270, 368, 384, 396; and Vespasian, 180–95, 199, 204, 212, 215, 220, 225, 230, 263, 272, 275–6, 279–80, 366, 371–2; sent to Alexandria, 180, 185; at Ptolemais, 185, 188; at Jotapata, 199, 206; at Japha, 204; and Trajan, 204; and Josephus, 211–12, 272, 285, 306, 310, 332, 334; at Scythopolis, 215; speech by, 217–18; at Tarichaeae, 217–20; and Mucianus, 225; at Gamala, 228; at Gischala, 230–33; and Galba, 263; sent to destroy Jerusalem, 275; at the siege of Jerusalem, 279–86, 288, 296, 299–306, 310, 312, 314–24, 327–9, 331–2, 334–7, 343–6, 351–3, 356, 358–60, 362–3, 367; and Castor, 302; and Antiochus, 316; and Mannaeus, 324; speech by, 327–9; and Julian, 331; reproaches John, 334–5; and Pedanius, 337; and Ananus and Archelaus, 343–4; victory speech, 351–3; and Idumaeans, 356; at Antioch, 369; returns to Rome, 370–72; and Jonathan, 395
Tityus, 129
Tobias, 27
Tomb of Memnon, 132
Trachonitis, 74, 111, 119, 122, 135, 138, 156, 184, 220, 223
Traill, 15
Trajan, 203–4, 216, 218, 259

Tripolis, 78
Trypho, guardian of Antiochus, 29
Trypho, barber, 95
Tyrannus, 92
Tyre and Tyrians, 40, 51–4, 69, 78, 94, 132, 137, 160–61, 164, 173, 183, 231

Valens, 266
Valerian, decurion, 215–16
Valley of Cheese-Makers, 287
Valley of Thorns, 280
Varro, 74
Varus, legate of Syria, 138; mediates between Herod and Antipater, 104–8; and Sabinus, 114–15, 117–20; and revolt in Judaea, 117–21, and Gaius, 120
Ventidius, 60, 63–4
Vespasian, 10, 12, 23–4, 250, 252–3, 281, 292n., 310, 347, 363, 365–6, 378, 384, 401; and Titus, 180–95, 199, 204, 212, 215, 220, 225, 230, 263, 272, 275–6, 279–80, 366, 371–2; and Nero, 180, 262–3; in command at Syria, 180; and Agrippa, 182, 215–16; and Caesennius Gallus, 182; at Ptolemais, 182, 185, 188–9, 213; at Sepphoris, 182–5; and Josephus, 185, 189–95, 196–212, 272; at Jotapata, 189, 191–203, 205–7; at Gabara, 190; at Japha, 203–4; and Trajan 203–4, 259; conquering advance of, 213–29; at Joppa, 213–14; at Tarichaeae, 216–20, 222; at Tiberias, 222–4; at Gamala, 224–9; at Mount Tabor, 227–8; at Scythopolis, 230; and Jerusalem, 230, 240–58, 262–3, 269, 275, 360; at Jamnia and Azotus,

233; and Ananus, 240–41; at Gadara, 256; Emperor, 259–75, 350; and rising in Gaul, 259; at Bethleptepha, 259; at Dead Sea, 261; and Galba, 263; at Gophna and Acrabetta, 266; and Vitellius, 269–74; and Egypt and Alexandria, 270–75, 367; received at Rome, 367, 370–73; and Germany, 367–8; and Antiochus, 379; and Jonathan, 395
Vienne, 124
Vindex, 259
Virgil, 13
Vitellius, 263, 266, 269–74
Vologeses, king of Parthia, 369, 379
Volumnius, 94

Whiston, 15, 401
White Cliff, 384
Women's Towers, 280, 284

Xaloth, 183
Xerxes, 121, 149

Zachariah, son of Amphicalleus, 241
Zachariah, son of Baruch, 250
Zealots, 179, 236, 238–41, 246–51, 253–4, 262, 264, 266–8, 276–7, 284, 296, 305, 321, 332, 336, 381
Zebulon, 164, 183
Zedekiah, King, 308
Zeno, Cotulos, 30, 33
Zeno (Zenodorus), 74, 122
Zephyrium, 83
Zeugma, 369
Zeus, 77
Zion, 287
Zoar, 262

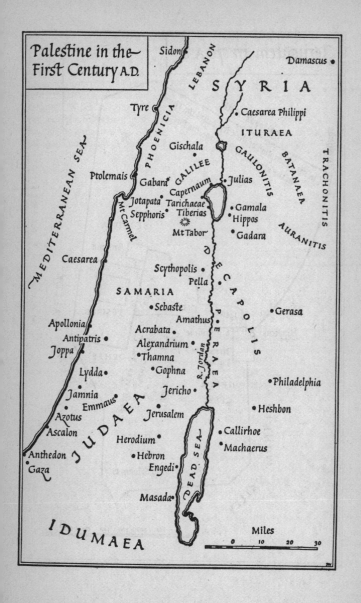

Palestine in the First Century A.D.

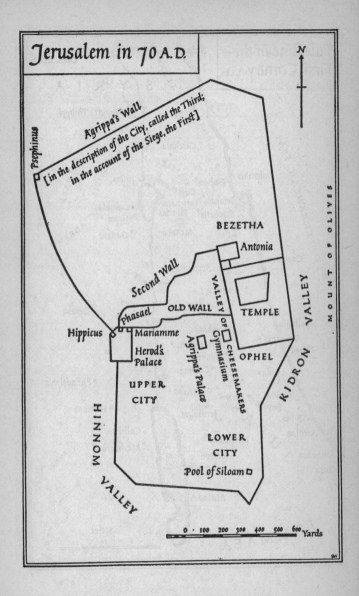

Jerusalem in 70 A.D.

N

Agrippa's Wall

[in the description of the City, called the Third; in the account of the Siege, the First]

Psephinus

BEZETHA

Antonia

Second Wall

VALLEY OF CHEESEMAKERS

TEMPLE

Phasael

OLD WALL

MOUNT OF OLIVES

Hippicus

Mariamme

Herod's Palace

Gymnasium

Agrippa's Palace

OPHEL

UPPER CITY

KIDRON VALLEY

HINNOM VALLEY

LOWER CITY

Pool of Siloam

0   100   200   300   400   500   600   Yards

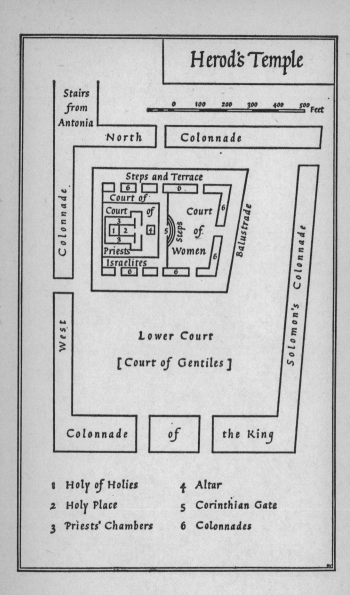

Herod's Temple

Stairs from Antonia

North Colonnade

Colonnade.

Steps and Terrace

Court of

Court of of Court of Women

Priests Israelites

Balustrade

Solomon's Colonnade

West

Lower Court

[Court of Gentiles]

Colonnade of the King

0 100 200 300 400 500 Feet

1 Holy of Holies
2 Holy Place
3 Priests' Chambers
4 Altar
5 Corinthian Gate
6 Colonnades

MORE ABOUT PENGUINS
AND PELICANS

Penguinews, which appears every month, contains details of all the new books issued by Penguins as they are published. From time to time it is supplemented by *Penguins in Print*, which is our complete list of almost 5,000 titles.

A specimen copy of *Penguinews* will be sent to you free on request. Please write to Dept EP, Penguin Books Ltd, Harmondsworth, Middlesex, for your copy.

In the U.S.A.: For a complete list of books available from Penguins in the United States write to Dept CS, Penguin Books, 625 Madison Avenue, New York, New York 10022.

In Canada: For a complete list of books available from Penguins in Canada write to Penguin Books Canada Ltd, 2801 John Street, Markham, Ontario L3R 1B4.

SENECA

LETTERS FROM A STOIC

Translated by Robin Campbell

The Stoic philosophy professed by Seneca the Younger (*c.* 4 B.C.–A.D. 65) in his writings and later supported by Marcus Aurelius provided Rome with a passable bridge to Christianity. The correspondence between Seneca, who was Nero's minister, and St Paul is now known to be a forgery, but the letters in this volume (selected from *Epistulae Morales ad Lucilium*) advertise the humane and upright ideals admired by Stoics and extol the good way of life as seen from their standpoint. Philosophical in tone and written in the 'pointed' style of the Latin Silver Age, these 'essays in disguise' were plainly aimed by Seneca at posterity.

SUETONIUS
THE TWELVE CAESARS

Translated by Robert Graves

The Twelve Caesars of Suetonius (born A.D. 69), covering the Roman rulers from Julius Caesar to Domitian, remains one of the richest and most fascinating of all Latin histories. Suetonius gathered much of his information from eye-witnesses, checking his facts carefully and quoting conflicting evidence without bias. But his history is also the most vivid and the raciest account we have of scandalous and amusing incidents in the domestic lives of the first Caesars.

TACITUS
THE AGRICOLA AND THE GERMANIA

Translated with an Introduction by
H. MATTINGLY
Translation revised by S. A. Handford

P. Cornelius Tacitus, soldier, senator, colonial administrator, and historian of the Roman Empire, was born about A.D. 55 and died about 120. His *Agricola* is a eulogistic description of the career of his father-in-law, probably the most famous of the governors of Roman Britain, and contains the first detailed account of the British Isles. The *Germania* is a study of the character, customs, and geography of the German tribes; in it Tacitus frequently contrasts the primitive virtues of the Germans with the degeneracy of contemporary Rome.

Also published
THE ANNALS OF IMPERIAL ROME

THE PENGUIN CLASSICS

Some recent volumes

CICERO
MURDER TRIALS
Michael Grant

DEMOSTHENES AND AESCHINES
A. N. W. Saunders

STENDHAL
LOVE
Gilbert and Suzanne Sale

ALARCÓN
THE THREE-CORNERED HAT
M. Alpert

MAUPASSANT
BEL-AMI
Douglas Parmée

CORNEILLE
THE CID, CINNA,
THE THEATRICAL ILLUSION
J. Cairncross

BIRDS THROUGH A CEILING OF
ALABASTER: THREE ABBASID POETS
G. B. H. Wightman and A. Y. al-Udhari